Data Warehousing in the Age of Big Data

Data Warehousing in the Age of Big Data

Krish Krishnan

Framingham State University
Framingham, MA

AMSTERDAM • BOSTON • HEIDELBERG • LONDON
NEW YORK • OXFORD • PARIS • SAN DIEGO
SAN FRANCISCO • SINGAPORE • SYDNEY • TOKYO
Morgan Kaufmann is an imprint of Elsevier

Acquiring Editor: *Andrea Dierna*
Development Editor: *Heather Scherer*
Project Manager: *Punithavathy Govindaradjane*
Designer: *Maria Inês Cruz*

Morgan Kaufmann is an imprint of Elsevier
225 Wyman Street, Waltham, MA, 02451, USA

Library of Congress Cataloging-in-Publication Data
Krishnan, Krish.
  Data warehousing in the age of big data / Krish Krishnan.
      pages cm
    Includes bibliographical references and index.
  ISBN 978-0-12-405891-0 (pbk.)
  1. Data warehousing.   2. Big data.   I. Title.
  QA76.9.D37K75 2013
  005.74'5—dc23
                                    2013004151

British Library Cataloguing-in-Publication Data
A catalogue record for this book is available from the British Library

Printed and bound in the United States of America

13 14 15 16 17   10 9 8 7 6 5 4 3 2 1

For information on all MK publications visit our website at *www.mkp.com*

This book is dedicated to

William Harvey Inmon, a dear friend, mentor, teacher, advisor, and business partner—you are an inspiration for generations to come.

My wonderful wife and our sons, who are my source of motivation and inspiration—without your unquestioning support, chasing my dreams would have been dreams.

Contents

PART 2 THE DATA WAREHOUSING

CHAPTER 8   Workload Management in the Data Warehouse............ 163

CHAPTER 9   New Technologies Applied to Data Warehousing 179

PART 3 BUILDING THE BIG DATA – DATA WAREHOUSE

Acknowledgments

This book would not have been possible without the support of many people, and I would like to acknowledge them and thank them for all the support and help in publishing this book.

First and foremost, I would like to thank my ever-supportive family of my wife and my two sons, who sacrificed many weekends, holidays, movies, school events, and social events (where I was absent) to provide me the quality time needed to think in developing the content of this book. Without your help and support, I would have never been able to dream and write this book.

Next is my dear friend, advisor, and business partner Bill Inmon, whose support and encouragement provided me the endurance to write this book while doing a full-time consulting job, working on a start-up company, and doing a zillion things. Bill, thanks for always being there and ready to help.

A very special thank you to the three best friends I have (and I'm blessed to have these guys as my friends), Todd Nash, Hans Hultgren, and Shankar Radhakrishnan, who spent hours of time (during evenings, weekends, and on airplanes) reviewing the draft material and providing feedback at every step. Without their tireless contribution, we would not have made it through in time. Gentlemen, you are all amazing and your readiness to be a part of this incredible journey is not something that can be described in words. You guys are just incredible and it is great to have such friends who can do anything that it takes to make you feel special.

No book can be written based on theories alone—here is where many industry veterans came to help in the form of vendor support. Glenn Zimmerman of IBM, you were truly supportive in getting me all the case studies and even rewriting them to Word formats. Kim Dossey of Teradata, how much I thank you for all the support and quick turnaround of many case studies. Alan and Kate from Cloudera, you two were just wonderful in letting me choose as many case studies as needed without any hesitation. I would like to thank the Microsoft SQL Server team for the Klout case study. There are more case studies coming from Rainstor, Composite Software, and HortonWorks that will be added to the companion website. I would like to formally thank all these vendors for their undying support and readiness to help.

There are several friends who supported me in this journey with words of encouragement who I would like to mention and thank: Paul Kautza, Philip Russom, Dave Stodder, Dave Wells, Claudia Imhoff, Jill Dyche, Mark Madsen, Jonathan Seidman, Kylie Clement, Dave Nielsen, Shawn Rogers, John Myers, John O'Brien, William McKinght, Robert Eve, Tony Shaw, and John Onder.

Last, but not least, my thanks to my editors Andrea Dierna, Heather Scherer, and the entire team at Morgan Kauffman for all the help, guidance, and support in this process—without you, none of this was possible.

Thanks!

About the Author

Krish Krishnan is a recognized expert worldwide in the strategy, architecture, and implementation of high-performance data warehousing solutions and unstructured data. A sought-after visionary and data warehouse thought-leader and practitioner, he is ranked as one of the top strategy and architecture consultants in the world in this subject. Krish is also an independent analyst and a speaker at various conferences around the world on Big Data, and teaches at The Data Warehousing Institute (TDWI) on this subject. Krish, along with other experts, is helping drive the industry maturity on the next generation of data warehousing, focusing on Big Data, Semantic Technologies, Crowd Sourcing, Analytics, and Platform Engineering.

Krish is the founder president of Sixth Sense Advisors Inc., who provide industry analyst services covering the Data Warehouse, Analytics, Cloud Computing, Social Media and Business Intelligence. Krish also provides strategy and innovation consulting services with partner organizations across the globe.

Introduction

Web 2.0 has changed the way we conduct business, interact with customers, share information with friends and family, measure success in terms of business revenue and customer wallet share, and define brand management, and, most importantly, it has created a revenue channel like none other. Whether you plan your vacation, buy the newest television, switch your mobile service provider, or want to buy the best meat for your cookout, you turn to the Internet and look for customer reviews and reader recommendations. It is same situation in your personal life today when you want to share your music, movies, photographs, and videos—you have Facebook, YouTube, iTunes, Instagram, and Flickr.

Personalization of products and services by enterprises today has created many opportunities for the consumer and has also driven the volume of data, the formats (variety) of data, and the velocity of production of the data. The key value of this data is the vast amount of intelligence that is found within the data when modeled with geographic and demographic data to create a cluster of personalities, behaviors, and their influence on similar populations.

This move toward offering personalization of services and customer-centric business models created three distinct trends:

- *Crowdsourcing*. A term coined by Jeff Howe in 2006 in *Wired Magazine*, crowdsourcing is the process of using collaborative intelligence to study human behaviors in the modern world, where information management and sharing of peer-level recommendations at a personal level amounts to trends in the industry.
- Crowdsourcing has evolved into a powerful tool where businesses today look for competitive research, consumer sentiments, and causal analysis, and have deployed other analytical models such as collaborative filtering and recommender and machine learning algorithms.
- Then-senator Barack Obama's campaign demonstrated one of the best examples of using crowdsourcing to raise the funds for his campaign for the 2008 presidential candidate nomination. By using the Internet and social media as a personalized channel of connect, he clearly outpaced all the other candidates in raising the funds to run a very effective campaign.
- *Social media analytics*. Today's consumers rely on data and information that is available through social media channels and relies on their individual decision making from this platform as their "personal decision support platform." This has led to the rise of using social media as a direct and indirect communication channel with customers, partners, and vendors. Today, if you do not have a social media presence, you are obsolete, especially with the generation X and millennial customer base.
- How do you measure the effectiveness of your social media channel and communications strategy? This is where you start implementing a social media analytics strategy. The strategy should be measuring both from an inside-out and outside-in perspective. There are multiple stages of maturity and evolution in this subject area that an enterprise will often need to go through. There are several success stories of business transformation with this strategy that you can read in the news and Internet today.
- *Gamification*. Another hot trend today is the use of gamification strategies both within and outside an enterprise to engage employees, customers, prospects, and just about anybody who is interested in your business and services.

- Gamification is based on a combination of game theory and statistical models, and has proven to be a very effective tool in the model of getting results from the "long tail," another Web 2.0–era term that was coined by Chris Andersson, who also wrote the book on the subject.
- The best example of this strategy is its use in the 2012 U.S. presidential elections where the campaign strategists effectively used a combination of gamification and statistical models to target voters and were very effective. The campaign of incumbent President Barack Obama especially used this combination as a very potent and disruptive strategy to create the much needed connect between the candidate and the voter at a personal level.

The common thread among all the trends, theories, and outcomes from Web 2.0 point toward two things:

- The volume of data needed for using the Web 2.0 platform is far greater than anything that has been used in enterprises today.
- The need for using statistical models and analytics than ever before in the history of computing.

Both of these facts have been demonstrated in success stories by companies like Facebook, Groupon, Google, Yahoo, Apple, and other Fortune 500 companies.

Along with the data came the problem of how to compute all this volume and variety, and how to handle the volume of the data. This is where Google, Facebook, and Yahoo clearly showed the way; the former created a new computing model based on a file system and a programming language called MapReduce that scaled up the search engine and was able to process multiple queries simultaneously. In 2002, architects Doug Cutting and Mike Carafella were working on an open-source search engine project Nutch, which led to them modeling the underlying architecture based on the Google model. This led to the development of the Nutch project as a top Apache project under open source, which was adopted by Yahoo in 2006 and called Hadoop. Hadoop has in the last few years created a whole slew of companies that are both commercial solutions and commit back features to the base open-source project, a true collaboration-based software and framework development.

The other technology that has evolved into a powerful platform is the NoSQL (not only SQL) movement. The underpinnings of this platform are based on a theorem proposed by Eric Brewer in 2002 called the CAP theorem. According to the CAP theorem, a database cannot meet all the rules of ACID compliance at any point in time and yet be scalable and flexible. However, in the three basic properties of consistency, availability, and partition tolerance, a database can meet two of the three, thereby creating a scalable and distributed architecture that can evolve into meeting scalability requirements in a horizontal scaling and provide higher throughput, as the compute in this environment is very close to the storage and is a distributed architecture that can allow for multiple consistency levels.

Facebook was one of the earliest evangelists of the NoSQL architecture, as they needed to solve the scalability and usability demands of a user population that was only third behind China and India in terms of number of people. The popular NoSQL database Cassandra was developed and used at Facebook for a long time (now it has been abandoned by Facebook due to greater scalability needs), and is used across many other companies in conjunction with Hadoop and other traditional RDBMS solutions. It remains a top-level Apache project and is evolving with more features being added.

With the advent of these new technologies and business models, there also has occurred a lot of noise, which has led to chaos. One of these trends or noise factors was the "death of the data warehouse," which caused a lot of caustic reaction across the globe, as enterprises have not only invested millions of dollars into building this decision support platform, but have also created several downstream systems that are based on outcomes from it.

As a data practitioner and consultant, having experience in the traditional data warehouse world and the Big Data world, I started teaching courses at The Data Warehousing Institute (TDWI) and speaking at a number of international summits and conferences on the subjects of Big Data and data warehousing, allaying the fears of the "death" of the data warehouse. Over the last four years, after having logged several miles across the globe on the topic, I decided to write this book and discuss Big Data, who uses it, how it impacts the world of data warehousing, the future of analytics, and, most importantly, the next-generation data warehouse and how it will be architected.

Frankly speaking, we will continue to build and use the data warehouse and it will be still the "single version of truth," but we will move away from using the RDBMS as the platform for the data warehouse and analytics. At the time of writing this book, we are seeing the evolution of Hadoop, MapReduce, and NoSQL with changes and new features coming out of the woodwork every few months and sometimes weeks. These architectures are being designed and built to handle large and complex data volumes and can process effectively in a batch-oriented environment and have limited real-time or interactive capabilities that are found in the RDBMS. The end state of the architecture will include a heterogeneous combination of all these architectures to create a powerful and ginormous decision support architecture that will still be called the data warehouse.

As you read this book, you will find three distinct parts. Part 1 is a discussion on Big Data, technologies of Big Data, and use cases from early adopters of Big Data. Part 2 regards data warehousing, why it failed, and the new architecture options, workloads, and defining a workload-driven architecture, as well as integration techniques for Big Data and the data warehouse. Part 3 deals with data governance, data visualization, information life-cycle management, data scientists, and implementing a Big Data–ready data warehouse. The appendixes include case studies from vendor implementations and a special segment on how we can build a healthcare information factory.

The overall goal of the book is to help you navigate through the complex layers of Big Data and data warehousing while providing you information on how to effectively think about using all these technologies and the architectures to design the next-generation data warehouse.

The chapters and how the book is organized are described here to provide you a roadmap to your reading. The chapters are integrated to provide you concise insights as you move from one chapter to the next.

Part 1: Big Data

Chapter 1: Introduction to Big Data. This chapter focuses on providing you with a thorough understanding of Big Data. We go beyond the buzzwords and explore the emerging world of Big Data and its importance to your enterprise.

Chapter 2: Working with Big Data. This chapter focuses on the underlying complexities of Big Data, the three v's—volume, velocity, and variety—and ambiguity, and how to deal with these characteristics and what are the potential hidden traps in these subject areas.

Chapter 3: Big Data Processing Architectures. This chapter focuses on what architectures are needed or designed to process Big Data. Discussions include algorithmic approaches, taxonomies, clusters, and more.

Chapter 4: Introducing Big Data Technologies. This chapter focuses on the core technologies that have evolved to solve large-scale data processing, including Hadoop and its ecosystem, NoSQL databases, and other technologies. This chapter is an extremely condensed treatment on the technologies and it is recommended that you expand your reading to some of the core books on these subjects.

Chapter 5: Big Data Driving Business Value. This chapter discusses various use cases on how real-life companies have realized value from Big Data. We discuss use cases across B2B, B2C, and C2C segments, and how each segment defines and realizes value.

Part 2: The Data Warehousing

Chapter 6: Data Warehousing Revisited. This chapter focuses on a throwback to the origins of the data warehouse and its evolution through the years. We discuss the pitfalls of the early editions leading to the failure of the data warehouse and how to identify and avoid these pitfalls.

Chapter 7: Reengineering the Data Warehouse. This chapter focuses on how and why to modernize your data warehouse architecture. It provides you with ideas on the concept and some options on the implementation aspects.

Chapter 8: Workload Management in the Data Warehouse. This chapter focuses on workloads, what they mean in the world of data warehousing and Big Data, the importance of understanding workloads, and creating the architecture of the data warehouse based on workloads. This is one of the most important and critical aspects of the future-state architecture for any data management solution.

Chapter 9: New Technologies Applied to Data Warehousing. This chapter focuses on the new and emerging technologies that have been steadily making in-roads into enterprises, especially dealing with the performance and scalability of the data warehouse. We discuss the data warehouse appliance, cloud computing, data virtualization, and in-memory.

Part 3: Building the Big Data – Data Warehouse

Chapter 10: Integration of Big Data and Data Warehousing. This chapter focuses on integrating the data warehouse with Big Data and the associated techniques that can be used based on the data type, your current state of evolution, and the incumbent technologies that are within the enterprise.

Chapter 11: Data-Driven Architecture for Big Data. This chapter focuses on creating data-driven architecture in the world of Big Data by deploying an effective MDM and metadata strategy. It emphasizes the need for these two pillars of data management, especially in the world of Big Data. We discuss semantic layers and semantic web-based approaches.

Chapter 12: Information Management and Life Cycle for Big Data. This chapter focuses on managing the life cycle of Big Data, including which data is essential and how and where the data will be stored both pre- and postprocessing. What are the gotchas with not implementing a robust ILM strategy within the enterprise for Big Data?

Chapter 13: Big Data Analytics, Visualization, and Data Scientists. This chapter deals with the end-state goal of using Big Data, which is the delivery of powerful visualizations, the creation of

analytics, and, most importantly, the emerging role of a data scientist. The goal here is to provide you the conceptual idea behind these topics and how they impact the Big Data strategy overall.
Chapter 14: Implementing the Big Data – Data Warehouse – Real-Life Situations. This chapter focuses on the end-state architecture from real-life implementation of a next-generation data warehouse by Fortune 500 companies. The goal is to provide you some ideas for future thinking as your enterprise evolves into this new world of data.

Appendixes

A: Customer Case Studies
B: Building the HealthCare Information Factory

Companion website

A companion website with supplementary material can be found at:
http://booksite.elsevier.com/9780124058910

Big Data

Introduction to Big Data

INTRODUCTION

The biggest phenomenon that has captured the attention of the modern computing industry today since the "Internet" is "Big Data". These two words combined together was first popularized in the paper on this subject by McKinsey & Co., and the foundation definition was first popularized by Doug Laney from Gartner.

The fundamental reason why "Big Data" is popular today is because the technology platforms that have emerged along with it, provide the capability to process data of multiple formats and structures without worrying about the constraints associated with traditional systems and database platforms.

Big Data

Data represents the lowest raw format of information or knowledge. In the computing world, we refer to data commonly in terms of rows and columns of organized values that represent one or more entities and their attributes. Long before the age of computing or information management with electronic processing aids, data was invented with the advent of counting and trade, preceding the Greeks. Simply put, it is the assignment of values to numerals and then using those numerals to mark the monetary value, population, calendars, taxes, and many historical instances to provide ample evidence to the fascination of the human mind with data and knowledge acquisition and management.

Information or data management according to a series of studies by Carnegie Mellon University entails the process of organizing, acquiring, storing, retrieving, and managing data. Data collected from different processes is used to make decisions feasible to the understanding and requirements of those executing and consuming the results of the process. This administrative behavior was the underlying theme for Herbert Simon's view of bounded rationality[1], or the limited field of vision in human minds when applied to data management. The argument presented in the decision-making behaviors and administrative behaviors makes complete sense, as we limit the data in the process of modeling, applying algorithmic applications, and have always been seeking discrete relationships within the data as opposed to the whole picture.

In reality, however, decision making has always transcended beyond the traditional systems used to aid the process. For example, patient treatment and management is not confined to computers and programs. But the data generated by doctors, nurses, lab technicians, emergency personnel, and medical devices within a hospital for each patient can now, through the use of unstructured data integration techniques and algorithms, be collected and processed electronically to gain mathematical or

---

[1] March, J. G., & Simon, H. A. (1958) Organizations (*http://www.amazon.com/Organizations-James-G-March/dp/063118631X*).

statistical insights. These insights provide visible patterns that can be useful in improving quality of care for a given set of diseases.

Data warehousing evolved to support the decision-making process of being able to collect, store, and manage data, applying traditional and statistical methods of measurement to create a reporting and analysis platform. The data collected within a data warehouse was highly structured in nature, with minimal flexibility to change with the needs of data evolution. The underlying premise for this comes from the transactional databases that were the sources of data for a data warehouse. This concept applies very well when we talk of transactional models based on activity generated by consumers in retail, financial, or other industries. For example, movie ticket sales is a simple transaction, and the success of a movie is based on revenues it can generate in the opening and following weeks, and in a later stage followed by sales from audio (vinyl to cassette tapes, CDs', and various digital formats), video ('DVDs and other digital formats), and merchandise across multiple channels. When reporting sales revenue, population demographics, sentiments, reviews, and feedback were not often reported or at least were not considered as a visible part of decision making in a traditional computing environment. The reasons for this included rigidity of traditional computing architectures and associated models to integrate unstructured, semi-structured, or other forms of data, while these artifacts were used in analysis and internal organizational reporting for revenue activities from a movie.

Looking at these examples in medicine and entertainment business management, we realize that decision support has always been an aid to the decision-making process and not the end state itself, as is often confused.

If one were to consider all the data, the associated processes, and the metrics used in any decision-making situation within any organization, we realize that we have used information (volumes of data) in a variety of formats and varying degrees of complexity and derived decisions with the data in nontraditional software processes. Before we get to Big Data, let us look at a few important events in computing history.

In the late 1980s, we were introduced to the concept of decision support and data warehousing. This wave of being able to create trends, perform historical analysis, and provide predictive analytics and highly scalable metrics created a series of solutions, companies, and an industry in itself.

In 1995, with the clearance to create a commercial Internet, we saw the advent of the "dot-com" world and got the first taste of being able to communicate peer to peer in a consumer world. With the advent of this capability, we also saw a significant increase in the volume and variety of data.

In the following five to seven years, we saw a number of advancements driven by web commerce or e-commerce, which rapidly changed the business landscape for an organization. New models emerged and became rapidly adopted standards, including the business-to-consumer direct buying/selling (website), consumer-to-consumer marketplace trading (eBay and Amazon), and business-to-business-to-consumer selling (Amazon). This entire flurry of activity drove up data volumes more than ever before. Along with the volume, we began to see the emergence of additional data, such as consumer review, feedback on experience, peer surveys, and the emergence of word-of-mouth marketing. This newer and additional data brings in subtle layers of complexity in data processing and integration.

Along the way between 1997 and 2002, we saw the definition and redefinition of mobility solutions. Cellular phones became ubiquitous and the use of voice and text to share sentiments, opinions, and trends among people became a vibrant trend. This increased the ability to communicate and create a crowd-based affinity to products and services, which has significantly driven the last decade of technology innovation, leading to even more disruptions in business landscape and data management in terms of data volumes, velocity, variety, complexity, and usage.

The years 2000 to 2010 have been a defining moment in the history of data, emergence of search engines (Google, Yahoo), personalization of music (iPod), tablet computing (iPad), bigger mobile solutions (smartphones, 3 G networks, mobile broadband, Wi-Fi), and emergence of social media (driven by Facebook, MySpace, Twitter, and Blogger). All these entities have contributed to the consumerization of data, from data creation, acquisition, and consumption perspectives.

The business models and opportunities that came with the large-scale growth of data drove the need to create powerful metrics to tap from the knowledge of the crowd that was driving them, and in return offer personalized services to address the need of the moment. This challenge was not limited to technology companies; large multinational organizations like P&G and Unilever wanted solutions that could address data processing, and additionally wanted to implement the output from large-scale data processing into their existing analytics platform.

Google, Yahoo, Facebook, and several other companies invested in technology solutions for data management, allowing us to consume large volumes of data in a short amount of time across many formats with varying degrees of complexity to create a powerful decision support platform. These technologies and their implementation are discussed in detail in later chapters in this book.

Defining Big Data

Big Data can be defined as volumes of data available in varying degrees of complexity, generated at different velocities and varying degrees of ambiguity, that cannot be processed using traditional technologies, processing methods, algorithms, or any commercial off-the-shelf solutions.

Data defined as Big Data includes machine-generated data from sensor networks, nuclear plants, X-ray and scanning devices, and airplane engines, and consumer-driven data from social media. Big Data producers that exist within organizations include legal, sales, marketing, procurement, finance, and human resources departments.

Why Big Data and why now?

These are the two most popular questions that are crossing the minds of any computing professional: Why Big Data? Why now? The promise of Big Data is the ability to access large volumes of data that can be useful in gaining critical insights from processing repeated or unique patterns of data or behaviors. This learning process can be executed as a machine-managed process with minimal human intervention, making the analysis simpler and error-free. The answer to the second question—Why now?—is the availability of commodity infrastructure combined with new data processing frameworks and platforms like Hadoop and NoSQL, resulting in significantly lower costs and higher scalability than traditional data management platforms. The scalability and processing architecture of the new platforms were limitations of traditional data processing technologies, though the algorithms and methods existed.

The key thing to understand here is the data part of Big Data was always present and used in a manual fashion, with a lot of human processing and analytic refinement, eventually being used in a decision-making process. What has changed and created the buzz with Big Data is the automated data processing capability that is extremely fast, scalable, and has flexible processing.

While each organization will have its own set of data requirements for Big Data processing, here are some examples:

- *Weather data*—there is a lot of weather data reported by governmental agencies around the world, scientific organizations, and consumers like farmers. What we hear on television or radio is an analytic key performance indicator (KPI) of temperature and forecasted conditions based on several factors.
- *Contract data*—there are many types of contracts that an organization executes every year, and there are multiple liabilities associated with each of them.
- *Labor data*—elastic labor brings a set of problems that organizations need to solve.
- *Maintenance data*—records from maintenance of facilities, machines, non-computer-related systems, and more.
- *Financial reporting data*—corporate performance reports and annual filing to Wall Street.
- *Compliance data*—financial, healthcare, life sciences, hospitals, and many other agencies that file compliance data for their corporations.
- *Clinical trials data*—pharmaceutical companies have wanted to minimize the life cycle of processing for clinical trials data and manage the same with rules-based processing; this is an opportunity for Big Data.
- *Processing doctors' notes on diagnosis and treatments*—another key area of hidden insights and value for disease state management and proactive diagnosis; a key machine learning opportunity.
- *Contracts*—every organization writes many types of contracts every year, and must process and mine the content in the contracts along with metrics to measure the risks and penalties.

Big Data example

In order to understand the complexities of the different types of data and their associated content including integration challenges, let us examine a sample of text and analytics mixed within content from different sources. In this example of a large and popular restaurant chain organization that wants to know the correlation between its sales and consumer traffic based on weather conditions. There are both historic patterns and current patterns that need to be integrated and analyzed, and added to this complexity is the social media sharing of consumer perspectives about shopping experiences and where weather is mentioned as a key factor. All this data needs to be added to the processing.

Upon deeper examination of the requirements, we find we need the data sets described in Table 1.1.

The complexities that exist in the data sets across the different sources in terms of data quality, volume, and variety make it difficult to integrate the same seamlessly. Let us examine the sample data to gain a better perspective. The next section discusses the example of Social Media posts and has several example websites that provide insight into the importance of content and context.

Social Media posts

Drive-Thru Windows Still Put the Fast in Fast Food Restaurants, May 30, 2012, *www.npd.com/wps/portal/npd/us/news/pressreleases/pr_120530a.*

> *Last year 12.4 billion visits were made through fast-food drive-thrus, a two percent. … In the total quick service/fast food restaurant segment, carry-out … about their drive-thru experience it's because they somehow lost time.*

Table 1.1 Sample Data Sets Needed for Restaurant Service Performance Analytics

Data	Features	Source	Complexity
Weather	Structured and semi-structured Available for all latitude and longitude codes Has 'weatherperson's editorial commentary and user shared data	Governmental agencies Public news channels Social media	Metadata Geo-coding Language Image and video formats
Customer sentiment	Voice Text Images Videos Blogs, forums, and other Internet channels	Call center Social media Campaign Databases Customer resource management (CRM)	Metadata Context Language Formats
Product	Corporate product data	In-house	HierarchiesMenu packaging
Competition	Available in structured formats from data federators Available unstructured from social media, forums, and Internet	Third party Social media Internal research	Metadata Data quality Context
Location	Structured Unstructured	Internal MDM Social media Third party Surveys	Metadata Data quality Formats: images and videos
Campaign	Structured	Internal	Multiple campaigns at any given time across geographies

Quick Fast Food Service Crucial to Success, *QSR Magazine, www.qsrmagazine.com/ordering/fast-food-fast.*

> *Fast Food Fast—The fast food industry is based on the principles of quality food … for customers who join the drive-thru or in-store queue: to get quality food fast … and it takes 10 minutes, you'll be annoyed by the time you get service.*

Drive Thru Study for Quick Serve Restaurants, *QSR Magazine,* March 16, 2011, *www2.qsrmagazine.com/reports/drive-thru-experience.*

> *Drive Thru Experience Study—You're fast, you're accurate, but today's. … In that same time frame, domestic and international same-store sales … when it comes to fast food or fast casual let alone any restaurant experience.*

Evolution Fast Food—Banker's Hill—San Diego, CA, *www.yelp.com› Restaurants › Vegetarian.*

> *I never realized how douchey using a drive-thru could make you look as a … much to say other than decent food, if a bit overpriced, friendly service, if a bit slow.*

Survey data analysis

The data shown in Figures 1.1, 1.2, and 1.3 represents a sample of consumer sentiment across three categories as measured. The trend from this data set shows the customers' expectations and the reality of service at a fast-food drive-thru.

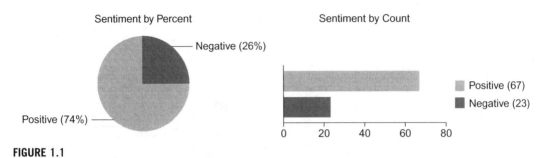

FIGURE 1.1

User sentiment analysis for burgers across the United States.

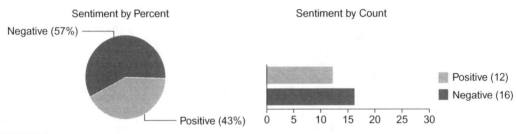

FIGURE 1.2

User sentiment analysis of drive-thru performance of U.S.-based fast-food restaurants.

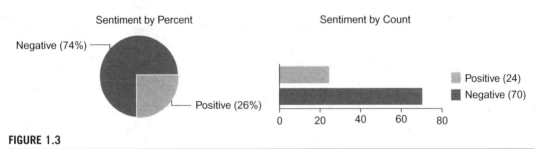

FIGURE 1.3

User sentiment analysis of fast-food quality in the United States.

Survey data

The data sample in Figure 1.4 is from a survey of fast-food restaurants from FoodSource (*www.food-source.com*). A survey typically will consist of hundreds of such responses and needs to be processed for creating a cluster from a population and their associated responses. Often the data becomes cumbersome to manage due to lack of demographics of the survey targets.

How do you make your fast food order a little healthier?	How often do you feed your family fast food rather than cooking at home?
Don't order large size 18%	about once a week 40%
I don't 16%	1-2 times per month 29%
Chicken instead of beef 13%	more than once a week 18%
No mayo/spread 12%	Never 13%
No cheese 11%	**How often do you eat fast food?**
Skip the side item 9%	more than once a week 52%
Low or no-calorie drink 9%	about once a week 28%
No bread (protein style) 4%	1-2 times per month 20%
Substitute veggies for fries 4%	**Where do you live?**
Eat half now, half later 3%	U.S. Southwest 35%
Saled instead of burger 3%	U.S. Midwest 24%
Other tricks to ordering more "healthy" fast food	U.S. Southeast 13%
Ask for knife and fork and ditch the bun after eating contents,	U.S. Northeast 11%
Double garden; double lettuce, tomato, pickles on sandwich; replacing mayo with juicy Vegetables,	U.S. Northwest 11%
If you order fries, get them with no salt.	U.S. South 4%
less fried	**Are you male or female?**
Moderations is the #1 tip	Male 55%
places that use fresh items	Female 45%
Whole wheat or multigrain bun	

(a)

Who makes your favorite burger?	Best chain for order accuracy	Least friendly chains
McDonald's 18%	Arby's 10%	McDonald's 20%
Burger King 16%	Carl's Jr. 10%	Burger King 12%
In-N-Out 11%	**Worst chain for order accuracy?**	**Best value**
Carl's Jr, 9%	Burger King 23%	McDonald's 20%
What's your favorite burger?	McDonald's 19%	Taco Bell 15%
Big Mac 13%	El Pollo Loco 11%	**Best quality**
Whopper 8%	Taco Bell 11%	McDonald's 11%
Whopper Jr, 8%	**Best chain for drive-thru speed**	Chipotle 9%
	McDonald's 38%	Chick-fil-a 9%
Who has the best french fries?	Taco Bell 10%	**Best chain for kids**
McDonald's 21%	**Worst drive-thru speed**	McDonald's 61%
Rallys/Checkers 9%	El Pollo Loco 11%	Dairy queen 7%
Wendy's 8%	**Friendlest chains**	*Note: This was the largest margin in the entire survey*
		How old are you?
Burger King 7%	Subway 9%	36-45 30%
Del Taco 7%	Taco Bell 9%	26-35 20%
Steak N Shake 6%	In-n-out 8%	18-25 15%
What's the best place for fast food? other than burgers?	Carl's Jr, 7%	Under 18 15%
Taco Bell 20%		Over 55 11%
Chick-fil-a 10%		46-55 9%
KFC 10%		

(b)

FIGURE 1.4

(a) Survey sample and (b) the data.

FIGURE 1.5

Sample weather data.

(Source: www.weatherbank.com.)

World Weather Map

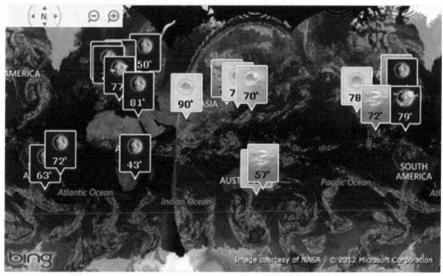

FIGURE 1.6

Sample weather map.

Weather data

Weather data is another common data type that companies today want to integrate in their data analysis and discovery platform. Presented in Figures 1.5 and 1.6 are common formats of weather data that is available for integration and consumption.

Twitter data

Another popular and most requested data for sentiments, trends, and other relevant topics is the social media channel Twitter. Twitter is a microblog and often contains less than 140 characters per tweet. The complexity is to understand the context of the flow and the associated content before proceeding with analysis (Figure 1.7). Twitter data has more complexity than any other web data, the reason being the cryptic notational format used by different consumers of the platform.

Integration and analysis

Based on the data examples discussed here, you can see that a lot of information is available in different sources and formats that can be harnessed into powerful analytics to create a disruptive differentiator for an organization. The fast-food company in the example that is observing the correlation between weather and food sales can answer the following types of questions more effectively:

- What sales occurred across the entire United States for a given day/week/month/quarter/year, and under what weather conditions?
- Did people prefer drive-thru in extreme weather conditions irrespective of the geography?

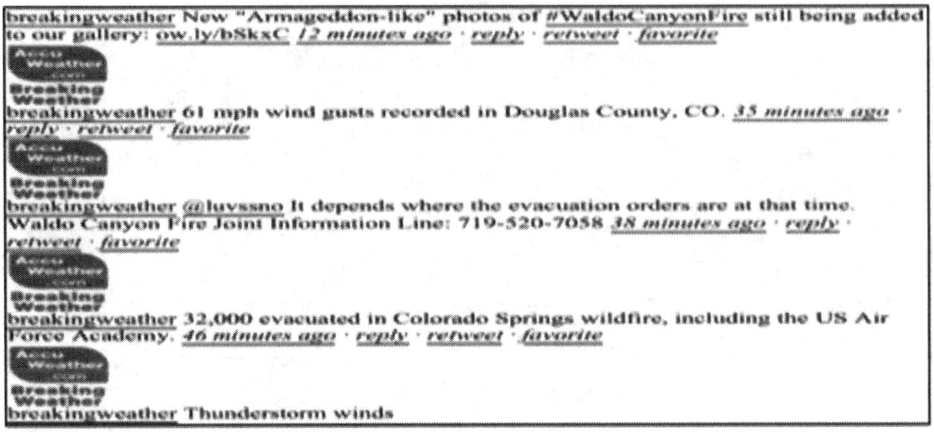

FIGURE 1.7

Tweets about weather.

- Did restaurants along the highway get more traffic in drive-thru during regular versus abnormal weather?
- Did service interruptions occur due to weather?
- What is the propensity for business impact in abnormal weather?
- Did customers wait at one zip code more than another zip code of the same population or demographics? More importantly, what factor did weather play?
- Does coffee sell more than burgers in the winter in Boston, and during the same time, do more cold beverages sell in Orlando?
- Do restaurants need to staff more in different weather conditions? What is the budget impact in such situations?
- What is the customer sentiment, especially during different weather patterns? What drives customers to the store in these circumstances? How can quality of service be improved and sustained?
- What are the customer expectations of pricing? Do they provide feedback by phone, email, or social media?
- What is the competition comparison by customers in social media?
- Do customers measure quality of service alone as the yardstick or are there other mentions in social media?
- Do customers differ in their purchase behaviors across geographies?

You might ask, can we not answer these questions without all this additional data? Or, do we not answer these questions today? The answer to both these questions is countered with another question: What is the effectiveness of the decisions you make today in your business? How aligned are these decisions to the market and, most importantly, your customer? Considering the agile requirements in decision making based on today's fast-paced market and changing economic conditions, every business needs to have a 360° view of data across their organization. A 360° view of your customer or your market or your organization is combined as inside-out (i.e., your view of the market

Table 1.2 Data Output

Source	Data	Metric
Weather	Latitude/longitude Temperature Forecast Time zone Date and hour	Average daily temperature Average snowfall/day Maximum temperature Minimum temperature
Customer sentiment	Sentiment: happy, disappointed, frustrated Tone Channel Influence Followers Posts	Total number of posts Average number of posts Average repost Total positive Total negative Total followers Amplification
Competition	Competitor name Product/service Channel Posts Authors	Total number of posts Total number of authors Average post/channel Average post/author Average compare/product Average compare/author
Contracts	Type Date range Liabilities	Total number of contracts Total type of contracts Contracts/date range—expiry Contract/type of liability
Location	Address Date and time Staff friendliness Cleanliness Quality of service	Number of visits Service time Wait time Quality of service Cleanliness

and customer) and outside-in (i.e., your customer or market's view of you) viewpoints in the form of data and its associated analytics and visualizations. This extends to including data such as contracts, compliance reporting, Excel spreadsheets, safety reports, surveys and feedback, and other data sets. The next section discusses examples of additional data and metrics associated with the data that form portions of the Big Data needed by an organization.

Additional data types

Let us proceed further and assume that all the data has been extracted and transformed from various sources. The output for each of them will look as outlined in Table 1.2.

When all the data is integrated with the data existing in the current business intelligence platforms, the fast-food company can get better insights into the following subject areas:

- Customers
- Markets
- Products

- Vendors/suppliers
- Contracts
- Labor management
- Campaign
- Location management

The analytics and trends that can be created with these additional metrics will provide analysts within the fast-food organization better insights into what drives business and how weather can form a powerful disruption to the business and, more importantly, the consumer. Additionally, in a business-to-business scenario, the data from contracts and liabilities provides context-related information that can aid in negotiations and renewal situations.

The promise of Big Data as seen from the fast-food example in this chapter proves one of the basic reasons why the entire industry is abuzz with wanting to adopt Big Data within their organization. Based on several examples we have discussed in this chapter, Big Data is complex, and this complexity is driven by three characteristics: volume, velocity, and variety. At this juncture, consider your organization and write down a list of missing information that is due to volume, velocity, variety, or complexity of processing issues.

SUMMARY

In this chapter, we discussed an example-driven approach to understanding Big Data. The issue of finding value is dwarfed when compared to the complexity and ambiguity associated with Big Data. In the next chapter, we will discuss the complexities associated with Big Data, and how to derive value from the complexity.

Further reading

Hedberg, B. (1981). How organizations learn and unlearn. In: Nyström, P. C., & Starbuck, W. H. (Eds.), *Handbook of Organizational Design*. Oxford University Press, USA.
Mullins, L. J. (1993). *Management and Organizational Behaviors*, (3rd ed.).
www.mckinsey.com
www.forrester.com
www.gartner.com
www.tdwi.org

Working with Big Data

Complexity is the prodigy of the world. Simplicity is the sensation of the universe. Behind complexity, there is always simplicity to be revealed. Inside simplicity, there is always complexity to be discovered.
—Gang Yu

INTRODUCTION

Why is Big Data tough to understand? What makes it complex? How can multiple layers of data and processes be inferred? How can meaningful insights through all this complexity be gained? These are some pivotal questions that arise repeatedly in Big Data programs. Let us take a step back and understand how we arrived at the definition of Big Data.

In 2001, META Group (now Gartner) analyst Doug Laney, in a research report that he published, defined data growth challenges and opportunities as three dimensional, characterized by increasing *volume* (amount of data), *velocity* (speed of data in and out), and *variety* (range of data types and sources)—the three V's. The industry today uses this definition as a standard to classify Big Data.

Data explosion

What has led to this explosive growth of data? One answer is innovation. Innovation has transformed the way we engage in business, provide services, and the associated measurement of value and profitability. Three fundamental trends that shaped up the data world in the last few years are business model transformation, globalization, and personalization of services. Let us examine these in detail.

- *Business model transformation.* Fundamental business models have been transformed by globalization and connectivity. Companies have moved from being product oriented to service oriented, where the value of the organization in its customers' view is measured by service effectiveness and not by product usefulness. What this transformation mandates to every business is the need to produce more data in terms of products and services to cater to each segment and channel of customers, and to consume as much data from each customer touch point, including social media, surveys, forums, direct feedback, call center, competitive market research, and much more. This trend exists across business-to-business (B2B), business-to-business-to-consumer (B2B2C), and business-to-consumer-to-consumer (B2C2C) models. The amount of data produced and consumed by every organization today exceeds what the same organization produced prior to the business transformation. The fundamental data that is central to the business remains, and

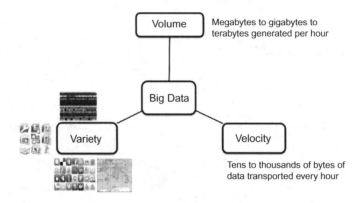

FIGURE 2.1

Big Data characteristics.

the supporting data that was needed but not available or accessible previously now exists and is accessible through multiple channels. This is where the volume equation of data exploding to Big Data comes to play. We will discuss this with examples in the later sections of this chapter.

- *Globalization.* Globalization is a key trend that has drastically changed the commerce of the world, from manufacturing to customer service. Globalization has also changed the variety and formats of data.
- *Personalization of services.* Business transformation's maturity index is measured by the extent of personalization of services and the value perceived by their customers from such transformation. This model is one of the primary causes for the velocity of data that is generated.
- *New sources of data.* With technology tipping points in the last decade, we now have data floating around in social media, mobile devices, sensor networks, and new media more than ever before. Along with this data there is now content within the corporation that was never tapped into decision support process from a Business Intelligence and Analytics perspective. The emergence of newer business models and the aggressive growth of technology capabilities over the last decade or more has paved the way for integrating all of the data across the enterprise into one holistic platform to create a meaningful and contextualized business decision support platform.

These trends have added complexities in terms of processes, and at the same time created the need for acquiring the data needed for the processes, which can provide critical insights into areas that were never possible. Technology also evolved in the last 20 years that provided the capability to generate data at extreme scales:

- Advances in mobile technology
- Large-scale data processing networks
- Commoditization of hardware
- Security
- Virtualization
- Cloud computing
- Open-source software

Let us now examine the definition that was published in the original META Group research report.

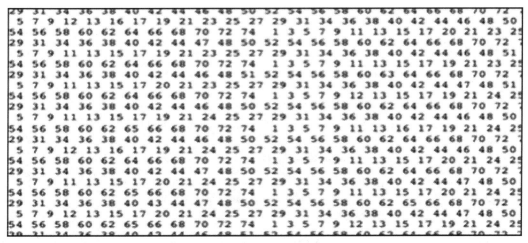

FIGURE 2.2

Machine data from an interactive gaming system.

Data volume

Data volume is characterized by the amount of data that is generated continuously. Different data types come in different sizes. For example, a blog text is a few kilobytes; voice calls or video files are a few megabytes; sensor data, machine logs, and clickstream data can be in gigabytes. Traditionally, employees generated data. Today, for a given organization, customers, partners, competitors, and anyone else can generate data.

The following sections outline some examples of data generated by different sources.

Machine data

Every machine (device) that we use today from industrial to personal devices can generate a lot of data. This data includes both usage and behaviors of the owners of these machines, and, in most cases, also includes detail activity logs (Figure 2.2). Machine-generated data is often characterized by a steady pattern of numbers and text, which occurs in a rapid-fire fashion. There are several examples of machine-generated data; for instance, a robotic arm that is on an assembly line at an automotive plant will be sending signals for every movement it makes, and that pattern will be steady, as opposed to a dredging machine that is doing roadwork and sending signals back on how much movement it had during the day, payload moved, and system and machine status. Sensors on top of buildings that regulate heating and cooling send different signals all through the day; though the structure may seem the same, the values differ depending on many factors. Sensors on automobiles send different signals depending on road type, driving speed, weight, and more to support centers. Radio signals, satellites, and mobile devices all transmit signals and can vary from small-volume bursts to large-volume bursts. The bottom line is the data is a write once in most cases and will not have an update for the same content except in case of corporate documents.

#Software: Microsoft Internet Information Services 7.0 #Version: 1.0 #Date: 2012-05-02 17:42:15 #Fields: date time c-ip cs-username s-ip s-port cs-method cs-uri-stem cs-uri-query sc-status cs(User-Agent) 2012-05-02 17:42:15 198.162.25.55 - 198.30.55.20 80 GET /images/picture.jpg - 30 Mozilla/6.0+(compatible;MSIE+5.5;+Windows+2012+Server)

FIGURE 2.3

Sample application log.

SHR89882,shirt,red,10.49,1
SHR89883,shirt,blue,10.49,2
PTB99943,pants,blue,32.1,1
GC010101,Gucci,Eyewear,100,1,1

FIGURE 2.4

Retail shopper clickstream data.

Application log

Another form of machine-generated data is an application log. Different devices generate logs at different paces and formats. The log shown in Figure 2.3 is generated every second by millions of servers across the world via Internet access by users on a popular operating system. We can add to this list CT scanners, X-ray machines, body scanners at airports, airplanes, ships, military equipment, commercial satellites, and the list goes on. Today, tablets, cellular phones, and automobile computers can all produce logs for each activity from the device at any time of the day, including geographic information, data type, access type, activity period, and much more.

Clickstream logs

The example shown in Figure 2.4 is a typical clickstream log from Internet portals and sites. The usage statistics of the web page are captured in clickstream data. This data type provides insight into what a user is doing on the web page, and can provide data that is highly useful for behavior and usability analysis, marketing, and general research. The biggest problem with the data is the volume, since the actions can be logged in multiple places, such as web servers, routers, proxy servers, ad servers, etc. Current tools can only glean partial information from this data today since data formats vary across the system and the sheer volume makes it hard for current technologies to process this data.

External or third-party data

There are multiple data sets that organizations purchase today or get as feeds from external sources. Though some of the data is structured, most of the data has different formats and often comes in heavy volumes. Examples include weather data, such as that shown in Figure 2.5.

Emails

Every enterprise has massive amounts of emails that are generated by its employees, customers, and executives on a daily basis. These emails are all considered an asset of the corporation and need to be managed as such. After Enron and the collapse of many audits in enterprises, the U.S. government mandated that all enterprises should have a clear life-cycle management of emails, and that emails should be available and auditable on a case-by-case basis. There are several examples that come to mind like insider trading, intellectual property, competitive analysis, and much more, to justify governance and management of emails.

Date	Time	TmpF	DPf	RH	Vis	CC	Pcpin	SnFall	SnDpth	WDir	Wind	NwWnd	S_Rain	S_Snow	S_Fog	S_TH	S_LT
6/1/09	0:00:00	54	42.1	64	10	25	0 N	N		200	3.5	3.5					
6/1/09	1:00:00	55	45	69	10	88	0 N	N		0	0	0					
6/1/09	2:00:00	53.1	42.1	66	10	0	0 N	N		40	6.3	6.9					
6/1/09	3:00:00	55	45	69	10	50	0 N	N		40	4.5	4.6					
6/1/09	4:00:00	55	43	64	10	100	0 N	N		340	4.5	4.6					
6/1/09	5:00:00	55.9	39.9	55	10	100	0 N	N		0	0	0					
6/1/09	6:00:00	55	39.9	57	10	100 T		N	N	300	4.5	4.6	Light Rain				
6/1/09	7:00:00	57.9	39	49	10	100 T		N	N	0	5.8	5.8	Light Rain				
6/1/09	8:00:00	53.1	46.9	80	10	88 T		N	N	160	5.8	5.8	Light Rain				
6/1/09	9:00:00	51.1	50	96	10	100	0.01 N	N		170	6.3	6.9	Light Rain				
6/1/09	10:00:00	52	50	83	7	100	0.02 N	N		170	8.1	8.1	Light Rain				
6/1/09	11:00:00	53.1	51.1	83	10	88	0.04 N	N		180	3.5	3.5	Light Rain				
6/1/09	12:00:00	54	52	83	10	88 T		N	N	170	9.2	9.2	Light Rain				
6/1/09	13:00:00	55	52	89	10	88	0 N	N		200	8.1	8.1					
6/1/09	14:00:00	57	52	83	10	100	0 N	N		200	3.5	3.5					

FIGURE 2.5

Sample weather data.

If enterprises do not understand the associated risks, liabilities, and penalties associated with email management, it is time to set policies in place. With the new information processing platforms, emails can be processed using text mining rules and algorithms, and flagged for risk, exposure, and noncompliance. Proactive management of this content is needed for every enterprise. There are several complexities associated with processing this content, including metadata, ambiguity of language, expression, and contextualization.

Contracts

Another data type that is generated every day by enterprises is contracts. While the types of contracts remain classified as human resources, legal, vendor, supplier, customer, etc., the content within each format can vary, and this creates volumes of data to parse in case of situations like bankruptcy or mergers and acquisitions. A sample contract template is shown in Figure 2.6; this employee agreement is filled out for each and every position in the organization and can contain changes based on level, title, and special contract addendums. The language and semantics within each contract mandate different types of legal implications. Legal teams spend hours on these documents and find value, which may be useful, or useless depending on the nature of the data discovered along with the relevance of the time of discovery. If legal teams can use a machine-learning type of approach, this data volume, complexity, and ambiguity can be managed, and valuable insights on risks in contracts by type, complexity, and duration can be analyzed with relative ease.

Geographic information systems and geo-spatial data

A popular device and smartphone application is the global positioning system (GPS), which uses geo-spatial data to guide anyone from point A to point B. Additionally, the GPS is built with features like guided voice navigation, points of interest (POI), and much more. This personalization aspect of a GPS has made smartphones even more popular, with GPS being a built-in feature. Another emerging

Employment Contract

This agreement is made and takes effect on MM/DD/YYYY between (company), a (State) corporation, hereafter called "Company" and (employee), hereafter called "Employee".

Witnesseth:

1. The Company hereby employs Employee for a term commencing on the date of this agreement and Employee hereby accepts such employment.

2. During the Employee's employment he/she will:

A. Devote such time and effort as may be reasonably required by the Company to perform his/her duties.

B. Not engage in any other employment or business activity without the Company's written consent.

C. Perform such duties as may reasonably be requires of him/her by the Company.

3. For services rendered by the Employee, the Company shall pay him/her as follows:

A. The annual sum of $X, calculated as follows (insert compensation formula)

B (Optional) A bonus of ($X, Y% of sales, etc.) payable (monthly, quarterly, annually) based upon (performance goals)

C. (Optional) Non-payroll benefits to include health insurance, travel and business entertainment expenses, and other items specified in Attachment A.

4. Employee agrees that during his/her term of employment by the Company and for a period of one year after termination of such employment, he/she will not act as an employee, agent, broker, shareholder, or otherwise engage in any business selling products similar to those customarily sold by the Company within the States of (specify).

5. Employee understands that he/she will acquire confidential information of business value to the Company during the course of his/her employment. Employee hereby agrees not to divulge such confidential information to any other party, or to use such information for his/her own profit except in performance of employment activities beneficial to the Company.

6. This agreement is an employment-at-will agreement. The Company may, at any time, with or without cause, discharge the Employee by giving him/her written notice of such discharge.

7. Employee's employment shall terminate upon his/her death; inability or failure to perform the duties required by his/her employment; or his/her written notice of resignation given to the Company.

8. Following termination of employment, all obligations under this agreement shall end except for the provisions of items 4 and 5, and any causes of action which may arise from the circumstances of the termination.

9. This agreement constitutes the entire agreement between Company and Employee.

10. This agreement shall be interpreted and, if necessary, adjudicated in accordance with the laws of (State, County).

FIGURE 2.6

Sample employment contract.

feature is the addition of GPS to cameras and camcorders. By this feature, one can set locations of where the picture was taken along with dates and other information. This is a hot trend, especially with journalists. But this kind of real-time data interaction requires a lot of data to transmit back and forth every second for millions of consumers across the globe. Figure 2.7 shows the different formats in which geographic information system (GIS) data is produced and consumed.

The most interesting data for any organization to tap into today is social media data. The amount of data generated by consumers every minute provides extremely important insights into choices, opinions, influences, connections, brand loyalty, brand management, and much more. Social media sites provide not only consumer perspectives, but also competitive positioning, trends, and access to communities formed by common interest. Organizations today leverage the social media pages to personalize marketing of products and services to each customer. Figure 2.8 shows the amount of

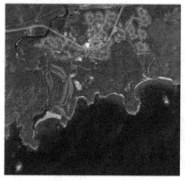

FIGURE 2.7

Geo-spatial data usage.

FIGURE 2.8

Social media channels.

social media channels available to interact with by users. A feed from each channel for each customer is low volume of data but an extremely high degree of complexity.

Example: Funshots, Inc.

From the preceding examples, we can see how the volume aspect of Big Data gets simply overwhelming. The complexity is not from the type of data but the size too—100 MB per every four hours versus 1 MB per second makes a lot of difference when you look at the amount of compute and associated process cycles. The most important point to think here is from your organization's point of view: What are some of the Big Data specifics that can fall into this category and what are the complexities associated with that data?

Let us examine another consumer-oriented corporation and how they looked at this situation within their organization.

Funshots, Inc. is a leading photography and videography equipment manufacturer since 1975, providing industry-leading equipment both for commercial and personal use. The company was thriving for over 20 years and was known for its superior customer service. Funshots employed traditional customer relationship management (CRM) techniques to maintain customer loyalty with incentives like club cards, discount coupons, and processing services. With the advent of Web 2.0 and the availability of the Internet, smartphones, and lower-priced competitive offerings, the customer base for Funshots started declining. The traditional decision support platform was able to provide trending, analytics, and KPIs, but was not able to point out any causal analysis. Funshots lost shares in their customer base and in the stock market.

The executive management of Funshots commissioned a leading market research agency to validate the weakness in the data that was used in the decision support platform. The research report pointed out several missing pieces of data that provided insights including sentiment data, data from clickstream analysis, data from online communities, and competitive analysis provided by consumers. Furthermore, the research also pointed to the fact that the company did not have a customer-friendly website and its social media presence was lacking, therefore, its connection with Gen X and Gen Y consumers was near nonexistent.

Funshots decided to reinvent the business model from being product-centric to customer-centric. As a part of the makeover, the CRM system was revamped, the customer-facing website was redone, and a strong social media team was formed and tasked with creating connections with Gen X and Gen Y customers. Product research and competitive intelligence were areas of focus with direct reporting to the executive leadership.

As the business intelligence team started understanding the data requirements for all the new initiatives, it became clear that additional data was needed, and the company had never dealt with this kind of data in its prior life cycle. The additional data sources documented included:

- Market research reports
- Consumer research reports
- Survey data
- Call center voice calls
- Emails
- Social media data
- Excel spreadsheets from multiple business units
- Data from interactive web channels

The bigger part of the problem was with identifying the content and the context within the new data and aligning it to the enterprise data architecture. In its planning phase, the data warehouse and business intelligence teams estimated the current data to be about 2.5 TB and the new data to be between 2 TB and 3 TB (raw data) per month, which would be between 150 GB and 275 GB post-processing. The team decided to adopt to a scalable platform that could handle this volatility with volume of data to be processed, and options included all the Big Data technologies and emerging database technologies. After the implementation cycle (we will discuss the implementation in later chapters in this book), the business intelligence teams across the enterprise were able to use the new platform to successfully plan the business model transformation.

The key learning points for the teams included:

- A new data architecture roadmap and strategy are essential to understand the data, especially considering the volume.
- Data volume will always be a challenge with Big Data.
- Data security will be determined only postprocessing.
- Data acquisition is first and then comes the analysis and discovery.
- Data velocity is unpredictable.
- Nontraditional and unorthodox data processing techniques need to be innovated for processing this data type.
- Metadata is essential for processing this data successfully.
- Metrics and KPIs are key to provide visualization.
- Raw data does not need to be stored online for access.
- Processed output is needs to be integrated into an enterprise level analytical ecosystem to provide better insights and visibility into the trends and outcomes of business exercises including CRM, Optimization of Inventory, Clickstream analysis and more.
- The enterprise data warehouse (EDW) is needed for analytics and reporting.

The business model transformation brought with it a tsunami of data that needed to be harnessed and processed for meaningful insights. With a successful change in the data architecture and strategy, Funshots was able to quickly reestablish itself as a leading provider of photography services including products. With the new business model, the company was able to gain better insights into its legacy and new-generation customer expectations, market trends and their gaps, competition from their view and their customers' view, and much more. There are nuggets of insights that are found in this extreme volume of information. The point to pause and ponder is, how might your own organization possibly adapt to new business models? What data might be out there that can help your organization uncover some of these possibilities?

Data velocity

Velocity can be defined as the speed and direction of motion of an object. Constant velocity of an object is the motion of an object at constant speed and direction.

With the advent of Big Data, understanding the velocity of data is extremely important. The basic reason for this arises from the fact that in the early days of data processing, we used to analyze data in batches, acquired over time. Typically, data is broken into fixed-size chunks and processed through different layers from source to targets, and the end result is stored in a data warehouse for further use in reporting and analysis. This data processing technique in batches or microbatches works great when the flow of input data is at a fixed rate and results are used for analysis with all process delays. The scalability and throughput of the data processing architecture is maintained due to the fixed size of the batches.

In the case of Big Data, the data streams in a continuous fashion and the result sets are useful when the acquisition and processing delays are short. Here is where the need becomes critical for an ingestion and processing engine that can work at extremely scalable speeds on extremely volatile sizes of data in a relatively minimal amount of time. Let us look at some examples of data velocity.

Amazon, Facebook, Yahoo, and Google

The business models adopted by Amazon, Facebook, Yahoo, and Google, which became the de-facto business models for most web-based companies, operate on the fact that by tracking customer clicks and navigations on the website, you can deliver personalized browsing and shopping experiences. In this process of clickstreams there are millions of clicks gathered from users at every second, amounting to large volumes of data. This data can be processed, segmented, and modeled to study population behaviors based on time of day, geography, advertisement effectiveness, click behavior, and guided navigation response. The result sets of these models can be stored to create a better experience for the next set of clicks exhibiting similar behaviors. The sheer volume of data that is processed by these four companies has prompted them to open their technologies to the rest of the world. The velocity of data produced by user clicks on any website today is a prime example for Big Data velocity.

Sensor data

Another prime example of data velocity comes from a variety of sensors like GPS, tire-pressure systems, On-Star-vehicle and passenger support services offered by General Motors, based on geospatial and location based intelligence associated with the sensor on the automobile, heating and cooling systems on buildings, smart-meters, mobile devices, biometric systems, technical and scientific application, and airplane sensors and engines. The data generated from sensor networks can range from a few gigabytes per second to terabytes per second. For example, a flight from London to New York generates 650 TB of data from the airplane engine sensors. There is a lot of value in reading this information during the stream processing and postgathering for statistical modeling purposes.

Mobile networks

The most popular way to share pictures, music, and data today is via mobile devices. The sheer volume of data that is transmitted by mobile networks provides insights to the providers on the performance of their network, the amount of data processed at each tower, the time of day, the associated geographies, user demographics, location, latencies, and much more. The velocity of data movement is unpredictable, and sometimes can cause a network to crash.

The data movement and its study have enabled mobile service providers to improve the QoS (quality of service), and associating this data with social media inputs has enabled insights into competitive intelligence.

Social media

Another Big Data favorite, different social media sites produce and provide data at different velocities and in multiple formats. While Twitter is fixed at 140 characters, Facebook, YouTube, or Flickr can have posts of varying sizes from the same user. Not only is the size of the post important, understanding how many times it is forwarded or shared and how much follow-on data it gathers is essential to process the entire data set. A post can go viral and have millions of posts and result in a huge volume to process, or a post may remain private yet generate additional data. The volatility of data generation is the data velocity problem experienced by social media. Let us examine the Funshots case study.

When the new website, social media presence, and interactive channels became reality for Funshots, the information technology (IT) team quickly realized that data velocity along with volume were going to be tricky issues to manage and be able to create an architecture using any of the known standard platforms. The relational database management system (RDBMS) would never be able to handle this situation, and creating silos of solutions to process each data type would mean no scalability in terms of scaling up or scaling out. The team decided that an elastic architecture was required to process the new data.

When the Funshots team started to look at different options for processing Big Data, the list of features for handling data velocity included that the:

- System must be elastic for handling data velocity along with volume.
- System must scale up and scale down as needed without increasing costs.
- System must be able to process data across the infrastructure in the least processing time.
- System throughput should remain stable independent of data velocity.
- System should be able to process data on a distributed platform.

After selecting the most appropriate architecture for data processing, the data velocity problem was handled by the IT team. The key takeaways from the exercise were:

- Data architecture needs to be based on workload.
- Metadata requirements need to be clearly documented.
- The data platform supports a wide range of real-time analytics.
- Result sets can be integrated easily with high-volume analytic data stores.
- Read and write latencies below 50 milliseconds.
- Scale out on commodity hardware.
- Database must automatically implement the defined partitioning strategy.

Data variety

Big Data comes in multiple formats as it ranges from emails to tweets to social media and sensor data (Figure 2.9). There is no control over the input data format or the structure of the data.

The processing complexity associated with a variety of formats is the availability of appropriate metadata for identifying what is contained in the actual data. This is critical when we process images, audio, video, and large chunks of text. The absence of metadata or partial metadata means processing delays from the ingestion of data to producing the final metrics, and, more importantly, in integrating the results with the data warehouse.

The platform requirements for processing new formats are:

- Scalability
- Distributed processing capabilities
- Image processing capabilities

FIGURE 2.9

New data formats.

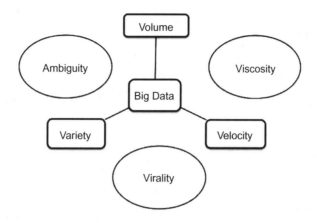

FIGURE 2.10

Additional Big Data characteristics.

- Graph processing capabilities
- Video and audio processing capabilities

From the discussions on the three V's associated with Big Data, you can see why there is intense complexity in processing Big Data. Along with the three V's, there also exists ambiguity, viscosity, and virality (the latter two have been contributed by an independent analyst community; Figure 2.10).

- *Ambiguity*—a lack of metadata creates ambiguity in Big Data. For example, in a photograph or in a graph, M and F can depict gender or can depict Monday and Friday. This characteristic manifests in the volume-variety category most times.
- *Viscosity*—measures the resistance (slow down) to flow in the volume of data. Resistance can manifest in dataflows, business rules, and even be a limitation of technology. For example, social media monitoring falls into this category, where a number of enterprises just cannot understand how it impacts their business and resist the usage of the data until it is too late in many cases.
- *Virality*—measures and describes how quickly data is shared in a people-to-people (peer) network. Rate of spread is measured in time. For example, re-tweets that are shared from an original tweet is a good way to follow a topic or a trend. The context of the tweet to the topic matters in this situation.

SUMMARY

In this chapter, we discussed the complexity associated with processing Big Data and the underlying characteristics of Big Data. Several examples in this chapter have been used in discussing the characteristics and there are several more that will be available in the companion website to this book (*http://booksite.elsevier.com/9780124058910*). Chapter 3 will focus on Big Data processing architecture and techniques.

Big Data Processing Architectures

And pluck till time and times are done
The silver apples of the moon,
The golden apples of the sun.
—**W. B. Yeats**

INTRODUCTION

Data processing has been a complex subject to deal with since the primitive days of computing. The underlying reason for this stems from the fact that complexity is induced from the instrumentation of data rather than the movement of data. Instrumentation of data requires a complete understanding of the data and the need to maintain consistency of processing (if the data set is broken into multiple pieces), the need to integrate multiple data sets through the processing cycles to maintain the integrity of the data, and the need for complete associated computations within the same processing cycle. The instrumentation of transactional data has been a challenge considering the discrete nature of the data, and the magnitude of the problem amplifies with the increase in the size of the data. This problem has been handled in multiple ways within the RDBMS-based ecosystem for online transaction processing (OLTP) and data warehousing, but the solutions cannot be extended to the Big Data situation. How do we deal with processing Big Data? Taking distributed processing, storage, neural networks, multiprocessor architectures, and object-oriented concepts, combined with Internet data processing techniques, there are several approaches that have been architected for processing Big Data.

Data processing revisited

Data processing can be defined as the collection, processing, and management of data resulting in information generation to end consumers. Broadly, the different cycles of activities in data processing can be described as shown in Figure 3.1.

Transactional data processing follows this life cycle, as the data is first analyzed and modeled. The data collected is structured in nature and discrete in volume, since the entire process is predefined based on known requirements. Other areas of data management, like quality and cleansing, are a non-issue, as they are handled in the source systems as a part of the process. Data warehouse data processing follows similar patterns as transaction data processing, the key difference is the volume of data to be processed varies depending on the source that is processed. Before we move onto Big Data processing, let us discuss the techniques and challenges in data processing

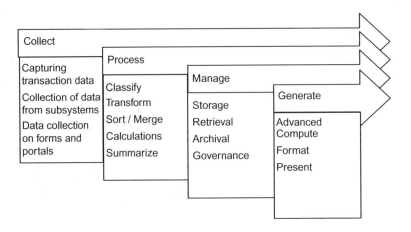

FIGURE 3.1

Data processing cycles.

Data processing techniques

There are two fundamental styles of data processing that have been accepted as de-facto standards:

- *Centralized processing*. In this architecture all the data is collected to a single centralized storage area and processed upon completion by a single computer with often very large architectures in terms of memory, processor, and storage.
  - Centralized processing architectures evolved with transaction processing and are well suited for small organizations with one location of service.
  - Centralized processing requires minimal resources both from people and system perspectives.
  - Centralized processing is very successful when the collection and consumption of data occurs at the same location.
- *Distributed processing*. In this architecture data and its processing are distributed across geographies or data centers, and processing of data is localized with the federation of the results into a centralized storage. Distributed architectures evolved to overcome the limitations of the centralized processing, where all the data needed to be collected to one central location and results were available in one central location. There are several architectures of distributed processing:
  - *Client–server*. In this architecture the client does all the data collection and presentation, while the server does the processing and management of data. This was the most popular form of data management in the 1980s, and this architecture is still in use across small and midsize businesses.
  - *Three-tier architecture*. With client–server architecture the client machines needed to be connected to a sever machine, thus mandating finite states and introducing latencies and overhead in terms of data to be carried between clients and servers. To increase processing efficiency and reduce redundancy while increasing reusability, client–server architecture evolved into three-tier systems, where the client's processing logic was moved to a middle tier of services, thereby freeing the client from having to be tethered to the server. This evolution

allowed scalability of each layer, but the overall connectedness of the different layers limited the performance of the overall system. This is predominantly the architecture of analytical and business intelligence applications.

- n-*tier architecture*. *n*-tier or multitier architecture is where clients, middleware, applications, and servers are isolated into tiers. By this architecture any tier can be scaled independent of the others. Web applications use this type of architecture approach.
- *Cluster architecture*. Refers to machines that are connected in a network architecture (software or hardware) to closely work together to process data or compute requirements in parallel. Each machine in a cluster is associated with a task that is processed locally and the result sets are collected to a master server that returns it back to the user.
- *Peer-to-peer architecture*. This is a type of architecture where there are no dedicated servers and clients; instead, all the processing responsibilities are allocated among all machines, known as peers. Each machine can perform the role of a client or server or just process data.
- Distributed processing has a lot of advantages and disadvantages.
  - Advantages:
    - Scalability of systems and resources can be achieved based on isolated needs.
    - Processing and management of information can be architected based on desired unit of operation.
    - Parallel processing of data reducing time latencies.
  - Disadvantages:
    - Data redundancy
    - Process redundancy
    - Resource overhead
    - Volumes
- The most popular distributed processing implementations in the data world are:
  - Peer to peer
  - Hub and spoke
  - Federated

Processing data in either the centralized processing or distributed processing style has a lot of infrastructure challenges that continue to dominate the space. The next section discusses the key areas of challenge in terms of data processing.

Data processing infrastructure challenges

Basic data processing architecture (computational units) as shown in Figure 3.2 has remained the same from the days of punch card to modern computing architectures. The following sections outline the four distinct areas that have evolved and yet prove challenging.

Storage

The first problem to manifest itself has been storage. With an increase in the volume of data, the amount of storage needed to process and store it increases by 1.5 times. You need the additional 0.5 times storage for intermediate result set processing and storage.

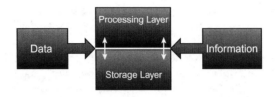

FIGURE 3.2

Computational units of data processing.

Let us look at an example. In the 1800s the first reported storage problem was the U.S. Census Bureau's inability to record and report statistics. The existing means of gathering data and calculating results were time consuming and error-prone, with no ability to correct errors and increase processing efficiency. Herman Hollerith created a card with holes specifying multiple data formats that when punched would create responses. Each set of holes punched created a pattern of answers to questions, along with the ability to cluster patterns into groups. With the aid of a processing machine he had developed, he was able to process data by reading the cards and store the input for repeated usage later. This is the primitive form of offline storage and processing of data. The problem became more challenging when the population increased and additional changes to questions had to be made. To manage this problem, Hollerith classified data as either static or changing, providing the basic master data and transaction data type of classification. As technology progressed, we moved from punch cards to magnetic tape to disk-based storage.

Storage has been a problem in the world of transaction processing and data warehousing. Due to the design of the underlying software, we do not consume all the storage that is available on a disk. Another problem with storage is the cost per byte—traditionally, fast-performing storage has been expensive (tier 1 SAN or NAS devices) and the cost drives up the overall total cost of ownership.

Transportation

One of the biggest issues that always confronted the data world is moving data between different systems and then storing it or loading it into memory for manipulation. This continuous movement of data has been one of the reasons that structured data processing evolved to be restrictive in nature, where the data had to be transported between the compute and storage layers. The continuous improvement in network technologies could not solve the problem, though it enabled the bandwidth of the transport layers to be much bigger and more scalable. Next, we discuss how different processing architectures evolved and how they were designed to take this data transport as one of the primary design requirements to develop the newer architecture.

Processing

Processing data required the ability to combine some form of logic and mathematical computes together in one cycle of operation. This area can be further divided into the following:

- *CPU or processor.* Computer processing units have evolved a long way from the early 1970s to today. With each generation the computing speed and processing power have increased, leading to more processing capabilities, access to wider memory, and have accelerated architecture evolution within the software layers.

- *Memory.* While the storage of data to disk for offline processing proved the need for storage evolution and data management, equally important was the need to store data in perishable formats in memory for compute and processing. Memory has become cheaper and faster, and with the evolution of processor capability, the amount of memory that can be allocated to a system, then to a process within a system, has changed significantly.

- *Software.* Another core data processing component is the software used to develop the programs to transform and process the data. Software across different layers from operating systems to programming languages has evolved generationally and even leapfrogged hardware evolution in some cases. In its lowest form the software translates sequenced instruction sets into machine language that is used to process data with the infrastructure layers of CPU + memory + storage. Programming languages that have evolved over time have harvested the infrastructure evolution to improve the speed and scalability of the system. Operating systems like Linux have opened the doors of innovation to enterprises to develop additional capabilities to the base software platform for leveraging the entire infrastructure and processing architecture improvements.

Speed or throughput

The biggest continuing challenge is the speed or throughput of data processing. Speed is a combination of various architecture layers: hardware, software, networking, and storage. Each layer has its own limitations and, in a combination, these limitations have challenged the overall throughput of data processing.

Data processing challenges continue to exist in the infrastructure architecture layers as an ecosystem, though the underlying software, processor, memory, storage, and network components have all evolved independently. In the world of database processing and data management this is a significant problem both from a value and a financial perspective. In the next section we discuss the architectures that were initially developed as shared-everything architecture and the problems that were solved as transaction processing on these platforms, and the newer evolution to shared-nothing architecture that has given us the appliance platform, which is providing the unlimited scalability that was always lacking in the world of data and its management.

Shared-everything and shared-nothing architectures

Data processing is an intense workload that can either scale dramatically or severely underperform and crash. The key to both the scenarios stems from the underlying infrastructure architecture, based on which a particular data architecture performance can be predicted. Two popular data processing infrastructure architectures that are regarded as industry standard are shared-everything and shared-nothing architectures.

Application software such as CRM, ERP, SCM, and transaction processing require software that can drive performance. Web applications require an architecture that is scalable and flexible. Data warehousing requires an infrastructure platform that is robust and scalable.

Based on the nature of the data and the type of processing, shared-everything architectures are suited for applications, while shared-nothing architecture lends itself to data warehouse and web applications.

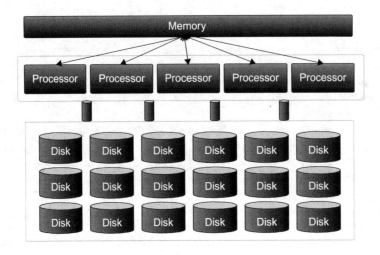

FIGURE 3.3

Shared-everything architecture.

Shared-everything architecture

Shared-everything architecture refers to system architecture where all resources are shared including storage, memory, and the processer (Figure 3.3). The biggest disadvantage of this architecture is the limited scalability. Two variations of shared-everything architecture are symmetric multiprocessing (SMP) and distributed shared memory (DSM).

In the SMP architecture, all the processors share a single pool of memory for read–write access concurrently and uniformly without latency. Sometimes this is referred to as uniform memory access (UMA) architecture. The drawback of SMP architecture is when multiple processors are present and share a single system bus, which results in choking of the bandwidth for simultaneous memory access, therefore, the scalability of such system is very limited.

The DSM architecture addresses the scalability problem by providing multiple pools of memory for processors to use. In the DSM architecture, the latency to access memory depends on the relative distances of the processors and their dedicated memory pools. This architecture is also referred to as nonuniform memory access (NUMA) architecture.

Both SMP and DSM architectures have been deployed for many transaction processing systems, where the transactional data is small in size and has a short burst cycle of resource requirements. Data warehouses have been deployed on the shared-everything architecture for many years, and due to the intrinsic architecture limitations, the direct impact has been on cost and performance. Analytical applications and Big Data cannot be processed on a shared-everything architecture.

Shared-nothing architecture

Shared-nothing architecture is a distributed computing architecture where multiple systems (called nodes) are networked to form a scalable system (Figure 3.4). Each node has its own private memory,

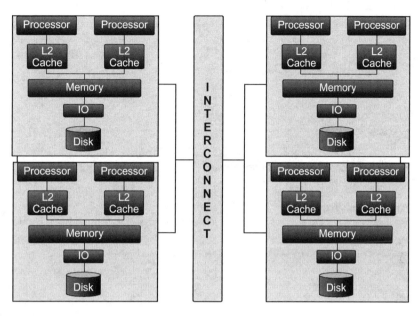

FIGURE 3.4

Shared-nothing architecture.

disks, and storage devices independent of any other node in the configuration, thus isolating any resource sharing and the associated contention. The flexibility of the architecture is its scalability. This is the underlying architecture for data warehouse appliances and large data processing. The extensibility and infinite scalability of this architecture makes it the platform architecture for Internet and web applications.

The key feature of shared-nothing architecture is that the operating system not the application server owns responsibility for controlling and sharing hardware resources. In a share-nothing architecture, a system can assign dedicated applications or partition its data among the different nodes to handle a particular task. Shared-nothing architectures enable the creation of a self-contained architecture where the infrastructure and the data coexist in dedicated layers.

OLTP versus data warehousing

OLTP and data warehouse processing architectures are designed and deployed on shared-everything architectures. In the case of transactional data, the structure and the volume of data are finite to the extent that shared-everything architecture–based database solutions satisfy the user needs for performance, throughput, and storage, while keeping a reasonable cost.

A data warehouse is architected to be the enterprise version of the truth and the data repository for the enterprise. With all the data from transactional systems to a third party and other data being processed into the data warehouse, and downstream reporting and analytics applications demanding access to data on a continuous basis, a shared-everything architecture does not lend itself to meet the data volume, user demands, and total cost. A shared-nothing data warehouse architecture like a data warehouse appliance is better suited for processing data in the data warehouse environment.

The world of Big Data processing differs completely from the transaction processing world, in terms of data type and architecture requirements to process the data.

Big Data processing

Big Data is neither structured, nor does it have a finite state and volume. As discussed in Chapter 2, we have seen examples of the different formats and sources of data that need to be processed as Big Data. The processing complexities in Big Data include the following:

1. *Data volume*—amount of data generated every day both within and outside the organization.
   * Internal data includes memos, contracts, analyst reports, competitive research, financial statements, emails, call center data, supplier data, vendor data, customer data, and confidential and sensitive data including HR and legal.
   * External data includes articles, videos, blogs, analyst reviews, forums, social media, sensor networks, and mobile data.
2. *Data variety*—different formats of data that are generated by different sources.
   * Excel spreadsheets and the associated formulas
   * Documents
   * Blogs and microblogs
   * Videos, images, and audio
   * Multilingual data
   * Mobile, sensor, and radio-frequency identification (RFID) data
3. *Data ambiguity*—complexity of the data and the ambiguity associated with it in terms of metadata and granularity.
   * Comma Separated Values (CSV) files may or may not contain header rows
   * Word documents have multiple formats (i.e., legal documents for patients versus pharmaceuticals by a hospital)
   * Sensor data from mobile versus RFID networks
   * Microblog data from Twitter versus data from Facebook
4. *Data velocity*—speed of data generation.
   * Sensor networks
   * Mobile devices
   * Social media
   * YouTube broadcasts
   * Streaming services such as Netflix and Hulu
   * Corporate documents and systems
   * Patient networks

Due to the very characteristics of Big Data, processing data of different types and volumes on traditional architectures like Symmetric Multi Processing (SMP) or Massive Parallel Processing (MPP) platforms, which are more transaction prone and disk oriented, cannot provide the required scalability, throughput, and flexibility. The biggest problem with Big Data is its uncertainty and the biggest advantage of Big Data is its nonrelational format.

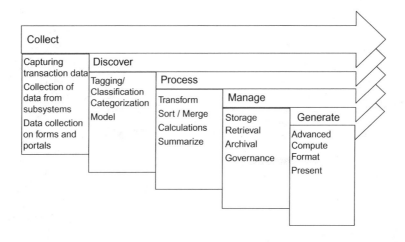

FIGURE 3.5

Big Data processing cycle.

The data processing life cycle for Big Data differs from transactional data (Figure 3.5). In a traditional environment you first analyze the data and create a set of requirements, which leads to data discovery and data model creation, and then a database structure is created to process the data. The resulting architecture is very efficient from the perspective of write performance, as data's finite shape, structure, and state are loaded in the end state.

Big Data widely differs in its processing cycle. The data is first collected and loaded to a target platform, then a metadata layer is applied to the data, and a data structure for the content is created. Once the data structure is applied, the data is then transformed and analyzed. The end result from the process is what provides insights into the data and any associated context (based on the business rules processed). To process the data in this flexible manner, a database-driven architecture will be unsuitable and will underperform. To process this volume and complexity, a file-driven architecture with a programming language interface is best suited. Based on this conclusion, we can specify the key requirements for infrastructure and processing architecture as follows:

- Data processing architecture requirements:
    - Data model-less architecture
    - Near-real-time data collection
    - Microbatch processing
    - Minimal data transformation
    - Efficient data reads
    - Multipartition capability
    - Store result in file system or DBMS (not relational)
    - Share data across multiple processing points
- Infrastructure requirements:
    - Linear scalability
    - High throughput

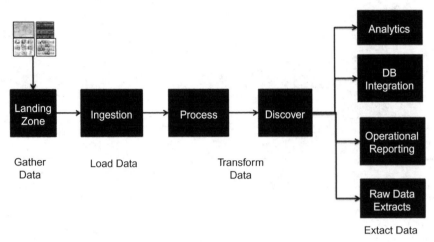

FIGURE 3.6

Big Data processing flow.

- Fault tolerance
- Auto recovery
- High degree of parallelism
- Distributed data processing
- Programming language interface

The key element that is not required for Big Data is the need for a relational database to provide the backend platform for data processing.

Interestingly, the architecture and infrastructure requirements for Big Data processing are closely aligned to web application architecture. Furthermore, there are several data processing techniques on file-based architectures including the operating systems that have matured over the last 30 years. Combining these techniques, a highly scalable and performing platform can be designed and deployed.

To design an efficient infrastructure and processing architecture, we need to understand the dataflow for processing Big Data. A high-level overview of Big Data processing is shown in Figure 3.6. There are four distinct stages of processing and each stage's requirement for infrastructure remains the same. Let us look at the processing that occurs in each stage.

- *Gather data.* In this stage, the data is received from different sources and loaded to a file system called the landing zone or landing area. Typically, the data is sorted into subdirectories based on the data type. Any file modifications like naming or extension changes can be completed in this stage.
- *Load data.* In this stage, the data is loaded with the application of metadata (this is the stage where you will apply a structure for the first time to the data) and readied for transformation. The loading process breaks down the large input into small chunks of files. A catalog of the

files is created and the associated metadata for the catalog is processed for that file. In this stage one can also partition the data horizontally or vertically depending on the user and processing requirements.

- *Transform data*. In this stage the data is transformed by applying business rules and processing the contents. This stage has multiple steps to execute and can quickly become complex to manage. The processing steps at each stage produce intermediate results that can be stored for later examination. The results from this stage typically are a few keys of metadata and associated metrics (a key-value pair).
- *Extract data*. In this stage the result data set can be extracted for further processing including analytics, operational reporting, data warehouse integration, and visualization purposes.

Based on the dataflow as described here, let us revisit the infrastructure and data processing architecture requirements as they relate to Big Data.

Infrastructure explained

- *Linear scalability*. Earlier in this chapter, we discussed the challenges of data processing infrastructure in terms of storage, memory, and processor. In a traditional system's architecture, when you add additional infrastructure, you achieve scalability, but it is not 100% linear and therefore becomes expensive. For example, when you add 1 TB storage, you get about half of that usable space with a RAID 5 configuration. In the case of Big Data, there is already inherent design to accommodate for the scalability of processing, and therefore the storage management and architecture of traditional data management techniques are obsolete. These architectures largely have been developed based on Google's original papers on storage and index management techniques.
- *High throughput*. Big Data's velocity mandates that data be ingested and processed at high speeds. This requires an infrastructure that is extremely fast across input/output (I/O), processing, and storage.
- *Fault tolerance*. Big Data because of its inherent complexity needs a fault-tolerant architecture. Any one portion of the processing architecture should be able to take over and resume processing from the point of failure in any other part of the system.
- *Auto recovery*. The processing architecture should be self-managing and recover from failure without manual intervention.
- *Programing language interfaces*. Big Data can be processed for multiple business scenarios. For example, a document can be processed for multiple subject areas and classified under more than one category of products or services. This processing cannot be done using any COTS (commercial off-the-shelf) software and needs custom coding and development.
- *High degree of parallelism*. By processing data in parallel, we can distribute the load across multiple machines, each having its own copy of the same data, but processing a different program.
- *Distributed data processing*. Since Big Data processing happens on a file-based architecture, to achieve extreme scalability, the underlying platform must be able to process distributed data. This is an overlapping requirement with parallel processing, but differs in the fact that parallelism can exist within multiple layers of the architecture stack.

Data processing explained

- *Data model-less architecture.* Due to the size and complexity of data, there is no fixed data model when you process Big Data. In other words, the data processing is on a schemaless or nonstructured data set.
- *Near-real-time data collection.* Big Data can be either collected as a batch or in real time. To process the landing of data very effectively, a highly scalable and performing storage platform is needed.
- *Microbatch processing.* Big Data can be processed as real time, batch, or microbatch data sets. The underlying platform must be capable of processing data in any of these formats, concurrently and in a scalable fashion.
- *Minimal data transformation.* Big Data processing with programming languages provides for some transformation. Most transformations are executed as a multistep derivation and complexity is kept to a minimal within each step. This feature is necessary to improve speed and design fault tolerance.
- *Efficient data reads.* The data processing design should be read-oriented, as there is no schema-based processing of data.
- *Multipartition capability.* The data processing architecture should be able to support vertical and horizontal partitions of the data. Due to the size and the volume of data, both the partitioning techniques will be implemented in the processing workflow.
- *Store result in file system or DBMS (not relational).* Big Data processing is file-based and therefore the result sets need to be stored in a file system architecture. Alternately, a DBMS platform can be integrated into the processing cycle, but not an RDBMS.
- *Share data across multiple processing points.* Replication and sharing of data is a key processing requirement. The reasons for this include the design of fault tolerance, multistep processing, and multipartitioning.

In a nutshell, Big Data processing can be summarized as a file system–based scalable and distributed data processing architecture, designed and deployed on a high-performance and scalable infrastructure.

Big Data architecture is not a fixed, one-size-fits-all architecture. As seen in Figure 3.7, each processing layer within the architecture has at least several solutions and techniques that can be implemented to create a robust environment. Each solution has its own advantages and disadvantages for a particular workload (this will be discussed in later chapters in this book).

To better understand the Big Data situation, let us discuss how a Telco organization will manage their requirements and create a robust architecture for data management.

Telco Big Data study

A very large Telco company has been working on a customer acquisition and retention strategy. In the current business intelligence and data warehouse architecture, they are able to understand the following metrics for every consumer:

- Call usage
- Noncall usage
- Charges

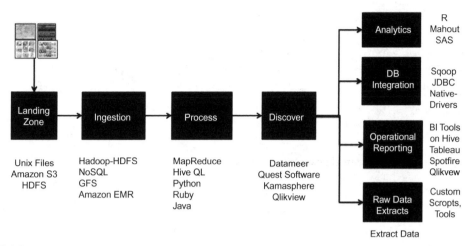

FIGURE 3.7

Conceptual Big Data processing platform.

- Three-month rolling average for usage and billing
- Customer Lifetime value (LTV)
- Customer profitability tier

The Telco has received complaints from a number of consumers on dropped calls or dropped packets, resulting in revenue leakage and customer attrition. The IT team believes that inspecting the data from the cell phone towers can give them a clue on whether the failure is due to poor infrastructure. The business team also wants to include the data from social media and newsprint about the quality of service, customer sentiments, competitive comparisons, and product and service reviews. To process this additional volume of data, the IT team undertook a study on the overall impact, the results of which are as follows:

- Current data in data warehouse: 5 TB (three years rolling)
- New data from towers: 400 MB log/day
- New data from social media and others: 250 MB/day
- Content from documents, contracts, and call center data: 200 MB/day
- Emails, forum posts, and social media: 100 MB/day

Based on the data analysis, the IT team concluded that a database cannot handle the type, volume, and processing complexity of the new data, for the following reasons:

- Data is stored in columns and table structures within a database. To process data, you need a finite structural definition first, called the data model.
- Relationships between different data structures are represented by data.
- Data manipulation language and data definition language are the two key mechanisms of processing data in the database.
- Databases are highly optimized for handling finite transactions.

- Databases can be abstracted from a physical layer for tuning the architecture.
- Databases cannot handle processing of document or semi-structured types of data.
- Procedural language or other programming language interfaces on the database add overhead in processing and often end up processing data outside the database, requiring cycles of moving vast amounts of data, and the problem will magnify with unstructured and other new data types.

To provide a robust processing approach for the additional data, the IT team recommended the following infrastructure and processing recommendations.

Infrastructure

To process data other than structured and additional volumes to current data, a combination of heterogeneous technologies is recommended. The solution architecture will include the following type of technologies:

- Hadoop, NoSQL, or similar data processing platforms, driven on nonrelational and file system–based architecture.
- MapReduce programming model will be implemented for managing data processing and transformation.
- Data discovery and analysis will be implemented using Tableau or Datameer software that abstracts the complexities of MapReduce and works directly on Hadoop for data integration and management.
- Analytics on Hadoop will be implemented using R, Predixion, and other competing technologies capable to MapReduce integration and management.
- In-memory data processing solutions like Qlikview need to be tested further for advanced reporting requirements, depending on the success and adoption of the new stack of technologies.
- Hardware infrastructure will be running on a commodity platform based on multicore processors and up to 96 GB RAM.
- Disk architecture for the new infrastructure will be not based on storage area network (SAN) but on direct attached storage (DAS).
- A redundant configuration will be set up for failover.
- A landing zone will be available on the existing server with unlimited storage. The storage will be designed for high capacity and not for high performance.
- Security for the raw data will be implemented on current disk storage access policies.
- Security rules for nonrelational data postprocessing will follow the existing rules in the LDAP repository (integrated single sign on security process) for EDW data.

Data processing

- Processing of different types of data will be assigned to different clusters of systems.
- Documents and text data will be processed using discovery rules. The result set will be a structured output of tags and keywords, occurrences, counts, and processing dates.
- Audit, balance, and control will be implemented for tracing data processing across layers.
- Business rules will be programmatically implemented with MapReduce and other programming languages that can scale and perform like Java or Ruby.

- Metadata for data loading and processing will be implemented in file systems. A catalog of such metadata will be versioned and stored using version control software.
- The designated software stack such as Karmasphere or Predixion will manage semantic layers for data output from the different data sets and their processes. The rules themselves will be stored in a central repository for source code management.
- All the preprocessing and processing of data will occur outside the data warehouse and other relational data environments.
- The hybrid data processing architecture will provide independent machine, software, and data scalability across the entire ecosystem.
- Any data integration between the new data outputs and the EDW will be done at a metric level using metadata,

Armed with these directives the teams proceeded to analyze the available technology choices and understand how they fit into the workload architecture they needed to design in order to create a dynamic and scalable Big Data processing architecture. In summary this chapter provided you with the fundamental insights into Big Data Processing Architectures and helped to learn the differences in processing structured data versus Big Data, and the case study has established the basic set of requirements, processes, and potential architectures. The next chapter will be focussing on technology choices for processing Big Data.

Introducing Big Data
Technologies

The first rule of any technology used in a business is that automation applied to an efficient operation will magnify the efficiency. The second is that automation applied to an inefficient operation will magnify the inefficiency.
—Bill Gates

INTRODUCTION

The first three chapters provided you an introduction to Big Data, the complexities associated with Big Data, and the processing techniques for Big Data. This chapter focuses on technologies that are available today and have been architected and developed to process Big Data, and the different architectures that can be adopted for processing vast amounts of data. While no one technology is a deep dive or a focus area, we have attempted to provide concise overviews of all the different technologies, distributed data processing, and Big Data processing requirements needed to select and implement the most appropriate Big Data technologies and architecture for your organization. We have referenced several whitepapers and the Apache Foundation website, apart from discussions with Hadoop teams at CloudEra and HortonWorks. The author thanks all those who provided time for these discussions.

Processing Big Data has several complexities in abstracted layers, as discussed in Chapter 3. We can quantify this into a finite realm of a three-dimensional problem with processing this data type, the dimensions being the volume of the data produced, the variety of formats, and the velocity of data generation. To handle any of these problems in traditional data processing architecture is not a feasible option. The problem by itself did not originate in the last decade and has been something that is being solved by various architects, researchers, and organizations over the years. A simplified approach to large data processing was to create distributed data processing architectures and manage the coordination by programming language techniques. This approach, while solving the volume requirement, did not have the capability to handle the other two dimensions. With the advent of the Internet and search engines, the need to handle the complex and diverse data became a necessity and not a one-off requirement. It is during this time in the early 1990s that a slew of distributed data processing papers and associated algorithms and techniques were published by Google; Stanford University; Dr. Stonebraker; Eric Brewer; and Doug Cutting (Nutch Search Engine); and Yahoo, among others.

Today, the various architectures and papers that were contributed by these and other developers across the world have culminated into several open-source projects under the Apache Software Foundation and the NoSQL movement. All of these technologies have been identified as Big Data processing platforms, including Hadoop, Hive, HBase, Cassandra, and MapReduce. NoSQL platforms

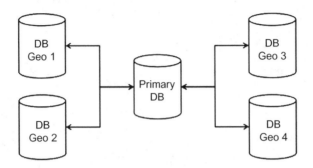

FIGURE 4.1

Distributed data processing in the RDBMS.

include MongoDB, Neo4J, Riak, Amazon DynamoDB, MemcachedDB, BerkleyDB, Voldemort, and many more. Though many of these platforms were originally developed and deployed for solving the data processing needs of web applications and search engines, they have evolved to support other data processing requirements. In the rest of this chapter, the intent is to provide you with how data processing is managed by these platforms. This chapter is not a tutorial for step-by-step configuration and usage of these technologies. There are also references provided at the end for further reading and reference.

Distributed data processing

Before we proceed to understand how Big Data technologies work and see associated reference architectures, let us recap distributed data processing.

Distributed data processing has been in existence since the late 1970s. The primary concept was to replicate the DBMS in a master–slave configuration and process data across multiple instances (Figure 4.1). Each slave would engage in a two-phase commit with its master in a query processing situation. Several papers exist on the subject and how its early implementations have been designed, authored by Dr. Stonebraker[1], Teradata, University of California at Berkley departments, and others.

Several commercial and early open-source DBMS systems have addressed large-scale data processing with distributed data management algorithms, however, they all faced problems in the areas of concurrency, fault tolerance, supporting multiple redundant copies of data, and distributed processing of programs. A bigger barrier was the cost of infrastructure.

Why did distributed data processing fail to meet the requirements in the relational data processing architecture? It can be called a hit or miss depending on the complexity of the architecture. The answer to this question lies in multiple dimensions:

- Dependency on RDBMS:
  - ACID (atomicity, consistency, isolation, and durability) compliance for transaction management
  - Complex architectures for consistency management
  - Latencies across the system

[1] DeWitt, D. J., & Stonebraker, M. (2008). MapReduce: a major step backwards. *The Database Column*, (*http:// homes.cs.washington.edu/~billhowe/mapreduce_a_major_step_backwards.html*).

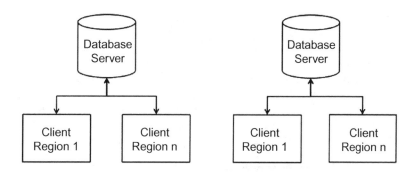

FIGURE 4.2

Client–server architecture.

- Slow networks
- RDBMS I/O
- SAN architecture
- Infrastructure cost
- Complex data processing and transformation requirements
- Minimal fault tolerance within infrastructure and expensive fault tolerance solutions

Due to the inherent complexities and the economies of scale, the world of data warehousing did not adopt to the concept of large-scale distributed data processing. On the other hand, the world of OLTP adopted and deployed distributed data processing architecture, using heterogeneous and proprietary techniques, though this was largely confined to large enterprises, where latencies were not the primary concern. The most popular implementation of this architecture is called client–server data processing (Figure 4.2).

The client–server architecture had its own features and limitations, but it provided limited scalability and flexibility:

- Benefits:
  - Centralization of administration, security, and setup.
  - Back-up and recovery of data is inexpensive, as outages can occur at the server or a client and can be restored.
  - Scalability of infrastructure by adding more server capacity or client capacity can be accomplished. The scalability is not linear.
  - Accessibility of the server from heterogeneous platforms locally or remotely.
  - Clients can use servers for different types of processing.
- Limitations:
  - The server is the central point of failure.
  - Very limited scalability.
  - Performance can degrade with network congestion.
  - Too many clients accessing a single server cannot process data in a quick time.

In the late 1980s and early 1990s there were several attempts at distributed data processing in the OLTP world, with the emergence of object-oriented programming and object store databases. We learned that with effective programing and nonrelational data stores, we could effectively scale up

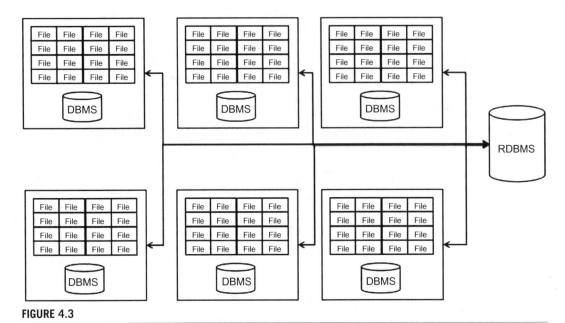

FIGURE 4.3

Generic new-generation distributed data architecture.

distributed data processing across multiple computers. It was at the same time the Internet was gaining adoption and web commerce or e-commerce was beginning to take shape. To serve Internet users faster and better, several improvements rapidly emerged in the field of networking with higher speeds and bandwidth while lowering costs. At the same time, the commoditization of infrastructure platforms reduced the cost barrier of hardware.

The perfect storm was created with the biggest challenges that were faced by web applications and search engines, which is unlimited scalability while maintaining sustained performance at the lowest computing cost. Though this problem existed prior to the advent of the Internet, its intensity and complexity were not comparable to what web applications brought about. Another significant movement that was beginning to gain notice was nonrelational databases (specialty databases) and NoSQL (not only SQL).

Combining the commoditization of infrastructure and distributed data processing techniques including NoSQL, highly scalable and flexible data processing architectures were designed and implemented for solving large-scale distributed processing by leading companies including Google, Yahoo, Facebook, and Amazon (Figure 4.3). The fundamental tenents that are common in this new architecture are:

- *Extreme parallel processing*—the ability to process data in parallel within a system and across multiple systems at the same time.
- *Minimal database usage*—the new approach to acquire, store, and manage data removes or bypasses the dependency on the database. This naturally removes the ACID compliance

limitations that exist in traditional RDBMS platforms. In the new architecture the RDBMS, DBMS, and NoSQL technologies have a role, and can be deployed as needed to solve that requirement.

- *Distributed file-based storage*—data is stored in files, which is cheaper compared to storing on a database. Additionally, data is distributed across systems, providing built-in redundancy.
- *Linearly scalable infrastructure*—every piece of infrastructure added will create 100% scalability from the CPU to storage and memory.
- *Programmable APIs*—all modules of data processing will be driven by procedural programming application programming interfaces (APIs), which allow for parallel processing without the limitations imposed by concurrency. The same data can be processed across systems for different purposes or the same logic can be processed across different systems. There are different case studies on these techniques.
- *High-speed replication*—data is able to replicate at high speeds across the network.
- *High availability*—data and the infrastructure are always available and accessible by the users.
- *Localized processing of data and storage of results*—the ability to process and store results locally, meaning compute and store occur in the same disk within the storage architecture. This means one needs to store replicated copies of data across disks to accomplish localized processing.
- *Fault tolerance*—with extreme replication and distributed processing, system failures could be rebalanced with relative ease, as mandated by web users and applications.

With the features and capabilities discussed here, the limitations of distributed data processing with relational databases are not a real barrier anymore. The new-generation architecture has created a scalable and extensible data processing environment for web applications and has been adopted widely by companies that use web platforms. Over the last decade many of these technologies have been committed back to the open-source community for further development by innovators across the world (see the Apache Foundation website at for committers across projects). The new-generation data processing platforms, including Hadoop, Hive, HBase, Cassandra, MongoDB, CouchDB, REDIS, Neo4J, DynamoDB, and more, are all products of these architectural pursuits, and are discussed in this chapter.

There is a continuum of technology development in this direction (by the time we are finished with this book, there will be newer developments that can be found on the companion website for this book (http://booksite.elsevier.com/9780124058910)).

Big Data processing requirements

What is unique about Big Data processing? What makes it different or mandates new thinking? To understand this better let us look at the underlying requirements. We can classify Big Data requirements based on its five main characteristics:

- Volume:
  - Size of data to be processed is large—it needs to be broken into manageable chunks.
  - Data needs to be processed in parallel across multiple systems.
  - Data needs to be processed across several program modules simultaneously.

- Data needs to be processed once and processed to completion due to volumes.
- Data needs to be processed from any point of failure, since it is extremely large to restart the process from the beginning.
- Velocity:
  - Data needs to be processed at streaming speeds during data collection.
  - Data needs to be processed for multiple acquisition points.
- Variety:
  - Data of different formats needs to be processed.
  - Data of different types needs to be processed.
  - Data of different structures needs to be processed.
  - Data from different regions needs to be processed.
- Ambiguity:
  - Big Data is ambiguous by nature due to the lack of relevant metadata and context in many cases. An example is the use of M and F in a sentence—it can mean, respectively, Monday and Friday, male and female, or mother and father.
  - Big Data that is within the corporation also exhibits this ambiguity to a lesser degree. For example, employment agreements have standard and custom sections and the latter is ambiguous without the right context.
- Complexity:
  - Big Data complexity needs to use many algorithms to process data quickly and efficiently.
  - Several types of data need multipass processing and scalability is extremely important.

Processing large-scale data requires an extremely high-performance computing environment that can be managed with the greatest ease and can performance tune with linear scalability.

Technologies for Big Data processing

There are several technologies that have come and gone in the data processing world, from the mainframes, to two-tier databases, to virtual storage access method (VSAM) files. Several programming languages have evolved to solve the puzzle of high-speed data processing and have either stayed niche or never found adoption. After the initial hype and bust of the Internet bubble, there came a moment in the history of data processing that caused an unrest in the industry—the scalability of the Internet search. Technology startups like Google, RankDex (now known as Baidu), and Yahoo, and open-source projects like Nutch, were all figuring out how to increase the performance of the search query to scale infinitely. Out of these efforts came the technologies that are now the foundation of Big Data processing. The focus of this section is to discuss the evolution and implementation of these technologies around

- Data movement
- Data storage
- Data management

Before we discuss the technology and architecture of Big Data platforms, let us take a few minutes to discuss one of the most powerful and game-changing technology innovations that revolutionized the landscape for Big Data platforms—the Google file system.

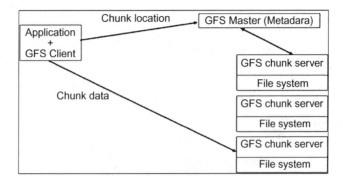

FIGURE 4.4

Google GFS.

Source: Google Briefing[2].

Google file system

In the late 1990s, Google was expanding the search processing capabilities to scale up effectively on massive volumes of data. In the quest for performance and scalability, Google discovered that its requirements could not be met by traditional file systems, and thus was born the need to create a file system that could meet the demands and rigor of an extremely high-performance file system for large-scale data processing on commodity hardware clusters.

Google subsequently published the design concepts in 2001, in a whitepaper titled the "Google File System" (GFS), which has revolutionized the industry today. The key pieces of the architecture as shown in Figure 4.4 include:

- A GFS cluster:
  - A single *master*
  - Multiple *chunk servers* (workers or slaves) per master
  - Accessed by multiple *clients*
  - Running on commodity Linux machines
- A file:
  - Represented as fixed-sized *chunks*
  - Labeled with 64-bit unique global IDs
  - Stored at chunk servers and three-way mirrored across chunk servers

In the GFS cluster, input data files are divided into chunks (64 MB is the standard chunk size), each assigned its unique 64-bit handle, and stored on local chunk server systems as files. To ensure fault tolerance and scalability, each chunk is replicated at least once on another server, and the default design is to create three copies of a chunk.

If there is only one master, there is a potential bottleneck in the architecture, right? The role of the master is to communicate to clients which chunk servers have which chunks and their metadata information. Clients' tasks then interact directly with chunk servers for all subsequent operations, and use the master only in a minimal fashion. The master, therefore, never becomes or is in a position to become the bottleneck.

[2] Google File System 19th ACM Symposium on Operating Systems Principles, Lake George, NY, October, 2003.

Another important issue to understand in the GFS architecture is the single point of failure (SPOF) of the master node and all the metadata that keeps track of the chunks and their state. To avoid this situation, GFS was designed to have the master keep data in memory for speed, keep a log on the master's local disk, and replicate the disk across remote nodes. This way if there is a crash in the master node, a shadow can be up and running almost instantly.

The master stores three types of metadata:

1. File and chunk names or *namespaces*.
2. Mapping from files to chunks (i.e., the chunks that make up each file).
3. Locations of each chunk's replicas. The replica locations for each chunk are stored on the local chunk server apart from being replicated, and the information of the replications is provided to the master at startup or when a chunk server is added to a cluster. Since the master controls the chunk placement, it always updates metadata as new chunks get written.

The master keeps track on the health of the entire cluster through handshaking with all the chunk servers. Periodic checksums are executed to keep track of any data corruption. Due to the volume and scale of processing, there are chances of data getting corrupt or stale.

To recover from any corruption, GFS appends data as it is available rather than updates an existing data set; this provides the ability to recover from corruption or failure quickly. When a corruption is detected, with a combination of frequent checkpoints, snapshots, and replicas, data is recovered with minimal chance of data loss. The architecture results in data unavailability for a short period but not data corruption.

The GFS architecture has the following strengths:

- Availability:
  - Triple replication–based redundancy (or more if you choose).
  - Chunk replication.
  - Rapid failovers for any master failure.
  - Automatic replication management.
- Performance:
  - The biggest workload for GFS is read-on large data sets, which based on the architecture discussion, will be a nonissue.
  - There are minimal writes to the chunks directly, thus providing auto availability.
- Management:
  - GFS manages itself through multiple failure modes.
  - Automatic load balancing.
  - Storage management and pooling.
  - Chunk management.
  - Failover management.
- Cost:
  - Is not a constraint due to use of commodity hardware and Linux platforms.

Google combined the scalability and processing power of the GFS architecture and developed the first versions of MapReduce programming constructs to execute on top of the file system. There are several other proprietary architectural advances that Google has since been deploying and continues to innovate and deploy that are outside the scope of the discussion for this book and this chapter.

The next few sections are focused on the Big Data platforms including Hadoop and NoSQL. The goal of these discussions is to provide you with a concise perspective on the subject. There are several other books, whitepapers, and material that are available on these topics if you need deeper details and technical insights.

Hadoop

The most popular word in the industry at the time of writing this book, Hadoop has taken the world by storm in providing the solution architecture to solve Big Data processing on a cheaper commodity platform with faster scalability and parallel processing.

Hadoop was started an open-source search engine project called Nutch in 2002 by Mike Cafarella and Doug Cutting. By early 2004, the team had developed an excellent crawler engine but hit a roadblock with the scalability of the search engine. Around the same time, Google announced the availability of GFS and MapReduce papers to open-source communities. The Nutch team developed the Nutch Distributed File System (NDFS), an open-source distributed file system, based on the architecture concepts of GFS. The NDFS architecture solved the storage and associated scalability issues. In 2005, the Nutch team completed the port of Nutch algorithms to the MapReduce programming model. The new architecture could enable processing of large and unstructured data with unsurpassed scalability.

In 2006, the Nutch team of Cafarella and Cutting created a subproject under Apache Lucene and called it Hadoop (named after Doug Cutting's son's toy elephant), and released the early version to the open-source community. Yahoo adopted the project and sponsored the continued development of Hadoop, which it widely adopted and deployed within Yahoo. In January 2008, Yahoo released the first complete project release of Hadoop under open source.

The first generation of Hadoop consisted of an HDFS (modeled after NDFS) distributed file system and MapReduce framework along with a coordinator interface and an interface to write and read from HDFS. When the first generation of Hadoop architecture was conceived and implemented in 2004 by Cutting and Cafarella, they were able to automate a lot of operations on crawling and indexing on search, and improved efficiencies and scalability. Within a few months they reached an architecture scalability of 20 nodes running Nutch without missing a heartbeat. This provided Yahoo the next move to hire Cutting and adopt Hadoop to become one of its core platforms. Yahoo kept the platform moving with its constant innovation and research. Soon many committers and volunteer developers/testers started contributing to the growth of a healthy ecosystem around Hadoop.

At the time of writing (2012), in the last three years we have seen two leading distributors of Hadoop with management tools and professional services emerge: CloudEra and HortonWorks. We have also seen the emergence of Hadoop-based solutions from IBM, Teradata, Oracle, and Microsoft, and HP, SAP, and DELL in partnerships with other providers and distributors.

The most current list at Apache's website for Hadoop lists the top-level stable projects and releases and also incubated projects that are evolving.

- Hadoop Common—the common utilities that support other Hadoop subprojects.
- Hadoop Distributed File System (HDFS™)—a distributed file system that provides high-throughput access to application data.
- Hadoop MapReduce—a software framework for distributed processing of large data sets on compute clusters.

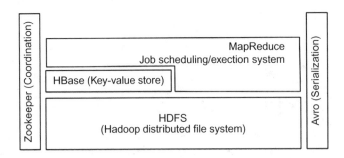

FIGURE 4.5

Core Hadoop components.

Other Hadoop-related projects include:

- Avro™—a data serialization system.
- Cassandra™—a scalable multimaster database with no single points of failure.
- Chukwa™—a data collection system for managing large distributed systems.
- HBase™—a scalable, distributed database that supports structured data storage for large tables.
- Hive™—a data warehouse infrastructure that provides data summarization and ad hoc querying.
- Mahout™—a scalable machine learning and data mining library.
- Pig™—a high-level data-flow language and execution framework for parallel computation.
- ZooKeeper™—a high-performance coordination service for distributed applications.

Hadoop core components

At the heart of the Hadoop framework or architecture there are components that can be called the foundational core. These components are shown in Figure 4.5 and discussed in detail in the following subsections.

HDFS

HDFS is a highly fault-tolerant, scalable, and distributed file system architected to run on commodity hardware.

The HDFS architecture was designed to solve two known problems experienced by the early developers of large-scale data processing. The first problem was the ability to break down the files across multiple systems and process each piece of the file independent of the other pieces and finally consolidate all the outputs in a single result set. The second problem was the fault tolerance both at the file processing level and the overall system level in the distributed data processing systems.

Some of the assumptions of HDFS design are

- *Redundancy*—hardware will be prone to failure and processes can run out of infrastructure resources, but redundancy built into the design can handle these situations.
- *Scalability*—linear scalability at a storage layer is needed to utilize parallel processing at its optimum level. Designing for 100% linear scalability.
- *Fault tolerance*—the automatic ability to recover from failure and complete the processing of data.

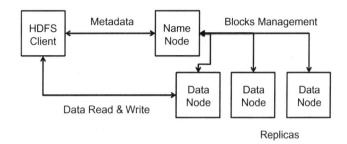

FIGURE 4.6

HDFS architecture.

- *Cross-platform compatibility*—the ability to integrate across multiple architecture platforms.
- *Compute and storage in one environment*—data and computation colocated in the same architecture removing redundant I/O and excessive disk access.

The three principle goals of HDFS architecture are:

1. Process extremely large files ranging from multiple gigabytes to petabytes.
2. Streaming data processing to read data at high-throughput rates and process data on read.
3. Capability to execute on commodity hardware with no special hardware requirements.

HDFS architecture evolved from the NDFS architecture, which is based on the GFS architecture. The next section discusses the HDFS architecture.

HDFS architecture

Figure 4.6 shows the overall conceptual architecture of HDFS. The main building blocks of HDFS are:

- NameNode (master node)
- DataNodes (slave nodes)
- Image
- Journal
- Checkpoint

NameNode The NameNode is a single master server that manages the file system namespace and regulates access to files by clients. Additionally, the NameNode manages all the operations like opening, closing, moving, naming, and renaming of files and directories. It also manages the mapping of blocks to DataNodes.

DataNodes DataNodes represent the slaves in the architecture that manage data and the storage attached to the data. A typical HDFS cluster can have thousands of DataNodes and tens of thousands of HDFS clients per cluster, since each DataNode may execute multiple application tasks simultaneously. The DataNodes are responsible for managing read and write requests from the file system's clients, and block maintenance and perform replication as directed by the NameNode. The block management in HDFS is different from a normal file system. The size of the data file equals the actual length of the block. This means if a block is half full it needs only half of the space of the full block on the local drive, thereby optimizing storage space for compactness, and there is no extra space consumed on the block unlike a regular file system.

HDFS is a file system and, like any other file system architecture, it needs to manage consistency, recoverability, and concurrency for reliable operations. These requirements have been addressed in the architecture by creating image, journal, and checkpoint files.

Image An image represents the metadata of the namespace (inodes and lists of blocks). On startup, the NameNode pins the entire namespace image in memory. The in-memory persistence enables the NameNode to service multiple client requests concurrently.

Journal The journal represents the modification log of the image in the local host's native file system. During normal operations, each client transaction is recorded in the journal, and the journal file is flushed and synced before the acknowledgment is sent to the client. The NameNode upon startup or from a recovery can replay this journal.

Checkpoint To enable recovery, the persistent record of the image is also stored in the local host's native files system and is called a *checkpoint*. Once the system starts up, the NameNode never modifies or updates the checkpoint file. A new checkpoint file can be created during the next startup, on a restart, or on demand when requested by the administrator or by the CheckpointNode (described later in this chapter).

HDFS startup

HDFS manages the startup sequence based on the image file, which is an in-memory persistence. During initial startup, every time the NameNode initializes a namespace image from the checkpoint file and replays all the changes from a journal file. Once the startup sequence completes the process, a new checkpoint and an empty journal are written back to the storage directories and the NameNode starts serving client requests. For improved redundancy and reliability, copies of the checkpoint and journal should be made at other servers.

Block allocation and storage in HDFS

Data organization in the HDFS is managed similar to GFS. The namespace is represented by inodes, which represent files, directories, and records attributes like permissions, modification and access times, and namespace and disk space quotas. The files are split into user-defined block sizes (default is 128 MB) and stored into a DataNode and two replicas at a minimum to ensure availability and redundancy, though the user can configure more replicas. Typically, the storage location of block replicas may change over time and therefore are not part of the persistent checkpoint.

HDFS client

A thin layer of interface that is used by programs to access data stored within HDFS is called the client. The client first contacts the NameNode to get the locations of data blocks that comprise the file. Once the block data is returned to the client, subsequently the client reads block contents from the DataNode closest to it.

When writing data, the client first requests the NameNode to provide to the DataNodes where the data can be written. The NameNode returns the block to write the data. When the first block is filled, additional blocks are provided by the NameNode in a pipeline. A block for each request might not be on the same DataNode.

One of the biggest design differentiators of HDFS is the API that exposes the locations of file blocks. This allows applications like MapReduce to schedule a task to where the data is located, thus improving the I/O performance. The API also includes functionality to set the replication factor for each file. To maintain file and block integrity, once a block is assigned to a DataNode, two files are created to represent each replica in the local host's native file system. The first file contains the data itself and the second file is the block's metadata including checksums for each data block and generation stamp.

Replication and recovery

In the original design of HDFS there was a single NameNode for each cluster, which became the single point of failure. This has been addressed in the recent releases of HDFS where NameNode replication is now a standard feature like DataNode replication.

Communication and management

The most critical component within the HDFS architecture is the communication and management between a NameNode and DataNodes. This aspect is implemented as a protocol of handshakes and system IDs. Upon initial creation and formatting, a namespace ID is assigned to the file system on the NameNode. This ID is persistently stored on all the nodes across the cluster. DataNodes similarly are assigned a unique storage ID on the initial creation and registration with a NameNode. This storage ID never changes and will be persistent event if the DataNode is started on a different IP address or port.

During the startup process, the NameNode completes its namespace refresh and is ready to establish the communication with the DataNode. To ensure that each DataNode that connects to the NameNode is the correct DataNode, there is a series of verification steps:

- The DataNode identifies itself to the NameNode with a handshake and verifies its namespace ID and software version.
- If either does not match with the NameNode, the DataNode automatically shuts down.
- The signature verification process prevents incorrect nodes from joining the cluster and automatically preserves the integrity of the file system.
- The signature verification process also is an assurance check for consistency of software versions between the NameNode and DataNode, since an incompatible version can cause data corruption or loss.
- After the handshake and validation on the NameNode, a DataNode sends a block report. A block report contains the block ID, the length for each block replica, and the generation stamp.
- The first block report is sent immediately upon the DataNode registration.
- Subsequently, hourly updates of the block report are sent to the NameNode, which provide the view of where block replicas are located on the cluster.
- When a new DataNode is added and initialized, since it does not have a namespace ID, it is permitted to join the cluster and receive the cluster's namespace ID.

Heartbeats

The connectivity between the NameNode and a DataNode are managed by the persistemt heartbeats that are sent by the DataNode every three seconds. The heartbeat provides the NameNode confirmation about the availability of the blocks and the replicas of the DataNode. Additionally, heartbeats also carry information about total storage capacity, storage in use, and the number of data transfers currently in progress. These statistics are by the NameNode for managing space allocation and load balancing.

During normal operations, if the NameNode does not receive a heartbeat from a DataNode in ten minutes the NameNode, it considers that DataNode to be out of service and the block replicas hosted to be unavailable. The NameNode schedules the creation of new replicas of those blocks on other DataNodes.

The heartbeats carry roundtrip communications and instructions from the NameNode, including commands to:

- Replicate blocks to other nodes.
- Remove local block replicas.
- Re-register the node.
- Shut down the node.
- Send an immediate block report.

Frequent heartbeats and replies are extremely important for maintaining the overall system integrity even on big clusters. Typically, a NameNode can process thousands of heartbeats per second without affecting other operations.

CheckpointNode and BackupNode

There are two roles that a NameNode can be designated to perform apart from servicing client requests and managing DataNodes. These roles are specified during startup and can be the CheckpointNode or the BackupNode. The primary reason for the additional roles are to create a native recovery mechanism for the NameNode in both a journal-based architecture and image based architecture.

CheckpointNode The CheckpointNode serves as a journal-capture architecture to create a recovery mechanism for the NameNode. The CheckpointNode combines the existing checkpoint and journal to create a new checkpoint and an empty journal in specific intervals. It returns the new checkpoint to the NameNode. The CheckpointNode runs on a different host from the NameNode since it has the same memory requirements as the NameNode.

By creating a checkpoint, the NameNode can truncate the tail of the current journal. HDFS clusters run for prolonged periods of time without restarts, resulting in the journal growing very large, increasing the probability of loss or corruption. This mechanism provides a protection.

BackupNode The BackupNode can be considered as a read-only NameNode. It contains all file system metadata information except for block locations. It accepts a stream of namespace transactions from the active NameNode and saves them to its own storage directories, and applies these transactions to its own namespace image in its memory. If the NameNode fails, the BackupNode's image in memory and the checkpoint on disk are a record of the latest namespace state and can be used to create a checkpoint for recovery. Creating a checkpoint from a BackupNode is very efficient as it processes the entire image in its own disk and memory.

A BackupNode can perform all operations of the regular NameNode that do not involve modification of the namespace or management of block locations. This feature provides the administrators the option of running a NameNode without persistent storage, delegating responsibility for the namespace state persisting to the BackupNode. This is not a normal practice, but can be used in certain situations.

File system snapshots

Like any file system, there are periodic upgrades and patches that might need to be applied to the HDFS. The possibility of corrupting the system due to software bugs or human mistakes always

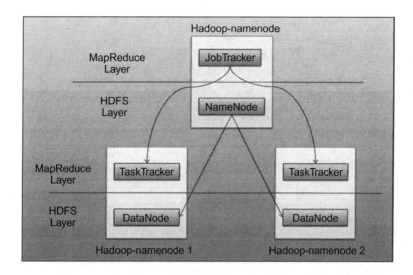

FIGURE 4.7

Job executions in Hadoop.

exists. To avoid system corruption or shutdown, we can create snapshots in HDFS. The snapshot mechanism lets administrators save the current state of the file system to create a rollback in case of failure.

JobTracker and TaskTracker

Hadoop by design is built to handle a large volume of data processing and throughput. It is primarily developed in Java and most of the processes that are executing within Hadoop typically follow the same base architecture of Java and execute within their Java Virtual Machines (JVMs). Figure 4.7 shows the processing of jobs within the Hadoop architecture that are managed by JobTrackers and TaskTrackers.

JobTracker is a daemon service within the Hadoop environment that controls the job execution and processing. For a given Hadoop cluster, there is only one JobTracker process that executes all the job requests submitted by client applications. JobTracker runs on its own JVM process. The detailed sequence of how jobs are executed in Hadoop is as follows:

- Client submits a job request.
- Job request is processed by the JobTracker.
  - The JobTracker talks to the NameNode to determine the locations of the data within the cluster.
  - Once the data locations are identified, the JobTracker finds TaskTracker nodes that are available to it and issues the work to these nodes.
  - The TaskTracker notifies the JobTracker of the status of the processes upon completion.
- When the job and its processes are completed, the JobTracker updates its status and signals the client application for completion of processing. Client applications can poll the JobTracker for status information during the execution of the job.

A TaskTracker is a node in the cluster that accepts tasks from a JobTracker. By design, every TaskTracker is configured with a set of *slots*, which indicate the total number of tasks that it can accept at any given point in time. The key features with which TaskTracker works are:

- The TaskTracker creates and manages separate JVM processes to execute the actual work assigned by the JobTracker. By creating a new JVM process the success or failure of any particular piece of work remains isolated and does not affect the entire TaskTracker.
- The TaskTracker monitors all the processes that were created by it for job execution and it captures all the output and exit codes. When the process finishes execution, the JobTracker is notified of the status.
- The TaskTracker communicates periodic signals called heartbeats to the JobTracker to notify that it is still alive. These messages additionally inform the JobTracker of the number of available slots, so the JobTracker can be updated about the availability of nodes within the cluster where work can be delegated.
- When a TaskTracker fails executing and notifies the JobTracker, there are three possibilities that a JobTracker can choose:
  1. It can resubmit the job elsewhere in the cluster.
  2. It can mark that specific record as something to avoid and not process that portion of data.
  3. It can blacklist the TaskTracker as unreliable and move on.

The combination of these two processes and their management of job execution is how Hadoop executes MapReduce processes. The JobTracker is a single point of failure for processing MapReduce services on Hadoop. If it goes down, all executing and queued jobs are halted.

HDFS is a file system that also provides load balancing, disk management, block allocation, and advanced file management within its design. For further details on these areas, refer to the HDFS architecture guide on Apache's HDFS Project page (http://hadoop.apache.org/).

Based on the brief architecture discussion of HDFS in this section, we can see how Hadoop manages all its data management functions, implemented through a series of API calls. Due to its file-based architecture, HDFS achieves unlimited scalability and can deliver sustained performance when infrastructure is expanded within the cluster.

MapReduce

MapReduce is a programming model for processing extremely large data sets and was originally developed by Google in the early 2000s for solving the scalability of search computation. Its foundations are based on principles of parallel and distributed processing without any database dependency. The flexibility of MapReduce lies in the ability to process distributed computations on large amounts of data on clusters of commodity servers, with simple task-based models for management of the same.

The key features of MapReduce that make it the interface on Hadoop or Cassandra include:

- Automatic parallelization
- Automatic distribution
- Fault-tolerance
- Status and monitoring tools
- Easy abstraction for programmers
- Programming language flexibility
- Extensibility

MapReduce programming model

MapReduce is based on functional programming models largely from Lisp. Typically, the users will implement two functions:

- `Map (in_key, in_value) -> (out_key, intermediate_value) list`
  - The `Map` function written by the user will receive an input pair of keys and values, and after the computation cycles, will produce a set of intermediate key-value pairs.
  - Library functions then are used to group together all intermediate values associated with an intermediate key I and passes them to the `Reduce` function.
- `Reduce (out_key, intermediate_value list) -> out_value list`
  - The Reduce function written by the user will accept an intermediate key I, and the set of values for the key.
  - It will merge together these values to form a possibly smaller set of values.
  - Reducer outputs are just zero or one output value per invocation.
  - The intermediate values are supplied to the Reduce function via an iterator. The Iterator function allows us to handle large lists of values that cannot be fit in memory or a single pass.

The MapReduce framework consists of a library of different interfaces. The major interfaces used by developers are Mapper, Reducer, JobConf, JobClient, Partitioner, OutputCollector, Reporter, InputFormat, OutputFormat, and OutputCommitter.

Figure 4.8 shows the overall architecture of MapReduce. The main components of this architecture include:

- Mapper—maps input key-value pairs to a set of intermediate key-value pairs. For an input pair the mapper can map to zero or many output pairs. By default the mapper spawns one map task for each input.
- Reducer—performs a number of tasks:
  - Sort and group mapper outputs.
  - Shuffle partitions.

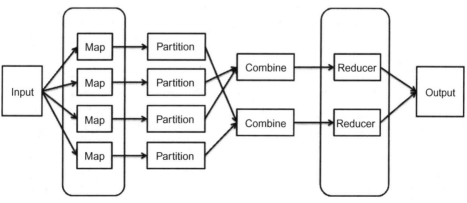

FIGURE 4.8

MapReduce architecture.

- Perform secondary sorting as necessary.
- Manage overrides specified by users for grouping and partitioning.
- Reporter—is used to report progress, set application-level status messages, update any user set counters, and indicate long running tasks or jobs are alive.
- Combiner—an optional performance booster that can be specified to perform local aggregation of the intermediate outputs to manage the amount of data transferred from the Mapper to the Reducer.
- Partitioner—controls the partitioning of the keys of the intermediate map outputs. The key (or a subset of the key) is used to derive the partition and default partitions are created by a *hash function*. The total number of partitions will be same as the number of reduce tasks for the job.
- Output collector—collects the output of Mappers and Reducers.
- Job configuration—is the primary user interface to manage MapReduce jobs.
  - It is typically used to specify the Mapper, Combiner, Partitioner, Reducer, InputFormat, OutputFormat, and OutputCommitter for every job.
  - It also indicates the set of input files and where the output files should be written.
  - Optionally used to specify other advanced options for the job such as the comparator to be used, files to be put in the DistributedCache, and compression on intermediate and/or final job outputs.
  - It is used for debugging via user-provided scripts, whether job tasks can be executed in a *speculative* manner, the maximum number of attempts per task for any possible failure, and the percentage of task failures that can be tolerated by the job overall.
- Output committer—is used to manage the commit for jobs and tasks in MapReduce. Key tasks executed are:
  - Set up the job during initialization. For example, create the intermediate directory for the job during the initialization of the job.
  - Clean up the job after the job completion. For example, remove the temporary output directory after the job completion.
  - Set up any task temporary output.
  - Check whether a task needs a commit. This will avoid overheads on unnecessary commits.
  - Commit of the task output on completion.
  - On failure, discard the task commit and clean up all intermediate results, memory release, and other user-specified tasks.
- Job input:
  - Specifies the input format for a Map/Reduce job.
  - Validate the input specification of the job.
  - Split up the input file(s) into logical instances to be assigned to an individual Mapper.
  - Provide input records from the logical splits for processing by the Mapper.
- Memory management, JVM reuse, and compression are managed with the job configuration set of classes.

MapReduce program design

MapReduce programming is based on functional programming, where the dataflow from one module to another is not based on a specific control but rather behaves like a directed acyclic graph (DAG), where value changes in the currently executing step cause the successors to recalculate values. This

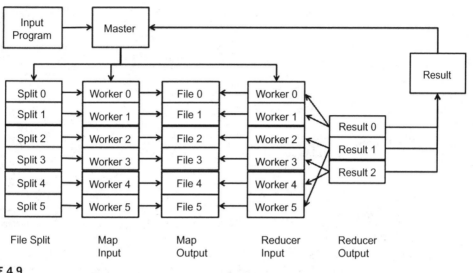

FIGURE 4.9

MapReduce implementation.

provides the dataflow consistency between Maps, Reduces, and Combiners. This is a very key concept to remember, as the DAG will be referenced in a MapReduce architecture and design often.

MapReduce implementation architecture

MapReduce transcends beyond the Mapper and Reducer functions. Since the fundamentals of its architecture are derived from programming languages and the original problem it was addressing was large-scale search enablement, which needed parsing of millions of documents, images, and video metadata, newsfeeds, and more at excessive speeds for millions of users across the globe at the same instance of time in one or more languages, MapReduce programs have been architected to function in a master–slave mode, where the master has a list of arrays of equal size and the arrays are processed across in parallel by multiple slaves that get the equal allocation of portions of the array. Finally, the master collates the results to return to the invoker.

The design of the architecture in the master–slave or master–worker configuration enables scalability for processing in a single or a small cluster of machines. The master manages the splitting or sharding of the input data and its distribution to the workers. Once the worker is assigned a task, the next set of activities for the tasks are tracked at each worker level, and upon completion the results are sent to the master. This concept is shown in Figure 4.9.

There are a number of built-in functions within MapReduce to manage the execution and program control. You can also add custom functions as needed, should you decide to add some layers of customization to the architecture.

MapReduce job processing and management

MapReduce master node communicates with all worker nodes via heartbeats. If a worker node does not respond to heartbeats in time, the node is marked as failed and the tasks are reexecuted from the point of failure to a different worker whether it was a Map or a Reduce task.

MapReduce limitations (Version 1, Hadoop MapReduce)

- Scalability:
  - Maximum cluster size: 4,000 nodes
  - Maximum concurrent tasks: 40,000
  - Coarse synchronization in JobTracker
- Single point of failure:
  - NameNode or JobTracker can become the choking point
  - Failure kills all queued and running jobs
  - Jobs need to be resubmitted by users
- Restart is very tricky due to complex state
- Hard partition of resources into Map and Reduce slots

MapReduce v2 (YARN)

At the time of writing this book, MapReduce v2 known as YARN is about six months into a stable release. There are a number of limitations of v1 that have been addressed in this release.

One issue that has been addressed is the JobTracker is a major component in data processing as it manages key tasks of resource marshaling and job execution at individual task levels (Figure 4.10). This interface has deficiencies in:

- Memory consumption
- Threading model
- Scalability

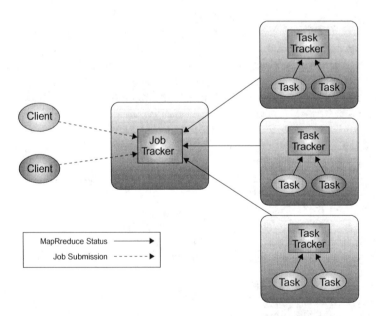

FIGURE 4.10

MapReduce classic JobTracker architecture.

Source: Apache Foundation.

- Reliability
- Performance

These issues have been addressed by individual situations and several tweaks in design were done to circumvent the shortcomings. The problem manifests in large clusters where it becomes difficult to manage the issue.

Other overall issues have been observed in large clustered environments in the following areas:

- Reliability
- Availability
- Scalability—clusters of 10,000 nodes or/and 200,000 cores
- Evolution—ability for customers to control upgrades to the grid software stack
- Predictable latency—a major customer concern
- Cluster utilization
- Support for alternate programming paradigms to MapReduce

The two major functionalities of the JobTracker are resource management and job scheduling/monitoring. The load that is processed by JobTracker runs into problems due to competing demand for resources and execution cycles arising from the single point of control in the design. The fundamental idea of YARN is to split up the two major functionalities of the JobTracker into separate processes (Figure 4.11). In the new-release architecture, there are two modules: a global ResourceManager (RM) and per-application ApplicationMaster (AM).

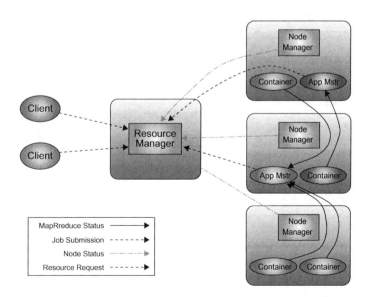

FIGURE 4.11

MapReduce v2 JobTracker architecture.

Source: Apache Foundation.

The primary components and their focus areas are:

1. ResourceManager (RM), which has two main components:
   - Scheduler:
     - The Scheduler is responsible for allocating resources to the various running applications and manages the constraints of capacities, availability, and resource queues.
     - The Scheduler is responsible for purely schedule management and will be working on scheduling based on resource containers, which specify memory, disk, and CPU.
     - The Scheduler will not assume restarting of failed tasks either due to application failure or hardware failures.
   - Application Manager:
     - Responsible for accepting job submissions.
     - Negotiates the first container for executing the application-specific AM.
     - Provides the service for restarting the AM container on failure.
     - The Application Manager has three subcomponents:
       a. Scheduler Negotiator—component responsible for negotiating the resources for the AM with the Scheduler.
       b. AMContainer Manager—component responsible for starting and stopping the container of the AM by talking to the appropriate NodeManager.
       c. AM Monitor—component responsible for managing the aliveness of the AM and responsible for restarting the AM if necessary.

   The ResourceManager stores snapshots of its state in the Zookeeper. In case of failure, a very transparent restart is feasible and ensures availability.

2. NodeManager:
   - The NodeManager is a per-machine agent and is responsible for launching containers for applications once the Scheduler allocates them to the application.
   - Container resource monitoring for ensuring that the allocated containers do not exceed their allocated resource slices on the machine.
   - Setting up the environment of the container for the task execution including binaries, libraries, and jars.
   - Manages local storage on the node. Applications can continue to use the local storage even when they do not have an active allocation on the node, thus providing scalability and availability.

3. ApplicationMaster (AM):
   - Per application.
   - Negotiates resources with the RM.
   - Manages application scheduling and task execution with NodeManagers.
   - Recovers the application on its own failure. Will either recover the application from the saved persistent state or just run the application from the very beginning, depending on recovery success.

YARN scalability

The resource model for YARN v1 or MapReduce v2 is memory-driven. Every node in the system is modeled to be consisting of multiple containers of minimum size of memory. The ApplicationMaster can request multiples of the minimum memory size as needed.

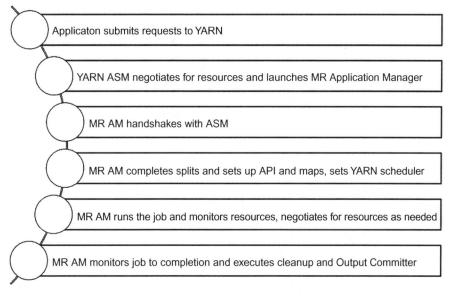

FIGURE 4.12

YARN execution flow.

What this means to any application is the memory slots required to run a job can be accessed from any node, depending on the availability of memory. This provides simple chunkable scalability especially in a cluster configuration. In classic Hadoop MapReduce the cluster is not artificially segregated into Map and Reduce slots, and the application jobs are bottlenecked on Reduce slots limiting scalability in job execution in the dataflow (Figure 4.12).

Comparison between MapReduce v1 and v2

Presented here is a simple comparison between the two releases of MapReduce:

- Classic MapReduce:
  - Job request submitted to JobTracker.
  - Jobtracker manages the execution with tasks.
  - Resources are allocated on availability basis, some jobs get more and others less.
  - No scalable resource allocation across a cluster.
  - Multiple single points of failure.
- YARN:
  - Application executed by YARN.
  - Resources negotiated and allocated prior to job execution.
  - Map-based resource request setup for the entire job.
  - Resource monitor tracks usage and requests additional resources as needed from across a cluster in a clustered setup.
  - Job completion and cleanup tasks are executed.

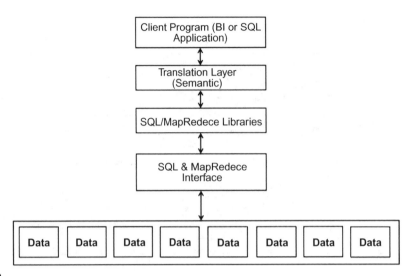

FIGURE 4.13

Conceptual SQL/MapReduce architecture.

SQL/MapReduce

Business intelligence has been one of the most successful applications in the last decade, but severe performance limitations have been a bottleneck, especially with detail data analysis. The problem becomes compounded with analytics and the need for 360° perspective on customers and products with ad-hoc analysis demands from users. The powerful combination of SQL when extended to MapReduce enables users to explore larger volumes of raw data through normal SQL functions and regular business intelligence tools. This is the fundamental concept behind SQL/MapReduce. There are a few popular implementations of SQL/MapReduce including Hive, AsterData, Greenplum, and HadoopDB.

Figure 4.13 shows a conceptual architecture of a SQL/MapReduce implementation. There are a few important components to understand:

- Translator—this is a custom layer provided by the solution. It can simply be a library of functions to extend in the current database environment.
- SQL/MapReduce interface—this is the layer that will create and distribute the jobs at the lowest MapReduce execution layer.
- SQL/MapReduce libraries—catalog of library functions.

The overall benefits of combining SQL/MapReduce include:

- Use of SQL for powerful postresult analytics and MapReduce to perform large-scale data processing on unstructured and semi-structured data.
- Effectively use the sharding capabilities of MapReduce to scale up and scale out the data irrespective of volume or variety.
- Provide the business user all the data with the same interface tool that runs on SQL.

The downside of the technology in evolution includes:

- Heavy dependency on custom libraries.
- Current support on certain analytic functions.

The next generation of SQL/MapReduce interfaces and libraries will solve a number of evolutionary challenges.

The combination of HDFS and MapReduce creates an extreme architecture. What is important to note here is:

- Files once processed cannot be processed from a midpoint. If a new version of the data is sent by files, the entire file has to be processed.
- MapReduce on large clusters can be difficult to manage.
- The entire platform by design is oriented to handle extremely large files and therefore is not suited for transaction processing.
- When the files are broken for processing, the consistency of the files completing processing on all nodes in a cluster is a soft state model of eventual consistency.

Zookeeper

Developing large-scale applications on Hadoop or any distributed platform mandates that a resource and application coordinator be available to coordinate the tasks between nodes. In a controlled environment like the RDBMS or SOA programming, the tasks are generated in a controlled manner and the coordination simply needs to ensure successful network management without data loss and the health check on the nodes in a distributed system. In the case of Hadoop, the minimum volumes of data start with multiterabytes and the data is distributed across files on multiple nodes. Keeping user queries and associated tasks mandates a coordinator that is as flexible and scalable as the platform itself.

Zookeeper is an open-source, in-memory, distributed NoSQL database that is used for coordination services for managing distributed applications. It consists of a simple set of functions that can be used to build services for synchronization, configuration maintenance, groups, and naming. Zookeeper has a file system structure that mirrors classic file system tree architectures, and it is natively developed and deployed in Java and has bindings for Java and C.

Because of its NoSQL origins, the architecture of Zookeeper is based on a hierarchical namespace structure called zNode. It uses the zNode architecture to allow distributed processes to coordinate and have interprocess communication mechanisms, in a low-latency, high-throughput, and ordered access environment. Sophisticated synchronization is implemented at the client by using a feature called ordering based on vector clocks and timestamps. Zookeeper is primarily designed to store coordination data—status information, configuration, location information, etc.—and not large data volumes. By default Zookeeper has a built-in check for a maximum size of 1 MB.

Zookeeper features

A Zookeeper data model is simple to understand:

- A parent namespace called zNode:
  - Contains children and further levels of zNodes.
  - Can have data associated with any level.

- Has access control lists.
- A session-based node called the ephemeral node can be created and destroyed by a session.
- zNodes can be sequential; this ordering helps manage complex interconnected tasks.
- zNodes can have watches to provide for callbacks. This helps when data is distributed and tasks are distributed in a large cluster.

- Zookeeper has a simple set of API commands to work with:
  - `string create(path, data, acl, flags)`
  - `delete(path, expected_version)`
  - `stat set_data(path, data, expected_version)`
  - `(data, stat) get_data(path, watch)`
  - `stat exists(path, watch)`
  - `string get_children(path, watch)`

- Zookeeper offers a data consistency model to provide guarantees with its services:
  - Sequential consistency—updates from a client are applied in the order sent.
  - Atomicity—updates either succeed or fail.
  - Single system image—unique view, regardless of the server.
  - Durability—updates once succeeded will not be undone.
  - Timeliness—lag is bounded, read operations can lag behind leaders.

- Used for:
  - Configuration service—get the latest configuration and get notified when changes occur.
  - Lock service—provide mutual exclusion
  - Leader election—there can be only one.
  - Group membership—dynamically determine members of a group.
  - Queue producer/consumer paradigm.

In the Hadoop ecosystem, Zookeeper is implemented as a service to coordinate tasks. Figure 4.14 shows the implementation model for Zookeeper.

Zookeeper as a service can be run in two modes:

- *Standalone mode.* There is a single Zookeeper server, and this configuration is useful for development or testing but provides no guarantees of high availability or resilience.

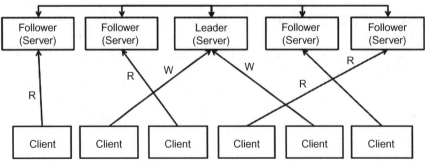

FIGURE 4.14

Zookeeper ensemble.

- *Replicated mode*. This is the mode of deployment in production, on a cluster of machines called an ensemble. Zookeeper achieves high availability through replication, and can provide a service as long as a majority of the machines in the ensemble are up and running. For example, as seen in Figure 4.12, in a five-node ensemble, any two machines can fail and the service will still work because a majority of three remain (a quorum), whereas in a six-node ensemble, a failure of three means a loss of majority and shutdown of service. It is usual to have an odd number of machines in an ensemble to avoid such situations.

Zookeeper has one task or goal, to ensure all the zNode changes across the system are updated to the leader and followers. When a failure occurs in a minority of machines, the replicas need to bring up the machines to catch up from the lag. To implement the management of the ensemble, Zookeeper uses a protocol called Zab that runs in two steps and can be repetitive:

1. *Leader election*. The machines in an ensemble go through a process of electing a distinguished member, called the leader. Clients communicate with one server in a session and work on a read or write operation. As seen here, writes will be only accomplished through the leader, which is then broadcast to the followers as an update. Reads can be from the leader or followers and happen in memory. Followers sometimes lag in read operations and eventually become consistent. This phase is finished once a majority (or quorum) of followers have synchronized their state with the leader. Zab implements the following optimizations to circumvent the bottleneck of a leader:
   - Clients can connect to any server, and servers have to serve read operations locally and maintain information about the session of a client. This extra load of a follower process (a process that is not a leader) makes the load more evenly distributed.
   - The number of servers involved is small. This means that the network communication overhead does not become the bottleneck that can affect fixed sequencer protocols.
2. *Atomic broadcast*. Write requests and updates are committed in a two-phase approach in Zab. To maintain consistency across the ensemble, write requests are always communicated to the leader. The leader broadcasts the update to all its followers. When a quorum of its followers (in Figure 4.12 we need three followers) have persisted the change (phase 1 of a two-phase commit), the leader commits the update (phase 2 of the commit), and the requestor gets a response saying the update succeeded. The protocol for achieving consensus is designed to be atomic, so a change either succeeds or fails completely.

Locks and processing

One of the biggest issues in distributed data processing is lock management, when one session has an exclusive lock on a server. Zookeeper manages this process by creating a list of child nodes and lock nodes and the associated queues of waiting processes for lock release. The lock node is allocated to the next process that is waiting based on the order received.

Lock management is done through a set of watches. If you become overzealous and set a large number of locks, it will become a nightmare and creates a herd effect on the Zookeeper service. Typically, a watch is set on the preceding process that is currently holding a lock.

Failure and recovery

A common issue in coordinating a large number of processes is connection loss. When there is a failover process, it needs information on the children affected by the connection loss to complete the failover. To manage this, the client session ID information is associated with child zNodes and locks, which will enable the failover client to synchronize.

Zookeeper is a highly available system, and it is critical that it can perform its functions in a timely manner. It is recommended to run Zookeeper on dedicated machines. Running it in a shared-services environment will adversely impact performance.

In Hadoop deployment, Zookeeper serves as the coordinator for managing all the key activities:

- *Manage configuration across nodes.* Zookeeper helps you quickly push configuration changes across dozens or hundreds of nodes.
- *Implement reliable messaging.* A guaranteed messaging architecture to deliver messages can be implemented with Zookeeper.
- *Implement redundant services.* Managing a large number of nodes with a Zab approach will provide a scalable redundancy management solution.
- *Synchronize process execution.* With Zookeeper, multiple nodes can coordinate the start and end of a process or calculation. This approach can ensure consistency of completion of operations.

Please see the Zookeeper configuration and administrators guide for further details (http://zookeeper.apache.org/doc/r3.1.2/zookeeperAdmin.html).

Pig

Analyzing large data sets introduces dataflow complexities that become harder to implement in a MapReduce program as data volumes and processing complexities increase. A high-level language that is more user friendly, is SQL-like in terms of expressing dataflows, has the flexibility to manage multistep data transformations, and handles joins with simplicity and easy program flow, was needed as an abstraction layer over MapReduce.

Apache Pig is a platform that has been designed and developed for analyzing large data sets. Pig consists of a high-level language for expressing data analysis programs and comes with infrastructure for evaluating these programs. At the time of writing, Pig's current infrastructure consists of a compiler that produces sequences of MapReduce programs. Pig's language architecture is a textual language platform called Pig Latin, of which the design goals were based on the requirement to handle large data processing with minimal complexity and include:

- *Programming flexibility.* The ability to break down complex tasks comprised of multiple steps and interprocess-related data transformations should be encoded as dataflow sequences that are easy to design, develop, and maintain.
- *Automatic optimization.* Tasks are encoded to let the system optimize their execution automatically. This allows the user to have greater focus on program development, allowing the user to focus on semantics rather than efficiency.
- *Extensibility.* Users can develop user-defined functions (UDFs) for more complex processing requirements.

Programming with pig latin

Pig is primarily a scripting language for exploring large data sets. It is developed to process multiple terabytes of data in a half-dozen lines of Pig Latin code. Pig provides several commands to the developer for introspecting the data structures in the program, as it is written.

Pig Latin can be executed as statements in either in Local or MapReduce mode, either interactively or as batch programs:

- In Local mode, Pig runs in a single JVM and accesses the local file system. This mode is suitable only for small data sets and can be run on minimal infrastructure.
- In MapReduce mode, Pig translates programs (queries and statements) into MapReduce jobs and runs them on a Hadoop cluster. Production environments for running Pig are deployed in this mode.

Pig data types
Pig language supports the following data types:

- Scalar types: int, long, double, chararray, bytearray
- Complex types:
  - map: associative array
  - tuple: ordered list of data, elements may be of any scalar or complex type
  - bag: unordered collection of tuples

Running pig programs
Pig programs can be run in three modes, all of which work in both Local and MapReduce modes (for more details see Apache Pig Wiki at (http://pig.apache.org/)).

- Scripting driven—a Pig program can be run as a script file, processed from a command line.
- Grunt shell—an interactive shell for running Pig commands.
- Embedded—you can run Pig programs from Java, using Java DataBase Connectivity (JDBC) drivers like a traditional SQL program from Java.

Pig program flow
Pig program control has many built-in commands and syntax. We will take a look at the core execution model. Every Pig module has LOAD, DUMP, and STORE statements:

- A LOAD statement reads data from the file system.
- A series of "transformation" statements process the data.
- A STORE statement writes output to the file system.
- A DUMP statement displays output to the screen.

Common pig command
LOAD: Read data from file system.
STORE: Write data to file system.
FOREACH: Apply expression to each record and output one or more records.
FILTER: Apply predicate and remove records that do not return true.
GROUP/COGROUP: Collect records with the same key from one or more inputs.
JOIN: Join two or more inputs based on a key.
ORDER: Sort records based on a key.
DISTINCT: Remove duplicate records.
UNION: Merge two data sets.

SPLIT: Split data into two or more sets, based on filter conditions.
STREAM: Send all records through a user-provided binary.
DUMP: Write output to stdout.
LIMIT: Limit the number of records.

During program execution, Pig first validates the syntax and semantics of statements and continues to process them; when it encounters a DUMP or STORE it completes the execution of the statement. For example, a Pig job to process compliance logs and extract words and phrases will look like the following"

```
A = load 'compliance_log';
B = foreach A generate
flatten(TOKENIZE((chararray)$0)) as word;
C = filter B by word matches '\\w+';
D = group C by word;
E = foreach D generate COUNT(C), group;
store E into 'compliance_log_freq';
```

Now let us say that we want to analyze how many of these words are in FDA mandates:

```
A = load 'FDA_Data';
B = foreach A generate
flatten(TOKENIZE((chararray)$0)) as word;
C = filter B by word matches '\\w+';
D = group C by word;
E = foreach D generate COUNT(C), group;
store E into 'FDA_Data_freq';
```

We can then join these two outputs to create a result set:

```
.compliance = LOAD 'compliance_log_freq' AS (freq, word);
 FDA = LOAD 'FDA_Data_freq' AS (freq, word);
 inboth = JOIN compliance BY word, FDA BY word;
 STORE inboth INTO 'output';
```

In this example the Food and Drug Administration (FDA) data is highly semi-structured and compliance logs are generated by multiple applications. Processing large data sets with simple lines of code is what Pig brings to MapReduce and Hadoop data processing.

Though Pig is very powerful, it cannot be used on small data sets or a transactional type of data. Its adoption to mainstream is still evolving. In the near future, I think Pig will be used more in data collection and preprocessing environments and in streaming data processing environments.

HBase

HBase is an open-source, nonrelational, column-oriented, multidimensional, distributed database developed on Google's BigTable architecture. It is designed with high availability and high performance as drivers to support storage and processing of large data sets on the Hadoop framework. HBase is not a database in the purist definition of a database. It provides unlimited scalability and performance and supports certain features of an ACID-compliant database. HBase is classified as a NoSQL database due to its architecture and design being closely aligned to Base (Being Available and Same Everywhere).

Why do we need HBase when the data is stored in the HDFS file system, which is the core data storage layer within Hadoop? For operations other than MapReduce execution and operations that aren't easy to work with in HDFS, and when you need random access to data, HBase is very useful. HBase satisfies two types of use cases:

- It provides a database-style interface to Hadoop, which enables developers to deploy programs that can quickly read or write to specific subsets of data in an extremely voluminous data set, without having to search and process through the entire data set.
- It provides a transactional platform for running high-scale, real-time applications as an ACID-compliant database (meeting standards for atomicity, consistency, isolation, and durability) while handling the incredible volume, variety, and complexity of data encountered on the Hadoop platform. HBase supports the following properties of ACID compliance:
  - Atomicity: All mutations are atomic within a row. For example, a read or write operation will either succeed or fail.
  - Consistency: All rows returned for any execution will consist of a complete row that existed or exists in the table.
  - Isolation: The isolation level is called "read committed" in the traditional DBMS.
  - Durability: All visible data in the system is durable data. For example, to phrase durability, a read will never return data that has not been made durable on disk.

HBase is different from the RDBMS and DBMS platforms and is architected and deployed like any NoSQL database.

HBase architecture

Data is organized in HBase as rows and columns and tables, very similar to a database; however, here is where the similarity ends. Let us look at the data model of HBase and then understand the implementation architecture.

- Tables:
  - Tables are made of rows and columns.
  - Table cells are the intersection of row and column coordinates. Each cell is versioned by default with a timestamp. The contents of a cell are treated as an uninterpreted array of bytes.
  - A table row has a sortable row key and an arbitrary number of columns.
- Rows:
  - Table row keys are also byte arrays. In this configuration anything can serve as the row key as opposed to strongly typed data types in the traditional database.
  - Table rows are sorted byte-ordered by row key, the table's primary key, and all table accesses are via the table primary key.
  - Columns are grouped as families and a row can have as many columns as loaded.
- Columns and column groups (families):
  - In HBse row columns are grouped into column families.
  - All column family members will mandatorily have a common prefix, for example, the columns person:name and person:comments are both members of the person column family, whereas email:identifier belongs to the email family.
  - A table's column families must be specified upfront as part of the table schema definition.
  - New column family members can be added on demand.

Row key	TS	Column "recipe:"	
"www.foodie.com"	t10	"recipe: foodie.com"	"FOODIE"
"www.foodtv.com"	t9	"recipe: foodtv.com"	"FOODTV.COM"
	t8	"recipe: foodtv.com/ spicy/curry"	"FOODTV.COM"

FIGURE 4.15

HBase data model example.

The flexibility of this type of a data model organization allows HBase to store data as column-oriented grouped by column families by design. The columns can be expanded based on the data loaded as long as it belongs to the row that it is loaded to and has predefined column groups in the data model.

As shown in Figure 4.15 there are multiple records for one row key and one row for the other. The flexibility to store this data in column groups allows us to store more data and query more data in the same query cycle. These are the powerful data model structures that are implemented within a larger architecture of Hadoop, where the data processing outputs are stored.

HBase components

There are four main components that together form the HBase architecture from an implementation model perspective:

- The HBase master is the key controller of operations in HBase. The main functions of the master include:
  - Responsible for monitoring region servers (one or more clusters).
  - Load balancing for regions.
  - Redirect client to correct region servers.

  To manage redundancy the master can be replicated. Like the master in MapReduce, the master in HBase stores no data and only has metadata about the region servers.
- The HBase region server is the slave node in the HBase architecture. Its primary functions include:
  - Storing the data and its metadata.
  - Serving requests (write/read/scan) of the client.

- Send heartbeats to master.
- Manage splits and synchronize with the master on the split and data allocation.
- The HBase client is a program API that can be executed from any language like Java or C++ to access HBase.
- Zookeeper is used to coordinate all the activities between master and region servers.

How does HBase internally manage all the communication between the Zookeeper, master, and region servers? HBase maintains two special catalog tables named ROOT and META. It maintains the current list, state, and location of all regions afloat on the cluster in these two catalogs. The ROOT table contains the list of META table regions, and the META table contains the list of all user-space regions. Entries in ROOT and META tables are keyed by region names, where a region name is made of the table name the region belongs to, the region's start row, its time of creation, and a hash key value. Row keys are sorted by default and finding the region that hosts a particular row is a matter of a lookup to find the first entry where the key is greater than or equal to that of the requested row key. As regions are split, deleted, or disabled, the ROOT and META tables are constantly refreshed and thus the changes are immediately reflected to user requests.

Clients connect to the Zookeeper and get the access information to the ROOT table. The ROOT table provides information about the META table, which points to the region of which the scope covers that of the requested row. The client then gets all the data about the region, user space, the column family, and the location details by doing a lookup on the META table. After the initial interaction with the master, the client directly starts working with the hosting region server.

HBase clients cache all the information they gather traversing the ROOT and META tables by caching locations as well as the user space, and the region start and stop rows. The cached data provides all the details about the regions and the data available there, avoiding roundtrips to read the META table. In a normal mode of operation, clients continue to use the cached entries as they perform tasks, until there is a failure or abort. When a failure happens, it is normally due to the movement of the region itself causing the cache to become stale. When this happens, the client first queries the META table and if it has moved to another location, the client traverses back to the ROOT table to get further information.

Write-ahead log

When clients write data to HBase tables, this data is first processed in memory. When the memory becomes full, the data is flushed to a log file. The file is available on HDFS for use by HBase in crash-recovery situations. This design is called the write-ahead log architecture and its goal is to ensure resiliency to failures. In the normal course of processing, region servers keep data in memory until enough is collected to flush to a disk. When the data is eventually flushed to a disk, the following sequence is followed:

- Every data update is first written to a log.
- The log is persisted (and replicated, since it resides on HDFS).

Only when the log file is completely written is the client notified of a successful operation from the system.

HBase is a powerful column-oriented data store, which is truly a sparse, distributed, persistent, multidimensional-sorted map. It is the database of choice for all Hadoop deployments as it can hold the key-value outputs from MapReduce and other sources in a scalable and flexible architecture.

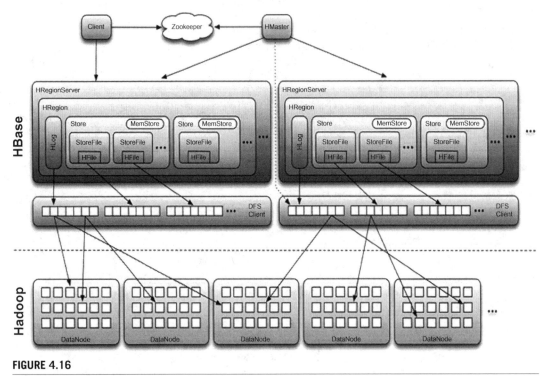

FIGURE 4.16

HBase components.

(Source: George Lars, @HUG Talk).

Hive

The scalability of Hadoop and HDFS is unparalleled based on the underlying architecture and the design of the platform. While HBase provides some pseudo-database features, business users working on Hadoop did not adopt the platform due to lack of SQL support or SQL-like features on Hadoop. While we understand that Hadoop cannot answer low-latency queries and deep analytical functions like the database, it has large data sets that cannot be processed by the database infrastructure and needs to be harnessed with some SQL-like language or infrastructure that can run MapReduce in the internals. This is where Hive comes into play.

Hive is an open-source data warehousing solution that has been built on top of Hadoop. The fundamental goals of designing Hive were:

- To build a system for managing and querying data using structured techniques on Hadoop.
- Use native MapReduce for execution at HDFS and Hadoop layers.
- Use HDFS for storage of Hive data.
- Store key metadata in an RDBMS.
- Extend SQL interfaces, a familiar data warehousing tool in use at enterprises.
- High extensibility: user-defined types, user-defined functions, formats, and scripts.
- Leverage extreme scalability and performance of Hadoop.
- Interoperability with other platforms.

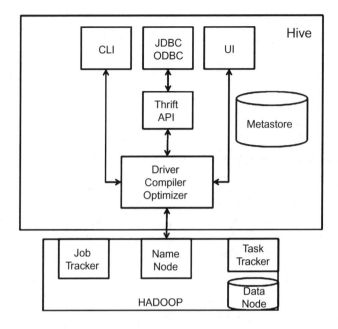

FIGURE 4.17

Hive architecture.

Hive supports queries expressed in an SQL-like declarative language, HiveQL, which are compiled into MapReduce jobs executed on Hadoop. Hive also includes a system catalog, the metastore, which contains schemas and statistics and is used in data exploration and query optimization.

Hive was originally conceived and developed at Facebook when the data scalability needs of Facebook outpaced and outgrew any traditional solution. Over the last few years, Hive has been released as an open-source platform on the Apache Hadoop Project. Let us take a quick look at the Hive architecture.

Hive architecture
The Hive system architecture is shown in Figure 4.17. The main architecture components that form the building blocks are as follows:

- *Metastore*—stores the system catalog and metadata about tables, columns, and partitions.
- *Driver*—maintains session details, process handles, and statistics, and manages the life cycle of a HiveQL statement as it moves through Hive.
- *Query compiler*—compiles HiveQL into Map and Reduce tasks (follows a DAG model).
- *Execution engine*—processes and executes the tasks produced by the compiler in a dependency order. The execution engine manages all the interactions between the compiler and Hadoop.
- *Thrift server*—provides a thrift interface, a JDBC/ODBC server, and a rich API to integrate Hive with other applications.
- *CLI and web UI*—two client interfaces. the command line interface (CLI) allows command-line execution and the web user interface is a management console.

- *Interfaces*—extensibility interfaces include the SerDe (implemented as Lazy SerDe in Hive) and ObjectInspector, UDF, and UDAF (user-defined aggregate function) interfaces that enable users to define their own custom functions.

The next section describes in detail the functionality of the components, broken down into infrastructure and execution.

Infrastructure

- *Metastore.* The metastore is the system catalog, which contains metadata about the tables stored in Hive. Metadata is specified during table creation and reused every time the table is used or specified in HiveQL. The metastore can be compared to a system catalog in a traditional database speak. The metastore contains the following entries.
- *Database.* This is the default namespace for tables. Users can create a database and name it. The database default is used for tables when there is no user-supplied database name.
- *Table.* A Hive table is made up of the data being stored in it and the associated metadata metastore.
  - In the physical implementation the data typically resides in HDFS, although it may be in any Hadoop file system, including the local file system.
  - Metadata for the table typically contains the list of columns and their data types, owner, user-supplied keys, storage, and SerDe information.
  - Storage information includes the location of the table's data in the file system, data formats, and bucketing information.
  - SerDe metadata includes the implementation class of serializer and serializer methods and any supporting information required by that implementation.
  - All this information can be specified during the initial creation of the table.
- *Partition.* To gain further performance and scalability, Hive organizes tables into partitions.
  - A partition contains parts of the data, based on the value of a partition column, for example, Date or Lat-Long.
  - Tables or partitions can be further subdivided into buckets. A bucket is akin to a subpartition. An example is to bucket a partition of customers by Customer_ID.
  - Each partition can have its own columns, SerDe, and storage information.

Execution: how does hive process queries?

A HiveQL statement is submitted via the CLI, the web UI, or an external client using the Thrift, ODBC, or JDBC API. The driver first passes the query to the compiler where it goes through parse, type check, and semantic analysis using the metadata stored in the metastore. The compiler generates a logical plan that is then optimized through a simple rule-based optimizer. Finally, an optimized plan in the form of a DAG of MapReduce and HDFS tasks is generated. The execution engine then executes these tasks in the order of their dependencies, using Hadoop.

We can further analyze this workflow of processing as shown in Figure 4.18:

- The Hive client triggers a query.
- The compiler receives the query and connects to the metastore.
- The compiler receives the query and initiates the first phase of compilation:
  - Parser—converts the query into parse tree representation. Hive uses Antlr to generate the abstract syntax tree (AST).

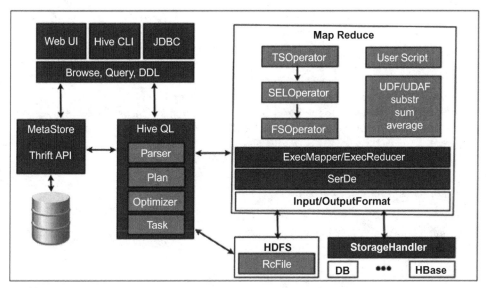

FIGURE 4.18

Hive process flow.

Source: HUG Discussions.

- Semantic analyzer—in this stage the compiler builds a logical plan based on the information that is provided by the metastore on the input and output tables. Additionally, the complier also checks type compatibilities in expressions and flags compile-time semantic errors at this stage. The next step is the transformation of an AST to intermediate representation that is called the query block (QB) tree. Nested queries are converted into parent–child relationships in a QB tree during this stage.
- Logical plan generator—in this stage the compiler writes the logical plan from the semantic analyzer into a logical tree of operations.
- Optimization—this is the most involved phase of the complier as the entire series of DAG optimizations are implemented in this phase. There are several customizations that can be done to the complier if desired. The primary operations done at this stage are as follows:
  - Logical optimization—perform multiple passes over the logical plan and rewrites in several ways.
  - Column pruning—this optimization step ensures that only the columns that are needed in the query processing are actually projected out of the row.
  - Predicate pushdown—predicates are pushed down to the scan if possible so that rows can be filtered early in the processing.
  - Partition pruning—predicates on partitioned columns are used to prune out files of partitions that do not satisfy the predicate.
  - Join optimization.
  - Grouping and regrouping.
  - Repartitioning.

- – The physical plan generator converts logical plan into physical.
  - – The physical plan generator creates the final DAG workflow of MapReduce.
- • Execution engine gets the compiler outputs to execute on the Hadoop platform:
  - – All the tasks are executed in the order of their dependencies. Each task is only executed if all of its prerequisites have been executed.
  - – A MapReduce task first serializes its part of the plan into a plan.xml file.
  - – This file is then added to the job cache for the task and instances of ExecMapper and ExecReducers are spawned using Hadoop.
  - – Each of these classes deserializes the plan.xml file and executes the relevant part of the task.
  - – The final results are stored in a temporary location and, at the completion of the entire query, the results are moved to the table if inserts or partitions, or returned to the calling program at a temporary location.

The comparison between how Hive executes versus a traditional RDBMS shows that due to the schema on a read design, the data placement, partitioning, joining, and storage can be decided at the execution time rather than planning cycles.

Hive data types

Hive supports the following data types: TinyInt, Int, SmallInt, BigInt, Float, Boolean, String, and Double. Special data types include Array, Map(key_value pair), and Struct (collection of names fields).

Hive query language (HiveQL)

The Hive query language (HiveQL) is an evolving system that supports a lot of SQL functionality on Hadoop, abstracting the MapReduce complexity to the end users.

The traditional SQL features are select, create table, insert, "from clause" subqueries, various types of joins (inner, left outer, right outer, and outer), "group by" and aggregations, union all, create table as select, and many other useful functions.

The following is a Hive example for counting rows in a table:

```
SELECT COUNT(1) FROM table2;
SELECT COUNT(*) FROM table2;
Order By - colOrder: ( ASC | DESC )
orderBy: ORDER BY colName colOrder? (',' colName colOrder?)*
query: SELECT expression (',' expression)* FROM src orderBy
```

Do you use HBase, Hive, or both to implement a database on Hadoop? The answer to this lies in the operations that you wish to execute on Hadoop. Hive is great for executing batch operations and can perform analytical workloads on Hadoop efficiently. HBase is a key-value store and can scan and process fetches from ranges of rows at high speeds. Depending on the need, either technology can serve the need or a combined platform can be configured and deployed to process data and analytics effectively.

Chukwa

Chukwa is an open-source data collection system for monitoring large distributed systems. Chukwa is built on top of HDFS and MapReduce frameworks. There is a flexible and powerful toolkit for displaying, monitoring, and analyzing results to make the best use of the collected data available in Chukwa.

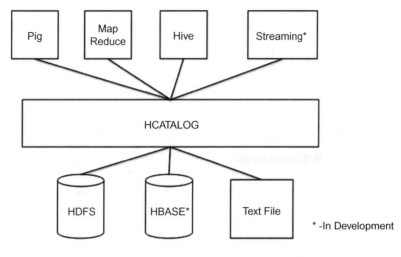

FIGURE 4.19

HCatalog concept.

Source: HortonWorks.

Flume

Flume is a distributed, reliable, and available service for efficiently collecting, aggregating, and moving large amounts of log data. It has a simple and flexible architecture based on streaming dataflows. It is robust and fault-tolerant with tunable reliability mechanisms and many failover and recovery mechanisms. It uses a simple extensible data model that allows for online analytic application.

Oozie

Oozie is a workflow/coordination system to manage Apache Hadoop jobs. Oozie workflow jobs are DAGs of actions like a MapReduce model. Oozie coordinator jobs are recurrent Oozie workflow jobs triggered by time (frequency) and data availability. Oozie is integrated with the rest of the Hadoop stack supporting several types of Hadoop jobs out of the box (Java MapReduce, Streaming MapReduce, Pig, Distcp, etc.). Oozie is a scalable, reliable, and extensible system.

HCatalog

A new integrated metadata layer called HCatalog was added to the Hadoop ecosystem in late 2011. It is built on top of the Hive metastore currently and incorporates components from Hive DDL. HCatalog provides read and write interfaces for Pig and MapReduce, and Hive in one integrated repository. By an integrated repository the users can explore any data across Hadoop using the tools built on its platform. The conceptual architecture of HCatalog is shown in Figure 4.19.

HCatalog's abstraction presents users with a relational view of data in HDFS and ensures that users need not worry about where or in what format their data is stored. HCatalog currently supports reading and writing files in any format for which a SerDe can be written. By default, HCatalog supports RCFile, CSV, JSON, and sequence file formats, which is supported out of the box. To use a custom format, you must provide the InputFormat, OutputFormat, and SerDe, and the format will be

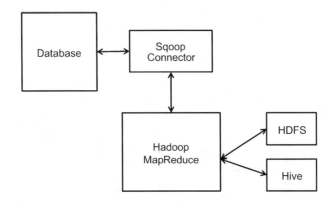

FIGURE 4.20

Sqoop1 architecture.

implemented as it can be in the current Hadoop ecosystem. (For further details on HCatalog, please see the Apache Foundation and HortonWorks websites.)

Sqoop

As the Hadoop ecosystem evolves, we will find the need to integrate data from other existing "enterprise" data platforms including the data warehouse, metadata engines, enterprise systems (ERP, SCM), and transactional systems. All of this data cannot be moved to Hadoop as their nature of small volumes, low latency, and computations are not oriented for Hadoop workloads. To provide a connection between Hadoop and the RDBMS platforms, Sqoop has been developed as the connector. There are two versions, Sqoop1 and Sqoop2. Let us take a quick look at this technology.

Sqoop1

In the first release of Sqoop, the design goals were very simple (Figure 4.20):

- Export/import data from the enterprise data warehouse, relational databases, and NoSQL databases.
- Connector-based architecture with plugins from vendors.
- No metadata store.
- Use Hive and HDFS for data processing.
- Use Oozie for scheduling and managing jobs.

Currently you can download and install Sqoop from the Apache Foundation website or from any Hadoop distribution. The installation is manual and needs configuration steps to be followed without any miss.

Sqoop is completely driven by the client-side installation and heavily depends on JDBC technology as the first release of Sqoop was developed in Java. In the workflow shown in Figure 4.20, you can import and export the data from any database with simple commands that you can execute from a command-line interface (CLI), for example:

```
Import syntax - sqoop import --connect jdbc:mysql://localhost/testdb \--table
PERSON --username test --password ****.
```

This command will generate a series of tasks:

- Generate SQL code.
- Execute SQL code.
- Generate MapReduces jobs.
- Execute MapReduce jobs.
- Transfer data to local files or HDFS.

```
Export syntax - sqoop export --connect jdbc:mysql://localhost/testdb \ --table
CLIENTS_INTG --username test --password **** \ --export-dir /user/localadmin/CLIENTS
```

This command will generate a series of tasks:

- Generate MapReduce jobs.
- Execute MapReduce jobs.
- Transfer data from local files or HDFS.
- Compile SQL code.
- Create or insert into CLIENTS_INTG table.

There are many features of Sqoop1 that are easy to learn and implement, for example, on the command line you can specify if the import is directly to Hive, HDFS, or HBase. There are direct connectors to the most popular databases: Oracle, SQL Server, MySQL, Teradata, and PostGres.

There are evolving challenges with Sqoop1, including:

- Cryptic command-line arguments.
- Nonsecure connectivity—security risk.
- No metadata repository—limited reuse.
- Program-driven installation and management.

Sqoop2

Sqoop2 is the next generation of data transfer architecture that is designed to solve the limitations of Sqoop1, namely:

- Sqoop2 has a web-enabled user interface (UI).
- Sqoop2 will be driven by a Sqoop server architecture.
- Sqoop2 will provide greater connector flexibility; apart from JDBC, many native connectivity options can be customized by providers.
- Sqoop2 will have a Representational State Transfer (REST) API interface.
- Sqoop2 will have its own metadata store.
- Sqoop2 will add credentials management capabilities, which will provide trusted connection capabilities.

The proposed architecture of Sqoop2 is shown in Figure 4.21. For more information on Sqoop status and issues, please see the Apache Foundation website.

Hadoop summary

In summary, as we see from this section and the discussion on Hadoop and its ecosystem of technologies, there are a lot of processing capabilities in this framework to manage, compute, and store large

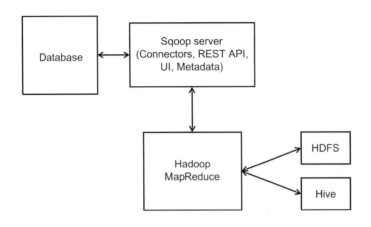

FIGURE 4.21

Sqoop2 architecture.

volumes of data efficiently. The next section discusses another popular set of technologies classified as NoSQL.

NoSQL

Relational databases cannot handle the scalability requirements of large volumes of transactional data, and often fail when trying to scale up and scale out. The vendors of RDBMS-based technologies have tried hard to address the scalability problem by replication, distributed processing, and many other models, but the relational architecture and the ACID properties of the RDBMS have been a hindrance in accomplishing the performance requirements of applications, such as sensor networks, web applications, trading platforms, and much more. In the late 1980s there were a number of research papers that were published about newer models of SQL databases, but not based on ACID requirements and the relational model. Fast forward to 1998 when there was the emergence of a new class of databases that could support the requirements of high-speed data in a pseudo-database environment but were not oriented completely toward SQL. The name NoSQL (not only SQL) database was coined by Eric Evans for the user group meeting to discuss the need for nonrelational and non-SQL-driven databases. This name has become the industry-adopted name for a class of databases that work on similar architectures but are purpose-built for different workloads.

There were three significant papers that changed the NoSQL database from being a niche solution to become an alternative platform:

- "Google Publishes the BigTable Architecture" (*http://labs.google.com/papers/bigtable.html*).
- "Eric Brewer discusses the CAP Theorem" (*http://lpd.epfl.ch/sgilbert/pubs/BrewersConjecture-SigAct.pdf*).
- "Amazon publishes Dynamo" (*http://www.allthingsdistributed.com/2007/10/amazons_dynamo.html*).

Dynamo presented a highly available key-value store infrastructure and BigTable presented a data storage model based on a multidimensional sorted map, where a three-dimensional intersection between a row key, column key, and timestamp provides access to any data in petabytes of data. Both these scalable architectures had concepts where a distributed data processing system can be deployed on a large scale to process different pieces of workload, with replication for redundancy and computations being driven programmatically. Both of these papers are the basis for further evolution of the architecture into multiple classes of databases. These architectures, in conjunction with CAP theorem, will be a discussion in the later sections of this book, when we talk about architecture of the future data warehouse and next-generation analytics.

CAP theorem

In 2000, Eric Brewer presented a theory that he had been working for a few years at University of California, Berkley, and at his company *iktonomi*, at the Symposium on Principles of Distributed Computing. He presented the concept that three core systemic requirements need to be considered when it comes to designing and deploying applications in a distributed environment, and further stated the relationship among these requirements will create shear in terms of which requirement can be given up to accomplish the scalability requirements of your situation. The three requirements are *consistency*, *availability*, and *partition tolerance*, giving Brewer's theorem its other name: CAP.

In simple terms, the CAP theorem states that in a distributed data system, you can guarantee two of the following three requirements: consistency (all data available at all nodes or systems), availability (every request will get a response), and partition tolerance (the system will operate irrespective of availability or a partition or loss of data or communication). The system architected on this model will be called BASE (basically available soft state eventually consistent) architecture as opposed to ACID.

Combining the principles of the CAP theorem and the data architecture of BigTable or Dynamo, there are several solutions that have evolved: HBase, MongoDB, Riak, Voldemort, Neo4J, Cassandra, HyperTable, HyperGraphDB, Memcached, Tokyo Cabinet, Redis, CouchDB, and more niche solutions. Of these, the most popular and widely distributed are:

- HBase, HyperTable, and BigTable, which are architected on CP (from CAP).
- Cassandra, Dynamo, and Voldemort, which are architected on AP (from CAP).

Broadly, NoSQL databases have been classified into four subcategories:

1. *Key-value pairs.* This model is implemented using a hash table where there is a unique key and a pointer to a particular item of data creating a key-value pair; for example, Voldemort.
2. *Column family stores.* An extension of the key-value architecture with columns and column families, the overall goal was to process distributed data over a pool of infrastructure; for example, HBase and Cassandra.
3. *Document databases.* tThis class of databases is modeled after Lotus Notes and similar to key-value stores. The data is stored as a document and is represented in JSON or XML formats. The biggest design feature is the flexibility to list multiple levels of key-value pairs; for example, Riak and CouchDB.
4. *Graph databases.* Based on the graph theory, this class of database supports the scalability across a cluster of machines. The complexity of representation for extremely complex sets of documents is evolving; for example, Neo4J.

Let us focus on the different classes of NoSQL databases and understand their technology approaches. We have already discussed HBase as part of Hadoop earlier in this chapter.

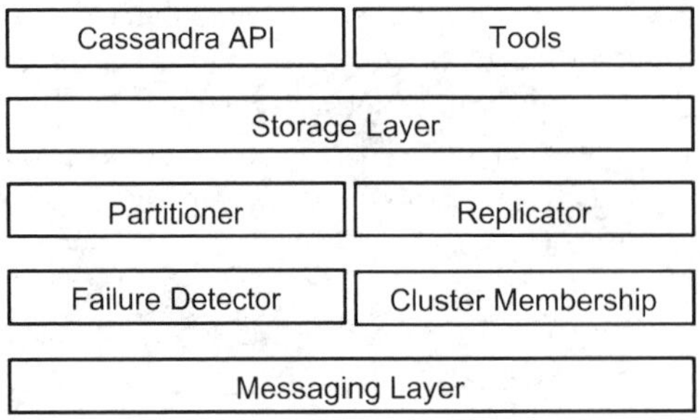

FIGURE 4.22

Cassandra architecture.

Key-value pair: Voldemort

Voldemort is a project that originated in LinkedIn. The underlying need at LinkedIn was a highly scalable lightweight database that can work without the rigidness of ACID compliance. Dynamo and Memcached inspired the database architecture. Data is stored as a key with values in conjunction as a pair. Data is organized in a ring topology with redundancy and range management built into each node of the ring. The architecture is very niche in solving problems and therefore did not get wide adoption outside of LinkedIn. It is still being evolved and updated at the time of writing this book.

Column family store: Cassandra

Facebook in the initial years had used a leading commercial database solution for their internal architecture in conjunction with some Hadoop. Eventually the tsunami of users led the company to start thinking in terms of unlimited scalability and focus on availability and distribution. The nature of the data and its producers and consumers did not mandate consistency but needed unlimited availability and scalable performance. The team at Facebook built an architecture that combines the data model approaches of BigTable and the infrastructure approaches of Dynamo with scalability and performance capabilities, named Cassandra. Cassandra is often referred to as hybrid architecture since it combines the column-oriented data model from BigTable with Hadoop MapReduce jobs, and it implements the patterns from Dynamo like eventually consistent, gossip protocols, a master–master way of serving both read and write requests. Cassandra supports a full replication model based on NoSQL architectures. Figure 4.22 shows the conceptual architecture of Cassandra.

The Cassandra team had a few design goals to meet, considering the architecture at the time of first development and deployment was primarily being done at Facebook. The goals included:

- High availability
- Eventual consistency
- Incremental scalability
- Optimistic replication
- Tunable trade-offs between consistency, durability, and latency

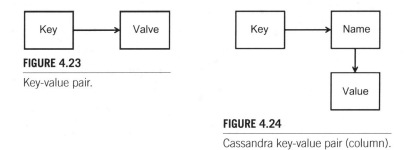

FIGURE 4.23

Key-value pair.

FIGURE 4.24

Cassandra key-value pair (column).

- Low cost of ownership
- Minimal administration

Data model

The Cassandra data model is based on a key-value model, where we have a key that uniquely identifies a value, and this value can be structured or completely unstructured or can also be a collection of other key-value elements. This is very similar to pointers and linked lists in the world of programming. Figure 4.23 shows the basic key-value structure.

A key-value pair can represent a simple storage for Person →→Name type of data but cannot scale much. An alteration to the basic model is done to create a name and value in the key-value pair, and this would provide a structure to create multiple values and associate a key to the name-value pair. This creates a tablelike structure described in Figure 4.24.

In the updated structure of the key-value notation, we can store Person → Name → John Doe, add another column called Person → Age → 30, and create multiple storage structures. This defines the most basic structure in the Cassandra data model called column.

- *Column.* A column is an ordered list of values stored as a name-value pair. It is composed of a column name, a column value, and a third element called timestamp. The timestamp is used to manage conflict resolution on the server, when there is a conflicting list of values or columns to be managed. The client sets the timestamp that is stored along with the data, and this is an explicit operation.
- The column can hold any type of data in this model, varying from characters to Globally Unique Identifiers (GUID) to blobs. Columns can be grouped into a row called a rowkey. A simple column by itself limits the values you can represent; to add more flexibility, a group of columns belonging to a key can be stored together, called a column family. A column family can be loosely compared to a table in the database comparison.
- *Column family.* A column family is a logical and physical grouping of a set of columns that can be represented by a single key. The flexibility of a column family is the names of columns can vary from a row to another and the number of columns can vary over a period of time. Figure 4.25 shows a sample column family.

There is no limitation with creating different column structures in a column family, except the maintenance of the same is dependent on the application that is creating the different structures. Conceptually, it is similar to overloading in the object-oriented programming language.

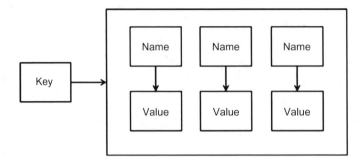

FIGURE 4.25

Column family representation.

If we wanted to further group column families together to create or manage the relationship between the column families, the Cassandra model provides a super column family:

- *Super column family.* A super column family is a logical and physical grouping of column families that can be represented by a single key. The flexibility of this model is you can represent relationships, hierarchies, and treelike traversal in a simple and flexible manner.

To create a meaningful data structure or architecture, a column family, super column family, or multiples of the same need to be grouped in one set or under a common key. In Cassandra, a keyspace defines that set of column families grouped under one key. Typically, we can decompose this as follows: Excel document → sheet 1 → columns/formulas → sheet2 (columns/formulas) → sheet 2 (other columns/formulas), and so on. You can define a keyspace for an application; this is a preferred approach rather than to create thousands of keyspaces for an application.

A keyspace has configurable properties that are critical to understand:

- *Replication factor*—refers to the number of nodes that can be copies or replicas for each row of data. If your replication factor is 2, then two nodes will have copies of each row. Data replication is transparent. The replication factor is the method of controlling consistency within Cassandra and is a tunable parameter in deciding performance and scalability balance.
- *Replica placement strategy*—refers to how the replicas will be placed in the deployment ring (we will discuss this in the architecture section). There are two strategies provided to configure which node will get copies of which keys: SimpleStrategy (defined in the keyspace creation) and NetworkTopologyStrategy (replications across data centers).
- *Column families*—each keyspace has at least one or more column families. A column family has configurable parameters, described in Table 4.1.

As we have learned so far, a keyspace provides the data structure for Cassandra to store the column families and the subgroups. To store the keyspace and the metadata associated with it, Cassandra provides the architecture of a cluster, often referred as the ring. Cassandra distributes data to the nodes by arranging them in a ring that forms the cluster.

Table 4.1 Column Family Parameters

Parameter	Default Value
column_type	Standard
compaction_strategy	SizeTieredCompactionStrategy
comparator	BytesType
compare_subcolumns_with	BytesType
dc_local_read_repair_chance	0
gc_grace_seconds	864000 (10 days)
keys_cached	200000
max_compaction_threshold	32
min_compaction_threshold	4
read_repair_chance	0.1 or 1 (see description below)
replicate_on_write	TRUE
rows_cached	0 (disabled by default)

Data partitioning

Data partitioning can be done either by the client library or by any node of the cluster and can be calculated using different algorithms. There are two native algorithms that are provided with Cassandra:

- *Random-Partitionner*—a hash-based distribution, where the keys are more equally partitioned across the different nodes, providing better load balancing. In this partitioning, each row and all the columns associated with the row key are stored on the same physical node and columns are sorted based on their name.
- *OrderPreserving-Partitioner*—creates partitions based on the key and data grouped by keys, which will boost performance of range queries since the query will need to hit lesser number of nodes to get all the ranges of data.

Data sorting

When defining a column, you can specify how the columns will be sorted when results are returned to the client. Columns are sorted by the "compare with" type defined on their enclosing column family. You can specify a custom sort order; the default provided options are:

- BytesType—simple sort by byte value; no validation is performed.
- AsciiType—similar to BytesType, but validates that the input can be parsed as US-ASCII.
- UTF8Type—a string encoded as UTF8.
- LongType— 64 bits long.
- LexicalUUIDType—a 128-bit, compared lexically (by byte value).
- TimeUUIDType—a 128-bit version 1 University Unique Identifiers (UUID), compared by timestamp.
- Integer—faster than a log, and supports fewer or longer lengths.

Consistency management

The architecture model for Cassandra is Availability and Partitioning (AP) with eventual consistency. Cassandra's consistency is measured by how recent and concurrent all replicas are for one row of data. Though the database is built on an eventual consistency model, real-world applications will mandate consistency for all read and write operations. To manage the user interaction and keep the consistency, Cassandra provides a model called tunable consistency. In this model, the client application decides the level of consistency desired by that application. This allows the user the flexibility to manage different classes of applications at different levels of consistency. There are additional built-in repair mechanisms for consistency management and tuning. A key point to remember is consistency depends on replication factor implementation in Cassandra.

Write consistency

Since consistency is a configuration setting in Cassandra, a write operation can specify its desired level of consistency. Cassandra lets you choose between weak and strong consistency levels. The consistency levels shown in Table 4.2 are available.

Read consistency

The read consistency level specifies how many replicas must respond before a result is returned to the client application. When a read request is made, Cassandra checks the specified number of replicas for the most recent data based on the timestamp data, to satisfy the read request.

Note: Local and each quorum are defined in large multi–data center configurations.

Specifying client consistency levels

The consistency level is specified by the client application when a read or write request is made. For example,

```
SELECT * FROM CUSTOMERS WHERE STATE='IL' USING CONSISTENCY QUORUM;
```

Built-in consistency repair features

Cassandra has a number of built-in repair features to ensure that data remains consistent across replicas:

- *Read repair.* A read repair is a technique that ensures that all nodes in a cluster are synchronized with the latest version of data. When Cassandra detects that several nodes in the cluster are out of sync, it marks the nodes with a read repair flag. This triggers a process of synchronizing the stale nodes with the newest version of the data requested. The check for inconsistent data is implemented by comparing the clock value of the data and the clock value of the newest data. Any node with a clock value that is older than the newest data is effectively flagged as stale.
- *Anti-entropy node repair.* This is a process that is run as a part of maintenance and called a NodeTool process. This is a sync operation across the entire cluster where the nodes are updated to be consistent. It is not an automatic process and needs manual intervention. During this process, the nodes exchange information represented as Merkle trees, and if the tree information is not consistent, a reconciliation exercise needs to be carried out. This feature comes from Amazon Dynamo, with the difference being that in Cassandra each column family maintains its own Merkle tree.
- *Note:* A *Merkle tree* is a hash key hierarchy verification and authentication technique. When replicas are down for extended periods, the Merkle tree keeps checking small portions of the replicas until the sync is broken, enabling a quick recovery. (For more information on Merkle trees, check Ralph Merkle's website at *www.merkle.com.*)

Table 4.2 Cassandra Consistency Levels

Consistency Level	Write Consistency	Read Consistency
ANY	A write must be written to at least one node. If a replica is down, a live replica or current node can store a hint and update the node when it comes back live. If all replica nodes for the given row key are down, the write can still succeed once it has been written by storing the hint and the data in the coordinator. Not a preferred model. *Note:* If all replica nodes are down an ANY write will not be readable until the replica nodes for that row key have been restored.	Not applicable
ONE	A write must be written to the commit log and memory table of at least one replica node.	Returns a response from the closest replica
QUORUM	A quorum is defined as the minimum number of replicas that need to be available for a successful read or write. A quorum is calculated as (rounded down to a whole number): (replication_factor/2) + 1. For example, with a replication factor of 5, a quorum is 3 (can tolerate 2 replicas down). A quorum is a middle ground between weak and strong consistency. A write must be written to the commit log and memory table on a quorum of replica nodes to be successful. Local quorum: A write must be written to the commit log and memory table on a quorum of replica nodes in the *same* data center as the coordinator node. Each quorum: A write must be written to the commit log and memory table on a quorum of replica nodes in *all* data centers.	
ALL	A write must be written to the commit log and memory table on all replica nodes in the cluster for that row key. The highest and strongest level of consistency brings latencies in the architecture. Not a preferred method until complexity and volumes are low.	Data is returned once all replicas have responded. The read operation will fail if a replica does not respond.

- *Hinted handoff.* During a write operation, data is set to all replicas by default. If a node is down at that time, data is stored as a hint to be repaired when the node comes back. If all nodes are down in a replica, the hint and the data are stored in the coordinator. This process is called a hinted handoff. No operation is permitted in the node until all nodes are restored and synchronized.

Cassandra ring architecture

Figure 4.26 shows the ring architecture we described earlier. In this configuration, we can visualize how Cassandra provides for scalability and consistency.

In the ring architecture, the key is the connector to the different nodes in the ring, and the nodes are replicas. For example, A can be replicated to B and C, when N = 3. And D can be replicated to D and E or D and F when N = 2.

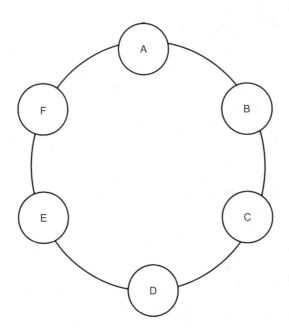

FIGURE 4.26

Cassandra ring architecture.

Data placement

Data placement around the ring is not fixed in any default configuration. Cassandra provides two components called snitches and strategies, to determine which nodes will receive copies of data.

- *Snitches* define the proximity of nodes within the ring and provide information on the network topology.
- *Strategies* use the information snitches provide them about node proximity along with an implemented algorithm to collect nodes that will receive writes.

Data partitioning

Data is distributed across the nodes by using partitioners. Since Cassandra is based on a ring topology or architecture, the ring is divided into ranges equal to the number of nodes, where each node can be responsible for one or more ranges of the data. When a node is joined to a ring, a token is issued, and this token determines the node's position on the ring and assigns the range of data it is responsible for. Once the assignment is done, we cannot undo it without reloading all the data.

Cassandra provides native partitioners and supports any user-defined partitioner. The key feature difference in the native partitioner is the order preservation of keys.

- *Random partitioner.* This is the default choice for Cassandra. It uses an MD5 hash function to map keys into tokens, which will evenly distribute across the clusters. Random partition hashing techniques ensure that when nodes are added to the cluster, the least possible set of data is affected. While the keys are evenly distributed, there is no ordering of the data, which will need the query to be processed by all nodes in an operation.

- *Ordered preserving partitioners.* As the name suggests, preserve the order of the row keys as they are mapped into the token space. Since the key is placed based on an ordered list of values, we can run efficient range-based data retrieval techniques. The biggest drawback in this design is a node with its replicas may become unstable over time, especially with large reads or writes being done in one node.

Peer-to-Peer: simple scalability

Cassandra by design is a peer-to-peer model of architecture, meaning in its configuration there are no designated master or slave nodes. The simplicity of this design allows nodes to be taken down from a cluster or added to a cluster with ease. When a node is down, the processing is taken over by the replicas and allows for a graceful shutdown. Similarly, when a node is added to a cluster, upon being designated with its keys and tokens, the node will join the cluster and understand the topology before commencing operations.

Gossip protocol: node management

In Cassandra architecture, to manage partition tolerance and decentralization of data, managing intranode communication becomes a key feature. This is accomplished by using the gossip protocol. Alan Demers, a researcher at Xerox's Palo Alto Research Center, who was studying ways to route information through unreliable networks, originally coined the term *gossip protocol* in 1987.

In Cassandra, the gossip protocol is implemented as a gossiper class. When a node is added to the cluster it also registers with the gossiper to receive communication. The gossiper selects a random node and checks it for being live or dead, by sending messages to the node. If a node is found to be unresponsive, the gossiper class triggers the "hinted handoff" process if configured. For the gossiper class to distinguish between failure detection and long running transactions, Cassandra implements another algorithm called the Phi Accrual Failure Detection algorithm (based on the popular paper by Naohiro Hayashibara, et al.[3]). According to the algorithm, a node can be marked as suspicious based on the time it takes to respond, and the longer the delays, the higher the suspicion that the node is dead. This delay or accrued value is calculated by Phi and compared to a threshold, which will be used by the gossiper to determine the state of the node. The implementation is accomplished by the FailureDetector class, which has three methods:

- isAlive(node_address)—what the detector will report about a given node's aliveness.
- interpret(node_address)—this method is used by the gossiper to make a decision on the health of the node, based on the suspicion level reached by calculating Phi (the accrued value of the state of responsiveness).
- report(node_address)—when a node receives a heartbeat, it invokes this method.

With the peer-to-peer and gossip protocols implementation, we can see how the Cassandra architecture keeps the nodes synced and the operations on the nodes scalable and reliable. This model is derived and enhanced from Amazon's Dynamo paper. Based on the discussion of Cassandra so far, we can see how the integration of two architectures from BigTable and Dynamo has created a row-oriented column store that can scale and sustain performance. At the time of writing, Cassandra is a top-level project in Apache. Facebook has already moved on to proprietary techniques for large-scale

---

[3] Hayashibara, N., (2011). Towards Persistent Connections Using Failure Detectors. Parallel and Distributed Processing Workshops and Phd Forum (IPDPSW), 2011 IEEE International Symposium. (http://www.researchgate.net/publication/224257250_Towards_Persistent_Connections_Using_Failure_Detectors?ev=prf_pub).

data management, but there are several large and well-known companies that have adopted and implemented Cassandra for their architectural needs of large data management, especially on the web, with continuous customer or user interactions.

Document database: Riak

Riak is a document-oriented database. It is similar in architecture to Cassandra, and the default is set up as a four-node cluster. It follows the same ring topology and gossip protocols in the underpinning architecture. Each of the four nodes contains eight nodes or eight rings, thus providing a 32-ring partition for use. A process called vnodes (virtual nodes) manages the partitions across the four-node cluster. Riak uses a language called Erlang and MapReduce. Another interesting feature of Riak is the concept of links and link walking. Links enable you to create metadata to connect objects. Once you create links, you can traverse the objects and this is the process of link walking. The flexibility of links allows you to determine dynamically how to connect multiple objects. More information on Riak is available at Basho's (the company that designed and developed Riak) website (http://basho.com/).

Other popular NoSQL implementations are document databases (CouchBase, MongoDB, and others) and graph databases (Neo4J). Let us understand the premise behind the document database and graph database architectures.

Document-oriented databases or document databases can be defined as a schemaless and flexible model of storing data as documents, rather than relational structures. The document will contain all the data it needs to answer specific query questions. Benefits of this model include:

- Ability to store dynamic data in unstructured, semi-structured, or structured formats.
- Ability to create persisted views from a base document and store the same for analysis.
- Ability to store and process large data sets.

The design features of document-oriented databases include:

- *Schema free*—there is no restriction on the structure and format of how the data needs to be stored. This flexibility allows an evolving system to add more data and allows the existing data to be retained in the current structure.
- *Document store*—objects can be serialized and stored in a document, and there is no relational integrity to enforce and follow.
- *Ease of creation and maintenance*—a simple creation of the document allows complex objects to be created once and there is minimal maintenance once the document is created.
- *No relationship enforcement*—documents are independent of each other and there is no foreign-key relationship to worry about when executing queries. The effects of concurrency and performance issues related to the same are not a bother here.
- *Open formats*—documents are described using JSON, XML, or some derivative, making the process standard and clean from the start.
- *Built-in versioning*—documents can get large and messy with versions. To avoid conflicts and keep processing efficiencies, versioning is implemented by most solutions available today.

Document databases express the data as files in JSON or XML formats. This allows the same document to be parsed for multiple contexts and the results scrapped and added to the next iteration of the database data.

Example usage: A document database can be used to store the results of clicks on the web. For each log file that is parsed a simple XML construct with the Page_Name, Position_Coordinates, Clicks, Keywords, Incoming and Outgoing sites, and Date_Time will create a simple model to query the number of clicks, keywords, date, and links. This processing power cannot be found in an RDBMS. If you want to expand and capture the URL data, the next version can add the field.

The emergence of document databases is still ongoing at the time of writing this book, and the market adoption for this technology will happen soon. We will discuss the integration architecture for this technology later in this book.

Graph databases

Social media and the emergence of Facebook, LinkedIn, and Twitter have accelerated the emergence of the most complex NoSQL database, the graph database. The graph database is oriented toward modeling and deploying data that is graphical by construct. For example, to represent a person and their friends in a social network, we can either write code to convert the social graph into key-value pairs on a Dynamo or Cassandra, or simply convert them into a node-edge model in a graph database, where managing the relationship representation is much more simplified.

A graph database represents each object as a node and the relationships as an edge. This means person is a node and household is a node, and the relationship between them is an edge.

Like the classic ER model for RDBMS, we need to create an attribute model for a graph database. We can start by taking the highest level in a hierarchy as a root node (similar to an entity) and connect each attribute as its subnode. To represent different levels of the hierarchy we can add a subcategory or subreference and create another list of attributes at that level. This creates a natural traversal model like a tree traversal, which is similar to traversing a graph. Depending on the cyclic property of the graph, we can have a balanced or skewed model. Some of the most evolved graph databases include Neo4J, infiniteGraph, GraphDB, and AllegroGraph.

NoSQL summary

In summary, NoSQL databases are quickly evolving to be the platform for deploying large-scale data stores. There are several architectures and techniques to design and deploy the NoSQL solution, and any solution will require periodic tuning and maintenance as the volume of data being processed is very high and complex.

Hadoop, NoSQL, and their associated technologies are excellent platforms to process Big Data, but they all require some amount of MapReduce integration and are not completely architected to be self-service driven by business users in any enterprise. The next section provides you with a brief overview on text mining approaches–based architecture to process Big Data called textual ETL.

Textual ETL processing

Business users have always wanted to process unstructured data by interrogating the data with many different types of algorithms and modeling techniques, while creating the processing rules in an English-like interface. The outputs of processing unstructured data will be similar to a key-value pair

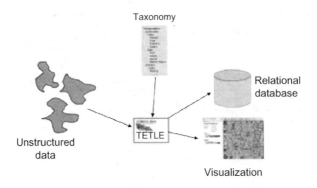

FIGURE 4.27

Textual ETL processing.

that is generated into a structured database for further analytical processing. The concept of textual ETL processing is shown in Figure 4.27.

Textual ETL consists of the following processing components:

- *Textual ETL rules engine*. This is the core processing engine to parse large unstructured data and extract value from the parsing for integration. The rules engine executes a series of data processing steps and processes the data. The following are the algorithms that are incorporated into the rules engine:
  - Classification
  - Clustering
  - Affinity
  - Proximity

  The additional integration processing techniques include taxonomy integration, metadata integration, and master data integration.
- *User interface*. The business users can create data processing rules in a drag-and-drop interface and in an free-form text interface that supports 16 languages for processing.
- *Taxonomies*. There are several categories of data that can be processed by any enterprise, and the most effective way to processes a multistructured and multihierarchical data is by integrating third-party taxonomy libraries. Textual ETL supports over 40,000 known taxonomies in 16 languages for data enrichment and processing.
- *Output database*. Textual ETL can write the output to any RDBMS or NoSQL databases. The result sets are key-value pairs that can be used to integrate the structured and unstructured databases.

Textual ETL is currently developed and architected on Microsoft technologies and can support Hadoop and NoSQL technologies. There is a special chapter on implementing a healthcare information factory at the end of this book.

As we conclude this chapter we see the different technologies that are available to process Big Data, their specific capabilities, and their architectures. In Chapter 5, we study some use cases from real-life implementations of solutions from early adopters of these technologies to solve the large-scale data processing. In Part 2 of this book, we see how these technologies will enrich the data warehouse and data management with Big Data integration.

Further reading

Blanas, S., Patel, J.M., Ercegovac, V., Rao, J., Shekita, E.J., & Tian, Y. A Comparison of Join Algorithms for Log Processing in MapReduce.

Dean, J., & Ghemawat, S. (2010). MapReduce: a data processing tool. *Communications of the ACM, 53*(1), 72–77.

Facebook Data Infrastructure Team. (2009). Hive: A Data Warehousing Solution over a MapReduce Framework. *Journal Proceedings of the VLDB Endowment, 2*(2), 1626–1629.

Friedman, E., Pawlowski, P., & Cieslewicz, J. (2009). SQL/MapReduce: a practical approach to self-describing, polymorphic, and parallelizable user-defined functions. *Proceedings of the VLDB Endowment, 2*(2), 1402–1413.

Ghemawat, S., Gobio, H., & Leung, S. (Oct. 2003). The google file system. *SIGOPS Operating Systems Review, 37*, 29–43.

Gilbert, S., & Lynch, N. A. (2012). Perspectives on the CAP Theorem. *IEEE Computer*, 30–36.

Lakshman, A., & Malik, P. (2010). Cassandra: A Decentralized Structured Storage System. ACM SIGOPS Operating Systems Review, vol. 44, pp. 35–40. SIGOPS ACM Special Interest Group on Operating Systems. NY, USA: ACM. ISSN: 0163-5980, doi: 10.1145/1773912.1773922

Lamport, L. (1978). Time, Clocks, and the Ordering of Events in a Distributed System. *Communications of the ACM, 21*(7), 558–565. Reprinted in several collections, including Distributed Computing: Concepts and Implementations, McEntire et al., eds. IEEE Press, 1984.

O'Malley, O., & Murthy, A. C. (2009). Hadoop Sort Benchmarks. <http://sortbenchmark.org/Yahoo2009.pdf>

Pavlo, A., Paulson, E., Rasin, A., Abadi, D. J., Dewitt, D. J., Madden, S., et al. (2009). A comparison of approaches to large-scale data analysis. In SIGMOD '09: Proceedings of the 35th SIGMOD international conference on Management of data.

Pavlo, A., Paulson, E., Rasin, A., Abadi, D. J., Dewitt, D. J., Madden, S., et al. A comparison of approaches to large-scale data analysis. Brown University. Retrieved Jan. 1, 2010, from communications of the ACM January 2010 vol. 53 no. 1.

Ranger, C., Raghuraman, R., Penmetsa, A., Bradski, G., Kozyrakis, C., Evaluating MapReduce for Multi-core and Multiprocessor Systems. *High Performance Computer Architecture, 2007. HPCA 2007. IEEE 13th International Symposium on, pp.13,24, 10–14 Feb. 2007. doi: 10.1109/HPCA.2007.346181. (http:// ieeexplore.ieee.org/stamp/stamp.jsp?tp=&arnumber=4147644&isnumber=4147636).*

Ronnie, C., Bob, J., Per-Åke, L., Bill, R., Darren, S., Simon, W., & Jingren, Z. (2008). SCOPE: easy and efficient parallel processing of massive data sets. *Proceedings of the VLDB Endowment, 1*(2), 1265–1276.

Thusoo, A., Sarma, J. S., Jain, N., Shao, Z., Chakka, P., & Anthony, S., et al. (2009). Hive: a warehousing solution over a MapReduce framework. *Proceedings of the VLDB Endowment, 2*(2), 1626–1629.

Big Data Driving Business Value

Technology is like a fish. The longer it stays on the shelf, the less desirable it becomes.
—Andrew Heller

INTRODUCTION

The world we live in today is accelerated by no single business or product, but by us—the consumers, the drivers of demand for specific products or services. The advances in mobile technologies coupled with the advent of smart devices and the rise of generation Z have created a perfect storm for companies to transform themselves from being product-centric to being a service-centric organization. But how successful can the transformation strategy be for an organization? And, more importantly, how does your organization make decisions on what areas to transform, and what is the timing of this transformation? How does a customer behavior or a market trend introduce disruption in the current strategy?

This chapter focuses on the emergence of social media, sensor networks, and other Big Data sources that provide a deeper and factual insight on the metrics that are used in decision analytics and how companies have adopted these different data artifacts to create better services for their customers in a B2B and B2C environment.

The case studies discussed in this chapter focus on the following areas:

- The business problem—what are real-world companies looking to solve when data is available in an integrated ecosystem across the enterprise.
- The data problem—what issues confront the companies from a data perspective: volume, availability, granularity, or formats.
- The business case—how these companies have approached developing the business case and what return on investment (ROI) have they been able to associate with the overall solution.

As you read this chapter, you will realize that your organization and many others will have a wish-list of problems you would like to solve. Different vendors who are integrating Hadoop and NoSQL into their solution ecosystem have provided the case studies that you will read in this chapter. While some of these solutions are ground-breaking architectures, there are more details in the following chapters that will help and guide your thinking when you set out to build your own solutions.

The author would like to extend thanks to all vendors who readily shared these case studies for the benefit of the readers.

Case study 1: Sensor data

This is a case study provided by IBM and adapted to this book. In this case study we see how Vestas uses Big Data processing techniques using the BigInsights and Hadoop platforms for harnessing climate data to predict the most optimal use of wind energy to its customers.

Summary

The challenge with the processing of data from around the world to track wind movement and weather to predict optimal use of turbines to harness energy was a challenge to Vestas. Processing large volumes of data constantly was not a feasible exercise on incumbent platforms and methodologies. This is when they turned to using Hadoop and the IBM BigInsights solution stack, to create a Big Data platform and leverage the processing techniques that made the entire requirements from data volume and complexity nearly disappear or rather become a very manageable challenge. As you read this case study look carefully at how the business case and the ROI were aligned in the entire exercise.

Vestas

Turning climate into capital with Big Data.

Overview

Vestas wants to pinpoint the optimal location for wind turbines to maximize power generation and reduce energy costs. Precise placement of a wind turbine can affect its performance and its useful life. For Vestas, the world's largest wind energy company, gaining new business depends on responding quickly and delivering business value. To succeed, Vestas uses one of the largest supercomputers worldwide along with a new Big Data modeling solution to slice weeks from data processing times and support ten times the amount of data for more accurate turbine placement decisions. Improved precision provides Vestas customers with greater business case certainty, quicker results, and increased predictability and reliability in wind power generation.

For centuries, sailors have seen how fickle the wind can be. It ebbs and flows like the tide and can allow ships to travel great distances or remain becalmed at sea. But despite the wind's capricious nature, new advances in science and technology enable energy producers to transform the wind into a reliable and steadfast energy source—one that many believe will help alleviate the problems of the world's soaring energy consumption. Lars Christian Christensen, vice president of Vestas Wind System A/S, states:

> *Wind energy is one of today's most important renewable energy sources. Fossil fuels will eventually run out. Wind is renewable, predictable, clean, and commercially viable. By 2020 as much as 10% of the world's electricity consumption will be satisfied by wind energy, and we believe that wind power is an industry that will be on par with oil and gas.*

Producing electricity from wind

Making wind a reliable energy source depends greatly on the placement of the wind turbines used to produce electricity. The windiest location may not generate the best output and revenue for energy companies. Turbulence is a significant factor, as it strains turbine components, making them more likely to fail. Avoiding pockets of turbulence can extend the service life of turbines and lower operating costs, which reduces the cost per kilowatt hour of energy produced.

Selecting wind turbine sites is a science that Vestas understands well. Since 1979, this Danish company has been engaged in the development, manufacture, sale, and maintenance of wind power systems to generate electricity. The company has installed more than 43,000 land-based and offshore wind turbines in 66 countries on six continents.

Today, Vestas installs an average of one wind turbine every 3 hours, 24 hours a day, and its turbines generate more than 90 million megawatt-hours of energy per year, which is enough electricity to supply millions of households. Christensen, who heads the company's division responsible for determining the placement of wind turbines, states:

> Customers want to know what their return on investment will be and they want business case certainty. For us to achieve business case certainty, we need to know exactly how the wind is distributed across potential sites, and we need to compare this data with the turbine design specifications to make sure the turbine can operate at optimal efficiency at that location.

What happens if engineers pick a suboptimal location? According to Christensen, the cost of a mistake can be tremendous:

> First of all, if the turbines do not perform as intended, we risk losing customers. Secondly, placing the turbines in the wrong location affects our warranty costs. Turbines are designed to operate under specific conditions and can break if they are operating outside of these parameters.

For Vestas, the process of establishing a location starts with its wind library, which incorporates data from global weather systems with data collected from existing turbines. Combined, this information helps the company not only select the best site for turbine placement, but also helps forecast wind and power production for its customers. Christensen explains:

> We gather data from 35,000 meteorological stations scattered around the world and from our own turbines. That gives us a picture of the global flow scenario. Those models are then cobbled to smaller models for the regional level, called mesoscale models. The mesoscale models are used to establish our huge wind library so we can pinpoint a specific location at a specific time of day and tell what the weather was like.

The company's previous wind library provided detailed information in a grid pattern with each grid measuring 17 × 17 miles (about 27 × 27 kilometers). Using computational fluid dynamics models, Vestas engineers can then bring the resolution down even further—to about 32 × 32 feet (10 × 10 meters)—to establish the exact wind flow pattern at a particular location.

However, in any modeling scenario, the more data and the smaller the grid area, the greater the accuracy of the models. As a result, Christensen's team wanted to expand its wind library more than tenfold to include a larger range of weather data over a longer period of time. Additionally, the company needed a more powerful computing platform to run global forecasts much faster. Often company executives had to wait up to three weeks for feedback regarding potential sites—an unacceptable amount of time for Vestas and its customers in this competitive industry. "In our development strategy, we see growing our library in the range of 18 to 24 petabytes of data," says Christensen. "And while it's fairly easy to build that library, we needed to make sure that we could gain knowledge from that data."

Turning climate into capital

Working with IBM, Vestas today is implementing a Big Data solution that is slicing weeks from data processing time and helping staff more quickly and accurately predict weather patterns at potential sites to increase turbine energy production. Data currently stored in its wind library comprises nearly 2.8 petabytes and includes more than 178 parameters, such as temperature, barometric pressure, humidity, precipitation, wind direction, and wind velocity from the ground level up to 300 feet, along with the company's own recorded historical data. Future additions for use in predictions include global deforestation metrics, satellite images, historical metrics, geospatial data, and data on phases of the moon and tides. Christensen states:

> *We could pose the questions before, but our previous systems were not able to deliver the answers, or deliver the answers in the required timeframe. Now, if you give me the coordinates for your back-yard, we can dive into our modeled wind libraries and provide you with precise data on the weather over the past 11 years, thereby predicting future weather and delivering power production prognosis. We have the ability to scan larger areas and determine more quickly our current turbine coverage geographically and see if there are spots we need to cover with a type of turbine. We can also assess information on how each turbine is operating and our potential risk at a site.*

IBM® InfoSphere® BigInsights software running on an IBM System x® iDataPlex® system serves as the core infrastructure to help Vestas manage and analyze weather and location data in ways that were not previously possible. For example, the company can reduce the base resolution of its wind data grids from a 17 × 17 mile area to a 1.8 × 1.8 mile area (about 3 × 3 kilmometers)—a nearly 90% reduction that gives executives more immediate insight into potential locations. Christensen estimates this capability can eliminate a month of development time for a site and enable customers to achieve a ROI much earlier than anticipated. He continues:

> *IBM InfoSphere BigInsights helps us gain access to knowledge in a very efficient and extremely fast way and enables us to use this knowledge to turn climate into capital. Before, it could take us three weeks to get a response to some of our questions simply because we had to process a lot of data. We expect that we can get answers for the same questions now in 15 minutes.*

For customers, the detailed models mean greater business case certainty, quicker results, and increased predictability and reliability on their investment. Christensen states:

> *Our customers need predictability and reliability, and that can only happen using systems like InfoSphere BigInsights. We can give customers much better financial warrantees than we have been able to in the past and can provide a solid business case that is on par with any other investment that they may have.*

Tackling Big Data challenges

Vestas and IBM worked together to implement IBM's InfoSphere BigInsights software, designed to enable organizations to gain insight from information flows that are characterized by variety, velocity, and volume. The solution combines open-source Apache Hadoop software with unique technologies and capabilities from IBM to enable organizations to process very large data sets—breaking up the data into chunks and coordinating the processing across a distributed environment for rapid, efficient analysis and results. Christensen explains:

> *IBM gave us an opportunity to turn our plans into something that was very tangible right from the beginning. IBM had experts within data mining, Big Data, and Apache Hadoop, and it was clear to us from the beginning if we wanted to improve our business, not only today, but also prepare for the challenges we will face in three to five years, we had to go with IBM.*

Maintaining energy efficiency in its data center

For a company committed to addressing the world's energy requirements, it's no surprise that as Vestas implemented its Big Data solution, it also sought a high-performance, energy-efficient computing environment that would reduce its carbon footprint. Today, the platform that drives its forecasting and analysis comprises a hardware stack based on the IBM System x iDataPlex supercomputer. This supercomputing solution—one of the world's largest to date—enables the company to use 40% less energy while increasing computational power. Twice the number of servers can be run in each of the system's 12 racks—reducing the amount of floor space required in its data center.

"The supercomputer provides the foundation for a completely new way of doing business at Vestas, and combined with IBM software, delivers a smarter approach to computing that optimizes the way we work," says Christensen.

Overall, the deployment of Hadoop-based processing has become a game changer for Vestas and provided critical insights that differentiate their services and capabilities. This kind of solution architecture is not a mandatory approach for every situation or organization, but the architecture approach can be used to design scalable platforms for Big Data problems that need agility and flexibility.

Case study 2: Streaming data

This case study is also contributed by IBM and republished with permission. This case study is on streaming data.

Summary

This case study deals with the extreme volume of data that needed to be processed prior to its reaching storage after the acquisition process. The volume of data to process is approximately 275 Mb of acoustic data from 1,024 individual sensor channels, which translates to 42 TB/day of new data. The data has to be processed through some statistical algorithms and current processing takes hours when the need is subsecond. As you read the case study, you will see how combining unconventional approaches to data processing data with structured techniques solves the architecture needs of TerraEchos.

Surveillance and security: TerraEchos

Streaming data technology supports covert intelligence and surveillance sensor systems.

The need

A U.S. Department of Energy National Lab needed a solution to detect, classify, locate, and track potential threats to secure its perimeters and border areas.

The solution

The solution is for IBM business partner, TerraEchos, to implement an advanced security and covert surveillance system based on the TerraEchos Adelos® S4 System with IBM InfoSphere® Streams and an IBM System x® 3650 server.

The benefit

The benefit is the system reduces time to process 275 Mb of data from hours to just one-fourteenth of a second, and captures and analyzes huge volumes of data in real time, providing unprecedented insight to detect, classify, locate, track, and deter potential threats.

A leading provider of covert intelligence and surveillance sensor systems, TerraEchos, Inc. provides organizations with advanced security solutions for critical infrastructures and extended borders. One TerraEchos client is a science-based, applied engineering national laboratory dedicated to supporting the mission of the U.S. Department of Energy (DOE) in nuclear and energy research, science, and national defense. Securing the scientific intelligence, technology, and resources related to these initiatives is vital. To this end, this national lab recognized the need for a technology solution that would detect, classify, locate, and track potential threats—above and below ground—to secure its perimeters and border areas. This solution would provide lab personnel and security staff with more situational awareness and enable a faster and more intelligent response to any threat, detecting and analyzing a wide range of sounds—even from miles away.

The requirements of the ideal solution were considerable. The solution would have to continuously consume and analyze massive amounts of digital acoustic data from biological, mechanical, and environmental objects in motion. In addition, because lab personnel lacked time to record the data and listen to it later, the solution had to gather and analyze information simultaneously. The analysis could extract meaningful intelligence, as well as verify and validate the data, such as distinguishing between the sounds of a trespasser versus a grazing animal. To put the sophistication of the needed technology into perspective, the data consumption and analytical requirements would be akin to listening to 1,000 MP3 songs simultaneously and successfully discerning the word "zero" from every song—within a fraction of a second. The solution would also serve as the lab's central nervous system and would have to meet strict technical requirements, including:

- Interoperability, enabling lab personnel to collect and analyze an array of data from video, acoustic, and other types of sensors to create a holistic view of a situation.
- Scalability to support new requirements as the lab's fiber-optic arrays, surveillance areas, and security perimeters change.
- Extensibility, serving as a framework to fit into the lab's existing IT architecture and integrating with signal processors and mobile and mapping applications.

Advanced fiber optics combine with real-time streaming data

To meet these requirements, the lab turned to IBM business partner TerraEchos to implement an advanced, covert security and surveillance system, based on the TerraEchos Adelos S4 System, an IBM System x 3650 server, and IBM InfoSphere Streams software, part of the IBM Big Data platform. The TerraEchos Adelos S4 solution offers advanced fiber-optic acoustic sensor technology licensed from the U.S. Navy. InfoSphere Streams is the engine that processes digital acoustic data in motion continuously from fiber-optic sensor arrays.

Solution components

> Software: IBM InfoSphere® Streams
> Server: IBM System x® 3650

Serving as the underlying analytics platform, the processing capacity of InfoSphere Streams enables the Adelos S4 solution to analyze and classify streaming acoustic data in real time. InfoSphere Streams collects data from multiple sensor types and enables associated streams of structured and unstructured data to be integrated into an intelligence system for threat detection, classification, correlation, prediction, and communication by means of a service-oriented architecture (SOA). Based on this technology, TerraEchos provides one of the most robust surveillance classification systems in the industry, and is the first fiber-optic sensor company to incorporate InfoSphere Streams as the computational platform for sensor data analytics.

Extending the security perimeter creates a strategic advantage

Because the solution captures and transmits real-time streaming acoustical data from around the lab premises, security staff has unprecedented insight into any event. The system enables lab and security personnel to "hear" what is going on—even when the disturbance is miles away. In this way, it is possible to confidently identify and classify a potential security threat—and take appropriate action. Dr. Philp (Dr. Alex Philp, Founder and CTO, TerraEchos, Inc) states:

> We use the fiber-optic cable as a sensing array. The listening devices are actually virtual segments of the cable, so think of a cable a mile long. We break it down digitally into individual microphones or individual listening areas of one meter, and these distances can change. The beauty of this extended perimeter security system is that it is completely passive. Using miles of fiber-optic cables and thousands of listening devices buried underground, the lab can extend its perimeter security and gain a strategic advantage.

Correlating sensor data delivers a zero false-positive rate

The solution is part of a more comprehensive security system. With the ability to integrate and collect data from video and airborne surveillance systems, lab personnel gain a holistic view of potential threats and issues—or nonissues. Dr. Philp explains:

> In addition to detection, classification, localization, and tracking, correlating the analysis from acoustic sensors and video cameras provides for verification and validation and a zero

false-positive rate. With these results, security staff can make confident decisions about responding to a threat—such as how many officers to deploy and which tactics to use—and can also thwart any plans intruders have to breach the property.

Finally, in addition to meeting the lab's requirements for extensibility, interoperability, and scalability, the solution saves the lab costs associated with data storage because data does not have to be stored before being analyzed. Dr. Philp states:

Capturing approximately 42 terabytes of data each day adds up fast and would be challenging and costly to store. InfoSphere Streams offers advantages, especially when you have to capture data continuously in real time and analyze it as it passes by. Organizations can realize huge savings in storage. Given the data processing and analytical challenges addressed using our Adelos Sensor Array, InfoSphere Streams is the right solution for us and our customers. We look forward to growing our strategic relationship with IBM across various sectors and markets to help revolutionize the concept of "sensor as a service."

Stream analytics will be a mandate for working with data on the wire. This case study shows the overall approach that was designed for solving the problem at TerraEchos. Similar techniques can be used for financial services—credit card fraud, trading floor systems, and retail banking—where the data processing before a fraud or illegal situation arises is of the highest priority.

Case study 3: The right prescription: improving patient outcomes with Big Data analytics

This case study is on managing patients proactively and increasing quality of healthcare, while reducing risk for both the patient and the provider. This is a case study from Teradata-Aster on the Big Data platform. The author would like to thank them for sharing this interesting case study.

Summary

Aurora Health Care had a major initiative to improve the patient care outcome by using predictive analytics from all the data available in the organization.

Business objective

The objective is to increase the effectiveness of treatment and contain costs by identifying and matching predictive health patterns.

Challenges

- Improve the quality of patient care by integrating patient records for a more comprehensive view of the patient's overall health.
- No data warehouse infrastructure.
- Slow queries.
- No reporting infrastructure.
- Gigabytes of clickstream data in flat files.

Overview: giving practitioners new insights to guide patient care

An integrated nonprofit medical provider in the midwest, Aurora Health Care serves communities throughout eastern Wisconsin and northern Illinois, meeting the needs of 1.2 million people and coordinating the operations of more than 30,000 caregivers. Given strict regulatory compliance issues, Aurora deals with significant responsibilities to keep patient data private. But there's an enormous incentive to use its data more effectively to improve the health and well-being of its patients.

One way to improve patient health outcomes is to identify the top treatment patterns that lead to better outcomes, and put those insights into the hands of medical professionals to make better real-time decisions about the treatments they recommend to their patients. This became a priority for Aurora Health Care as the organization began a major initiative to evaluate the critical technologies that could meet this objective quickly and more efficiently. However, as one of the nation's largest healthcare organizations, Aurora deals with huge amounts of data from multiple sources and varying formats—it has 18 data feeds, ranging from financial information and procedures, to pharmacy, to laboratory services, and many other operational areas.

Challenges: blending traditional data warehouse ecosystems with Big Data

Aurora's challenges include:

- Multiple sources of siloed data that need to be synchronized.
- Lack of an analytics and discovery platform that could scale and generate the insights needed.
- Gigabytes of clickstream data stored in flat files, resulting in extremely slow queries.

Dave Brown, senior director of enterprise business intelligence, explained:

The challenges Big Data brings to our existing data integration and analytics platforms are … huge. The shared business imperative is to reduce IT expenses, while simultaneously maintaining that the BI service quality is ever-present. However, the "new" business value of analyzing Big Data must be pursued to remain competitive.

Most Big Data implementations are external, or run alongside existing EDW platforms. Because this can add more people, more processes, and more cost, Aurora decided to adopt a new model that blends the technologies of a traditional EDW ecosystem with that of a Big Data discovery platform.

One initiative that Aurora began was to enhance the functionality of its nearly $900 million supply chain. With new technology in place, Aurora will manage supplies from the purchase order all the way through to the inventory process, and then follow up to monitor actual utilization within a procedure to give doctors a peer-to-peer comparison on outcomes and cost savings.

Solution: getting ready for Big Data analytics

To meet its goals, Aurora embarked on a strategic and comprehensive program to recreate a completely new enterprise business intelligence platform from scratch. This took the form of a hybrid business intelligence ecosystem that combines a RDBMS for traditional business intelligence reporting with a Big Data discovery platform for next-generation Big Data analytics. The ecosystem includes a message-centric ETL methodology, and leverages an RDBMS to perform all dimension and fact table processing. This, in turn, integrates with a big analytics and discovery platform that enables analytics on Big Data using the Aster SQL/MapReduce framework and Aster *n*Path, a prebuilt analytic function that discovers patterns in rows of sequential data.

By unlocking new data-driven insights, while gaining substantial query performance increases, Aurora will enjoy both improved performance and a lower total cost of ownership. Because the Teradata Aster platform is built on the patented SQL/MapReduce framework, the Aurora IT team was able to achieve a "paradigm shift" of being able to "break apart" a particular problem into many smaller tasks and operate them across a cluster on a massively parallel processing platform. Brown explains:

> *The total cost of ownership was our initial reason for moving forward with the Teradata Aster platform. And that was a compelling story for our financially minded decision makers to say, "Well, we can actually do more with less. We can actually ready ourselves for Big Data analytics."*

Results: eliminating the "Data Trap"

Working with Teradata Aster, Aurora was able to improve the patient experience by deeply understanding the interactions of patients and medical providers, test facilities, and hospitals to identify patterns that lead to positive outcomes, and incorporate the findings into business processes without significant complexity or facing a steep learning curve. Results include:

- Instant real-time decisions, using predictions from the master patient index for whether a patient should stay in the hospital or be discharged, improving outcomes and care.
- Potential savings of up to $60 million that Aurora now pays in losses due to patient readmissions.
- Lower total cost of ownership by using a classic enterprise data warehouse on top of Teradata Aster.
- Quick implementation with no large learning curve between SQL and SQL/MapReduce.

Aurora is planning additional improvements to the continuum of patient care, through electronic medical records that follow the patient, and are updated no matter what provider they see, even when out of network. Brown states:

> *We're looking at going back to how we integrate the decisions that come off of this platform and streaming that into our electronic health record in near real time. What we found most compelling about Big Data and the solution that Teradata Aster has in place is the ability for us to leverage existing talent into this discovery platform immediately. There isn't much of a learning curve from SQL to SQL/MapReduce. It is a bit of a mind shift but it's one that's not difficult to overcome.*

Why aster?

- Advanced analytics execution and data in one location.
- Provides 360° view of patient treatment and care given.
- Minimal movement of data.
- Fast access to information Aurora needs to run its business.
- Ability to analyze massive amounts of internally generated data.
- Information at the speed of thought ersus the speed of the infrastructure.
- Elimination of redundant environments, tasks, and data.
- Significant cost savings.

About aurora

- Private, nonprofit integrated healthcare provider
- 31 counties, 90 communities
- 15 hospitals
- 185 clinic sites
- 1,516 employed physicians
- Largest homecare organization in eastern Wisconsin and northern Illinois
- More than 70 pharmacies
- 30,000 caregivers
- 1.2 million individual patients treated annually
- 91,000 inpatient discharges
- 2 million hospital and outpatient visits
- 4 million ambulatory care visits
- $4.3 billion in annual revenue

As we can see from this use case, the out-of-the-box thinking provided Aurora Health Care the ability to create a platform to harness the benefits from Big Data analytics. This type of approaches to solve platform related limitations is where Big Data processing will continue to create impacts and benefits.

Case study 4: University of Ontario, institute of technology: leveraging key data to provide proactive patient care

This case study is from a healthcare segment where the organization decided to use Streams technology to solve a data problem.

Summary

The University of Ontario wanted to create a platform to monitor patients around the clock based on the medical devices that were used to treat the patients. This meant processing real-time signals from the devices and detecting subtle changes on-the-fly, and respond before a critical event or adverse event strikes. A first-of-its-kind, stream-computing platform was developed to capture and analyze real-time data from medical monitors, alerting hospital staff to potential health problems before patients manifest clinical signs of infection or other issues.

What makes it smart is that early warning gives caregivers the ability to proactively deal with potential complications, such as detecting infections in premature infants up to 24 hours before they exhibit symptoms.

As you read the case study pay attention to the business-use case pieces, which is what your organizations will need to articulate clearly.

Overview

The rapid advance of medical monitoring technology has done wonders to improve patient outcomes. Today, patients are routinely connected to equipment that continuously monitors vital signs such as blood pressure, heart rate, and temperature. The equipment issues an alert when any vital sign goes out of the normal range, prompting hospital staff to take action immediately, but many life-threatening conditions do not reach critical level right away. Often, signs that something is wrong begin to appear long before the situation becomes serious, and even a skilled and experienced nurse or physician might not be able to spot and interpret these trends in time to avoid serious complications. Unfortunately, the warning indicators are sometimes so hard to detect that it is nearly impossible to identify and understand their implications until it is too late.

One example of such a hard-to-detect problem is nosocomial infection, which is contracted at the hospital and is life threatening to fragile patients such as premature infants. According to physicians at the University of Virginia, an examination of retrospective data reveals that, starting 12–24 hours before any overt sign of trouble, almost undetectable changes begin to appear in the vital signs of infants who have contracted this infection. The indication is a pulse that is within acceptable limits, but not varying as it should—heart rates normally rise and fall throughout the day. In a baby where infection has set in, this doesn't happen as much, and the heart rate becomes too regular over time. So, while the information needed to detect the infection is present, the indication is very subtle; rather than being a single warning sign, it is a trend over time that can be difficult to spot, especially in the fast-paced environment of an intensive care unit.

Business benefits

- Holds the potential to give clinicians an unprecedented ability to interpret vast amounts of heterogeneous data in real time, enabling them to spot subtle trends.
- Combines physician and nurse knowledge and experience, with technology capabilities to yield more robust results than can be provided by monitoring devices alone.
- Provides a flexible platform that can adapt to a wide variety of medical monitoring needs.

The monitors continuously generate information that can give early warning signs of an infection, but the data is too large for the human mind to process in a timely manner. Consequently, the information that could prevent an infection from escalating to life-threatening status is often lost. Dr. Andrew James, staff neonatologist at The Hospital for Sick Children (SickKids) in Toronto, Canada, states:

> The challenge we face is that there's too much data. In the hectic environment of the neonatal intensive care unit, the ability to absorb and reflect upon everything presented is beyond human capacity, so the significance of trends is often lost.

Making better use of the data resource

The significance of the data overload challenge was not lost on Dr. Carolyn McGregor, Canada research chair in health informatics at the University of Ontario Institute of Technology (UOIT):

> As someone who has been doing a lot of work with data analysis and data warehousing, I was immediately struck by the plethora of devices providing information at high speeds—information that went unused. Information that's being provided at up to 1,000 readings per second is summarized into one reading every 30 to 60 minutes, and it typically goes no further. It's stored for up to 72 hours and is then discarded. I could see that there were enormous opportunities to capture, store, and utilize this data in real time to improve the quality of care for neonatal babies.

With a shared interest in providing better patient care, Dr. McGregor and Dr. James partnered to find a way to make better use of the information produced by monitoring devices. Dr. McGregor visited researchers at the IBM T.J. Watson Research Center's Industry Solutions Lab (ISL), who were extending a new stream-computing platform to support healthcare analytics.

Smarter healthcare

- *Instrumented*—using streaming data to help clinicians spot infections. Instrumented patient's vital-sign data is captured by bedside monitoring devices up to 1,000 times per second.
- *Interconnected*—monitoring device data and integrated clinician knowledge are brought together in real time for an automated analysis using a sophisticated, streamlined computing platform.
- *Intelligent*—detecting medically significant events even before patients exhibit symptoms will enable proactive treatment before the condition worsens, eventually increasing the success rate and potentially saving lives.

Solution components

Software: IBMInfoSphere™ Streams and IBMDB2®
Research: IBM T.J. Watson Research Center

A three-way collaboration was established, with each group bringing a unique perspective: the hospital's focus on patient care, the university's ideas for using the data stream, and IBM providing the advanced analysis software and information technology expertise needed to turn this vision into reality. The result was Project Artemis, part of IBM's First-of-a-Kind program, which pairs IBM's scientists with clients to explore how emerging technologies can solve real-world business problems.

Project Artemis is a highly flexible platform that aims to help physicians make better, faster decisions regarding patient care for a wide range of conditions. The earliest iteration of the project is focused on early detection of nosocomial infection by watching for reduced heart rate variability along with other indications. For safety reasons, in this development phase the information is being collected in parallel with established clinical practice and is not being made available to clinicians. The early indications of its efficacy are very promising.

Project Artemis is based on IBMInfoSphere Streams, a new information processing architecture that enables near-real-time decision support through the continuous analysis of streaming data using sophisticated, targeted algorithms. The IBMDB2® relational database provides the data management required to support future retrospective analyses of the collected data.

Project Artemis was a consequence of the unique and collaborative relationship between SickKids, UOIT, and IBM. "To gain its support, we needed to do our homework very carefully and show that all the bases were covered. The hospital was cautious, but from the beginning we had its full support to proceed," says Dr. Andrew James, staff neonatologist at The Hospital for Sick Children (SickKids) in Toronto. Even with the support of the hospital, there were challenges to be overcome. Because Project Artemis is more about information technology than about traditional clinical research, new issues had to be considered.

For example, the hospital CIO became involved because the system had to be integrated into the existing network without any impact. Regulatory and ethical concerns are part of any research at SickKids, and there were unique considerations here in terms of the protection and security of the data. The research team's goal was to exceed provincial and federal requirements for the privacy and security of personal health information—the data had to be safeguarded and restricted more carefully than usual because it was being transmitted to both the University of Ontario Institute of Technology and to the IBM T.J. Watson Research Center. After the overarching concerns were dealt with, the initial tests could begin.

Two infant beds were instrumented and connected to the system for data collection. To ensure safety and effectiveness, the project is being deployed slowly and carefully, notes Dr. James:

> We have to be careful not to introduce new technologies just because they're available, but because they really do add value. It is a stepwise process that is still ongoing. It started with our best attempt at creating an algorithm. Now we're looking at its performance, and using that information to fine-tune it. When we can quantify what various activities do to the data stream, we'll be able to filter them out and get a better reading.

The ultimate goal is to create a robust, valid system fit to serve as the basis for a randomized clinical trial.

Merging human knowledge and technology

The initial test of the Project Artemis system captured the data stream from bedside monitors and processed it using algorithms designed to spot the telltale signs of nosocomial infection. The algorithm concept is the essential difference between the Artemis system and the existing alarms built into bedside monitors. Although the first test is focused on nosocomial infection, the system has the flexibility to handle any rule on any combination of behaviors across any number of data streams. Dr. James notes:

> What we've built is a set of rules that reflects our best understanding of the condition. We can change and update them as we learn more, or to account for variations in individual patients. Artemis represents a whole new level of capability.

The truly significant aspect of the Project Artemis approach is how it brings human knowledge and expertise together with device-generated data to produce a better result. The system's outputs are based on algorithms developed as collaboration between the clinicians themselves and programmers. This inclusion of the human element is critical, because good patient care cannot be reduced to mere data points. Validation of these results by an experienced physician is vital since the interpretation of these results has to do with medical knowledge, judgment, skill, and experience. As part of the project, the rules being used by Project Artemis are undergoing separate clinical research to support evidence-based practice.

Artemis also holds the potential to become much more sophisticated. For example, eventually it might integrate a variety of data inputs in addition to the streaming data from monitoring devices—from lab results, to observational notes about the patient's condition, to the physician's own methods for interpreting information. In this way, the knowledge, understanding, and even intuition of physicians and nurses will become the basis of the system that enables them to do much more than they could on their own. Dr. James explains:

> In the early days, there was a lot of concern that computers would eventually "replace" all healthcare providers. But now we understand that human beings cannot do everything, and it's quite helpful to develop tools that enhance and extend the physicians' and nurses' capabilities. I look to a future where I'm going to receive an alert that provides me with a comprehensive, real-time view of the patient, allowing me to make better decisions on the spot.

Broadening the impact of artemis

The flexibility of the platform means that in the future, any condition that can be detected through subtle changes in the underlying data streams can be the target of the system's early-warning capabilities. Also, since it depends only on the availability of a data stream, it holds the potential for use outside the ICU and even outside the hospital. For example, the use of remote sensors and wireless connectivity would allow the system to monitor patients wherever they are, while still providing life-saving alerts in near-real time. Dr. James states:

> *I think the framework would also be applicable for any person who requires close monitoring— children with leukemia, for example. These kids are at home, going to school, participating in sports—they're mobile. It leads into the whole idea of sensors attached to or even implanted in the body and wireless connectivity. Theoretically, we could ultimately monitor these conditions from anywhere on the planet.*

This case study shows the applicability of processing techniques to real-world situations where the ROI is visible and measurable. Extending the concept, you can also architect a machine learning system to make this architecture even more useful.

Case study 5: Microsoft SQL server customer solution

This case study is a new-generation solution combining the traditional RDBMS/SQL server along with Hadoop. This case study is provided by Microsoft Corporation.

Customer profile

Founded in 2007, Klout is a privately held firm of about 70 employees that helps individuals and companies gain a competitive advantage by filtering through and understanding the hundreds of terabytes of information generated each day on social media networks. Based in San Francisco, CA, Klout is recognized as a pioneer in Big Data solutions by leading organizations such as the *Wall Street Journal* and *Forbes* magazine. "When it comes to business intelligence, Microsoft SQL Server 2012 demonstrates that the platform has continued to advance and keep up with the innovations that are happening in Big Data," notes David Mariani, vice president of engineering at Klout.

Klout wanted to give consumers, brands, and partners faster, more detailed insight into hundreds of terabytes of social media network data. It also wanted to boost efficiency. To do so, Klout deployed a business intelligence solution based on Microsoft SQL Server 2012 Enterprise and Apache Hadoop. As a result, Klout processes data queries in near-real time, minimizes costs, boosts efficiency, increases insight, and facilitates innovation.

Solution spotlight

- Speeds efficiency and cuts costs by reducing complexity and speeding Big Data queries to near-real time.
- Increases insight and competitive advantage by providing more detailed information.
- Facilitates innovation.

Business needs

Klout helps clients make sense of the hundreds of terabytes of data generated each day by more than 1 billion signals on 15 leading social media networks, including Facebook and LinkedIn. "We take in raw data and make it into something that is actionable for our consumers, brands, and partners," says Mariani.

The data that Klout analyzes is generated by the more than 100 million people who are indexed by the firm. This includes Klout members and the people who they interact with on social sites. Individuals join Klout to understand their influence on the web, which is rated on a scale from 1 to 100. They also sign up to participate in campaigns where they can receive gifts and free services. More than 3,500 data partners also join Klout to better understand consumers and network trends, including changes in demand and how peoples' influence might affect word-of-mouth advertising.

To deliver the level of insight that customers seek and yet meet the budget constraints of a startup firm, Klout maintained a custom infrastructure based on the open-source Apache Hadoop framework, which provides distributed processing of large data sets. The solution included a separate silo for the data from each social network. To manage queries, Klout used custom web services, each with distinct business logic, to extract data from the silos and deliver it as a data mashup.

Maintaining Hadoop and the custom web services to support business intelligence (BI) was complex and time consuming for the team. The solution also hindered data insight. For example, accessing detailed information from Hadoop required extra development, and so mashups often lacked the detail level that users sought. In addition, people often waited minutes, or sometimes hours, for queries to process, and they could only obtain information based on predetermined templates.

Klout wanted to update its infrastructure to speed efficiency and support custom BI. Engineers sought technologies that could deliver mission-critical availability and still scale to meet Big Data growth and performance requirements.

Solution

In 2011, Klout decided to implement a BI solution based on Microsoft SQL Server 2012 Enterprise data management software and the open-source Hive data warehouse system. "When it comes to BI and analytics, open-source tool sets are just ineffective and there's really not a good choice," Mariani says. "Instead, Klout chose the best of both worlds by marrying the Microsoft BI platform with Hadoop and Hive." Based on employees' previous experience with the Microsoft BI platform, Klout also knew that SQL Server offers excellent compatibility with third-party software and it can handle the data scale and query performance needed to manage Big Data sets.

In August 2011, engineers implemented a data warehouse with Hive, which consolidates data from all of the network silos hosted by Hadoop. In addition, Klout deployed SQL Server 2012 on a system that runs the Windows Server 2008 R2.

Engineers use the operating system to manage all business logic required to facilitate multidimensional online analytical processing (MOLAP). Data is stored in multidimensional cubes, which help preserve detail and speed analysis. To provide high availability, Klout replicates the database to a secondary system using SQL Server 2012 AlwaysOn.

At the time that Klout was initially deploying its solution, SQL Server 2012 and Hive could not communicate directly. To work around this issue, engineers set up a temporary relational database that runs MySQL 5.5 software. It includes data from the previous 30 days and serves as a staging area for data exchange and analysis.

Klout engineers are currently working to implement the new open database connectivity driver in SQL Server 2012 to directly join Hive with SQL Server 202 Analysis Services. In addition, to enhance insight, Klout plans to work with Microsoft to incorporate other Microsoft BI tools into its solution, such as Microsoft SQL Server Power Pivot for Microsoft Excel.

Benefits

With its new solution, Klout expects to boost efficiency, reduce expenses, expand insight, and support innovation.

Speed efficiency and cut costs

By taking advantage of the Microsoft platform for BI, users will be able to get the data they seek in near-real time. Mariani says,

> By using SQL Server 2012 Analysis Services to create cubes, every day our MOLAP model can load 350 million rows of new Hive data, analyze 35 billion rows of information, and achieve an average query response time of less than 10 seconds.

He further explains how Klout can minimize costs and complexity with its new solution:

> By using open-source and commercial software, we don't have to build everything from the ground up and we get a great ecosystem of tools and support.

For example, Klout will spend less time managing business logic and data connections. Mariani explains,

> By creating a single warehouse on Hive, and putting all of our business logic in SQL Server 2012 Analysis Services, we can easily expose all of the data that was previously tucked away in Hadoop.

Increases insight and advantage

Once it is fully implemented, customers and employees can use the new BI solution to see the big picture and the details behind it—to gain competitive advantage and better manage social presence. Users will also have more control over data analysis. Mariani notes:

> SQL Server 2012 and Microsoft BI tools work well with Big Data. We can use SQL Server 2012 Analysis Services and Microsoft BI tools to perform ad-hoc queries of Big Data on Hadoop at sub-second response times.

Facilitates innovation

Klout is implementing the flexible and scalable infrastructure it needs to continue to push the limits of data analysis. Mariani explains:

> When it comes to business intelligence, Microsoft SQL Server 2012 demonstrates that the platform has continued to advance and keep up with the innovations that are happening in Big Data. We're very excited about working with Microsoft to develop solutions based on technologies like SQL Server PowerPivot for Excel and Hadoop so that we can continue to deliver unique services that transform what is possible with Big Data.

The case study shows how real-world organizations are using a combination of social media data and structured data to create a powerful analytical platform. The business case in this situation transcends beyond simple monetization—it is about brand value and market.

Case study 6: Customer-centric data integration

This case study is a representative of social media data integration in many large organizations. It is based on implementing a customer-centric business transformation program, popularly called voice of customer.

Overview

The world of social media and the revolution of mobile technology have changed the way we communicate and network forever. Prior to the advent of Facebook or MySpace and the smartphone, we did have channels to voice opinions and feedback through forums (needed a laptop with Internet), surveys, and call centers. The customer was important then, but more as a purchaser and a consumer of products and services. The opinion of the customer was important but measured in terms of market reach, wallet share, and overall brand presence. But the last decade has changed that landscape; the customer is now an integral part of any organization, considered as an important stakeholder in the business. The opinions of the customer across any channel and source are considered to be extremely valuable.

Integrating customer data across CRM, sales, call center, forums, sentiment analytics, and social media can benefit an organization to:

- Understand the customer.
- Understand the sentiments of a group of customers and apply the deviations to specific customers to bridge the gap between happy and unhappy customers.
- Understand the sentiments and trends in the market as applied to their products and services.
- Understand how the customer evaluates them against the competition.
- Understand the needs of a customer based on their current life events.
- Understand what the customer wants from a social crowd perspective.

The challenge is how to build a solution, and determining what the best kind of data is and how beneficial the analytics and metrics can be. The most important question is the measurement of ROI.

A large exercise like this has several critical phases of implementation:

- Data analysis
- Data architecture
- Data collection
  - Planning the listening posts
  - Implementing the listening posts
- Data quality
- Data processing
- Data classification
- Data integration

- Metrics processing
- Dashboards
  - Mashups
  - Heat maps
  - Clustering
  - Statistical

Why do we need these entire complex processing steps? The companies could have purchased third-party data from aggregators like Nielsen Buzzmetrics and integrated sentiments and trends into their data architecture. But the contexts of the sentiments, the categorization of the trends, and the ability to reprocess the data for several business situations will be near impossible because the data is already qualified and presented as metrics. To leverage the complete knowledge provided by the different touchpoints of data, these organizations have processed most of the steps outlined above and some more in certain situations.

Let us say we have third-party data and it provides the following:

- Number of posts
- Channels posted
- Sentiment tone by topic
- Word clouds
- Latitude, longitude, and geographic data
- Demographic data
- Social media user identification:
  - Twitter handle
  - Facebook user name
  - Any other user identification
  - Influencer status:
    - Peer index
    - Klout score
    - Likes
    - InShare
    - ReTweets
    - G+ score
- Opinions:
  - Percentage of tones:
    - Positive
    - Negative
    - Neutral
  - Category of subjects
  - Direct versus indirect sharing

While integrating all this data is a huge step in connecting the customer behaviors, sentiments, and trends, the unfortunate scenario here is the lack of an integrated approach. The customer sentiment expressed in the conversation is not categorized based on the context of the event, and here is the gap that needs to be addressed.

For example, consider that a customer makes the following statement:

I have been very frustrated with a particular service offering from Acme Inc. and the number of times I had to follow up for completing this service to my satisfaction. I'm not going to engage in the pursuit any further as there is minimal support from their customer care. I'm very disappointed. I will take my business elsewhere.

Analyzing this data for pure sentiment provides a limited perspective on the situation. You can identify that the:

- Customer sentiment is negative.
- The tone of the conversation is negative.
- There is a process failure that has caused this issue.

What you cannot see is:

- Why the customer is unhappy.
- The context of the conversation that has been happening:
  - Service delays
  - Lack of follow up
  - Customer care failed to communicate and engage

Further, if you process this data and integrate it with call center records, you can simply see:

- The nature of service calls the customer called for.
- The number of follow-up calls that he or she did to close the loop.
- The organization response and status:
  - This provides the overall context of the customer sentiment and the impact when integrated with financial data.
  - The bigger picture to worry about is the impact of this conversation in a forum.
  - How many more services does this customer hold and the potential risk that he or she might cancel all services.
  - How many other people in his or her network might this customer influence and what is the loss of revenue.
  - How many more customers have expressed such concerns and canceled services that might result in a legal situation.

Unless this gap is addressed, the value from the voice of customer initiative is deemed primitive. Another channel is that customers will follow up the conversation with a real person at a call center or with emails. For example, a customer writes the following email:

From: john.doe@myfreecountry.com
To: msvcs@Acme Inc.com
Subject: Customer Services Feedback

Dear Acme Inc., I have been a customer for the last 30 years of your services. While the relationship has had its share of highs and lows, in recent times your customer services team has been performing very poorly. The response times have been lagging, there is a lack of urgency to close questions, and the intent is to sell more services and not address issues. While we appreciate the self-service channels you have opened, the services provided by direct channels have deteriorated. Should this trend continue, I would be forced to consider other alternatives.

Sincerely,
John Doe

In this email, there are several key issues, associated sentiments, and comparisons that need to be analyzed carefully. If the customer had written this email and then in a 30-day timeframe followed up with a call to let Acme Inc. know that they are moving on and terminating all the relationships, there was time to react had the email been parsed and an alert raised on a potential attrition situation.

Why is this analysis and proactive action important? Because if John Doe has 50 friends who hear this story, chances are a potential loss of all 50 customers, or over a period of time a loss of groups of customers, all of which lead to a negative impact on the revenue. If John Doe expresses these sentiments and experiences in social media channels, the impact is viral and irreparable. There is brand reputation at stake and more customer attrition that will follow the social media posts.

As we can see from this short discussion, there is a lot of hidden value in Big Data, and not harnessing this in the right time and providing the results to the right business users will have a negative impact. However, the same situation, if provided in the right time to the business users, can result in a proactive reaction to the customer resulting in more favorable outcomes.

To get an all-round level of information, and gain near-perfect and accurate actionable insights, these companies decided to go beyond just sentiment analytics, to integrate data across multiple channels including email and social media analytics. Not only will this bring better insights, it will provide the organizations with the ability to predict and model customer behavior and be prepared to react better at such situations. Additionally, the data and analytics will enable the business user community to better address their knowledge base and learnings, and better aid their customer interactions.

Solution design

Figure 5.1 shows a high-level integration approach where we combine processing structured data from online transaction processing (OLTP)/operational data store (ODS) systems and process the extract, transform, and load (ETL) rules, and alongside, process unstructured data from sentiments, emails, and social media channels. The advantage of combining the data from both the sources is we can get a holistic view of the customer. The linkage between the different data types will be enabled by the existing master data management (MDM) and metadata collections, which can be augmented with taxonomies and ontologies from vendor solutions.

Enabling a better cross-sell and upsell opportunity

After implementing this solution, say Acme Inc. has concluded a campaign for a new integrated portfolio services plan to its customers, who were segmented with newer algorithms and sent specific offers based on their buying trends, life situation, and socioeconomic situations in the geography. The campaign has resulted in several calls from the customer community to call center and business services teams.

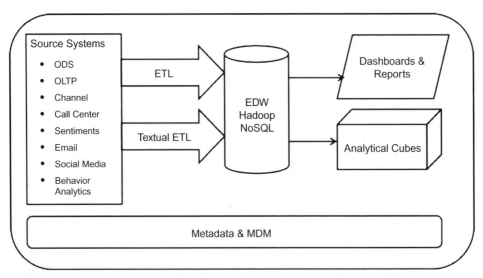

FIGURE 5.1

Solution design for social media and multichannel data integration.

To process each call, the call center is equipped with data about the customer, the offers, benefits of signing an offer, and overall ratings. The call center teams are now achieving better conversion from the customers and have a better quality of conversation. This will result in better customer experiences and drive a true customer-centric approach. The end result will be measured in gains in revenue for the organization.

Example

> Caller customer name: John Doe; ID: 123456AZFSCST
> Campaign: NMSCSWW-3456XX2011

When the customer calls, the system loads in the information and provides the following data:

- Customer LTV
- Last transaction date
- Last product purchased
- Last campaign responded to
- Customer stickiness
- Customer life events
- Customer cross-sell opportunity
- Customer social media affiliations and presence (as traceable or a generic customer behavior model)
- Trends of customer clusters with similar characteristics
- Top demography for affinity to promotions

- Cross-geography analysis
- Heat map of customer satisfaction indexes
- Most effective campaigns
- Least effective campaigns
- Most trending topics on sentiment analytics

With all the data available to the call center staff in visual mashups, analytics, and on-demand reports, the relationship management on the phone with the customer results in a positive experience that contributes to increasing the overall profitability and bottom line of the company.

Companies who have implemented social media data integration into the data warehouse as discussed in this case study include fortune 500 enterprises ranging from financial services corporations, software vendors, healthcare providers, pharmaceutical companies, insurance companies, manufacturing industries, and e-commerce retailers, and all of them benefited by improving the bottom line and by gaining better insights about their customers and prospects. The insights are enabling the enterprises to provide near-real-time customer-focused conversations, aligning to the sentiment and the expectations of the customers, which results in constant and measureable growth. Another benefit of this data integration is the ability to model and predict the outcomes of campaigns and the competitive insights into other brands and their impact on the customer.

SUMMARY

As seen from these sample case studies there is a lot of knowledge, behavior, sentiment, and other types of insights in the world of Big Data, whether you look at machine data, sensor data, social data, or clickstream data. The data can be processed and the outputs provided for analysis and research by the business users to create more value and opportunities in new and existing markets and customers. There are several additional case studies available in Appendix A at the end of this book that will provide insights into how many other real-world companies have integrated Big Data in their organizations.

The chapters in Part 2 focus on data warehousing and its evolution, analytics, limitations, and how the new world of data will include both Big Data and the data in the data warehouse on one integrated platform called the next-generation data warehouse.

The Data Warehousing

Data Warehousing Revisited

The information links are like nerves that pervade and help to animate the human organism. The sensors and monitors are analogous to the human senses that put us in touch with the world. Databases correspond to memory; the information processors perform the function of human reasoning and comprehension. Once the postmodern infrastructure is reasonably integrated, it will greatly exceed human intelligence in reach, acuity, capacity, and precision.

—**Albert Borgman,** *Crossing the Postmodern Divide.* **Chicago: University of Chicago Press, 1992.**

INTRODUCTION

The first part of this book introduced the world of Big Data; its complexities, processing techniques, and technologies; and case studies on Big Data. This chapter reintroduces you to the world of data warehousing. We look at the concept and evolution of the data warehouse over the last three decades. Since the days of punch cards to the writing of this book, there has been one fundamental struggle: managing data and deriving timely value. The last three decades have created many tipping points in technology that have evolved the growth of data management including data warehousing. Companies have invested millions of dollars into creating data warehouses and these investments need to be leveraged for solving the right problems.

Prior to the advent of electronic data processing, companies used to manage their customers more by customer loyalty of making purchases at the same store for products, and used to track inventory using traditional bookkeeping methods. At that time, population demographics were small and buying trends for products and services were limited. When the early days of electronic data processing came about in the early 1950s, initial systems were based on punch cards. The benefit of the systems was their ability to start managing pockets of businesses in electronic formats. The downside was the proliferation of multiple stores of data on punch cards that reflected different values, and damage to the paper would mean loss of data. We quickly evolved from the punch cards to magnetic tapes that gave better data storage techniques, yet were not able to control the proliferation of different formats of data. From magnetic tapes we evolved to disks where we could store data. Along the way the applications that generated and controlled data production from the front-end perspective moved quickly from simple niche languages to declarative programming languages.

Tracking along the progress of the storage and programming languages, the applications to manage customers, employees, inventory, suppliers, finances, and sales evolved. The only issue with the data was it could not be analyzed for historical trends, as the data was updated in multiple cycles.

Thus evolved the first generation of OLTP applications. Around the same time in the 1970s, Edgar. F. Codd published his paper on the relational model of systems for managing data.[1] The paper was pivotal in several ways:

- It introduced for the first time a relationship-based approach to understanding data.
- It introduced the first approach to modeling data.
- It introduced the idea of abstracting the management and storage of data from the user.
- It discussed the idea of isolating applications and data.
- It discussed the idea of removing duplicates and reducing redundancy.

Codd's paper and the release of System R, the first experimental relational database, provided the first glimpse of moving to a relational model of database systems. The subsequent emergence of multiple relational databases, such as Oracle RDB, Sybase, and SQL/DS, within a few years of the 1980s were coupled with the first editions of SQL language. OLTP systems started emerging stronger on the relational model; for the first time companies were presented with two-tier applications where the graphical user interface (GUI) was powerful enough to model front-end needs and the underlying data was completely encapsulated from the end user.

In the late 1970s and early 1980s, the first concepts of data warehousing emerged with the need to store and analyze the data from the OLTP. The ability to gather transactions, products, services, and locations over a period of time started providing interesting capabilities to companies that were never there in the OLTP world, partially due to the design of the OLTP and due to the limitations with the scalability of the infrastructure.

Traditional data warehousing, or data warehousing 1.0

In the early days of OLTP systems, there were multiple applications that were developed by companies to solve different data needs. This was good from the company's perspective because systems processed data quickly and returned results, but the downside was the results from two systems did not match. For example, one system would report sales to be $5,000 for the day and another would report $35,000 for the day, for the same data. Reconciliation of data across the systems proved to be a nightmare.

The definition of a data warehouse by Bill Inmon that is accepted as the standard by the industry states that the data warehouse is a subject-oriented, nonvolatile, integrated, time-variant collection of data in support of management's decision.[2]

The first generation of data warehouses that we have built and continue to build are tightly tied to the relational model and follow the principles of Codd's data rules. There are two parts to the data warehouse in the design and architecture. The first part deals with the data architecture and processing; per Codd's paper, it answers the data encapsulation from the user. The second part deals with the database architecture, infrastructure, and system architecture. Let us take a quick overview of the data architecture and the infrastructure of the data warehouse before we discuss the challenges and pitfalls of traditional data warehousing.

[1] Codd, E. F. (1970). A Relational Model of Data for Large Shared Data Banks. *Communications of the ACM, 13*(6), 377–387. doi:10.1145/362384.362685.

[2] http://www.inmoncif.com/home/

Data architecture

From the perspective of the data warehouse, the data architecture includes the key steps of acquiring, modeling, cleansing, preprocessing, processing, and integrating data from the source to the EDW outlined here:

1. Business requirements analysis:
   - In this step the key business requirements are gathered from business users and sponsors.
   - The requirements will outline the needs for data from an analysis perspective.
   - The requirements will outline the needs for data availability, accessibility, and security.
2. Data analysis:
   - In this step the data from the OLTP is analyzed for data types, business rules, quality, and granularity.
   - Any special requirements for data are discovered and documented in this step.
3. Data modeling:
   - In this step the data from the OLTP models are converted to a relational model. The modeling approach can be 3NF, star schema, or snowflake.
   - The key subject areas and their relationships are designed.
   - The hierarchies are defined.
   - The physical database design is foundationally done in this step.
   - The staging schema is created.
   - The EDW schema is created.
   - If an ODS is defined and modeled, the ODS data model is defined and created.
4. Data movement:
   - In this step the process of extracting, loading, and transformation of data is designed, developed, and implemented.
   - There are three distinct processes developed typically; some designs may do less and others will do more, but the fundamental steps are:
     - Source extract
     - Staging loading
     - Staging extract and EDW loading
   - Data transformations are applied in this phase to transform from the OLTP to the EDW model of data.
   - Any errors occurring in this stage of processing are captured and processed later.
   - Data movement and processing will need to be audited for accuracy and a count of data along each step of the process. This is typically accomplished by implementing an audit, balance, and control process to trace data from the point of arrival into the data warehouse to its final delivery to datamarts and analytical data stores.
5. Data quality:
   - In this step, typically done both in the ETL steps and in the staging database, the data from the source databases is scrubbed to remove any data-quality issues that will eventually lead to data corruption or referential integrity issues.
   - To enable data quality, there are special third-party tools that can be deployed.
   - Errors in this step are critical to be discovered and marked for reprocessing.

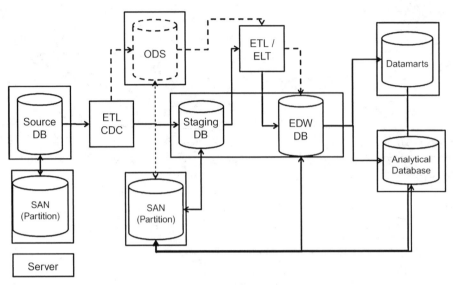

FIGURE 6.1

Data warehouse 1.0 infrastructure layers.

6. Data transformation:
   - In this step all the key staging to EDW data transformation rules are processed.
   - Data aggregations and summarizations are applied.
   - Data encryption rules are applied.
7. Data presentation:
   - In this step the data presentation layers including views and other semantic layers are readied for user access.
   - Data security rules are applied.

Infrastructure

The data architecture of a data warehouse is the key to the castle of knowledge that lies within, but the infrastructure of a data warehouse is the castle. The data warehouse architecture from an infrastructure perspective consists of the following as shown in Figure 6.1:

- *Source systems*—these represent the various source feeds for the data warehouse.
- *Data movement* (ETL/CDC) —this represents the primary programming techniques of moving data within the ecosystem.
- *Databases*—there are several databases created and deployed within the data warehouse:
  - *Staging areas*—these databases (in some instances, there is more than one staging database to accommodate data from different sources) are the primary landing and preprocessing zone for all the data that needs to be moved into the data warehouse.

- *Operational data store*—this database represents the database structure extremely close to the source systems and is used as an integration point for daily data processing. Not all data warehouses have an ODS.
- *(Enterprise) data warehouse*—the data warehouse is arguably one of the largest databases in the enterprise. It holds many years of data from multiple sources combined into one giant structure.
- *Datamarts*—these are specialty databases that are designed and developed for use by specific business units and line of business in the enterprise. In a bottom-up approach to data warehousing, enterprises build multiple datamarts and integrate them.
- *Analytical database*—these are databases that extract or copy data from the data warehouse and support analytical platforms for data mining and exploration activities.

The analytical databases are deployed on a combination of infrastructure technologies including:

- Database technologies:
  - Traditional data warehouses are developed on RDBMS technologies like Oracle, SQL Server, DB2, and Teradata.
  - There are niche solutions built on DBMS technologies like Ingres, PostGres, and Sybase.
- Networks:
  - Enterprise network connections based on 10 MB/100 MB pipes.
- Storage hardware:
  - SAN (storage area network) is the most common storage platform.
  - All the data across the enterprise typically shares the SAN in a partitioned allocation.
  - Smaller data warehouses can be stored on NAS (network-attached storage).
- Server hardware:
  - Data warehouse, datamart, and analytical database server infrastructure can be deployed on
    - Unix operating systems: 32-/64-bit with 4, 8, or 16 dual-core CPUs, some use quad-core processors, 8, 16, 64, or 128 GB of DDR3 RAM.
    - Linux operating systems: 32-/64-bit with 4, 8, or 16 dual-core CPUs, some use quad-core processors, 8, 16, 64, or 128 GB of DDR3 RAM.
    - Windows operating systems: 32-/64-bit with 4, 8, 16 dual-core CPUs, some use quad-core processors, 8, 16, 64, or 128 GB of DDR3 RAM.
  - There are instances where a large server is partitioned into multiple virtual servers and shared between the different components.

These are all the different moving parts within any data warehouse, and upkeep of performance of these components is a major deterrent for enterprises today.

Pitfalls of data warehousing

Is your data warehouse implementation and adoption a success? When asked this question, a large number of data warehouse implementations often cite failure with the implementation because performance becomes a real challenge over a period of time, depending on the size and complexity of transformations within the processing layers in the data warehouse. The underlying reason for performance and scalability issues is the sharing of resources in the infrastructure layer and the database layers. In Figure 6.1, you can see the following layers of shared infrastructure:

- Storage:
  - The source database is isolated in its own storage, though it is a partition of a larger storage cluster.
  - The ODS (if deployed), staging, and EDW databases are all normally connected to one storage architecture.
  - The physical servers for the staging and EDW are the same system and database servers.
  - This shared infrastructure creates scalability and performance issues:
    - The I/O is constrained in the same enterprise network pipe.
    - The I/O between the source, staging, and EDW databases needs to travel from source, to staging, to ETL, to storage, to ETL, to EDW. A lot of system resources and the network are dedicated to managing this dataflow and it introduces natural time latencies.
    - Timeouts on connections, slow-moving transactions, and outages on disk architecture are other common side effects that occur in this environment.
- Server hardware:
  - The server hardware can be a set of virtual partitions on a large physical server.
  - The staging and EDW databases are normally in one server.
  - Analytical databases are normally installed in their own server environment.

Performance

What is the limitation of sharing-everything architecture? The answer to this lies in understanding the shared-everything architecture as shown in Figure 6.2. In this architecture:

- Memory, CPU, and system bus are shared by all programs running on the systems.
- Storage is shared across the programs.
- The network is a common enterprise network and not a direct tethered connection in most cases.

The architecture approach described in Figure 6.2 is not the optimal architecture to handle the large volume of data, the processing complexities, and users defined for the data warehouse. This architecture will scale well and perform with consistency on an OLTP or transaction processing platform, since the transactions are discrete in size and occur in small bursts. The system can be tuned and maintained for optimal performance and managed to accommodate the growth needs of a transactional environment.

The data warehouse is a collection of transactional data over a period of time and by definition is a larger data set, which will be used for a variety of query and analysis purposes by multiple users in an enterprise.

In a shared-services environment, there are several issues that limit the performance and scalability of the data warehouse. Let us examine the performance aspect of the data warehouse versus the OLTP platforms in the shared environment.

In an OLTP query execution, classic transactional queries are discrete like:

- Insert into `Sales(date, gross_sales_amt, location_id, product_code, tax_amt)`
- Update customer set `email='someone.somemail.com"`
- Delete from inventory where `sku = 'q12345'`

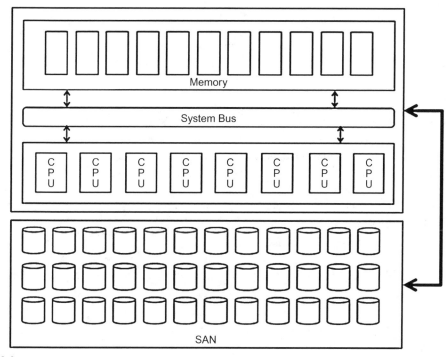

FIGURE 6.2

Shared-everything architecture.

If you observe the query pattern, you can discern that for each of these query actions a particular record in a table will be affected. This activity typically generates a roundtrip across the different infrastructure layers and does not timeout or abruptly quit processing, since the data activity is record by record and each activity is maintained in a buffer until the transaction commit is accomplished. There can be many such small queries that can be processed on the OLTP system, since the workload performed in this environment is small and discrete.

The amount of CPU cycles, memory consumed, and data volume transported between the server and storage can be collectively expressed as a unit of "workload" (remember this definition, as we will discuss it over the next few chapters in greater depth).

Now let us look at the execution of a query on the data warehouse data set. Typically, the query will take a longer processing cycle and consume more resources to complete the operation. This can be attributed to the size of the data set and the amount of cycles of transportation of data across the different layers for processing, compiling, and processing the final result set, and presentation of the same to the process or user requesting the query. The data warehouse can handle many such queries and process them, but it needs a more robust workload management design, as the resources to process the data of this size and scale will differ from the OLTP environment. There is a different class of workload that will be generated when you process data from web applications within the data warehouse environment and another class of workload for analytical query processing.

Continuing on understanding how workloads can impact the performance, for a transactional query the workload is streamlined and can be compared to automobiles on expressways. There is a smooth flow of traffic and all drivers follow lane management principles. The flow is interrupted when a breakdown, accident, or large volume of big rigs merge in the traffic. On a similar note, you will see a slowdown or failure of query processing if there is an infrastructure breakdown or a large and complex query that might have been generated by an ad-hoc user, which will resemble traffic jams on any large-city expressway when an accident occurs.

The hidden complexities of data warehouse queries are not discernable by visual inspection. The reason for this is the design and architecture of the semantic layers built on top of the data warehouse, which allows the user to navigate the relationships in the underlying data and ask questions that can drive workload and optimization demands in multiple layers, and sometimes creates conflicts between the optimization and its workload model in the database.

For example, to determine the sales dollars per month and year for each customer in a household, the query on a data warehouse will look as follows:

```
Select   cust.customer_name,   cust.cust_id,   household.household_id,   household.
state,   sum(sales.net_sales_amt)   net_sales,   sales.month_num,   sales.year_num   from
cust,household,sales where cust.household_id = household.household_id and cust.cust_
id = sales.cust_id group by cust.customer_name, cust.cust_id, household.household_id,
sales.month_num, sales.year_num
```

Let us assume the tables sizes are:

- Customer: 300,000 rows
- Household: 190,000 rows
- Sales: 75,000,000 rows

To execute this query, the data warehouse will perform several cycles of computational processing across layers of infrastructure, as shown in Figure 6.3:

- There are large data sets that will be read from the disk and moved to the memory and back to the disk. This will lead to excessive data swapping between different layers on a continued basis.
- Additionally, the same data may be needed multiple times and depending on how stale or fresh the data is, the query might have to repeat the processing steps since there is not enough space to persist the result sets.
- Depending on the configuration setting of the database and the server, the memory and CPU are divided between the multiple threads that are generated by the query for processing. For example, a dual-core CPU can execute four threads—two per CPU. In the case of an average server the CPU can execute 32 threads for eight CPUs. If there are 32 threads and eight users running, the CPU cycles will be divided for the eight users.
- If there are multiple queries executing operations in parallel, there will be contention for resources, as everybody will be on the same shared-everything architecture. Multiple threads of execution can decrease throughput and increase swapping of data and slowdown of execution.
- If the data warehouse load operations execute in parallel with the query processing, they can evolve into sync issues especially in circular references.
- A mix of query and load operations can cause the database to underperform in the shared architecture as it creates a mixed workload.
- Adding ad-hoc users and data mining type of operations can cause further underperformance.

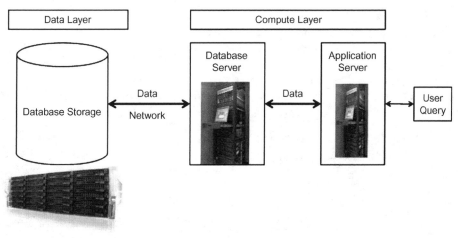

FIGURE 6.3

Data warehouse processing.

The challenge of the shared-everything architecture limits the usability of the data warehouse. The data warehouse can underperform due to growth of data, users, queries, load cycles, new applications like data mining, and online analytical processing (OLAP). The problem manifests after three to six months in a high-volume database, and in a year in a lower-volume database. How do organizations address this situation? In addition to the performance issues, the scalability challenge is another area that is a constant threat.

Typically, the next step a database administrator and system administrator take is performance tuning the data warehouse. Adding indexes, storage, and server capacities are the most common techniques. With all this performance tuning, there are still challenges that limit the adoption of the data warehouse. The reason for this situation is that all these actions are being done in the same shared-everything infrastructure. The end result is momentary relief and not radical sustained performance. These issues remain whether you build the data warehouse using top-down or bottom-up approaches.

While performance is one major area that continues to challenge the data warehouse, scalability is another area that has been a significant challenge to the success of data warehouses. In the next section we will discuss the scalability issues and how they have been addressed.

Scalability

Database scalability is commonly used to define improvements in the infrastructure and data structure areas of the data warehouse to accommodate growth. Growth in the data warehouse happens in two areas: the volume of data and new data, and the growth of users across different user hierarchies. Both of these situations affect the performance and the scalability of the database. Common techniques to scale up performance in a shared-everything architecture include:

- Adding more server hardware. You need to scale up both the CPU and memory for achieving some benefit; scaling one component does not provide huge benefits.
- Adding more storage does not help if you cannot separate the data structures discreetly into their own specific substorage areas.

- Implementing a robust data management technique, by reducing the amount of data in the tables by archiving history, can help only if volumes are extremely high.
- Creating additional indexing strategies normally creates more overhead than help.
- Compressing data on storage with the available compression algorithms.
- Create aggregate tables or materialized views.
- Archiving data based on usage and access. This differs from the traditional archiving techniques where data is archived based on a calendar.

The performance of a database can be definitely improved by a combination of effective data management strategies, coupled with a boost in additional hardware and storage. By this technique you can achieve efficiencies of processing and execution of tasks.

In a shared-everything architecture, as you improve the efficiencies of processing on the server hardware, the storage layer also needs to be parallelized. Techniques for managing and improvising storage architecture include:

- Master–slave:
  - Another implementation of multinode concept.
  - All writes are written to the master.
  - All reads are performed against the replicated slave databases.
  - Is a limited success, as large data sets slow down the query performance as the master needs to duplicate data to the slaves.
  - Master and slave databases are synced on a continuous basis, causing query performance and result set consistency issues.
- Multimaster replication:
  - Create many nodes or clones.
  - Each node is a master and connects to peers.
  - Any node can service a client request.
  - Did not emerge as a big success for RDBMS:
    - Consistency was loosely coupled.
    - ACID principles violated data integrity.
- Partitioning of data has been a very popular option supported by the database vendors, even though the scalability achieved is limited due to inherent design limitations. With partitioning:
  - Data can be partitioned across multiple disks for parallel I/O.
  - Individual relational operations (e.g., sort, join, aggregation) can be executed in parallel in a partitioned environment, as resources can be bequeathed to the operation.
- Commonly used partitioning techniques are:
  - List partitioning:
    - Based on a list of values that are randomly applied.
  - Range-based partitioning:
    - Applied when a single table cannot sit on a server.
    - Split table onto multiple servers based on ranges of values; commonly used ranges are dates.
  - Key or hash-based partitioning:
    - In this technique, a key-value pair is used in the hash partitioning and the result set is used in the other servers.
  - Composite partitioning:

    – Hash: range partitioning:
  a. First partition of the table by hash keys.
  b. Subpartition by range of values.
    – Range: hash partitioning:
  a. First partition of the table by a range of values.
  b. Subpartition by hash keys.

The partitioning techniques introduce a different problem in the storage architecture, the skewing of the database. Certain partitions may be very large and others small, and this will generate suboptimal execution plans.

The following are partitioning methods that are used for large tables:

- Vertical partitioning:
  - Partition large tables by columns across the database, normally in the same database.
  - The biggest issue with this technique is that we have to balance the partition when the tables grow in columns.
  - Queries needing large columns will fail to perform.
  - The technique will not scale for data warehousing, but lends well for OLTP.
- Horizontal partitioning:
  - Tables are partitioned by rows and distributed across servers or nodes in a database.
  - Queries looking for more than one group of rows will have to read multiple nodes or servers.
  - Extremely large tables will be heavily skewed in this distribution.
  - Moderately sized tables will perform well.

Partitioning, adding infrastructure, and optimizing queries do not enable unlimited scalability in the data warehouse for extremely large data. The workarounds used to enhance scalability and performance include:

- Designing and deploying multiple data warehouses for different business units or line of business (defeats the purpose of an integrated data warehouse).
- Deploy multiple datamarts (increases architecture complexity).
- Deploy different types of databases to solve different performance needs (very maintenance-prone).

The evolution of the data warehouse appliance and cloud and data virtualization has created a new set of platforms and deployment options, which can be leveraged to reengineer or extend the data warehouse for sustained performance and scalability. We will be looking at these technologies and the reengineering techniques in the next few chapters.

Architecture approaches to building a data warehouse

The last area of overview in this chapter is the data warehouse building approaches with different architecture styles. In the data warehouse world today, there are two schools of thought in the architecture approach for building and deploying a data warehouse:

1. Information factory is a widely popular model conceived and designed by Bill Inmon. It uses a data modeling approach aligned with the third normal form where the data is acquired at

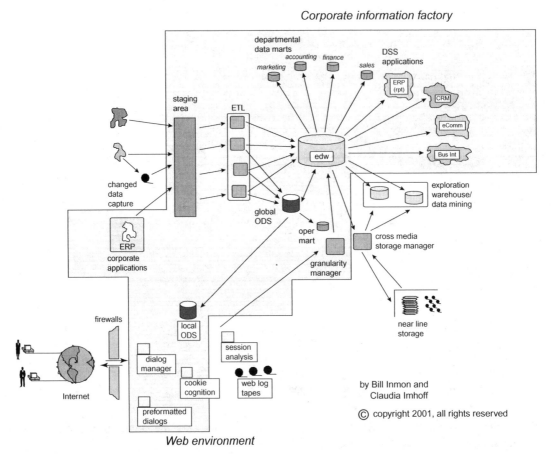

FIGURE 6.4

CIF architecture (reproduced here with explicit permission of authors).

its closest form to the source, and subsequent layers are added to the architecture to support analytics, reporting, and other requirements.

2. BUS architecture, also known as the Kimball architecture, is based on a set of tightly integrated datamarts that are based on a dimensional data model approach. The data model allows business to define and build datamarts for each line of business and then link the diverse datamarts by aligning the common set of dimensions.

In the information factory architecture shown in Figure 6.4, the data warehouse is built in a top-down model, starting with multiple source systems across the enterprise sending data to the centralized data warehouse, where a staging area collects the data, and the data quality and cleansing rules are applied. The preprocessed data is finally transformed and loaded to the data warehouse. The third normal form of the data model enables storing the data with minimal transformations in to the data

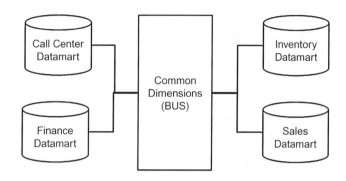

FIGURE 6.5

Datamart BUS architecture.

warehouse. After loading the data warehouse, depending on the needs of the business intelligence and analytical applications, there are several virtual layers built with views and aggregate tables that can be accessed by the applications. In most cases, a separate datamart is deployed to create further data transformations.

The datamart BUS architecture shown in Figure 6.5 builds a data warehouse from the bottom up. In this technique, we build multiple datamarts oriented per subject and join them together using the common BUS. The BUS is the most common data elements that are shared across the datamarts. For example, customer data is used in sales and call center areas; there will be two distinct datamarts— one for sales and one for call center. Using the BUS architecture we can create a data warehouse by consolidating the datamarts in a virtual layer. In this architecture the datamarts are based on a dimensional model of dimensions and facts.

Pros and cons of information factory approach
- Pros:
  - Provides an enterprise view of the data.
  - Centralized architecture.
  - Central rules and control.
  - Refresh of data happens at one location.
  - Extremely high performance.
  - Can build in multiple steps.
- Cons:
  - High risk of failure.
  - Data quality can stall processing data to the data warehouse.
  - Expensive to maintain.
  - Needs more scalable infrastructure.

Pros and cons of datamart BUS architecture approach
- Pros:
  - Faster implementation of multiple manageable modules.
  - Simple design at the datamart level.

- Less risk of failure.
- Incremental approach to build most important or complex datamarts first.
- Can deploy in smaller footprint of infrastructure.
- Cons:
  - A datamart cannot see outside of its subject area of focus.
  - Redundant data architecture can become expensive.
  - Needs all requirements to be completed before the start of the project.
  - Difficult to manage operational workflows for complex business intelligence.

As we can see from this section, neither architecture is completely good or bad. There have been mixes of both these architectures in the current world of data warehousing for creating and deploying solutions. An important aspect to note here is the shared-everything architecture is an impediment irrespective of whether you design a top-down or bottom-up architecture.

The challenges of a data warehouse can be categorized into the following:

- Dependence on RDBMS. The relational model restricts the ability to create flexible architectures. Enforcing relationships and integrity is needed to keep the quality of the data warehouse, but there is no rule that mandates this as a precursor to build a data warehouse.
- Shared-everything architecture. Except for Teradata, all the other databases are built on the shared-everything architecture.
- Explosive growth of data—new data types, volumes, and processing requirements.
- Explosive growth of complexity in querying.
- Evolving performance and scalability demands.
- Unpredictable dynamic workloads.
- Analytical support.
- User evolution from static report consumers to interactive analytical explorers.
- Data management limitations with sharding (partitioning in the database speak of RDBMS).

While the data warehouse 1.0 has been useful and successful, it cannot meet the demands of the user and data needs in the structured data world. If we were to create the Big Data processing architecture on this foundation, it is not feasible or conducive based on the challenges that have been outlined.

Data warehouse 2.0

The second generation of data warehouses has been designed on more scalable and flexible architecture models, yet in compliance with Codd's rules. With the emergence of alternative technology approaches, including the data warehouse appliance, columnar databases, and the creation of useful hub-and-spoke architectures, limitations of the first-generation architecture have been scaled back but have not completely gone away.

One of the key aspects of the second generation of the data warehouse is the classification of the data life cycle to create a scalable data architecture as proposed by Bill Inmon in Inmon's DW 2.0.[2] Another proposed solution is the DSS 2.0 data architecture described by Claudia Imhoff and Colin White.[3]

---

[3] DSS 2.0 -http://www.b-eye-network.com/view/8385.

Overview of Inmon's DW 2.0

The first-generation data warehouse challenges prompted a newer architecture for the next generation of the data warehouse. The architecture of DW 2.0 has to address three distinct components:

- *Data architecture*—based on information life cycle.
- *Infrastructure*—based on data architecture and life cycle.
- *Unstructured data*—new content of text, images, emails, and more.

Figure 6.6 describes the architecture approach of Inmon's DW 2.0. Based on this architecture and foundational elements that it addresses, let us examine the following differentiators in this architecture:

- Data is divided into four distinct layers, based on the type of data and the business requirements for the data. This concept is similar to information life-cycle management, but extends the metadata layer associated with data across the following different layers:
  - *Interactive sector*—very current data (e.g., transaction data).
  - *Integrated sector*—integrated data (e.g., current data that is relative to the business needs, including hourly, daily, or near real time).
  - *Near line sector*—integrated history (e.g., data older than three to five years from the integrated sector).
  - *Archival sector*—archived data from near line.
- Metadata is stored in each layer.
- Each layer has a corresponding unstructured data component.
- Each layer can be created on different platforms as metadata unites the layers.
- Data can be integrated across all the layers with metadata.
- Lower cost compared to DW 1.0.
- Lower maintenance compared to DW 1.0.
- Creates platform for strong governance.
- Provides for flexibility and scalability.

The architecture is relatively new (about five years) and is gaining attention with the focus on Big Data.

Overview of DSS 2.0

Another concept that has been proposed by Claudia Imhoff and Colin White is the DSS 2.0 or the extended data warehouse architecture shown in Figure 6.7.

In the DSS 2.0 model, the authors have suggested compartmentalizing the workload of the operational and analytical business intelligence (BI) and adding the content analytics as a separate module. The three different modules can be harnessed using corporate business rules deployed through a decision support integration platform called decision intelligence. The matrix in Figure 6.8 explains the different types of business intelligence needs that can be addressed by the DSS 2.0 approach. The authors explain in the matrix the different types of users, their data needs, and the complexity of processing, and introduce the concept of managing user expectations by understanding their query behaviors.

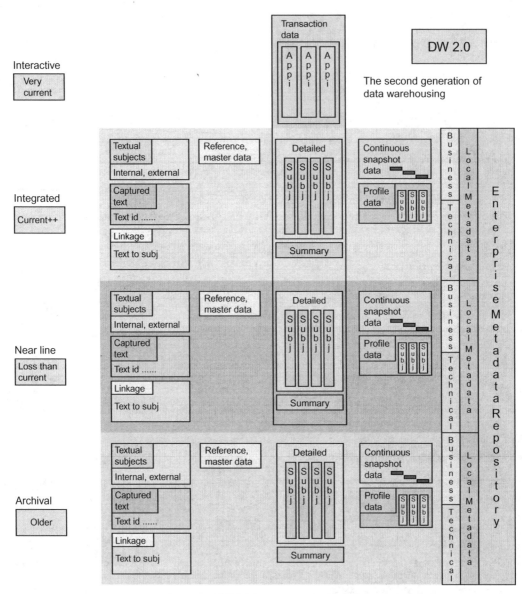

FIGURE 6.6

DW 2.0 architecture.

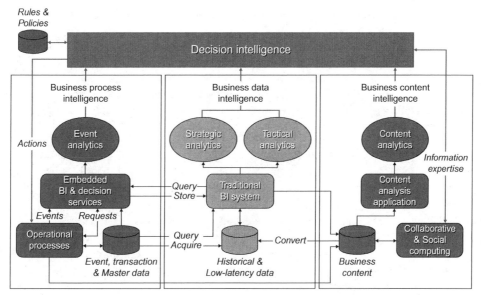

FIGURE 6.7

DSS 2.0 architecture.

Source:www.beyenetwork.com.

	Strategic BI	Tactical BI	Operational BI
Business focus	Achieve long-term business goals	Manage tactical initiatives to achieve strategic goals	Monitor & optimize operational business processes
Primary users	Executives & business analysts	Business analysts, & LOB managers	LOB managers, operational users & operational processes
Time-frame	Months to years	Days to weeks to months	Intra-day to daily
Data	Historical data	Historical data	Real-time, low-latency & historical data
Mode of operation	User driven Data centric	User driven Data centric	Event driven Process centric

FIGURE 6.8

DSS 2.0 matrix.

Source: Courtesy of Claudia Imhoff and Colin White.

DSS 2.0 is implemented more from the front-end solution with common metadata integration points in the industry today.

The challenge that faces data warehousing today is not the volume of data alone; the data types and data formats are issues that threaten to violate the data processing rules of the data warehouse. The rules that were designed for relational data cannot be enforced on text, images, video, machine-generated data, and sensor data. The future data warehouse will also need to handle complex event processing and streaming data and support object-oriented or Service Oriented Architecture (SOA) structures as part of data processing.

The future evolution of data warehousing will be an integration of different data types and their usage, which will be measured as the workload executed on the data warehouse. The next generation of the data warehouse design technique will be the workload-driven data warehouse, where the fundamental definition of the data warehouse remains as defined by the founding fathers, but the architecture and the structure of this data warehouse transcends into heterogeneous combinations of data and infrastructure architectures that are based on the underlying workloads.

While Inmon's DW 2.0 and DSS 2.0 architectures provide foundational platforms and approaches for the next-generation data warehouse, they focus on usability and scalability from a user perspective. The workload-driven data warehousing architecture is based on functionality and infrastructure scalability, where we can compartmentalize the workloads into discrete architectures. In a sense, the workload-driven architecture can be considered as a combination of Inmon's DW 2.0 and Google's Spanner architecture.

SUMMARY

As we conclude this chapter, readers need to understand the primary goals of a data warehouse will never change, and the need to have an enterprise repository of truth will remain as a constant. However, the advances in technology and the commoditization of infrastructure now provide the opportunity to build systems that can integrate all the data in the enterprise in a true sense, providing a holistic view of the behavior of the business, its customers, and competition, and much more decision-making insights to the business users.

Chapter 7 will focus on providing you with more details regarding workload-driven architecture and the fundamental challenges that can be addressed in this architecture along with the scalability and extensibility benefits of this approach.

Further reading

http://www.kimballgroup.com/
http://www.bitpipe.com/tlist/Data-Warehouses.html
http://ist.mit.edu/warehouse
http://tdwi.org/
http://www.b-eye-network.com/
http://research.itpro.co.uk/technology/data_management/data_warehousing

http://www.ithound.com/browse/business-management/business-intelligence/data-mining
http://www.teradata.com/resources.aspx?TaxonomyID=3534
http://www.idgconnect.com/browse_documents/109/it-systems-management/database-solutions/
data-warehousing
www.gartner.com
www.microsoft.com
www.oracle.com
www.emc.com

Reengineering the Data Warehouse

Simplicity is prerequisite for reliability.
—Edsger W. Dijkstra

INTRODUCTION

In Chapter 6 we discussed the different generations of data warehousing, the challenges of the data warehouse, and some modern thoughts on evolving the data warehouse. Earlier chapters have provided us with an in-depth look at Big Data, and its challenges, problems, and solutions. The big questions that stare at us at this juncture are: What will the data warehouse evolve to in the new architecture landscape? Is there even room for a data warehouse? Is there a future for the current investment? This chapter provides us an introduction to reengineering the data warehouse or modernizing the data warehouse. This is the foundational step in building the new architecture for the next-generation data warehouse.

The data warehouse has been built on technologies that have been around for over 30 years and infrastructure that is at least three generations old, compared to the advancements in the current-state infrastructure and platform options. There are several opportunities that are being missed by organizations, including:

- Gaining competitive advantage
- Reducing operational and financial risks
- Increasing revenue
- Optimizing core business efficiencies
- Analyzing and predicting trends and behaviors
- Managing brand presence, channels, and reputation
- Managing customer expectations proactively

One can argue that an enterprise data warehouse is not responsible for many of these types of insights, true and false. The promise of the data warehouse is an enterprise repository for data and a platform for the single version of truth. The issue, however, is due to complexities of users, processes, and data itself. The data warehouse performance has eroded over time steadily and degraded to the extent that it needs to be modernized by a combination of infrastructure and software upgrades to ensure that its performance can be sustained and maintained.

147

Enterprise data warehouse platform

In Chapter 6 we saw a few layers under the hood with respect to the limitations of a database, however, that makes only one component of the entire infrastructure platform called the enterprise data warehouse. There are several layers of infrastructure that make the platform for the EDW:

1. The hardware platform:
   - Database server:
     - Processor
     - Memory
     - BUS architecture
   - Storage server:
     - Class of disk
     - Controller
   - Network
2. Operating system
3. Application software:
   - Database
   - Utilities

A cross-section examination of this infrastructure platform is shown in Figure 7.1.

There are several layers of data distributed from transactional systems into the ODS or staging areas and finally into the data warehouse, to be passed downstream to analytical databases. Let us examine Figure 7.1.

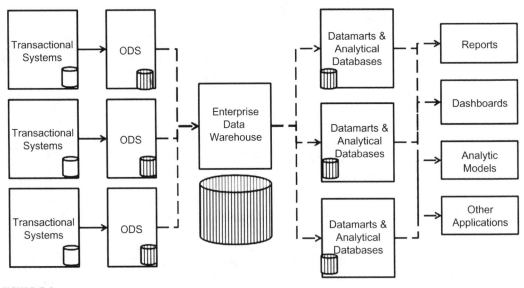

FIGURE 7.1

Data distribution in a data warehouse today.

Transactional systems

Transactional systems are the source databases from any application—web or client server—and are very small in size and have a lower degree of complexity of data processing. The data life cycle is not more than a day or a week at a maximum. Data is copied from this system to downstream databases including the ODS, staging area, and data warehouse. The databases here have very minimal latencies and are always tuned to perform extremely fast writes.

Operational data store

The ODS is an *optional* architecture component and is used for operational reporting purposes. The data collected in the ODS varies in weeks to months, sometimes even a year. The ODS is an aggregation of the data from the transactional systems. The data model undergoes minimal changes, but the complexity of the ODS is inherited from the integration of multiple data sources into one database. The ODS serves two operations: loading data from transactional systems, and running report queries from users. The mixture of two different types of operations causes data to be moved from disk to memory and back to disk in a repeated manner. This causes a lot of performance issues on the overall ODS. There are several potential possibilities to reengineer the ODS, which we will discuss later in this chapter. The ODS is one key area for the modernization exercise.

Staging area

The staging area is another database that is built and deployed in every data warehouse. The purpose of the staging area is to gather data for data quality and data preparation exercises for loading data into the data warehouse. While the data is scrubbed on a daily or every other day basis, maintaining the volumes at lower levels compared to the ODS or data warehouse, there is a lot of activity on the staging area, which often shares the same disk space on the storage layer with the rest of the data warehouse tables. This activity includes data quality and data preparation for loading to the data warehouse, apart from any specific data integration prior to data warehouse loading. These activities, while not creating any overhead from data volume, cause a lot of overhead from the data complexity perspective. The current dilemma for architects is whether to create a separate storage area for the staging area or to completely remove the staging area from the data warehouse data infrastructure, and relocate the same to the ODS or a separate preprocessing database. The disk activity generated by the staging area activities in terms of overloading the data warehouse, competes with the same memory, processor, disk, and network as the data warehouse. This causes several performance issues that database and system administrators have tuned for years. The platform is irrelevant, as the problem manifests across the board.

Data warehouse

The biggest and most complex data structures that has been built on the RDBMS platform is the data store for all the data deemed as an enterprise asset. The data warehouse contains not only current data, but also past history of several years online and offline. The data warehouse is the source of data for all downstream systems including reporting platforms, analytics, dashboards, and specialty applications like CRM, compliance reporting, and financial reporting.

The data structures within the data warehouse can range from simple tables that are reference data to complex aggregate tables and even multidimensional cubes. The data contained in these data structures is constantly changing either in the loading of new data from sources, or in the refresh of complex aggregate structures, while being simultaneously queried by downstream applications for refresh and other data requirements. This flurry of activity requires constant management of infrastructure to provide performance between the loading and the concurrent querying, generating heavy traffic across the infrastructure, which over a period of time becomes fragile and susceptible to failure, leading to performance issues, breakdown of data processing and query processing, and eventually resulting in the failure of the entire data warehouse.

Datamarts

Datamarts are specialty databases built for solving reporting and analysis needs of departmental users, and provide specific subject area–based views of the data to the users. In some organizations that follow BUS architecture for data warehousing, datamarts represent subject areas for that data warehouse. The activities on the datamart are very similar to the data warehouse with users constantly querying data and executing reports and analytics. There are two architectural impacts due to the datamart that can affect the performance of both the data warehouse and the datamart:

- *Data extraction for the datamart*—this is a load on the data warehouse, the underlying infrastructure, and the storage. The impact of this process can be minimal when completed during off hours, as opposed to report refresh or interactive analysis.
- *Querying and analytics on the datamart*—if the data warehouse and the datamart share the physical infrastructure layers, chances of network and storage contention is a very valid situation. These activities can create significant performance and scalability impacts on the data warehouse.

Analytical databases

Analytical databases are specialty databases that are used by analytical applications such as SAS, SPSS, SSAS, and R. These databases are highly complex and large in volume. In most RDBMS systems today, these databases are being natively supported in the same platform that supports the data warehouse. Whether separate or in the same database, the analytical database queries are extremely complex and long running, often creating multiple intermediate temporary data structures on-the-fly. The unpredictable nature of the underlying statistical model creates this complexity. If these databases are built as a separate instance, they still share the same storage and network layer as the data warehouse and the datamarts. When a user executes queries on the analytical database, it increases the contention for shared resources. The direct effect of this contention is the slowdown of the entire infrastructure. (*Note:* At this point in time we are still discussing a shared-everything architecture and its impacts, which are the foundational platform for traditional database architecture and deployment.)

Issues with the data warehouse

What Figure 7.1 depicts is the domino effect of data bottlenecks on the infrastructure, and the bottom line in this situation is the introduction of latencies across the entire infrastructure. The impact of the latencies transcends across multiple layers within the data warehouse and the dependent applications and cumulatively leads to business decision latencies. These latencies can be summed up as "opportunity costs" that often drive away the premise of competitive advantages, clinically precise insights, and opportunities to innovate new business trends. Quite often this is the core reason for the slow adoption or quick attrition from the data warehouse.

The second threat in these widespread silos of data comes in the form of data security. While the data warehouse is the designated corporate repository, due to the performance and scalability issues that surround the data warehouse from the discussion so far, we know that smaller footprints of the data exist in spreadmarts (Excel spreadsheets driving a pseudo-datamart), and datamarts and other data-consumption formats pose a threat to securing the data at rest, loss of data from the enterprise, and compliance violations in regards to data privacy.

The third threat that arises from the loosely coupled data is the reliability of data. The islands of data with minimal governance will provide multiple versions of truth even with a data warehouse being in the organization. The multiple versions of truth mean loss of confidence in the data and its associated metrics, which ultimately leads to reliability questions on the data.

The fourth threat of loose and multiple distributions of data is additional complexity of processing, which results in limited scalability across the spectrum. This lack of scalability due to processing complexities coupled with inherent data issues and limitations of the underlying hardware, application software, and other infrastructure, creates a multilayered scalability problem (we have discussed the scalability issues in Chapter 6 and will discuss more in Chapter 8). There is no one-size-fits-all solution possibility in this layer to counter the issues effectively.

The fifth threat that arises in this architecture is the portability of data. Due to multiple distributions, the data architecture is not uniform, and the additional lack of governance in many cases and nonmaintenance of governance in other cases creates issues with portability of data. The lack of portability leads to further islands of solutions in many enterprises, and this architecture often resembles the tower of Babel.

The last threat from distributed data silos is more tied to cost and total cost of ownership. Multiple silos of solutions require infrastructure, software, and personnel for maintenance. All of these items add to the cost, and in many organizations the budget for newer programs often gets consumed toward such maintenance efforts.

These threats and issues provide one of the fundamental reasons for reengineering the EDW. The other reasons for reengineering include:

- Lower cost of infrastructure.
- New data architectures.
- New business requirements.
- New data.
- Organic or inorganic growth of business.
- New technology advances and improvements that can be leveraged in combination with some of the reasons mentioned above.

The biggest issue that contributes to the current state of the data warehouse is the usage of technologies built for OLTP to perform data warehouse operations. Take a look at what we do in a transactional world. We run discrete transactions that are related to the purchase of a product or service or interactions of the customer at a ATM, for example, and in each of these situations, we do not have any volume or transformation. A database needs to simply log the information into a repository and we are done with a transaction commit. Extending the same concept to supply chain, sales, CRM, and ERP, we need to store a few more records at any given point in time from any of these transactions, and there is still minimal volume and complexity in this situation. The data from the OLTP with some transformations is what gets loaded into the data warehouse. What changes in the equation is data from all the different systems is loaded into the data warehouse, making it extremely complex to navigate through. It does not matter whether you have a star schema or third normal form (3NF)—the problem transcends all the underlying RDBMS. to make the data warehouse scalable and fit, there are multiple techniques that can be utilized with the options available from the modern architectures.

Choices for reengineering the data warehouse

The most popular and proven options to reengineer or modernize the data warehouse are discussed in the following sections. (*Note:* We will discuss cloud computing, data virtualization, data warehouse appliance, and in-memory in Chapter 9, after we discuss workload dynamics in Chapter 8.)

Replatforming

A very popular option is to replatform the data warehouse to a new platform including all hardware and infrastructure. There are several new technology options in this realm, and depending on the requirement of the organization, any of these technologies can be deployed. The choices include data warehouse appliances, commodity platforms, tiered storage, private cloud, and in-memory technologies. There are benefits and disadvantages to this exercise.

- Benefits:
    - Replatforming provides an opportunity to move the data warehouse to a scalable and reliable platform.
    - The underlying infrastructure and the associated application software layers can be architected to provide security, lower maintenance, and increase reliability.
    - The replatform exercise will provide us an opportunity to optimize the application and database code.
    - The replatform exercise will provide some additional opportunities to use new functionality.
    - Replatforming also makes it possible to rearchitect things in a different/better way, which is almost impossible to do in an existing setup.
- Disadvantages:
    - Replatforming takes a long cycle time to complete, leading to disruption of business activities, especially in large enterprises and enterprises that have traditional business cycles based on waterfall techniques. One can argue that this can be planned and addressed to not cause any interruption to business, but this seldom happens in reality with all the possible planning.
    - Replatforming often means reverse engineering complex business processes and rules that may be undocumented or custom developed in the current platform. These risks are often not considered during the decision-making phase to replatform.
    - Replatforming may not be feasible for certain aspects of data processing or there may be complex calculations that need to be rewritten if they cannot be directly supported by the functionality of the new platform. This is especially true in cross-platform situations.
    - Replatforming is not economical in environments that have large legacy platforms, as it consumes too many business process cycles to reverse engineer logic and documenting the same.
    - Replatforming is not economical when you cannot convert from daily batch processing to microbatch cycles of processing.

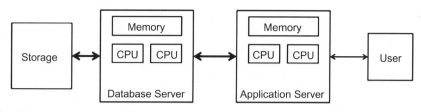

FIGURE 7.2

Data warehouse platform.

Platform engineering

With advances in technology, there are several choices to enable platform engineering. This is fundamentally different from replatforming, where you can move the entire data warehouse. With a platform engineering approach, you can modify pieces and parts of the infrastructure and get great gains in scalability and performance.

The concept of platform engineering was prominent in the automotive industry where the focus was on improving quality, reducing costs, and delivering services and products to end users in a highly cost-efficient manner. By following these principles, the Japanese and Korean automakers have crafted a strategy to offer products at very competitive prices while managing the overall user experience and adhering to quality that meets performance expectations. Borrowing on the same principles, the underlying goal of platform engineering applied to the data warehouse can translate to:

- Reduce the cost of the data warehouse.
- Increase efficiencies of processing.
- Simplify the complexities in the acquisition, processing, and delivery of data.
- Reduce redundancies.
- Minimize customization.
- Isolate complexity into manageable modular environments.

There are several approaches to platform engineering based on the performance and scalability needs of the data warehouse; the typical layers of a platform include those shown in Figure 7.2.

Platform reengineering can be done at multiple layers:

- *Storage level.* In this approach the storage layer of the data is engineered to process data at very high speeds for high or low volumes. This is not an isolation exercise. When storage is customized, often the network and the operating system are also modified to process data at twice the speed of the storage to manage multiple cycles of data transfer between the storage and the database servers. This is not a very popular option, as it needs large-scale efforts, the ROI question cannot be answered in simple math, and the total operating costs often surpass the baseline expectations.
- *Server reengineering.* In this approach the hardware and its components can be replaced with more modern components that can be supported in the configuration. For example, replacing processors, memory upgrades, and network card upgrades are all common examples of server platform reengineering. The issue with server reengineering is the scalability is limited by the processer design and flexibility and by the underlying operating system design that can leverage the processor capabilities. Due to the dual impact, the scalability from server upgrades is very limited. Though

commoditization of hardware components has brought down the cost of the upgrades, the benefits do not outweigh the costs at any point in time, if the server alone is reengineered as a component.

- *Network reengineering.* In this approach the network layout and the infrastructure are reengineered. In the last five years (2008 to present) we have seen a huge evolution in the network technologies from gigabit Ethernet to fiber-optic networks. Transporting data across the network and the associated firewalls has always been a challenge. With the availability of both higher-bandwidth cards and underlying network infrastructure, we can leverage the network upgrade or reengineering to circumvent long waits for data at application, database, and storage tiers in the architecture. This is a significant change that will provide a boost for performance whether implemented as a stand-alone or as a part of major reengineering.
- *Data warehouse appliances.* In this approach the entire data warehouse or datamart can be ported to the data warehouse appliance (the scope of this migration option does not include Big Data). The data warehouse appliance is an integrated stack of hardware, software, and network components designed and engineered to handle data warehouse rigors. There are several benefits to this approach:
  - Integrated stack, purpose built for the data warehouse.
  - Lower overhead costs in maintenance.
  - One-time migration cost depending on platform.
  - Better performance and scalability.
  - Incremental application migration based on phased deployment.
- *Application server.* In this approach the application server is customized to process reports and analytic layers across a clustered architecture. By creating a scalable architecture for the front end, the complexity of managing user loads is resolved, but this leads to an inverse problem with managing the data workloads—there are additional servers spawned. Once again we need to ensure that the back-end systems can scale along with front-end applications to handle the concurrency and the performance service levels.

Solution vendors want to provide the entire stack from the data acquisition layer to the business intelligence and analytics layer, and they all favor the platform engineering approach. This provides a lot of opportunity for the vendors to experiment and create a strong proprietary architecture. While this is innovative, it creates a lot of scalability problems, and if those problems need to be addressed, you need to remove the cost factor out of the equation.

While platform engineering is not a simple exercise, I do recommend separating the multiple layers in the architecture to create a robust application layer that can scale up and out independent of the underlying data. As a separate step, we can then reengineer or modernize the infrastructure for the data layers. To create this layer of abstraction and flexibility between the layers, we need to understand how each layer works on a workload architecture with the rest of the layers (see Chapter 8 for more on this).

Data engineering

Data engineering is a relatively new concept where the data structures are reengineered to create better performance. In this exercise, the data model developed as a part of the initial data warehouse is often scrubbed and new additions are made to the data model. Typical changes include:

- *Partitioning*—a table can be vertically partitioned depending on the usage of columns, thus reducing the span of I/O operations. This is a significant step that can be performed with minimal effect on the existing data, and needs a significant effort in ETL and reporting layers to refresh the changes. Another partition technique already used is horizontal partitioning where the table is partitioned by date or numeric ranges into smaller slices.

- *Colocation*—a table and all its associated tables can be colocated in the same storage region. This is a simple exercise but provides powerful performance benefits.
- *Distribution*—a large table can be broken into a distributed set of smaller tables and used. The downside is when a user asks for all the data from the table, we have to join all the underlying tables.
- *New data types*—several new data types like geospatial and temporal data can be used in the data architecture and current workarounds for such data can be retired. This will provide a significant performance boost.
- *New database functions*—several new databases provid native functions like scalar tables and indexed views, and can be utilized to create performance boosts.

Though there are several possibilities, data engineering can be done only if all other possibilities have been exhausted. The reason for this is there is significant work that needs to be done in the ETL and reporting layers if the data layer has changes. This requires more time and increases risk and cost. Therefore, data engineering is not often a preferred technique when considering reengineering or modernizing the data warehouse.

Modernizing the data warehouse

When you consider modernizing the data warehouse, there are several questions that need to be addressed.

- Migration options—a key question that needs to be answered for deciding the modernization strategy and approach is the selection of one of these choices:
  - Do we rip/replace the existing architecture? Depending on the choice of whether you are moving to a self-contained platform, such as the data warehouse appliance, or migrating the entire platform, this choice and its associated impact needs to be answered.
  - Do we augment the existing architecture? If you choose platform reengineering as the approach, this is a preferred approach to complete the migration process.
- Migration strategy—the following questions need to be articulated to formulate the strategy to build the roadmap for the reengineering or modernizing process:
  - What is the biggest problem that you are facing? A clear articulation on the nature of the problem and the symptoms of where the problem manifests needs to be documented. The documentation needs to include examples of the problem, including the SQL, formulas, and metrics.
  - How mature is your data warehouse? A documentation of the data warehouse processes and the associated business transformation rules needs to be analyzed for determining the maturity of the data warehouse. This will help in planning the migration process.
  - How complex is your ETL process? A documented analysis of the ETL process is needed to complete the ETL migration and determine the associated complexity. If the ETL process is the major reason for the reengineering, you need to determine if just changing the ETL process and its infrastructure will provide the performance and scalability.

- How complex is your BI and analytics? A documented analysis of the BI and analytics process and infrastructure is needed to complete the BI migration and determine the associated complexity. If the BI or analytics process is the major reason for the reengineering, you need to determine if just changing the BI and/or analytics process and its infrastructure will provide the performance and scalability.
- How complex is your security configuration? A critical component of the ETL and BI infrastructure is the associated security configuration. Depending on the migration option, the impact on the security infrastructure can be significant or minimal. If the impact of the security changes is significant, it will impact the overall performance in the new architecture and require extensive testing for the migration.
- How mature is your documentation? Often an ignored aspect in the data warehouse or BI, if your current state documentation is not updated and is legacy or dated, do not even step into the migration or modernization of your data warehouse.
- Cost-benefit analysis—consider the multiple perspectives discussed in this chapter and perform a detailed cost-benefit analysis. The cost should include all the following details by line item:
  - Acquisition costs of new infrastructure
  - Acquisition costs of new data
  - Migration costs:
    - One-time labor costs:
      a. Consultants
      b. Nonemployee staff
    - Ongoing labor costs:
      a. Consultants
      b. Employees
      c. New hires
  - Maintenance costs of current state infrastructure
  - Retirement costs of current state infrastructure
- Identification of pitfalls—conduct a detailed proof of concept (POC), which will provide the opportunity to identify the pitfalls and the areas of concern that need further validation in terms of reengineering or modernization. The pitfalls to verify include:
  - Memory performance
  - Disk architecture
  - Network architecture
  - Scalability of the overall infrastructure
  - Compression of data at rest
  - SQL optimization
  - SQL generation
- Develop a robust roadmap for the program that will include:
  - Timeline for the migration
  - IT and business teams' skills and people requirements
  - Migration execution by subject area or application
  - Testing and deployment plan
  - Backup and recovery plan
  - Rollback plan in case of issues
  - Business continuity plan

Once you have identified the approach, costs, pitfalls, and options for modernizing the data warehouse, you can implement a program. A critical question that we need to still discuss before the modernization aspect is complete is; Do you know the workload that is being addressed in the modernization, and does the modernization address scalability and can this architecture handle Big Data integration? Let us discuss this in a case study.

Case study of data warehouse modernization

A large retail/e-retail organization has been experiencing a slowdown in sales and the responses to their campaigns has been less than expected. The business teams, after a lot of analysis and introspection, have determined that many of their strategies were based on information retrieved from the enterprise data warehouse but significantly transformed to meet their specific requirements. Further analysis revealed that the EDW was not being used as the source for all the data required for decision support, the fundamental reason being the performance and availability of the EDW and its limitations to transform the data as required by a business team.

The Corporate Executives (CxO) team asked for an evaluation and recommendation on modernizing the EDW infrastructure. To enable this process to be completed in a timely manner, a special team of business stakeholders, IT stakeholders, and executives was formed, and an advisory external team was added to this group. The goals of the team were:

- Evaluate the current state of the infrastructure, processes, and usage of the data warehouse.
- Recommend a set of options for a new platform for the data warehouse.
- Recommend a set of optimizations that can be executed for the processes associated with managing the data in the data warehouse.
- Recommend a strategy to modernize the data warehouse to include current and future requirements from a data perspective.

The team executed a four-week exercise and presented the following findings on the performance and health of the EDW.

Current-state analysis

- The infrastructure for the EDW is over a decade old and has been severely underperforming.
- There are several years of data that need to be evaluated and archived from the production systems, as this is slowing down daily processing.
- The software versions for the database platform need upgrades and some of the upgrades cannot work on the current hardware.
- There are tables and aggregates that have not been used for a few years but keep getting processed on a daily basis. We need to have the business users validate if they do not require this data.
- The storage architecture is legacy and upgrading this will provide a lot of benefits.
- The data architecture needs a thorough evaluation, as there are computations from the semantic layers that create a lot of stress on the database from a performance perspective.
- There are several multidimensional storage structures that can be rearchitected with modern design approaches. This would need some additional skills in the team.

Recommendations

There are several options that can be explored to modernize the EDW and the two options that will meet the current needs are:

- Option 1: The traditional route of upgrading the infrastructure platform starting with the servers, operating system, database software, application software, network, and storage systems is one technique.
  - Pros:
    - No new technologies to evaluate.
    - Minimal learning curve.
  - Cons:
    - Longer migration due to infrastructure layers that need upgrades.
    - Costs can be prohibitive based on the requirements.
    - Performance benefits cannot be predictable due to heterogeneous layers of infrastructure.
- Option 2: Evaluate the data warehouse appliance solution from two to four leading vendors, conduct a POC to check for compatibility, and select that as a platform for the EDW.

  - Pros:
    - Integrated platform of infrastructure and storage.
    - Configured and designed to meet the demands of the EDW users.
    - Scalable architecture.
    - Requires minimal maintenance.
    - High availability by architecture design.
    - Self-managing.
  - Cons:
    - New technology configuration, requires some learning.
    - There will be some legacy functionality that may not be supported in the appliance.
    - Custom or user-defined functions may not be supported in the appliance platform, if the technology is different from the incumbent platform.
    - Longer testing cycles to migrate applications to the new platform.

The overall recommendation of the team is that option 2 be selected, and the modernization of the EDW will be developed and deployed on an appliance platform.

Business benefits of modernization

- Enterprise version of data is restored.
- Measure effectiveness of new products on the consumer experience.
- Increase employee productivity and collaboration with customer-facing processes.
- Measure and track business performance goals Key Performance Indicators (KPIs).
- Measure and track improvements in business processes.
- Drive innovation and top-line revenue growth.
- Increase operational efficiencies.
- Improve people efficiencies.
- Improve decision making.

The appliance selection process

The data warehouse appliance selection process was a 12-week exercise that included the following activities.

Request For Information/Request For Proposal (RFI/RFP)

The first step executed was an RFI/RFP that contained sections with the following information.

Vendor information

This section provides the information about the vendor organization and should contain the following:

- General
- Company financials
- Customer references

Product information

This section is regarding the product and its details and should contain the following:

- Product description
- Product history
- Product development
- Product service and support
- Product upgrades
- Documentation and online help
- Training
- User groups and communities
- Partnerships and alliances

Scorecard

Based on the response from the prior sections, a vendor scorecard was developed and evaluated by the teams. The scorecard looks like the following:

Category	Vendor A	Vendor B	Vendor C	Vendor D
Maturity	10	9	5	5
Financial	9	8	5	5
Reference	10	6	6	6
Architecture	9	8	7	6
Scalability	9	7	5	6
Interfaces	9	8	4	4
Support	10	8	3	4
Service	8	8	4	6
Cost	8	6	6	7
Total (scale of 0)	9	8	5	5

Proof of concept process

The proof of concept process was conducted as an onsite exercise with three vendors, and this included the transportation and setup of the actual appliance in the data center. The entire process of the infrastructure setup was also scored and recorded for a production execution. The remaining steps of the POC included the execution of a set of use cases on the appliance, which was loaded with all the current production data.

- Configuration and setup—the appliance vendors brought their infrastructure and set up the same in the data center. The key pieces of information that were used for creating a scorecard included:
  - Floor space requirements
  - Networking requirements
  - Setup process: ease of use
  - Administration tools
  - Monitoring tools
  - Data architect/Database administrator tools
- Data loading and setup—the appliance vendors were provided with the current data model and the complete backup of the current data in the EDW. The vendors were asked to load the data into the appliance and the process was timed and scored. The data loading and setup process included:
  - Data types and compatibility issues
  - Database functions supported and not supported
  - Data load scripts
  - Special tools used for loading the data
  - Storage layout and design
  - Data compression
- POC execution—the proof of concept execution included a set of reports (or report SQL), analytical queries, and queries that do not currently execute due to various reasons.
  - The use cases were scored based on response time, accuracy, number of concurrent users, data usage statistics, ease of execution, and number of queries executed concurrently.
  - Additional tests were executed by connecting the current ETL and BI applications.
  - There were multiple cycles of the use cases execution conducted on the appliance platform with the following constraints:
    - Appliance initial setup with no tuning—in this cycle the queries were executed on the appliance based on the initial setup.
    - Minimal tuning—in this cycle the appliance was tuned for minimal improvements.
    - Complete performance tuning—in this cycle the appliance was tuned to perform at its optimal best.
- Selection phase—the execution of the POC was completed and a final scorecard was created, which included scoring by the business users, scoring by data center teams, and scoring by the POC team. The final recommendation of the vendor was made based on the consensus among all stakeholders and the move to go ahead was taken.

Program roadmap

The next step of the modernization was to plan the migration program from the EDW to the appliance platform. This program roadmap included:

- Architecture analysis—based on the appliance architecture, there are changes that need to be made to the data model, the data architecture itself, the ETL process, and the aggregate tables management process. This analysis provided the gaps that needed to be managed in the migration process and the level of complexity along with the associated risks to be mitigated in the design process of the migration program.

- Skills—the architecture analysis provided a skills gap that needed to be managed with both skills training and additional staffing for the migration.
- Data architecture—the appliance architecture required the data model to be changed from its current state to a simpler 3NF of hybrid architecture. There were not too many changes that needed to be made, and the changes that were made were more aligned to the requirements from the BI layers.
- Infrastructure architecture—the appliance is a self-managing and highly available architecture based on its design principles. The infrastructure architecture that is the biggest change is the storage of the data changed from the traditional SAN to a distributed architecture, which is a one-time change and provides a significant performance boost.
- ETL migration—the appliance platform supported the ETL applications natively, minimizing the configuration and set up of the software on the new platform. There were changes in the ETL process due to changes in the data architecture that needed to be developed and tested. The additional changes that were made to the ETL layer included new modules that were designed and developed to accommodate the migration of custom functions that were not supported in the appliance platform.
- BI migration—the appliance platform supports the BI software and did not require additional setup or configuration process. The changes that were made to this application were in the semantic layers to reflect the changes in the data architecture, hierarchies, lookup and reference tables, additional functions, and data structures to accommodate any custom functions that were in the legacy platform.
- Analytics migration—the appliance platform supported all the analytical functions that were available in the legacy platform and there were no specific migration requirements in this process.
- Migration process—the overall migration process was done after data migration, in four parallel phases:
  1. Data migration—this was completed as a one-time migration exercise. New data model deployment and additional data structures were created as a part of the migration. This includes the additional transformations needed by each line of business for their requirements.
  2. ETL migration—this was initiated as a process that was implemented in parallel with the BI and analytics migration. There were no dependencies on the user layers to implement the ETL migration.
  3. Business intelligence migration—this was implemented in multiple phases within one large phase, in parallel with the ETL and analytics migration.
  4. Analytics migration—this was implemented in parallel with BI and ETL migration. The dependency for this phase to complete was the availability of data, which depended on the ETL migration completion, especially for the new data structures.
- Production rollout—the production rollout and operationalization of the appliance platform is a phased operation. This was implemented based on three critical factors:
  1. Business continuity—the most critical business applications were the first to be rolled out on this platform based on the priority provided by the governance team.
  2. Adoption readiness—the business units that were ready to move to the appliance platform became the second factor for the migration. For example, the financial line of business users were ready to use the new platform first though they had higher risks compared to other users.

3. Completion of migration—the migration of data, ETL, and BI processes had to be complete and signed off by the respective stakeholders.

- Support—the support for the new platform for infrastructure requirements was provided by the vendor teams for the first quarter and subsequently the internal teams:

  - Stabilization—the appliance rollout process included a stabilization phase of three months after the production kickoff. This phase provided the time required to mature the initial rollout.
  - Sunset legacy systems—the last phase of the migration process was to sunset the legacy hardware. This was done six months after the production rollout.

Modernization ROI

The corporation was able to demonstrate the benefits of the modernization in the first three months of the process, including:

- One version of truth—all the reports and analytics were driven from the central platform, with a certified data stamp of approval, which was provided the data governance organization.
- Auditable and traceable data—all the data in the organization was auditable and any associated traceability for lineage was easily available in a self-service portal of reports.
- Decision support accuracy—after migration to the appliance platform, the sales and marketing organizations were able to make informed decisions with improved accuracy, which was measured in the lift in the campaign response and increased volume of sales as indicated by improved margins for same-store sales.
- Process simplification—a large benefit that is not traditionally measured is the improvement of process times. This impact was very significant for the executives as the teams were able to conduct analysis of different outcomes and provide causal inputs with data and statistics, which was never possible in the legacy environment.

Additional benefits

The appliance platform has also enabled the organization to leapfrog and be ready to integrate data from new sources, including unstructured, semi-structured, and nontraditional sources.

SUMMARY

As seen from this chapter and case study, the modernization of the data warehouse is an exercise that many organizations are currently engaged in executing. There are several steps that need to be executed to complete a modernization program, and if these steps are executed with the appropriate amount of due diligence and the outcomes measured appropriately, there are large measurable benefits.

The next chapter will discuss in depth the workloads of data warehousing. What constitutes a workload? How much workload is the right size to consider for the data warehouse and Big Data? Is the workload architecture dependent on the data or the converse? The next-generation architecture will require these clarifications and forms the focus of the next chapter.

Workload Management in the Data Warehouse

For the machine meant the conquest of horizontal space. It also meant a sense of that space which few people had experienced before—the succession and superimposition of views, the unfolding of landscape in flickering surfaces as one was carried swiftly past it, and an exaggerated feeling of relative motion (the poplars nearby seeming to move faster than the church spire across the field) due to parallax. The view from the train was not the view from the horse. It compressed more motifs into the same time. Conversely, it left less time in which to dwell on any one thing.
—**Robert Hughes**, *The Shock of the New*

INTRODUCTION

There are several systems that have been built for data warehouses over the last 30 years. The primary goal of a data warehouse has evolved from being a rear-view look at the business and metrics for decision making to a real-time and predictive engine. The evolution has been really fast in the last 5 years compared to the 25 years prior, and such a pace of growth mandates several changes to happen in the entire data processing ecosystem to scale up and scale out to handle the user demands and data processing requirements. One of the key aspects to consider for designing the newer architectures is to understand what we are processing and what is required from a system perspective for this processing to happen in an acceptable performance time. Apart from the initial processing, we need to design the system to sustain the performance, remain scalable, and remain financially viable for any enterprise. The answer to this lies in understanding the workloads that happen in the system today and in the future, and create architectures that will meet these requirements.

Workload-driven data warehousing is a concept that will help the architects and system administrators to create a solution based on the workload of processing data for each data type and its final integration into the data warehouse. This is key to understanding how to build Big Data platforms that will remain independent of the database and have zero or very minimal dependency on the database. This is the focus of this chapter and the design and integration will be discussed in Chapters 11 and 12.

Current state

Performance, throughput, scalability, and flexibility are all areas that have challenged a data warehouse and will continue to be an area of challenge for data warehousing until we understand the grassroots of the problem and address it. To understand the problem, we need to go beyond just managing the database-related tuning and architectural nuances, and understand the workload aspects of the entire system, thereby managing the design process of both data and systems architecture to accomplish the goal of overcoming challenges and turning those into opportunities.

Defining workloads

According to Dictionary.com, *workload* is defined as the amount of work that a machine produces or can produce in a specified time period. By delving deeper and applying this definition to a data processing machine (we should include the application server, network, database server, and storage as one unit for this definition), we define the query processing of the database in terms of throughput or how many rows/second we have read or written or, in system terms, inserted, updated, or deleted. There are several benchmarks that one can conduct to determine throughput (please refer to Transaction Processing Council at *www.tpc.org*). This throughput, however, is constrained to one unit in the entire machine—the database—and the number of users and queries it can manage at any point in time (i.e., a multi-user work processing or multi-user workload constrained to a specific pattern of queries).

While the database definitely manages the number-crunching tasks on a data warehouse or OLTP platform, it has to rely on the capabilities of the network, the operating system, and the storage infrastructure to create a sustainable and scalable performance.

Why do we need to understand workloads better when we discuss data warehousing or analytics? Because the design of the next-generation data warehouses will be largely focused on building workload-characterized architectures, and integrating them through logical layers. Gartner calls this the logical data warehouse, and my definition is workload-driven data warehousing. For example, if we are designing a near-real-time integration between a traditional decision support platform and a web application or a point-of-sale (POS) kiosk, we are discussing two different types of system architectures that work at different response rates. Without understanding the workload capabilities of these systems, designing a platform will be delivering an underperforming system or often can lead to failure of adoption.

Another perspective to look at regarding workloads is to understand the need for static versus dynamic systems. A low-end digital camera is a static system. It is designed once and mass-produced with the only requirement being how many pictures it can take in different settings provided as options. There is not much room to change the basic architecture of a camera until you start talking about high-end devices or light-field cameras. Whereas, a data warehouse can receive different data types and process requests from different types of users in the same timeframe or across different times in a day. This requires a lot of dynamic data processing as opposed to a static system.

Figure 8.1 shows the classic system architecture and the associated behaviors of each portion of the system. If you closely follow the trail from the end-user application to the database storage, there are multiple steps of data movement and processing across the layers. Eventually, we also see that each layer has a wait on the subsequent layer before a final processing step can be accomplished. We often address a symptom when a problem manifests rather than take a holistic approach for the big

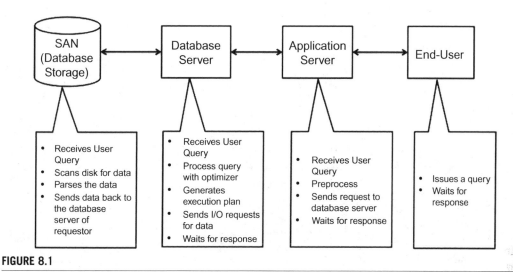

FIGURE 8.1

Classic systems architecture.

picture. This isolated problem addressing technique needs to change for designing and addressing scalability and performance demands of today's users.

An additional aspect to keep in perspective is the ever-changing nature of data and its associated structures. The impact of data itself is one of the most ignored areas that affect workloads of the data warehouse and datamarts. There are two categories of data that adversely affect workloads due to their volume and special needs for security in certain categories:

- *Persistent data*—data that is needed to be maintained for compliance and regulatory reasons and cannot be deleted or archived for a period of time; for example, customer data and sensitive data fall into this category.
- *Volatile data*—data that is of value for a shorter life span, but once the intelligence/analytics are drawn, the data is no longer useful to maintain; for example, a large portion of transactional data falls into this category.

Understanding workloads

In a classic systems architecture approach as shown in Figure 8.1, the workload management today is centered on the database. The primary reason for this situation is due to the fact that we can analyze what happens in the database when a query is submitted and, based on the results, interpret if the issues are within the database or outside the database. As a result of this approach, today we define workload from the database perspective alone regardless of what happens in the entire system. The results that are discussed for workload and throughput revolve around the statistics like CPU usage, elapsed time of query, the number of SQL executions, and total users on the database. Based on the

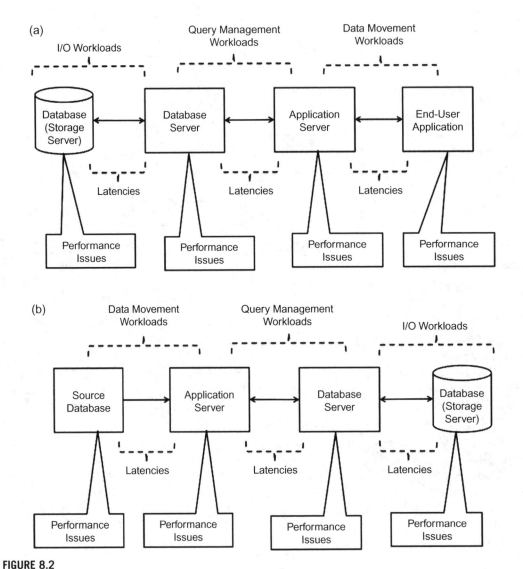

FIGURE 8.2

Classic data warehouse problem manifests: (a) outbound side and (b) inbound side.

results, we infer what performance impact is experienced in the current state and what can be experienced if there are spikes of increases or decreases of workloads. The resulting definitions from these exercises often fail to produce the right architectural decisions.

Figure 8.2 shows the problem areas that manifest in the data warehouse today. We can bucket these problems under each segment to understand the overall workload aspect of the system. The different aspects of the data warehouse affected by workloads are discussed in the following sections.

Data warehouse outbound

There are several recipients of data from the data warehouse, including end-user applications, data-marts, and analytical databases.

End-user application

This includes the reporting, analytics, web, and desktop applications that directly interact with the data warehouse. We include the web application since many reporting or analytic applications can be used on a pure-play web browser or a mobile application.

Data outbound to users

- Overheads—the end-user application layer adds security constraints to the data based on the user who is accessing the application. This constraint cannot be managed as a database-level filter in many situations, and the impact of this overhead is often data result sets that are larger than needed and will be filtered and discarded at the end-user system level.
- Dependencies—the processing capabilities of the application at the end user depend on the amount of disk, memory, cache, and processor available to the application. Large volumes of data mean multiple cycles of exchange between the application server and the end-user system, adding network traffic and waits.
- Issues—many a time, due to the volume of data and the amount of elapsed time when waiting on the data, the end user loses connection to the application server due to timeouts, the application goes into a sleep mode, or the priority of execution of the application is lowered on the end-user system.
- Note—the situation is similar or even worse when you remove the application server and directly connect to a datamart or data warehouse.
- Workarounds—current workarounds include:
  - Special tables and/or views (at the database layer).
  - Semantic layer filters and data structures.
  - Adding security filters to queries.
  - Adding infrastructure to process data and move data faster.
- Complexities—the data within the data warehouse is clearly articulated for usage by the enterprise. This imposes restrictions on the amount of transformation or data granularity level for the data warehouse. From an outbound perspective this is the biggest area of complexity, as many processing iterations from a transformation requirement and different types of calculations are worked upon to complete the query's requirement.
- Goal—the goal for creating an effective workload strategy at this layer is to minimize the amount of work to be done by this layer to manifest the dashboard, report, or metric.

Data inbound from users

End-user applications rarely send data directly to the data warehouse. The inbound data comes from ETL processes.

Datamarts

The behavior characteristics of a datamart are similar to the data warehouse but not with the same level of complexity.

Data outbound to users

- Overheads—the end-user application layer adds security constraints to the data based on the user who is accessing the application. This constraint cannot be managed as a database-level filter in many situations and the impact of this overhead is often data result sets that are larger than needed and will be filtered and discarded at the end-user system level.
- Dependencies—the processing capabilities of the application at the end user depend on the amount of disk, memory, cache, and processor available to the application. Large volumes of data mean multiple cycles of exchange between the application server and the end-user system, adding network traffic and waits.
- Issues—many times, due to the volume of data and the amount of elapsed time when waiting on the data, the end user loses connection to the application server due to timeouts, the application goes into a sleep mode, or the priority of execution of the application is lowered on the end-user system.
- Note—the situation is similar or even worse when you remove the application server and directly connect to a datamart.
- Workarounds—current workarounds include:
  - Special tables and/or views (at the database layer).
  - Semantic layer filters and data structures.
  - Adding security filters to queries.
  - Adding infrastructure to process data and move data faster.
- Complexity—the most complex operations at the datamart layer are a hierarchy-based processing of data and referential integrity management between data structures that need to integrate data across different layers of granularity and sometimes in nonrelational techniques.
- Goal—the goal for creating an effective workload strategy at this layer is to minimize the amount of work to be done by this layer to manifest the dashboard, report, or metric.

Data inbound from users

End-user applications rarely send data directly to the datamart. The inbound data comes from ETL processes.

Analytical databases

Analytical databases can be executed from within a data warehouse or outside as a separate infrastructure. The issue with a separate processing infrastructure is the tendency of extremely large data sets that need to be moved between the data warehouse and the analytical database in a bidirectional manner.

- Overheads—the end-user application adds minimal overhead from the analytical application.
- Dependencies—the processing capabilities of the application at the end user depend on the amount of disk, memory, cache, and processor available to the application. Large volumes of data mean multiple cycles of exchange between the application server and the end-user system, adding network traffic and waits.
- Issues—large volumes of data are moved back and forth between the analytical database and the data warehouse. This extremely large data extraction process adds a lot of burden to the processing database on both sides of the picture.

- Workarounds—current workarounds include:
  - Special aggregate structures at the data warehouse or datamart.
  - Special network connectors between the analytical database and the data warehouse to bypass the enterprise network and avoid clogging it.
  - Adding infrastructure to process data and move data faster.
- Goal—the goal for creating an effective workload strategy at this layer is to minimize the amount of work to be done by this layer by shifting the data processing to the data warehouse or the underlying database in a shared-server architecture with the data warehouse, and restricting the data volume to be moved across, thereby improving the overall performance of the application.

To summarize, the outbound data processing from the data warehouse generates workloads that will require processing of data several times to the same application and processing several such applications at the same period of time. The focus areas for workload management that impact performance include the database, storage servers, and network.

Data warehouse inbound

There are several sources of data that need to be processed into the data warehouse and stored for further analysis and processing. The primary application that manages the inbound processing of data into the data warehouse is the extract, transform, and load (ETL) application. There are different variations of ETL today with extract, load and transform (ELT) and change data capture (CDC) techniques and database replication.

Data warehouse processing overheads

The processing of data into the data warehouse has several overheads associated with it, depending on the technique.

- ETL—the most common processing model, the ETL design includes movement of data to an intermediate staging area, often shared in the same storage as the data warehouse and applying transformation rules including lookup processing. The data is often extracted from both the staging and data warehouse areas and compared in memory for processing. Depending on the volume of data from both ends, the process may spiral into an uncontrolled timespan causing a major impact on the data warehouse. A second continuum of overhead persists in the transformation of data within the data warehouse. There are several business rules to be completed for the processing of data and these rules can add workload overheads. Similarly, constraints on the tables within the data warehouse add to processing overheads when inserting or updating data within the data warehouse.
- Dependencies—the processing capabilities of the ETL application apart from the business rules and the data processing complexities depend on the amount of disk, memory, cache, and processor available to the application server. Large volumes of data mean multiple cycles of exchange between the application server and the database, adding network traffic and waits.
- Issues—large volumes of data are moved back and forth between the ETL application server and the data warehouse. This extremely large data extraction process adds a lot of burden to the processing database on both sides.

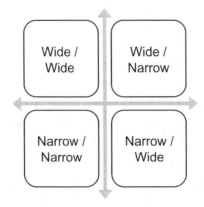

FIGURE 8.3

Workload categories.

- Workarounds—current workarounds include:
  - Minimizing data movement when processing large data sets by incorporating ETL and ETL-hybrid architectures.
  - Special network connectors between the ETL server and the data warehouse to bypass the enterprise network and avoid clogging it.
  - Adding infrastructure to process data and move data faster.
  - Implementing SOA-type architectures to data processing.
- Goal—the goal for creating an effective workload strategy at this layer is to minimize the amount of work to be done by either the ETL or the data warehouse or, in a different approach, maximize each processing or iteration cycle where the resources are effectively utilized.

Query classification

There are primarily four categories of workload that are generated today: wide/wide, wide/narrow, narrow/wide, and narrow/narrow (Figure 8.3).

Wide/Wide

Wide/wide workloads are queries from analytics or multidimensional analysis, and can also be triggered by ad-hoc users and return long sets of columns typically joining more than two tables in the result set. The resulting complexity from these queries are impacted by the:

- Length of the table
- Distribution of the table across the storage
- Data model
- Data relationship

Typically, these queries exhibit the following traits:

- Long running from a perspective of time
- A lot of I/O action
- Multiple cycles of read
- Heavily skewed joins
- Minimal computes

Wide/Narrow

Wide/narrow workloads are queries that are generated by standard reports and dashboards and run execution on wide columns from more than two tables returning a narrow set of columns in the result set. The resulting complexity from these queries are impacted by the:

- Length of the source table
- Distribution of the table across the storage
- Data model
- Data relationship
- Computation

Typically, these queries exhibit the following traits:

- Medium cycles of execution (running from a perspective of time)
- High memory consumption
- Mixed CPU utilization
- Lot of computes

Narrow/Wide

Narrow/wide workloads are queries generated by ad-hoc users or analytic users and run execution on a narrow set of columns from two to four tables returning a wide set of columns in the result set. The resulting complexity from these queries are impacted by the:

- Length of the table
- Distribution of the table across the storage
- Data model
- Data relationship
- Time dimension
- Semantic layer functionality

Typically, these queries exhibit the following traits:

- Long running (from a perspective of time)
- Mixed I/O
- Multiple cycles of read
- Heavily skewed joins
- Heavy computes

Narrow/Narrow

Narrow/narrow workloads are queries generated by standard reports and run execution on a narrow set of columns, summarized tables, or aggregate structures returning a narrow set of columns in the result set. The resulting complexity from these queries are impacted by the:

- Length of the table
- Distribution of the table across the storage
- Data model
- Time dimension
- Semantic layer functionality

  Typically, these queries exhibit the following traits:

- Smaller I/O
- High CPU consumption
- High memory utilization
- Multiple cycles of read
- Heavy computes

Unstructured/semi-structured data

   Another big impact on query performance comes from the integration of data in the query from a non-RDBMS structure like Excel files, CSV files, and other storage structures. The impact on the workload performance is the actual loading of the data into memory from the file for each cycle of operation and managing the intermediate data sets. The queries affected here are across all the different types of classifications discussed in this section, and they exhibit the following traits:

- Large I/O cycles
- High CPU consumption
- High memory utilization
- Heavy computes
- Long waits of execution (from a perspective of time)
- Lots of temporary storage

   File-based data in the traditional data management platform is a threat to increasing and skewing workloads since they are managed in a serial fashion in terms of reads and writes. In the traditional data integration architecture, there is no parallelism involved in file-based operations due to consistency management, which has been a big deterrent in the performance and negatively impacted workloads.

   While queries by themselves are a problem when it comes to workload management, the associated data integration challenges that are present in this layer of the architecture make it one of the most complex areas to design, maintain, and manage on an ongoing basis.

ETL and CDC workloads

Figure 8.4 shows the categorization of ETL and CDC workloads. Depending on the data type, the associated business rule for transformation, and the underlying data model and architecture, the

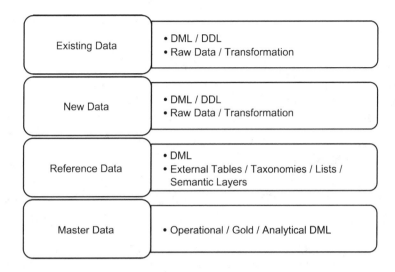

FIGURE 8.4

ETL/CDC workload categories.

processing of loading, updating, or deleting data to the tables can generate a lot of workload on the application and the database server.

The typical traits of ETL workloads are:

- Higher I/O for longer bursts of time
- High memory consumption
- Higher CPU utilization
- Large volumes of data moved across the network
- Large transaction cycles—leading to many flushes of log files and cache in the database, creating additional operating system–level workload
- Depending on the software and the programming model, additional file management can be necessary

CDC workloads exhibit the following traits:

- Higher I/O for shorter bursts of time
- Smaller volumes of data moved across the network
- Larger file-based operations
- Smaller transaction cycles
- More file management at the operating system level

Depending on the set of operations executed in the data warehouse at any given point in time, you can have multiple workloads being processed on the entire system. This is the underlying design concept that needs to be thought about when designing a data warehouse. Database vendors like Oracle, Teradata, and IBM have created workload management algorithms and toolsets to help users manage their database performance. These tools aid the database and system administrators to create a set of optimization rules based on which the database and the associated data architecture can be utilized to create an efficient execution map for querying and loading data.

In the early days of data warehouse implementation, data was always processed in a batch execution environment, and that process was always executed when the data warehouse was not utilized and there were no users on the system. This situation provided administrators to optimize the database and the servers to either load or query data within the data warehouse. In the last decade we have seen the trend change to load more real-time data to the data warehouse, which means there is no downtime for specifically loading data. This situation is called mixed-workload architecture where the data warehouse now has to be able to handle multiple types of query workloads while loading or transforming data. The challenge that confronts the architects is not about the infrastructure capability, but rather the data structure and architecture.

Measurement

Before we move on to discussing how we think of the modern data warehouse design, we need to understand how to measure the workload. In today's situation we focus on the database and the operations cycle time it takes to execute any unit of work, and multiply that unit of work by resource cost from the infrastructure to arrive at a query cost/minute and throughput/minute. From an OLTP perspective there are multiple types of measurement standards published by the Transaction Processing Council, and from a data warehouse perspective there is one called TPC-H (*http://www.tpc.org/tpch/default.asp*).

The most known technique to measure workload for a data warehouse is to calculate the sum of all parts:

- Load process:
  - Start time
  - Elapse time
  - Number of records affected: insert, update, delete
  - Indexes affected: build time
  - Network throughput
  - Disk throughput
  - CPU and memory utilization
  - Application server throughput
- Query process:
  - Start time
  - Elapse time
  - Number of tables affected
  - I/O cycles
  - I/O waits
  - CPU waits
  - Network throughput
  - Disk throughput
  - Memory utilization
  - Number of records moved
  - Application server throughput
  - Application server processing time

If we effectively measure and add all the different components, we will get a better picture that will help us to optimize the layers of architecture and better assist in the design of the newer architectures. By doing this exercise, we can determine which component has the most latencies and how to address its workload.

Current system design limitations

There are several design limitations in the current data warehouse architectures and we discussed them in Chapters 6 and 7. To recap:

- *Sharding.* The RDBMS cannot shard data efficiently due to the ACID compliance rules. The application of sharding concepts in data partitioning methods does not lend to scalability and workload reduction. Partitioning often tends to increase workloads.
- *Disk architecture.* The disk architecture for SAN underperforms and, due to the data architecture and data model issues, the data distribution is highly skewed, causing poor optimization to occur at the database layer.
- *Data layout architecture.* The data layout on the disk is a major performance inhibitor and contributes to higher workloads. Often there are large tables that are colocated in the same disk along with their indexes. Another issue is undersizing of disk or unit of storage, causing too many fragments of the same table and leading to excessive chaining.
- *Underutilization of CPU.* In many systems, the CPU is always underutilized and this needs to be corrected for efficient throughput and scalable thread management.
- *Underutilization of memory.* A large amount of data integration often bypasses usage of memory and relies on disk. These situations often use one or more smaller tables and two or more large tables in a join. Efficient design of the query can result in using the smaller tables in memory and the larger tables can be processed in a combination of memory and disk. This will reduce several roundtrips between the database server and storage, reducing disk workloads and network workloads.
- *Poor query design.* A silent contributor to the workload situation is poorly designed queries. Whether the queries are written by developers or generated based on the semantic layer integration in a reporting tool, when a query complies and has a large number of joins, the workload typically increases across the system and there are several opportunities to improve the reduction of the workload. One example is to generate star-schema types of queries on a third normal form (3NF) database model, albeit with some semantic layer in the database including aggregate table and summary views. This situation will always generate a high volume of I/O and tends to cause poor network throughput. If you add more operation to the query and you can see the workload increase greatly on disk I/O. Another example is to execute a query with a high number of aggregates on a database where you can utilize three or more tables in the query.

Though many architects and system designers try to create workarounds for the current state, since the system is already in place from a foundational perspective, the workarounds do not provide a clear workload optimization. It does not matter whether you have a world-class infrastructure or you have implemented your design on a commodity infrastructure, the current limitations add more weight to the already voluminous data warehouse from a workload perspective, causing overwhelming workloads and underperforming systems. Distributing the workload does not improve scalability and reduce workload, as anyone would anticipate since each distribution comes with a limited scalability.

New workloads and Big Data

Big Data brings about a new definition to the world of workloads. Apart from traditional challenges that exist in the world of data, the volume, velocity, variety, complexity, and ambiguous nature of Big Data creates a new class of challenges and issues. The key set of challenges and issues that we need to understand regarding data in the Big Data world include:

- Data does not have a finite architecture and can have multiple formats.
- Data is self-contained and needs several external business rules to be created to interpret and process the data.
- Data has a minimal or zero concept of referential integrity.
- Data is not relational.
- Data needs more analytical processing.
- Data depends on metadata for creating context.
- Data has no specificity with volume or complexity.
- Data is semi-structured or unstructured.
- Data needs multiple cycles of processing, but each cycle needs to be processed in one pass due to the size of the data.
- Data needs business rules for processing like we handle structured data today, but these rules need to be created in a rules engine architecture rather than the database or the ETL tool.
- Data needs more governance than data in the database.
- Data has no defined quality.

Big Data workloads

Workload management as it pertains to Big Data is completely different from traditional data and its management. The major areas where workload definitions are important to understand for design and processing efficiency include:

- Data is file based for acquisition and storage—whether you choose Hadoop, NoSQL, or any other technique, most of the Big Data is file based. The underlying reason for choosing file-based management is the ease of management of files, replication, and ability to store any format of data for processing.
- Data processing will happen in three steps:
  1. *Discovery*—in this step the data is analyzed and categorized.
  2. *Analysis*—in this step the data is associated with master data and metadata.
  3. *Analytics*—in this step the data is converted to metrics and structured.

- Each of these steps bring a workload characteristic:
  - Discovery will mandate interrogation of data by users. The data will need to be processed where it is and not moved across the network. The reason for this is due to the size and complexity of the data itself, and this requirement is a design goal for Big Data architecture. Compute and process data at the storage layer.
  - Analysis will mandate parsing of data with data visualization tools. This will require minimal transformation and movement of data across the network.
  - Analytics will require converting the data to a structured format and extracting for processing to the data warehouse or analytical engines.
- Big Data workloads are drastically different from the traditional workloads due to the fact that no database is involved in the processing of Big Data. This removes a large scalability constraint but adds more complexity to maintain file system–driven consistency. Another key factor to remember is there is no transaction processing but rather data processing involved with processing Big Data. These factors are the design considerations when building a Big Data system, which we will discuss in Chapters 10 and 11.
- Big Data workloads from an analytical perspective will be very similar to adding new data to the data warehouse. The key difference here is the tables that will be added are of the narrow/narrow type, but the impact on the analytical model can be that of a wide/narrow table that will become wide/wide.
- Big Data query workloads are more program execution of MapReduce code, which is completely opposite of executing SQL and optimizing for SQL performance.

The major difference in Big Data workload management is the impact of tuning the data processing bottlenecks results in linear scalability and instant outcomes, as opposed to the traditional RDBMS world of data management. This is due to the file-based processing of data, the self-contained nature of the data, and the maturity of the algorithms on the infrastructure itself.

Technology choices

As we look back and think about how to design the next generation of data warehouses with the concept of a workload-driven architecture, there are several technologies that have come into being in the last decade, and these technologies are critical to consider for the new architecture. A key aspect to remember is the concept of data warehousing is not changing but the deployment and the architecture of the data warehouse will evolve from being tightly coupled into the database and its infrastructure to being distributed across different layers of infrastructure and data architecture. The goal of building the workload-driven architecture is to leverage all the technology improvements into the flexibility and scalability of the data warehouse and Big Data processing, thereby creating a coexistence platform leveraging all current-state and future-state investments to better ROI. Another viewpoint to think about is that by design Big Data processing is built around procedural processing (more akin to programming language–driven processing), which can take advantage of multicore CPU and SSD or DRAM technologies to the fullest extent, as opposed to the RDBMS architecture where large cycles of processing and memory are left underutilized.

SUMMARY

The next chapter will focus on these technologies that we are discussing including Big Data appliances, cloud computing, data virtualization, and much more. As we look back at what we have learned from this chapter, remember that without understanding the workload of the system, if you create architectures, you are bound to have limited success. In conclusion, the goal is for us to start thinking like designers of space exploration vehicles, which mandate several calculations and optimization techniques to achieve superior performance and reusable systems. This radical change of thinking will help architects and designers of new solutions to create robust ecosystems of technologies.

New Technologies Applied to Data Warehousing

*Once a new technology rolls over you, if you're not part of the steamroller,
you're part of the road.*
—Stewart Brand

INTRODUCTION

The goal of building a data warehouse is to create an enterprise repository for truth, which can be consumed by the entire organization and not one user or user group. The underlying goal, however, does not mandate the physical architecture construct being on one unified layer. Why this statement needs to be re-read a number of times stems from the fact that we often get into a frenzy of building an integrated (read single stack) infrastructure platform for handling all the requirements of an enterprise data warehouse, resulting in underutilized and underperforming platforms. Chapters 7 and 8 discussed the issues that have been plaguing the data warehouse scalability and adoption from such architecture approaches. It is clear that we have arrived at crossroads of information technology where the need to build a heterogeneous platform that can match the requirements of the data warehouse while sustaining scalability is the future. This chapter will provide an overview of technologies that are shaping the landscape of the data warehouse, including data warehouse and Big Data appliances, solid-state drive (SSD) and in-memory technologies, cloud computing, and data virtualization.

Data warehouse challenges revisited

Speed is a single verb that can define the success of a data warehouse in the real world. The users of a data warehouse and the downstream business intelligence and analytics applications measure the efficiency and effectiveness as units of speed, both on the inbound and outbound sides of the data warehouse. The performance service-level agreements that are created for the data warehouse often tend to overlook the need for quality of data and information management in terms of volume and process complexities, which often comes back to haunt the data warehouse.

The key challenges that confront the data warehouse in terms of performance and capability include the following.

Data loading

A process that can range from simple to extremely complex, loading of data to the data warehouse has been a design challenge for the longest time. There are several issues that can be associated with data loading that create a challenge:

- *Data quality.* One of the biggest bottlenecks in processing data from source databases to staging or ODS or a data warehouse is the data quality processing. Whether you preprocess or postprocess data, in any stage of moving it to the data warehouse, bad data needs to be cleansed and qualified. This is a key area for benchmarking performance for the data warehouse infrastructure.
- *Slowly changing dimensional data.* Processing slowly changing data to the data warehouse is often a key area to verify performance. This type of processing involves several layers of hidden complexity from reference data, fact keys referential integrity, maintaining history, and if there is partitioning involved with either the update date or any specific data that changes as a dimension, moving the data across storage segments, and such. This is another key area for performance management.
- *Master data.* Master data management (MDM) is a key area of challenge for the data warehouse. Whenever there is a change in the MDM data, the changes need to be updated and completed in the data warehouse and often this also involves data at rest.
- *Metadata.* Metadata management and maintenance is often overlooked in the data warehouse. This is an area that can definitely benefit if the performance challenges are cleared. This is definitely needed for integrating data from structured and unstructured datasets.
- *Transformation and processing.* Data transformation and processing business rules involves several complexities across different stages in the data management layers of the data warehouse. These transformation rules often add layers of processing that may not be needed but are created to overcome shortcomings of the current architecture of the data or the platform. This is an area of huge opportunity to improve efficiencies in the data warehouse.

Availability

Data recency and availability have been a challenge to the data warehouse, both due to the loading process and the infrastructure as a whole. The nonavailability of timely data has impacted the usage and adoption of the data warehouse within the enterprise. There are several reasons for data to not be available in a timely manner, including the lack of documented requirements, underestimated data growth projections, data demand projections, data retention cycles, and associated query response service level agreements (SLAs). This is a very key area to benchmark when rearchitecting the data warehouse.

Data volumes

Data volumes in the data warehouse have been growing at an explosive rate of several terabytes per day. Reasons for this data explosion include:

- *Analytics.* Predictive and key performance analytics have emerged as a key requirement for any organization. These computations create additional volumes of data in the system.

- *Compliance requirements*. SAFE Harbor, SOX, HIPAA, GLBA, and PCI regulations require maintaining structured and unstructured data for an extended period of time.
- *Legal requirements*. To provide clearly auditable and valid data in legal lawsuits has created a data availability challenge online or offline.
- *Data security*. Encryption and storage of data at rest in the encrypted format is another requirement that creates additional overhead. This data sometimes is moved to another appliance outside the database and the encrypted result data is stored back into the database.
- *Business users*. With large enterprises moving from product- or service-centric business approaches to customer-centric approaches, they need real-time and historical data.
- *Social media*. With the advent of social media and smartphones, consumers have access to express their opinions.
- *Nonspecific requirements*. When there are no clearly documented requirements for data availability, organizations need to maintain data and provide its availability to users. The issue this creates is the negative impact on performance.

Storage performance

The performance of storage systems is a weak area for the data warehouse. The issue is both at the data architecture and storage architecture areas. The sharing of storage across all areas of a data warehouse infrastructure creates a huge penalty on both the availability and performance of the I/O system. In addition to the shared storage, data, indexes, and temporary tables all work with the same set of disks and controllers. On top of this, if we add mixed query workloads on the storage architecture, we are going to start seeing extended access times of disks and data, causing low performance. This area needs both data reengineering and storage reengineering to move from shared-systems architecture.

Query performance

Another area of performance that challenges the data warehouse is query performance. The queries that cause the most impact are ad-hoc queries and analytical queries, due to their nondeterministic nature. The queries can require a small but wide data set that needs access to multiple areas of the storage or a large data set that can be accessed in a smaller storage area. In either situation the impact of accessing and processing the data, including moving it across the network, impacts the overall performance of the query.

Data transport

A major processing overhead in the data architecture is the transportation of data from one layer to another and its subsequent availability for processing. This overhead is not often noticed or calculated as it is assumed to be a part of the bandwidth issues in the network or the capability limitations of the memory or disk architecture.

If we add the cycles of I/O and time spent on the transport of data between data at rest and the computing infrastructure, there are significant aspects of performance that can be improved for efficient processing of data. This is one of the design goals of the Big Data platforms, whether Hadoop or NoSQL.

These are the key impact areas that bring the data warehouse to its knees in performance. To overcome some of these limitations, we have technology approaches that will bring huge benefits if architected the right way for sustainable performance in the data warehouse. These include the data warehouse appliance, cloud computing, and data virtualization.

Data warehouse appliance

One of the key challenges of the infrastructure architecture is the shared-everything designs, where the underlying resources are shared among the users or applications. The uninhibited sharing of resources negatively impacts the scalability of the system with the increase in query and application complexity, compounded with the explosive growth of data.

To address the needs of a data warehouse scalability while keeping the overall cost at a manageable level, a preconfigured stack of hardware, operating system, RDBMS software, storage, interconnect, and applications programming interface were designed and developed, popularly known as the *data warehouse appliance* (DWA).

The primary design goals of the DWA are to overcome the bottlenecks caused by shared-everything approaches and ensure:

- Scalability
- Reliability
- Fault tolerance
- Self-managing and tuning
- Lower cost of entry and sustained managed costs

The underlying architecture tenents of the DWA include:

- Shared-nothing architecture
- Commodity hardware and storage
- Massively parallel processing engines
- Workload optimizers

The first commercial DWA was introduced by Netezza (now part of IBM) in 2001, though Teradata conceptually designed the architecture of an appliance for the first time almost 30 years before that, and their foray into the appliance market was much later in the timeline. This was soon followed by Greenplum (now EMC), Oracle, Vertica (now part of Hewlett Packard), DataAllegro (now part of Microsoft), Teradata, AsterData (now part of Teradata), ParAccel, KickFire (now part of Teradata), Kognitio, Extremedata, Infobright, and others. At the time of this writing we are seeing a fourth generation of the DWA (all within one decade).

What makes an appliance appealing? DWAs offer an integrated stack of solutions, including hardware, software, database, and storage, tuned to perform for the data warehouse at a fraction of the cost of a similar technical solution on a traditional platform. They are plug-and-play and efficient, while being scalable in a modular fashion.

Let us look at the architecture of the appliance and understand why this solution has gained acceptance and popularity.

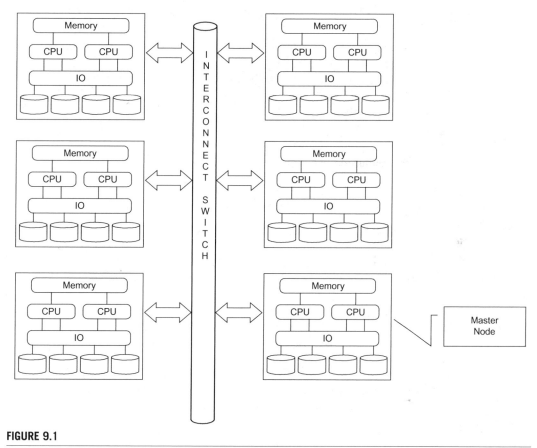

FIGURE 9.1

Generic appliance architecture.

Appliance architecture

The fundamental design of the appliance is to remove all configuration processes and any sizing requirements for the data warehouse by providing a preconfigured solution stack. The users typically need to establish a baseline for performance and another for scalability before beginning the deployment of an appliance.

Figure 9.1 shows the general architecture of a DWA. In the overall architecture, an appliance is made of two or more nodes with each node having its own set of processers, memory, I/O, and storage. Each node in the architecture is interconnected by a switch (GigE/Infiniband). There is a node designated as the "master" node (queen or leader node in some appliances), which is responsible for interfacing with the users to service client requests, manage the distribution of data, query or ETL workloads across the architecture, and marshal the resources pool and scalability needs.

The distinct advantages of this architecture approach include:

- All the data is stored locally across the nodes, and each node manages its portion of the data and query assigned to it by the master node.
- Data is striped and mirrored across two nodes at a minimum, which increases scalability when large query workloads are submitted.
- The advantage of data being mirrored is that it helps in achieving workload balance and can support failure in case of an unplanned outage.
- When the need arises for scalability the nodes can be used to divide the work in discrete chunks, and if needed, we can simply add more nodes that can be configured and used by the system with minimal intervention.
- A node can be assigned a specific role or set of roles to be available for querying, loading, and managing data.

The appliance architecture in a nutshell is a specialized configuration of multiple SMP nodes into one physical device with a custom operating system layer added to a Linux or Unix platform, which is managed by a smart controller and has its own internal network switch to move large data across the nodes, bypassing the outside network completely. Due to its self-managing nature, administrators or database administrators (DBAs) find minimal needs for intervention to maintain sustained performance and scalability. Appliances also provide the flexibility to deploy commodity hardware platforms, which lower the cost of operation and can increase time to market. The lower price point enables appliance users to add more nodes as needed without breaking the bank.

The other aspect of the appliance that is worth exploring and understanding before you launch on selecting an appliance or migrating to an appliance is the data architecture. The appliance can support third normal form (3NF), star schema, or hybrid data architecture depending on the user's needs. The data distribution and data storage techniques create the magic of scalability with workloads and users, which we discuss next.

Data distribution in the appliance

Figure 9.2 shows a typical data distribution across the data warehouse appliance. From this figure we see that data is distributed across multiple nodes, and in addition to this, typically nodes 1, 3, and 5 will mirror data slices, nodes 2, 4, and 6 will mirror data slices across, and nodes 7 and 8 are standby for usage if there is an outage with the other nodes.

This type of data layout definitely needs the designer or architect to:

- Understand the data and the special requirements for handling data.
- Understand the underlying relationships.
- Understand the data skew.
- Understand the data volume.
- Understand the data growth.

Once you have the data architecture mapped, the distribution of data, including the striping and mirroring, will create the boost needed for performance, which comes with data availability in more than one storage location, the optimization of the workload to execute on noncompeting infrastructure, and the minimal amount of data movement within the infrastructure.

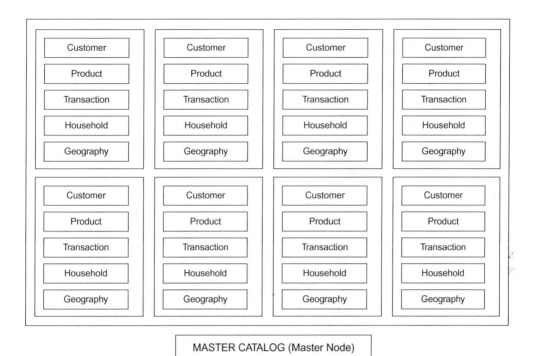

FIGURE 9.2

Appliance data distribution.

The other performance benefits include:

- Fault tolerance—if and when a node fails, a second node is available with the same data to process other workloads, and you can stand up a backup node replica in a lot less time.
- Workload management—data loading can be managed in different techniques across the products while data querying and analytics are being executed concurrently. Due to advancements in workload distribution beyond just setting parameters in the database, in the appliance configuration, we can keep sustained performance during mixed-workload execution.
- Another key workload management feature is the ability to dedicate resources across nodes on-the-fly to accommodate completion of tasks. Smarter management of resources without stopping the database or deleting job queues has created the flexibility for administrators to manage workload shifting or adjusting to shifting workloads with simple techniques.
- Node balancing—in a typical situation of adding more infrastructure resources, you do not get to use 100% of the resources, as not all of them are available to you. In the case of the DWA, each time you add a node, you get more self-contained infrastructure of memory, processor, and storage, and all the 100% of the resources are available at that node's disposal. It is up to the administrator to designate the node as a standby or replicate it to something specific. Once the replicate option is selected, the data is automatically extended to the node and loaded. After

the node is completely configured, it is added to the data set. The feature is handled in different techniques across the appliances available in the market today.

These architectural improvements coupled with new data and workload management techniques focused on data warehouse–driven workloads and have made the DWA a popular option.

Key best practices for deploying a data warehouse appliance

1. Clearly documented requirements:
   - Data availability requirements
   - Data scalability requirements
   - Query and analytics requirements
   - Performance requirements
   - Security requirements
   - Compression requirements
   - Data growth requirements
   - Mixed-workload requirements
2. Implementation architecture. DWAs can be architected and deployed as a fully functional replacement to the data warehouse or an augmentation to the current infrastructure. Plan this deployment architecture, as it can have a different impact on the outcome based on how it is created.
3. Data architecture. Always ensure that data is available at lower grains for the DWA. The architecture will provide for managing complex formulas and aggregate calculations on-the-fly. This approach will be very powerful when you look at implementing data virtualization as an additional integration layer.
4. Workload architecture. Workload optimization is a delicate art that needs to be handled with finesse with the type of workload, its frequency of occurrences, and the overall impact on the SLAs. Plan the workload architecture by documenting the individual workloads, and its infrastructure, data consumption, baseline performance, and mixed workload performance. Once you add more data, users, and queries, you can revisit and calibrate the architecture to sustain the overall baseline or reset the new numbers and amend the new numbers to business users as the new SLA.
5. Security architecture. Plan the data and user security architecture for the appliance. This is useful when migrating from other platforms into an appliance platform. It additionally provides a clear analysis of gaps and workarounds if they are needed.
6. Compression. Plan for data management by compressing data on a usage basis. If data older than 120 days is not needed at detailed levels and only summary data is accessed, then we can compress the data older than 120 days and reclaim space. In certain situations, we can alternatively use the appliance as a backup system and archive data and compress it upon acquisition.
7. Proof of concept. Execute a holistic proof of concept and perform it through reference checks from users before you buy a DWA.
8. BI tools integration. The DWA of today can support a wide variety of BI tools. Plan for utilizing the native functions in the appliance to perform complex functions. This will truly distribute the workload into the data layer and enable compute to happen where the data is located rather than move the data to layers where compute needs to be performed and thereby lose the advantage of a better architecture. While this means that some rewrites will happen in the current applications, the benefits outweigh the implementation costs in these situations.

9. Analytical functions. Appliances are good at performing number-crunching functions. Enable utilization of the native analytic functions to reap performance benefits when dealing with analytical data.
10. Data loading. Many of the leading ETL and CDC tools support the appliance out of the box with connectors. Plan your ETL migration depending on the connector and its associated performance. In some cases, an ELT technique may be a faster approach to load data to the appliance.

The best practices discussed here are based on implementation experiences and you can add more to this list for your own education and deployment.

To recap, the benefits of the DWA are:

- Complete black-box architecture built for the data warehouse and its applications.
- Redundancy and support for fault tolerance.
- Minimal user intervention needed for operation.
- Modular infrastructure scalability.
- Lower capital expense (CAPEX) costs when compared to traditional infrastructure costs.
- Higher ROI.
- Reuse of skills and personnel.

The DWA certainly is a good option when we discuss the next-generation data warehouse infrastructure. At the time of this writing most of the appliances also offer a connector to Hadoop distributions and these connectors are native drivers and therefore can be implemented with more ease than an odbc or jdbc connector. Extending the unstructured or Big Data integration to this platform is a better option than implementing it as an out-of-the-box preconfigured stack. It allows the users to try the business value of Big Data in a simpler setup while keeping the core functionality and purpose of the appliance intact.

There are several success stories and case studies on the DWA and there are some references in the case studies in Appendix A of this book.

Big Data appliances

A new trend recently has begun: a Big Data appliance. As the name suggests, this is an appliance-like architecture that is preconfigured and built to handle the needs of a Big Data program in any organization. There are solution offerings from all the leading vendors. A Big Data appliance much like the DWA can be a differentiator, but it is too early to predict a winner or a leader due to the time of presence in the market.

Cloud computing

Another option to create and deploy data warehouses, especially for small and midsize business groups, is to leverage cloud computing for both data and visualization infrastructure including analytics and reporting. This reduces the burden of managing infrastructure and keeping the business running, and helps businesses leverage the latest in hardware and software for infrastructure on a managed cost.

There are several business benefits for small and midsize businesses when deploying solutions on the cloud computing platform:

- Cloud computing services are provided over the Internet and can be accessed from anywhere in the world.
- Cloud computing reduces business latencies when developing or testing applications.
- Cloud computing can simplify and reduce process complexities.
- Cloud computing abstracts the complexities of underlying infrastructure and creates simple plug-and-play architecture.
- Cloud computing does not require you to determine the size of the footprint when you initially deploy a development process.
- Cloud computing can provide an adequately secure environment to host any data deemed critical by the organization.
- Cloud computing provides you a complete platform and frees IT to keep the business running.
- Cloud computing provides you with an option to conduct experiments on a small footprint on non-mission-critical and secure infrastructures.

There are different architectural styles of implementing cloud computing services both in general and as applied to data warehousing.

Infrastructure as a service

In infrastructure as a service (IaaS) architecture, we can specify the amount of infrastructure that is required, including storage, processing, and memory requirements. Once the configuration of the basic hardware is done, then networking, access, and security needs are added to the configuration. The biggest benefit to this architecture is the utility-based charge—that is, the amount of monies charged depends on the usage in terms of infrastructure consumption, data storage, and processing, and the number of hours such activities were performed. The key takeaway here is the software costs in terms of database licenses and application software licenses are dependent on the consumer and that price is not a part of the cost that you pay for.

Deploying IaaS on the cloud is a good option when you have no additional license spending—that is, you can either utilize an open-source tool or you have a zero footprint required for software licenses or. In other words, you have no BI or analytical compute and are deploying metrics and dashboards.

Platform as a service

In platform as a service (PaaS) architecture, we can deploy a data warehouse on a platform. For example, on Amazon EC2, we can deploy a functional analytical datamart on Vertica, Teradata, or Oracle, and host reports and analytics on that database, and we now have a PaaS architecture. Simply explained, IaaS plus the software platforms combined together is PaaS.

The PaaS architecture is best suited for small business organizations. It is also ideal for midsize organizations to deploy development and testing processes on this architecture, with an option to deploy production. The biggest benefit on this architecture is the fixed amount of cost based on data volume, software license, SLAs, and operational overheads. This predictability will enable users to decide which features to build and deploy, how many interactive users will access the system, and how much data needs to be moved to the cloud. Apart from the data, the operational cost of this solution is hundreds of dollars less expensive compared to the traditional solution and it delivers value on demand. Scalability can be elastic in this situation and users can pay as the usage increases or decreases on a monthly or weekly basis.

Applications that can utilize the PaaS option include social media analytics and text mining analytics.

Software as a service

The most popular option from a cloud perspective adopted in business intelligence is the software as a service (SaaS) platform. This is application-driven and less intrusive on data, which makes it easier to adopt. There are a variety of vendors providing an SaaS option today.

For the data warehouse deployment on the cloud we need platforms that are:

- *Scalable*. Elastic scalability is the primary need when we discuss data warehousing on the cloud. The data volume can dynamically shift on-the-fly.
- *Secure*. Data privacy issues often keep adopters of the technology worried about the security of data. As a general rule, public or hybrid clouds should never encourage any data that has compliance requirements to be loaded to the cloud.
- *Available*. Data availability around the clock is a user expectation.
- *Performing*. System performance and query performance are desired characteristics, though some providers may need to set up and charge extra for those SLAs.

If we can support these four pieces of a 2×2 quadrant, the primary requirements of the data warehouse users are resolved. The next question that comes up is what is the infrastructure components that make up my cloud.

Cloud infrastructure

A typical cloud infrastructure consists of the components shown in Figure 9.3.

- Applicationscan be classified into:
  - Services—Paypal or Google Maps falls into this category, where the application is a complete service.
  - Business—Salesforce.com and Microsoft Office 365 enable businesses to run their entire requirement on a cloud platform, eliminating the need for onsite software and infrastructure.
  - Collaboration—portals and forums are examples of a collaboration suite.
  - Mobile applications—another emerging cloud-based application footprint is the concept of corporate application stores.
- Services:
  - Include the different management tools and application suites provisioned to manage the cloud.
  - Software API layers for programming and deployment.
- Storage—includes multi tiered storage architectures including all types of disks and technologies
- Hardware—servers and network infrastructure
- Virtualization/operating system tools

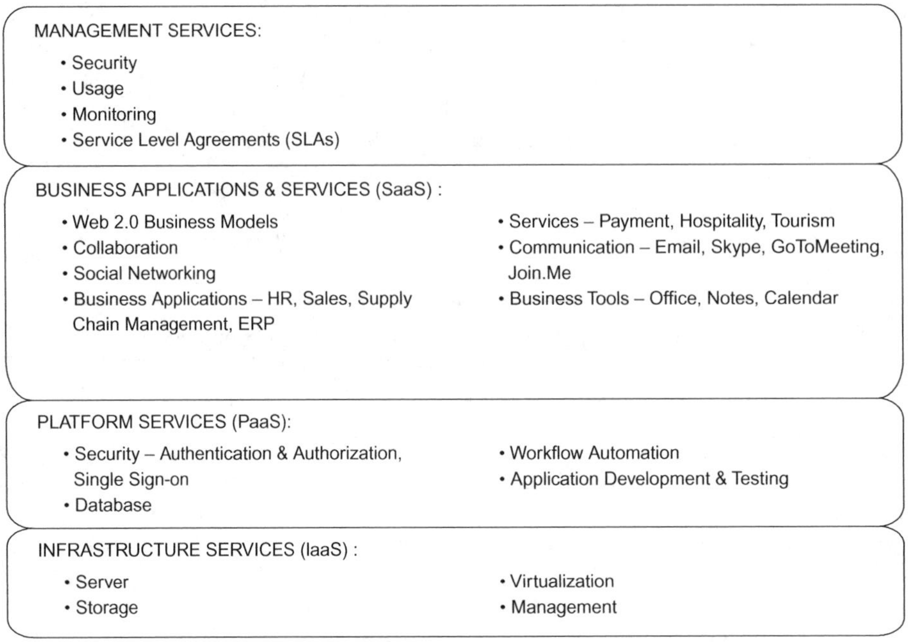

FIGURE 9.3

Cloud computing components.

These components remain the same whether you plan for a private cloud within your enterprise, a hybrid mix of public and private clouds, or a public cloud. Each component is available from most of the service providers, with Amazon leading the pack.

Benefits of cloud computing for data warehouse

- Infrastructure spending is not capital investment.
- Scalability is managed by the provider.
- Utility-based spending provides better budget management.
- Quick deployment increasing time to value.
- Multiple sandbox environments can be configured to realize the best approach for production in parallel.
- Reusable components.

Issues facing cloud computing for data warehouse

- Workload management is not flexible as resources are shared and managed.
- Data access from an end-user perspective requires overhead.
- Performance management is driven by tier and class of service.
- High volume of data movement to and from the cloud in nonsecure environments violates compliance requirements.

From a business intelligence and data warehouse perspective, the applicability of cloud computing can be extended to reports, analytics, and dashboards. The other areas are still in nascent stages of adoption to cloud computing. Big Data can be easily built on a cloud footprint and deployed by organizations, as most data types that will be classified as Big Data will not be an organizational asset, and rather will be a purchased data set from a third-party source; this includes social data, sensor data, and others.

Though cloud computing is in a mature state of evolution from an application perspective, there are still concerns on security and availability from a data warehouse perspective. In the next five years these issues will be nonissues and the cloud will be a vibrant platform in most organizations.

Another emerging technology for next-generation data warehouses is the data virtualization platform.

Data virtualization

Another approach to solving the data integration challenge while leveraging all the investments on the current infrastructure is by deploying data virtualization to create a semantic data integration architecture. While the concept of data virtualization itself is not new, it has evolved over the years from enterprise application integration (EAI) to enterprise information integration (EII) to service oriented architecture (SOA), with the difference being that as EAI and SOA platforms, the integration aspects were focused on applications and middleware, while the current engineering efforts have been focused on data and analytics.

The key features of data virtualization that make it an attractive proposition include:

- Data presentation as a single colocated layer to the consumer.
- Data formatting to a uniform presentation layer via semantic transformations.
- Infrastructure abstraction.
- Pushdown performance optimization based on the source platform.
- Data as a service (DaaS) implementation, providing extreme scalability.

What is data virtualization?

Figure 9.4 shows the current data and analytics architecture and landscape that exist in many organizations. Due to the intrinsic limitations of the database technology and its underutilization of the technology stack, we often build too manly silos of solutions and cannot scale up or integrate data in many situations. One technique that was tried to overcome these limitations was to create a data federation architecture. The shortcoming of the federated approach was the inability to scale the infrastructure when linking multiple instances of a database or datamarts. In the current-state architecture we lose a lot of business value and opportunities that can be harnessed from the current data. In addition, due to the nonstandard implementation of metadata across the layers, we cannot easily integrate any new data or Big Data without significant rework.

Figure 9.5 shows a potential future state based on implementing a data virtualization platform. In this architecture, with the data integration architecture shifting to a data virtualization layer, there are a few key platform features that can be leveraged for creating business value and scaling business intelligence:

- *Automated data discovery*. Data virtualization can perform an automated data discovery exercise across the current data sources and new data sources and integrate the outputs in a metadata repository.

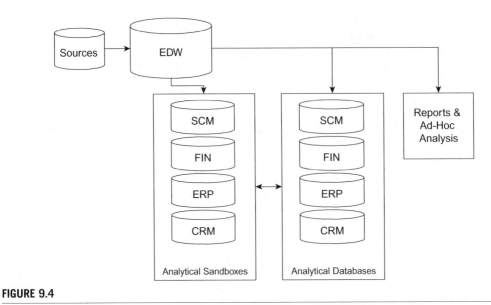

FIGURE 9.4

Current state of analytics and reporting.

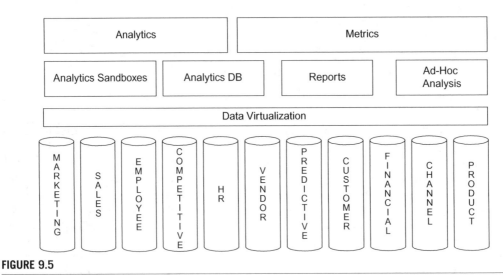

FIGURE 9.5

Data virtualization–based architecture.

- *Contextualization and resolution.* The context of data relationships across different data sources and systems can be complex and overwhelming. Data virtualization provides a mechanism by metadata integration to create contexts that can be applied to data sets as they are discovered for processing and integration. This creates a natural integration path to create relationship between data layers. The data virtualization process completes the resolution of the contexts and the relationships, and this can be an automated task reducing room for errors.

- *Data governance.* The data virtualization exercise needs a strong data governance process. By providing the business users an accelerated solution, the governance process provides a strong data life-cycle management process.
- *Taxonomy/ontology integration.* Data virtualization can create intelligent links with its metadata creation and integrate a wide range of discovery and navigation paths by incorporating taxonomies and ontologies into the solution. This integration also creates a powerful semantic layer to mine data outside the corporation.

These features of the data virtualization platform will complement ETL and MDM processes and provide a scalable data integration architecture delivering data to the users in an agile and sustained process.

Increasing business intelligence performance

Another feature of the data virtualization platform is an increase in business intelligence performance. The common processes for BI across any organization include:

- Data acquisition
- Data discovery and contextualization
- Data movement to the EDW
- Data customization in semantic layers
- Data presentation to consumers
- Data personalization for consumers

The biggest issue that remains unsolved is the integration of the data in other business systems, such as financial, ERP, SCM, and CRM, along with the BI data. This is the biggest weakness that every user faces in a decision-making situation, and this is the real value of a decision support platform. Data virtualization provides an integrated ecosystem for data integration, and this platform output can increase the performance of the BI solutions out of the box.

Workload distribution

The last architecture advantage of the data virtualization platform that we will discuss is the optimal utilization of the infrastructure. Data is not physically moved around in the data virtualization architecture; rather, it is stored in the native physical layer. The advantage of this integration is we can tune each database or data store to serve the native requirements of that platform, and those optimization rules can benefit the data when accessed from the data virtualization repository. This will enable optimal usage of the underlying infrastructure and leverage all the resources available within the infrastructure.

Implementing a data virtualization program

Implementing a data virtualization platform needs planning of the data architecture and an understanding of data relationships across systems within the organization. Once the data mapping and layout is complete, then metadata and contextualization can be designed, and lastly, the database and data infrastructure integration can be completed. The steps are as follows:

- Data inventory.
  - List all data inputs across the organization.
  - Create an auto-discovery search and scan the enterprise for new data and sources.
  - Create alters and processes to handle new data as it is discovered.
- MDM.
  - Data virtualization can complete the operational master data management process once it completes data discovery.
  - Use data virtualization to manage the gold-copy redistribution and replication.
- Data source management data virtualization can determine new data based on patterns and contexts. Once you have a new pattern discovered, create the data lineage and provide the data to the platform for use when executing queries.
- Data virtualization data delivery rules can be implemented to deliver data upon ingestion and preprocessing to a business user or group to accelerate discovery of any corporate or legal types of data.
- Agile development process and programs can effectively use data virtualization to manage agile development and testing of data integration.

Pitfalls to avoid when using data virtualization

- Overengineering—virtualizing everything is not a good idea; in some cases it may have a negative effect.
- Underengineering—the power of data virtualization lies in the fact that you can perform automated data discovery. Incorrect rules or poorly defined discovery contexts create an underperforming virtualization environment.
- Adding too many data quality rules to data virtualization can defeat the agility enabled by the platform.
- Adding too many sources at the same time can slow down data processing and acquisition.
- Incorrect configuration across databases and servers can lead to skewed performance.

As we see from the overview of data virtualization, it provides a compelling option for integrating data across the enterprise while leveraging current and new infrastructure investments. There are four known platforms in the market for you to try and select from, including IBM, Informatica, Composite Software, and Denodo Technologies.

In-memory technologies

The biggest benefit of commoditization of hardware is the advances of increasing infrastructure capabilities within the same form factors. What we mean by this statement is the fact that five years ago what you could purchase for hardware is still physically the same size but configuration-wise is 200× more faster, cheaper, and has more horsepower and storage. One of these advancements is a set of powerful hardware accelerators utilizing the power of flash memory, memory chips, and solid-state disks. Though the common term used for specialized memory-based computing is *in-memory computing*, the actual technology may include very high-speed solid-state disks along with pure memory.

There are several variants of in-memory architectures, and we will discuss briefly the common goals and benefits of in-memory computing as applied to Big Data and data warehouse solutions. In-memory technologies enable storage of vast amounts of data in an online storage and reduce the roundtrips between disk and memory, circumventing latencies to near zero. The ability to load and unload data at extremely high speeds in these architectures provides architects with options to create platforms for high-speed data movement and management.

Benefits of in-memory architectures

- Agility of analytics and number-crunching operations
- Lookup and MDM data management without disk operations
- Stream analytics implementation
- Inspect data on the wire before it reaches disk
- Persist standard reports and precalculated data in memory
- Near-real-time refresh
- Drill down, drill across, and roll up with extreme flexibility

Evolving areas of in-memory computing:

- Data security
- Scalability
- Compression

While there are several in-memory technologies and solutions available today, the user adoption is not as viral, and the reason for this is too much dependency on legacy solutions, fear of moving to in-memory computing, uncertainty of sustained performance, and user reluctance to move from an incumbent platform.

the most popular infrastructure solutions include Fusion IO; Violin Memory; business intelligence platforms like Qlikview, SAP, and HANA; and data warehouse platforms like MongoDB, Oracle, IBM, and Microsoft with Fusion IO or Violin Memory.

SUMMARY

This chapter provided some of the groundbreaking options in terms of infrastructure, where the data architecture and workload management capabilities combined together enable a robust infrastructure for the next-generation data warehouse. What exactly is the architecture for the next-generation data warehouse? How can we physicalize the infrastructure while retaining the foundation goals of the data warehouse? These questions are the focus of discussion in the next chapter.

Further reading

http://blogs.idc.com/ie/?p=190
http://www.infoworld.com/article/08/04/07/15FE-cloud-computing-reality_2.html
http://searchenterprisedesktop.techtarget.com/sDefinition/0,,sid192_gci1287881,00.html

http://en.wikipedia.org/wiki/Cloud_computing
http://techmagazine.ws/full-web-20-api-list/
http://news.cnet.com/8301-13846_3-10184457-62.html?part=rss&subj=news&tag=2547-1_3-0-5
http://www.davidchappell.com/CloudPlatforms--Chappell.pdf
http://download.boulder.ibm.com/ibmdl/pub/software/dw/wes/hipods/Cloud_computing_wp_final_8Oct.pdf
http://www.guardian.co.uk/technology/2008/sep/29/cloud.computing.richard.stallman

Building the
Big Data – Data
Warehouse

Integration of Big Data and Data Warehousing

INTRODUCTION

The data warehouse of today, while still building on the founding principles of an "enterprise version of truth" and a "single data repository," must address the needs of data of new types, new volumes, new data-quality levels, new performance needs, new metadata, and new user requirements. As discussed in earlier chapters, there are several issues in the current data warehouse environments that need to be addressed and, more importantly, the current infrastructure cannot support the needs of the new data on the same platform. We have also discussed the emergence of new technologies that can definitely enhance the performance needs of the current data warehouse and provide a holistic platform for the extended requirements of the new data and associated user needs. The big question is how do we go about integrating all of this into one data warehouse? And, more importantly, how do we justify the data warehouse of the future?

The focus of this chapter is to discuss the integration of Big Data and the data warehouse, the possible techniques and pitfalls, and where to leverage a technology. How do we deal with complexity and heterogeneity of technologies? What are the performance and scalabilities of each technology, and how can we sustain performance for the new environment?

If one were to take a journey back in history and look at the architectural wonders that were built, we often wonder what kind of blueprints the architects considered, how they decided on the laws of physics, and how they combined chemical properties of materials for the structures to last for centuries while supporting visitor volumes and climate changes. In building the new data warehouse, we need to adapt a radical thinking like the architects of the yore, where we will retain the fundamental definition of the data warehouse as stated by Bill Inmon, but we will be developing a physical architecture that will not be constrained by the boundaries of a single platform like the RDBMS.

The next-generation data warehouse architecture will be complex from a physical architecture deployment, consisting of a myriad of technologies, and will be data-driven from an integration perspective, extremely flexible, and scalable from a data architecture perspective.

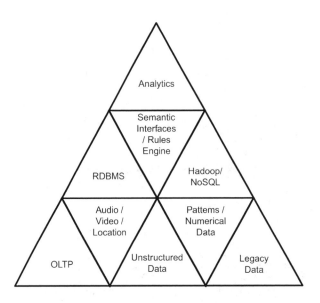

FIGURE 10.1

Components of the next-generation data warehouse.

Components of the new data warehouse

Figure 10.1 shows the high-level components that will be the foundational building blocks of the next-generation data warehouse, which is the integration of all the data in the enterprise including Big Data. The lowest tier represents the data, the next tier represents the technologies that will be used in integrating the data across the multiple types and sources of data, and the topmost layer represents the analytical layer that will be used to drive the visualization needs of the next generation of business intelligence and analytics. Let us first look at each layer of the components in detail and then move onto the physical architecture options.

Data layer

As discussed in prior chapters, the next-generation data warehouse will have data from across the enterprise that will be integrated and presented to the users for business decision-making and analysis purposes. The data layer in the new platform includes the following.

- *Legacy data*. Data from all legacy systems and applications that include structured and semi-structured formats of data, stored online or offline, can be integrated into the data architecture. There are lots of use cases for this data type. Seismic data, hurricane data, census data, urban planning data, and socioeconomic data are all forms of data that have been classified as legacy over a period of time.
- *Transactional (OLTP) data*. Data from transactional systems traditionally is loaded to the data warehouse. Due to scalability issues, transactional data is often modeled such that not all the data from the source systems is used in analysis. The new platform can be used to load and

analyze the data in its entirety as a preprocessing or second-pass processing step. Data from ERP, SCM, and CRM systems often gets left out in processing, and these segments of data can be used in creating a powerful back-end data platform that analyzes data and organizes it at every processing step.

- *Unstructured data.* Content management platforms are more oriented toward either producing and storing content or just storing content. Most of the content is not analyzed, and there are no standard techniques to create analytical metrics on content. Content of any nature is specific to the context in which it was created and to the organization that owns the content. The next-generation platform will provide interfaces to tap into the content by navigating it based on user-defined rules for processing. The output of content processing will be used in defining and designing analytics for exploration mining of unstructured data. The output from processing content data can be integrated using semantic technologies and used for visualization and visual data mining.

- *Video.* Corporations and government agencies alike have a need to harness into video-based data. There are three components in a video—the content, the audio, and the associated metadata—and processing techniques and algorithms for this data type is nascent and complex. The new data platforms, however, provide the infrastructure necessary to process this data. The next-generation data warehouse can integrate this data type and its associated analytics into the data warehouse architecture. The data will be needed as organizations start adopting gamification strategies in customer engagement, government agencies start using the data in managing multiple areas of defense and security, weather agencies use the data for analysis and reporting, and news and media agencies use multiple public and private videos to provide education to consumers on real-time and historical news in one mashup. The possibilities of how to leverage the data in commercial and noncommercial aspects are deep and wide to cover in this section. The next-generation data warehouse will be a holistic platform for processing and integrating all these one-off data types, which will be stored as contextualized data with associated metadata.

- *Audio.* Data from call centers to audio extracts from videos contains a lot of intelligence about customers, competition, and many more categories. While the current data warehouse has limitations on processing and integrating this data, the new data platforms and technologies have enabled processing of this data seamlessly and integrating it into the context of the data warehouse. Audio data extracts can be processed and stored as contextual data with the associated metadata in the next-generation data warehouse.

- *Images.* Static images carry a lot of data that can be very useful in government agencies (geospatial integration), healthcare (X-ray and CAT scans), and other areas. Integrating this data in the data warehouse will provide benefits in a large enterprise, where sharing such data can result in big insights and generate business opportunities where none existed due to lack of data availability.

- *Numerical/patterns/graphs.* Seismic data, sensor data, weather data, stock market data, scientific data, RFID, cellular tower data, automotive on-board computer chips, GPS data, streaming video, and other such data are either patterns, numeric data, or graphs that occur and repeat their manifests in periodic time intervals. Processing such data and integrating the results with the data warehouse will provide analytical opportunities to perform correlation analysis, cluster analysis, or Bayesian types of analysis, which will help identify opportunities in revenue leakage, customer segment behavior, and many other opportunities where business risk can be identified and processed by decision makers for business performance optimization.

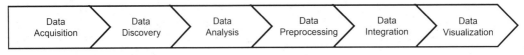

FIGURE 10.2

Big Data processing.

- *Social media data.* Typically classified as Facebook, LinkedIn, or Twitter data, the social media data transcends beyond those channels. This data can be purchased from third-party aggregators such as Datasift, Gnip, and Nielsen. The processing of this data in the data warehouse can be accomplished using the rules engine and semantic technologies. Output from the processing can be integrated with multiple dimensions of the data warehouse.

The data layer consists of data sets that are most commonly available to organizations as their asset or from third-party sources. The known data sets that can be processed today consist of 20% of the data that has been discussed in the data layer. How do we process the remaining data and how does the integration happen? To answer these questions, let us discuss the underlying algorithms that need to be integrated into the processing architecture and technology layers.

Algorithms

Big Data processing needs to happen in the order shown in Figure 10.2.

The first step after acquisition of data is to perform discovery of data. This is where the complexity of processing data lies especially in unstructured data. To accelerate the reduction of complexity, there are several algorithms that have evolved in commercial or open-source solutions. The key algorithms that are useful include:

- *Text mining.* These algorithms are available as commercial off-the-shelf software solutions and can be integrated into the data architecture with ease. The primary focus of the text mining algorithms are to process text based on user-defined business rules and extract data that can be used in classifying the text for further data exploration purposes. Semantic technologies play a vital role in integrating the data within the data warehouse ecosystem.
- *Data mining.* These algorithms are available as commercial software from companies like SAS and IBM, and open-source implementations like Mahout. The primary focus of data mining algorithms is to produce data output based on statistical data models that work on population clustering, data clustering, and segmentation based on dimensions and time called microsegmentation techniques. The data output is deep and wide, providing a cube-based environment for executing data exploration exercises.
- *Pattern processing.* These algorithms are developed for pattern processing, which includes patterns from credit card data; POS data; ATM data; stock market signals; sensor data from buildings, trains, trucks, automobiles, airplanes, ships, satellites, images, and audio; cryptographic data, and symbolic languages. When a pattern is detected the data is processed in a transactional manner for that single instance. The advantage of integrating this data in the data warehouse will be the ability to tap into these one-time occurrences and the entire data set to arrive at a more defined predictive model of data behaviors. The next-generation platforms offer the infrastructure

to store both the raw data and the output from the processing of pattern algorithms, to provide a holistic data architecture and exploration capability.

- *Statistical models.* These algorithms are models used largely in financial services and healthcare to compute statistical data for managing population segments. These algorithms are customized for every organization that uses them and produces outputs that today cannot be reused in computation due to the size of data and the associated processing complexity. In the next generation of the data warehouse these models can be computed and driven based on the data available in the data warehouse whether structured, semi-structured, unstructured, or a combination of all. These models can be developed in technologies like R and other open-source models as opposed to closed architectures like SAS or IBM SPSS.
- *Mathematical models.* These algorithms are models used for disease predictions, weather prediction, fraud analytics, and other nonstatistical computes that require mathematical models. The current-state data requirements of these algorithms cannot be met to the fullest extent by the existing infrastructure and compute technologies. In the next-generation data warehouse, the data required by these models and associated computing fabrics are both available within the data warehouse processing layers.

The next generation of data architecture and data processing activities will need to include the algorithms discussed in this section to solve the specific categories of data processing and reporting and analytics delivery from the data warehouse. Now that we have the data and the associated types of algorithms, before we discuss the integration strategies, let's revisit the technology layer.

Technology layer

In the preceding chapters we have discussed the different types of technologies that will be used to architect the next-generation data warehouse for supporting data processing of structured, semi-structured, and unstructured or Big Data. To recap the technologies that will be mixed and integrated into the heterogeneous architecture, the list includes:

- RDBMS
- Hadoop
- NoSQL
- MDM solutions
- Metadata solutions
- Semantic technologies
- Rules engines
- Data mining algorithms
- Text mining algorithms
- Data discovery technologies
- Data visualization technologies
- Reporting and analytical technologies

These technologies will present significant integration challenges in building the foundational architecture for the next-generation data warehouse from a solution architecture point of view. Each technology listed here has its own specific performance and scalability strengths and limitations, and one needs to understand the nuances of how to combine the strengths of the technologies to create a sustainable platform.

A key critical success factor in the design approach for the next-generation data warehouse architecture is a clearly documented and concise user requirement. With the appropriate user specification on the data and the associated processing requirements and outcomes, a program can be developed toward the implementation of the solution.

The next section's focus and discussion is on the integration strategy and architecture. There are two primary portions of the integration architecture: data integration and architecture, and the physical implementation architecture.

Integration strategies

Data integration refers to combining data from different source systems for usage by business users to study different behaviors of the business and its customers. In the early days of data integration, the data was limited to transactional systems and their applications. The limited data set provided the basis for creating decision support platforms that were used as analytic guides for making business decisions.

The growth of the volume of data and the data types over the last three decades, along with the advent of data warehousing, coupled with the advances in infrastructure and technologies to support the analysis and storage requirements for data, have changed the landscape of data integration forever.

Traditional data integration techniques have been focused on ETL, ELT, CDC, and EAI types of architecture and associated programming models. In the world of Big Data, however, these techniques will need to either be modified to suit the size and processing complexity demands, including the formats of data that need to be processed. Big Data processing needs to be implemented as a two-step process. The first step is a data-driven architecture that includes analysis and design of data processing. The second step is the physical architecture implementation, which is discussed in the following sections.

Data-driven integration

In this technique of building the next-generation data warehouse, all the data within the enterprise are categorized according to the data type, and depending on the nature of the data and its associated processing requirements, the data processing is completed using business rules encapsulated in processing logic and integrated into a series of program flows incorporating enterprise metadata, MDM, and semantic technologies like taxonomies.

Figure 10.3 shows the inbound data processing of different categories of data. This model segments each data type based on the format and structure of the data, and then processes the appropriate layers of processing rules within the ETL, ELT, CDC, or text processing techniques. Let us analyze the data integration architecture and its benefits.

Data classification

As shown in Figure 10.3, there are broad classifications of data:

- *Transactional data*—the classic OLTP data belongs to this segment.
- *Web application data*—the data from web applications that are developed by the organization can be added to this category. This data includes clickstream data, web commerce data, and customer relationship and call center chat data.

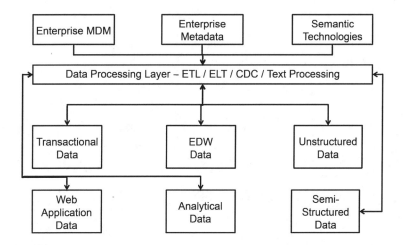

FIGURE 10.3

Inbound data processing.

- *EDW data*—this is the existing data from the data warehouse used by the organization currently. It can include all the different data warehouses and datamarts in the organization where data is processed and stored for use by business users.
- *Analytical data*—this is data from analytical systems that are deployed currently in the organization. The data today is primarily based on EDW or transactional data.
- *Unstructured data*—under this broad category, we can include:
  - Text—documents, notes, memos, contracts.
  - Images—photos, diagrams, graphs.
  - Videos—corporate and consumer videos associated with the organization.
  - Social media—Facebook, Twitter, Instagram, LinkedIn, Forums, YouTube, community websites.
  - Audio—call center conversations, broadcasts.
  - Sensor data—includes data from sensors on any or all devices that are related to the organization's line of business. For example, smart meter data makes a business asset for an energy company, and truck and automotive sensors relate to logistics and shipping providers like UPS and FedEx.
  - Weather data—is used by both B2B and B2C businesses today to analyze the impact of weather on the business; has become a vital component of predictive analytics.
  - Scientific data—this data applies to medical, pharmaceutical, insurance, healthcare, and financial services segments where a lot of number-crunching type of computation is performed including simulations and model generation.
  - Stock market data—used for processing financial data in many organizations to predict market trends, financial risk, and actuarial computations.
- *Semi-structured data*—this includes emails, presentations, mathematical models and graphs, and geospatial data.

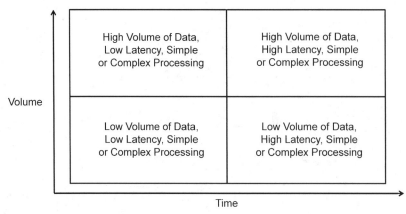

FIGURE 10.4

Workload category.

Architecture

With the different data types clearly identified and laid out, the data characteristics, including the data type, the associated metadata, the key data elements that can be identified as master data elements, the complexities of the data, and the business users of the data from an ownership and stewardship perspective, can be defined clearly.

Workload

The biggest need for processing Big Data is workload management, as discussed in earlier chapters. The data architecture and classification allow us to assign the appropriate infrastructure that can execute the workload demands of the categories of the data.

There are four broad categories of workload based on volume of data and the associated latencies that data can be assigned to (Figure 10.4). Depending on the type of category the data can then be assigned to physical infrastructure layers for processing. This approach to workload management creates a dynamic scalability requirement for all parts of the Data Warehouse, which can be designed by efficiently harnessing the current and new infrastructure options. The key point to remember at this juncture is the processing logic needs to be flexible to be implemented across the different physical infrastructure components since the same data might be classified into different workloads depending on the urgency of processing.

The workload architecture will further identify the conditions of mixed workload management where the data from one category of workload will be added to processing along with another category of workload.

For example, processing high-volume, low-latency data with low-volume, high-latency data creates a diversified stress on the data processing environment, where you normally would have processed one kind of data and its workload. Add to this complexity the user query and data loading happening at the same time or in relatively short intervals, and now the situation can get out of hand in a quick succession and impact the overall performance. If the same infrastructure is processing Big Data and traditional data together with all of these complexities, the problem just compounds itself.

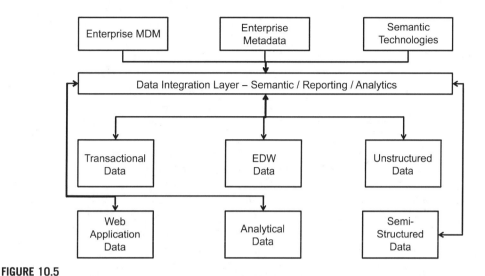

FIGURE 10.5

Semantic layer integration for data visualization.

The goal of using the workload quadrant is to identify the complexities associated with the data processing and how to mitigate the associated risk in infrastructure design to create the next-generation data warehouse.

Analytics

Identifying and classifying analytical processing requirements for the entire set of data elements at play is a critical requirement in the design of the next-generation data warehouse platform. The underpinning for this requirement stems from the fact that you can create analytics at the data discovery level, which is very focused and driven by the business consumer and not aligned with the enterprise version of the truth, and you can equally create analytics after data acquisition in the data warehouse.

Figure 10.5 shows the analytics processing in the next-generation data warehouse platform. The key architecture integration layer here is the data integration layer, which is a combination of semantic, reporting, and analytical technologies, which is based on the semantic knowledge framework, which is the foundation of next-generation analytics and business intelligence. This framework is discussed later in this chapter.

Finalizing the data architecture is the most time-consuming task, which once completed will provide a strong foundation for the physical implementation. The physical implementation will be accomplished using technologies from the earlier discussions including Big Data and RDBMS systems.

Physical component integration and architecture

The next-generation data warehouse will be deployed on a heterogeneous infrastructure and architectures that integrate both traditional structured data and Big Data into one scalable and performing environment. There are several options to deploy the physical architecture with pros and cons for each option.

The primary challenges that will confront the physical architecture of the next-generation data warehouse platform include data loading, availability, data volume, storage performance, scalability, diverse and changing query demands against the data, and operational costs of maintaining the environment. The key challenges are outlined here and will be discussed with each architecture option.

Data loading

- With no definitive format or metadata or schema, the loading process for Big Data is simply acquiring the data and storing it as files. This task can be overwhelming when you want to process real-time feeds into the system, while processing the data as large or microbatch windows of processing. An appliance can be configured and tuned to address these rigors in the setup as opposed to a pure-play implementation. The downside is a custom architecture configuration may occur, but this can be managed.
- Continuous processing of data in the platform can create contention for resources over a period of time. This is especially true in the case of large documents or videos or images. If this requirement is a key architecture driver, an appliance can be suitable for this specificity, as the guessing game can be avoided in the configuration and setup process.
- MapReduce configuration and optimization can be daunting in large environments and the appliance architecture provides you reference architecture setups to avoid this pitfall.

Data availability

- Data availability has been a challenge for any system that relates to processing and transforming data for use by end users, and Big Data is no exception. The benefit of Hadoop or NoSQL is to mitigate this risk and make data available for analysis immediately upon acquisition. The challenge is to load the data quickly as there is no pretransformation required.
- Data availability depends on the specificity of metadata to the SerDe or Avro layers. If data can be adequately cataloged on acquisition, it can be available for analysis and discovery immediately.
- Since there is no update of data in the Big Data layers, reprocessing new data containing updates will create duplicate data and this needs to be handled to minimize the impact on availability.

Data volumes

- Big Data volumes can easily get out of control due to the intrinsic nature of the data. Care and attention needs to be paid to the growth of data upon each cycle of acquisition.
- Retention requirements for the data can vary depending on the nature of the data and the recency of the data and its relevance to the business:
  - Compliance requirements: SAFE Harbor, SOX, HIPAA, GLBA, and PCI regulations can impact data security and storage. If you are planning to use these data types, plan accordingly.
  - Legal mandates: There are several transactional data sets that were not stored online and were required by courts of law for discovery purposes in class-action lawsuits. The Big Data infrastructure can be used as the storage engine for this data type, but the data mandates certain compliance needs and additional security. This data volume can impact the overall performance, and if such data sets are being processed on the Big Data platform, the appliance

configuration can provide the administrators with tools and tips to zone the infrastructure to mark the data in its own area, minimizing both risk and performance impact.

- Data exploration and mining is a very common activity that is a driver for Big Data acquisition across organizations, and also produces large data sets as output of processing. These data sets need to be maintained in the Big Data system by periodically sweeping and deleting intermediate data sets. This is an area that normally is ignored by organizations and can be a performance drain over a period of time.

Storage performance

- Disk performance is an important consideration when building Big Data systems and the appliance model can provide a better focus on the storage class and tiering architecture. This will provide the starting kit for longer-term planning and growth management of the storage infrastructure.
- If a combination of in-memory, SSD, and traditional storage architecture is planned for Big Data processing, the persistence and exchange of data across the different layers can be consuming both processing time and cycles. Care needs to be extended in this area, and the appliance architecture provides a reference for such complex storage requirements.

Operational costs

Calculating the operational cost for a data warehouse and its Big Data platform is a complex task that includes initial acquisition costs for infrastructure, plus labor costs for implementing the architecture, plus infrastructure and labor costs for ongoing maintenance including external help commissioned from consultants and experts.

External data integration

Figure 10.6 shows the external data integration approach to creating the next-generation data warehouse. In this approach the existing data processing and data warehouse platforms are retained, and a new platform for processing Big Data is created in new technology architecture. A data bus is developed using metadata and semantic technologies, which will create a data integration environment for data exploration and processing.

Workload processing is clearly divided in this architecture into processing Big Data in its infrastructure and the current-state data warehouse in its infrastructure. The streamlining of workload helps maintain performance and data quality, but the complexity increases in the data bus architecture, which can be a simple layer or an overwhelmingly complex layer of processing. This is a custom-built solution for each system that will be integrated into the data warehouse architecture, and needs a lot of data architecture skills and maintenance. Data processing of Big Data will be outside the RDBMS platform, and provides opportunities to create unlimited scalability at a lower price point.

- Pros:
  - Scalable design for RDBMS and Big Data processing.
  - Reduced overload on processing.
  - Complexity of processing can be isolated across data acquisition, data cleansing, data discovery, and data integration.

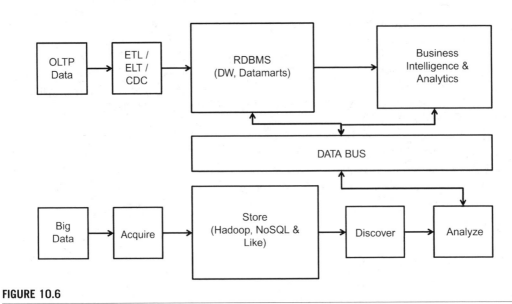

FIGURE 10.6

External data integration.

- Modular data integration architecture.
  - Heterogeneous physical architecture deployment, providing best-in-class integration at the data processing layer.
- Cons:
  - Data bus architecture can become increasingly complex.
  - Poor metadata architecture can creep due to multiple layers of data processing.
  - Data integration can become a performance bottleneck over a period of time.

Typical use cases for this type of integration architecture can be seen in organizations where the data remains fairly stable over a period of time across the Big Data spectrum. Examples include social media channels and sensor data.

- Data loading is isolated across the layers. This provides a foundation to create a robust data management strategy.
- Data availability is controlled to each layer and security rules can be implemented to each layer as required, avoiding any associated overhead for other layers.
- Data volumes can be managed across the individual layers of data based on the data type, the life-cycle requirements for the data, and the cost of the storage.
- Storage performance is based on the data categories and the performance requirements, and the storage tiers can be configured.
- Operational costs—in this architecture the operational cost calculation has fixed and variable cost components. The variable costs are related to processing and computing infrastructure and labor costs. The fixed costs are related to maintenance and data-related costs.

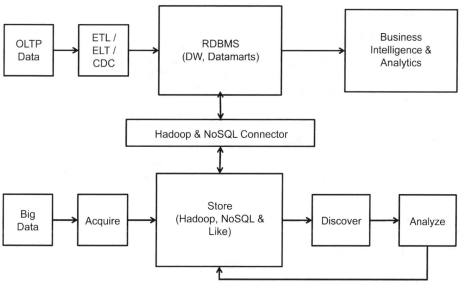

FIGURE 10.7

Integration-driven approach.

- Pitfalls to avoid:
  - Too much data complexity at any one layer of processing.
  - Poor metadata.
  - Incorrect data analysis within Big Data layers.
  - Incorrect levels of integration (at data granularity) within the Big Data layers.
  - Incorrect application of data bus integration.

Hadoop & RDBMS

Figure 10.7 shows the integration-driven approach to creating the next-generation data warehouse. To create the next-generation data warehouse we combine the Big Data processing platform created in Hadoop or NoSQL and the existing RDBMS-based data warehouse infrastructure by deploying a connector between the two systems. This connecter will be a bridge to exchange data between the two platforms. At the time of writing, most of the RDBMS, BI, analytics, and NoSQL vendors have developed Hadoop and NoSQL connectors.

Workload processing is this architecture blends data processing across both platforms, providing scalability and reducing complexity. The streamlining of workload creates a scalable platform across both the infrastructure layers, where data discovery can be seamlessly enabled in either platform. The complexity of this architecture is the dependency on the performance of the connector. The connectors largely mimic a JDBC behavior, and the bandwidth to transport data will be a severe bottleneck, considering the query complexity in the data discovery process.

- Pros:
    - Scalable design for RDBMS and Big Data processing.
    - Modular data integration architecture.
    - Heterogeneous physical architecture deployment, providing best-in-class integration at the data processing layer.
    - Metadata and MDM solutions can be leveraged with relative ease across the solution.
- Cons:
    - Performance of the Big Data connector is the biggest area of weakness.
    - Data integration and query scalability can become complex.

Typical use case for this type of integration architecture can be seen in organizations where the data needs to be integrated into analytics and reporting. Examples include social media data, textual data, and semi-structured data like emails.

- Data loading is isolated across the layers. This provides a foundation to create a robust data management strategy.
- Data availability is controlled to each layer and security rules can be implemented to each layer as required, avoiding any associated overhead for other layers.
- Data volumes can be managed across the individual layers of data based on the data type, the life-cycle requirements for the data, and the cost of the storage.
- Storage performance—Hadoop is designed and deployed on commodity architecture and the storage costs are very low compared to the traditional RDBMS platform. The performance of the disks for each layer can be configured as needed by the end user.
- Operational costs—in this architecture the operational cost calculation has fixed and variable cost components. The variable costs are related to processing and computing infrastructure and labor costs. The fixed costs are related to RDBMS maintenance and its related costs.
- Pitfalls to avoid:
    - Too much data complexity at any one layer of processing.
    - Executing large data exchanges between the different layers.
    - Incorrect levels of integration (at data granularity).
    - Applying too many transformation complexities using the connectors.

Big Data appliances

Data warehouse appliances emerged as a strong black-box architecture for processing workloads specific to large-scale data in the last decade. One of the extensions of this architecture is the emergence of Big Data appliances. These appliances are configured to handle the rigors of workloads and complexities of Big Data and the current RDBMS architecture.

Figure 10.8 shows the conceptual architecture of the Big Data appliance, which includes a layer of Hadoop and a layer of RDBMS. While the physical architectural implementation can differ among vendors like Teradata, Oracle, IBM, and Microsoft, the underlying conceptual architecture remains the same, where Hadoop and/or NoSQL technologies will be used to acquire, preprocess, and store Big Data, and the RDBMS layers will be used to process the output from the Hadoop and NoSQL layers. In-database MapReduce, R, and RDBMS specific translators and connectors will be used in the integrated architecture for managing data movement and transformation within the appliance.

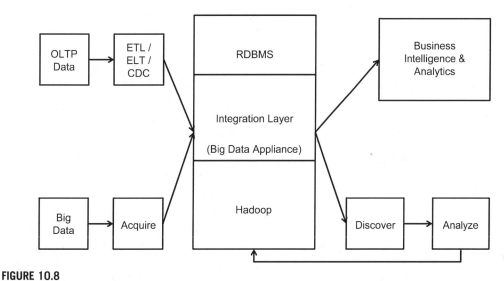

FIGURE 10.8

Conceptual Big Data appliance.

The Big Data appliance is geared to answer some key areas that emerge as risks or challenges when dealing with extremely large data processing. The primary areas include data loading, availability, data volume, storage performance, scalability, diverse and changing query demands against the data, and operational costs of the next-generation data warehouse platform. The risks can be applied to both the structured and the unstructured data that will be coexisting in this platform.

- Data loading is isolated across the layers. This provides a foundation to create a robust data management strategy.
- Data availability is controlled to each layer and security rules can be implemented to each layer as required, avoiding any associated overhead for other layers.
- Data volumes can be managed across the individual layers of data based on the data type, the life-cycle requirements for the data, and the cost of the storage.
- Storage performance is based on the data categories and the performance requirements, and the storage tiers can be configured.
- Operational costs—the appliance architecture enables a quick way to calculate the total cost of ownership and especially operational costs, since the configuration of the appliance is focused on satisfying all the known requirements as documented.

The areas discussed here are some key considerations for looking at the appliance as a solution rather than building out your own architecture.

Workload processing in this architecture is configured to the requirements as specified by the users, including data acquisition, usage, retention, and processing. The complexity of this architecture is the configuration and initial setup, which will need significant rework if the specifications are not clear or tend to change over time, since the initial configuration is customized.

- Pros:
  - Scalable design and modular data integration architecture.
  - Heterogeneous physical architecture deployment, providing best-in-class integration at the data processing layer.
  - Custom configured to suit the processing rigors as required for each organization.
- Cons:
  - Customized configuration is the biggest weakness.
  - Data integration and query scalability can become complex as the configuration changes over a period of time.

This architecture can be deployed to process all types of Big Data, and is the closest to a scalable and integrated next-generation data warehouse platform.

- Pitfalls to avoid:
  - Custom configuration can be maintenance-heavy.
  - Executing large data exchanges between the different layers can cause performance issues.
  - Too much dependency on any one transformation layer creates scalability bottlenecks.
  - Data security implementation with LDAP integration should be avoided for the unstructured layers.

Data virtualization

Data virtualization technology can be used to create the next-generation data warehouse platform. As shown in Figure 10.9, the biggest benefit of this deployment is the reuse of existing infrastructure for the structured portion of the data warehouse. This approach also provides an opportunity to distribute workload effectively across the platforms thereby allowing for the best optimization to be executed in the architectures. Data Virtualization coupled with a strong semantic architecture can create a scalable solution.

- Pros:
  - Extremely scalable and flexible architecture.
  - Workload optimized.
  - Easy to maintain.
  - Lower initial cost of deployment.
- Cons:
  - Lack of governance can create too many silos and degrade performance.
  - Complex query processing can become degraded over a period of time.
  - Performance at the integration layer may need periodic maintenance.
- Data loading is isolated across the layers. This provides a foundation to create a robust data management strategy.
- Data availability is controlled to each layer and security rules can be implemented to each layer as required, avoiding any associated overhead for other layers.
- Data volumes can be managed across the individual layers of data based on the data type, the life-cycle requirements for the data, and the cost of the storage.
- Storage performance is based on the data categories and the performance requirements, and the storage tiers can be configured.

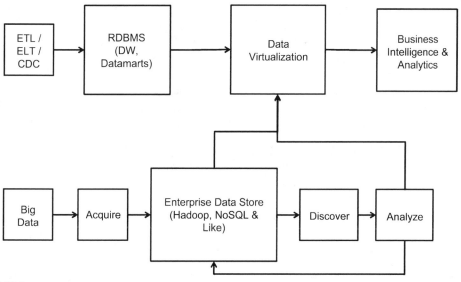

FIGURE 10.9

Data virtualization–based Big Data integration.

- Operational costs—in this architecture the operational cost calculation has fixed and variable cost components. The variable costs are related to processing and computing infrastructure and labor costs. The fixed costs are related to maintenance of the data virtualization platform and its related costs.
- Pitfalls to avoid:
  - Loosely coupled data integration.
  - Incorrect data granularity across the different systems.
  - Poor metadata across the systems.
  - Lack of data governance.
  - Complex data integration involving too many computations at the integration layer.
  - Poorly designed semantic architecture.

There are many more possible architectural deployments to integrate Big Data and create the next-generation data warehouse platform. This chapter's goal is to provide you a starter kit to begin looking at what it will take for any organization to implement the next-generation data warehouse. In the next section we discuss the semantic framework approach.

Semantic framework

Building the next-generation data warehouse requires strong metadata architecture for data integration, but that does not solve the data exploration requirements. When data from multiple sources and systems is integrated together, there are multiple layers of hierarchies including jagged and skewed hierarchies, data granularity at different levels, and data quality issues especially with unstructured

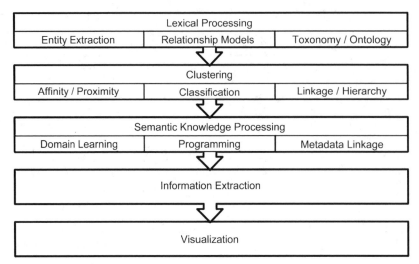

FIGURE 10.10

Semantic Framework.

data, including text, image, video, and audio data. Processing data and presenting data for visualization at both ends requires a more robust architecture, which is the semantic framework.

Figure 10.10 shows the concept of the semantic framework architecture. The framework consists of multiple layers of processing and data integration techniques that will be deployed as a part of the next-generation data warehouse. The layers and their functions include the following.

Lexical processing

This layer can be applied to both input data processing of Big Data and the processing of data exploration queries from the visualization layer. Lexical processing includes processing tokens and streams of text. The three main subcomponents of lexical processing include:

- *Entity extraction*—a process to identify key data tokens that can include keys and master data elements. For example, identifying "product_name" from a twitter feed.
- *Taxonomy*—a process to navigate across domains within the text stream to identify the contexts in the text that may be feasible, and discover relationship attributes for cross-hierarchy navigation.
- *Relationship models*—a process to derive the relationship between different data elements and layers resulting in an exploration roadmap. This process will use outputs from the prior components in this process.

Clustering

In this process all the data from lexical processing will be clustered to create a logical grouping of data processed in the Big Data layers and from any data exploration queries. The subcomponents in this layer include:

- *Affinity/proximity*—in this process there are two components:
  1. Affinity—this feature will determine the affinity of data across different formats. For example, a group of videos, audio, and documents containing data about cardiac diseases.
  2. Proximity—the occurrence of specific data elements within a given unstructured text.
- *Classification*—in this process that is more back-end oriented, the data can be classified into multiple groups of topics or be aligned to subject areas similar to the structured data in the data warehouse.
- *Linkage/hierarchy*—in this process the output from the classification stage is linked in a lexical map including the associated hierarchy information.

Semantic knowledge processing

This process consists of integrating the data outputs from lexical and clustering layers to provide a powerful architecture for data visualization. This process consists of the following subcomponents:

- *Domain learning*—in this process the data from different domains is paired and integrated with semantic technologies. The data at this stage includes structured and Big Data.
- *Programming*—in this process software programs are created and deployed to complete the semantic integration process. This section also includes machine learning techniques and additional lexical processing to complete the integration as needed for visualization.
- *Metadata linkage*—a last step in the semantic processing is the integration of data with metadata links that will be used in visual exploration and mining.

Information extraction

In this process the visualization tools extract the data from the prior layers of processing and load it for visual exploration and analytics. The data at this stage can be loaded into technology like in-memory for further analysis.

Visualization

In this process the data can be visualized using new technologies like Tableau and Spotfire, or with R, SAS, or traditional technologies like Microstrategy, Business Objects, or Cognos. These tools can directly leverage the semantic architecture from their integration layers and create a scalable interface.

SUMMARY

In summary, as observed in this chapter, heterogeneity is permanent in the future of the data warehouse, and the concept remains the same as defined 40 years ago by Bill Inmon, but the physical implementation will be different from the prior generations of data warehousing. In the next chapter we will focus on the data-driven integration architecture, and the impact of data governance, metadata, and master data in creating the next-generation data warehouse.

Data-Driven Architecture for Big Data

11

What information consumes is rather obvious: it consumes the attention of its recipients.
Hence a wealth of information creates a poverty of attention, and a need to allocate that
attention efficiently among the overabundance of information sources that might consume it.
—Herbert Simon

INTRODUCTION

Data is one of the biggest assets of any enterprise, large or small. With the right set of information, you can make business decisions with higher levels of confidence, as you can audit and attribute the data you used for the decision-making process. The complexities of managing data in structured environments have been a challenge that enterprises struggle with, and things will be worse when you look at adding Big Data into this situation. Enterprises that have paid attention to data management as an asset will be winners when building out the next-generation data warehouse.

To goal of this chapter is to provide readers with data governance in the age of Big Data. We will discuss the goals of what managing data means with respect to the next generation of data warehousing and the roles of metadata and master data in integrating Big Data into a data warehouse.

Data management refers to the process of collecting, processing, storing, and distributing data. The data management techniques that we have been using today in the modern database world are based on requirements that were developed for legacy systems dating back from punch cards, to mainframes, to analytical data processing systems.

Figure 11.1 shows the fundamental stages of data management across enterprises. There are several cycles of activities within each stage of processing that create complexities for managing the entire process end to end. Before we look into the details of these processes, let us take a brief look at metadata and master data.

Metadata

Metadata is defined as data about data or, in other words, information about data within any data environment. The origins of metadata can be traced to library systems from many years ago, where the classification, tagging, and cataloging of books provided the fundamental information classification and retrieval. Applied to information technology, metadata provides a natural way to integrate data and interrogate data.

219

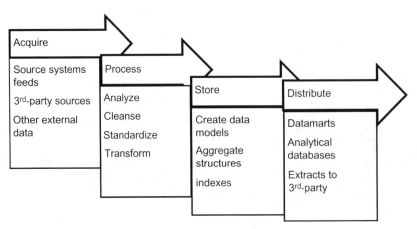

FIGURE 11.1

Data management stages.

Why is metadata so valuable? The answer to this question can be explained by a simple example. Let us assume you make a trip to the local hardware store to buy some sheets of wood. Without any label describing the wood, its dimensional attributes, and the price, you will be lost for hours waiting for someone to help you. This little label of information is what the value of metadata is all about.

From a database perspective, metadata describes the content of every attribute in every table as defined during the design phase of the database. This provides the developers, data architects, business intelligence architects, analysts, and users a concise roadmap of what data is stored within the database and in which table.

Metadata changes in the lifetime of a database when changes occur within the business, such as mergers and acquisitions, new systems deployment, integration between legacy, and new applications. To maintain the metadata associated with the data, we need to implement business and technology processes and governance policies. Many enterprises today do not track the life cycle of metadata, which will cost them when data is brought back from backups or data is restored from an archive database, and nobody can quite decipher the contents and its relationships, hierarchies, and business processing rules.

The value of having metadata can be easily established in these situations by measuring the cost impact with and without metadata:

- Cost of commissioning new applications
- Learning curve for new employees
- Troubleshooting application problems
- Creating new business intelligence and analytics applications
- Data auditing
- Compliance auditing

Traditionally in the world of data management, metadata has been often ignored and implemented as a postimplementation process. When you start looking at Big Data, you need to create a strong metadata library, as you will be having no idea about the content of the data format that you need to process. Remember in the Big Data world, we ingest and process data, then tag it, and after these steps, consume it for processing.

Let us revisit the metadata subject area first and then understand how it integrates into the world of Big Data. Sources of metadata include:

- Metadata generated automatically for data and business rules
- Metadata created by the designer of the systems
- Metadata procured from third-party sources

There are fundamentally nine types of metadata that are useful for information technology and data management across the enterprise from transaction processing to analytical and reporting platforms.

Technical metadata

Technical metadata consists of metadata that is associated with data transformation rules, data storage structures, semantic layers, and interface layers.

- Metadata for data model and physical database includes length of a field, the shape of a data structure, the name of a table, the physical characteristics of a field, the number of bytes in a table, the indexes on a table, and data definition language (DDL) for a table.
- Business processing metadata includes information about:
  - The system of record for a specific piece of data.
  - Transformations that were performed on which source data to produce data in the data warehouse/datamart.
  - Tables and columns used in the particular process in the data warehouse/datamart and what the transformations mean.
- Administrative metadata.

Business metadata

Business metadata refers to the data describing the content available in the data warehouse/datamart, including:

- The structure of the data.
- The values that are stored within the attributes.
- Create and update date and time.
- Processing specifics if any for the field or attribute.

Contextual metadata

Contextual metadata is data that sets the "context" of your data. This is more related to processing large objects like text, images, and videos. Examples of contextual metadata include newsfeeds, tags on images, etc. Contextual metadata is the hardest to collect.

Process design–level metadata

Process design–level metadata consists of the following:

- Source table
- Target table

- Algorithms
- Business rules
- Exception
- Lookup or master data or reference data

Program-level metadata

Program-level metadata consists of the following:

- History of transformation changes
- Business rules
- Source program
- System name
- Source program author
- Extract program name and version
- Load scripts
- Script-specific business rules
- Load frequency
- Extract dependencies
- Transformation dependencies
- Load dependencies
- Load completion date/time stamp
- Load completion record count
- Load status

Infrastructure metadata

Infrastructure metadata includes:

- Source system platform
- Source system network address
- Source system support contact
- Target system platform
- Target system network address
- Target system support contact
- Estimated size (tables/objects)

Core business metadata

Core business metadata includes:

- Field/object description
- Confidence level
- Frequency of update
- Basic business metadata
- Source system name
- Valid entries (i.e., "There are four valid reply flags: Y, N, N/A, DNR")

- Formats (i.e., Contract DateTime: 20-Nov-2012 18:00:00)
- Business rules used to calculate or derive the data
- Changes in business rules over time
- Additional metadata:
  - Data owner
  - Data owner contact information
  - Typical uses
- Level of summarization
- Related fields/objects
- Existing queries/reports using this field/object

Operational metadata

Operational metadata is information about application runs, including:

- Frequency
- Record counts
- Usage
- Processing time
- Security

Business intelligence metadata

BI metadata contains information about how data is queried, filtered, analyzed, and displayed in business intelligence and analytics software tools. This includes:

- Data mining metadata—the descriptions and structures of data sets, algorithms, and queries.
- OLAP metadata—the descriptions and structures of dimensions, cubes, measures (metrics), hierarchies, levels, and drill paths.
- Reporting metadata—the descriptions and structures of reports, charts, queries, data sets, filters, variables, and expressions.
- Business intelligence metadata can be combined with other metadata to create a strong auditing and traceability matrix for data compliance management.

The impact of metadata in the Big Data environment is discussed in later sections. The next section discusses master data management and its impact on the world of data management.

Master data management

Master data management (MDM) is the process of standardization of key business entities and its associated data processing rules across multiple operational applications and data consumption applications like a data warehouse and datamarts within an organization into a central data management platform referred to as an MDM database. MDM primarily focuses on processing "reference or dimensional" data for key business entities (e.g., customer, products, policy, agent, location, employee) that have been agreed on by all stakeholders as a "corporate shared asset" and is shared across an organization.

Why is MDM important? In the traditional world of data and information management, we used to build data and applications in silos across an enterprise. The addition of new systems and applications resulted in not only data volumes and transactions, but also created redundant copies of data, and in many cases the same data structure contained disparate values. The end-state architecture resulted in systems that did not interface and integrate with each other. The complexity of processing disparate data into a common reference architecture required hours of manual effort and did not provide a clean and auditable result set. Each system could give you a fractured insight into what was happening in the enterprise, but you could not create a clear and concise view of data as a centralized system.

This is where the need for a centralized MDM system begins. With a centralized system, the enterprise can create, manage, and share information among systems and applications seamlessly. The efforts to manage and maintain such a system are very simple and flexible compared to a decentralized platform. This approach can save an enterprise time and opportunity costs, while ensuring data quality and consistency. MDM is driven to handle each subject area as its own system within the enterprise. The underlying architecture of the system allows multiple source systems to be integrated and each system can alter the attribute values for the subject area. The final approval of the most accurate value is determined by a data steward and a data governance team, after which the business rules are executed to process the data modifications. The results are then shared back with the source systems, applications, and downstream analytical applications and databases, and called the "gold copy" of the data definition.

MDM is not about technology. The critical success factor of this initiative is the subject matter experts in data within the business teams, who can understand and define the processing rules and complex decision-making process regarding the content and accuracy of the data. MDM is not implementing a technology; as the role of any technology platform in this process, it is that of a facilitator and an enabler.

MDM is about defining business processes and rules for managing common data within disparate systems in an enterprise. In implementing these processes, the data governance and stewardship teams collectively determine the policies, validation, and data-quality rules, as well as service level agreements for creating and managing master data in the enterprise. These include:

- A standardized definition of data common to all the systems and applications.
- A standardized definition of metadata.
- A standardized definition of processes and rules for managing data.
- A standardized process to escalate, prioritize, and resolve data processing issues.
- A standardized process for acquiring, consolidating, quality processing, aggregating, persisting, and distributing data across an enterprise.
- A standardized interface management process for data exchange across the enterprise internally and externally.
- A standardized data security process.
- Ensuring consistency and control in the ongoing maintenance and application use of this information.

Master data sets are used across transactional databases, operational databases, web applications and databases, data warehouses, datamarts, and analytical databases. There are several techniques to implement a master data repository and, depending on the nature of the applications and databases involved, enterprises choose their custom implementation process. MDM transcends all architecture schools of data warehousing and is not exclusively confined to dimensional models alone. The two most popular applications of master data are a single view of the customer, called customer data integration (CDI), and a single view of the product, called product information management (PIM).

Metadata about master data is a key attribute that is implemented in every style of master data implementation. This helps resolve the business rules and processing conflicts that are encountered by teams within organizations and helps the data governance process manage the conflicts and resolve them in an agile approach.

There are several books and best practices documents about master data and the readers are encouraged to peruse them.[1–5]

Processing data in the data warehouse

The challenge with data has always been the ability to discern the content within the structure. There are two distinct parts of data that every data model shows: the physical attributes and data types, and the relationships between different data elements across an enterprise. What we miss out with is the attribution of content within the data structure, also known as metadata. The lack of metadata creates a confusion when nomenclature of the attribute versus the values stored differ; for example, Customer_Id can mean a unique machine-generated key for the table or the actual loyalty program identification for the customer. Storing a mix of values or one type of value when you meant the other is where a lack of data governance is observed.

With the world of Big Data there is a lot of ambiguity with data that makes it complex to process and navigate. To make this processing simple and agile, a data-driven architecture needs to be designed and implemented. This architecture will be the blueprint of how business will explore the data on the Big Data side and what they can possibly integrate with data within the RDBMS that will evolve to become the analytical data warehouse. Data-driven architecture is not a new concept; it has been used in business decision making for ages, except for a fact that all the touchpoints of data we are talking about in the current state are present in multiple silos of infrastructure and not connected in any visualization, analytic, or reporting activity today.

Figure 11.2 shows the data touchpoints in an enterprise prior to the Big Data wave. For each cycle of product and service from ideation to fulfillment and feedback, data was created in the respective system and processed continuously. The dataflow is more of a factory model of information processing. There are data elements that are common across all the different business processes, which have evolved into the master data for the enterprise, and then there is the rest of the data that needs to be analyzed for usage, where the presence of metadata will be very helpful and accelerates the data

[1] Loshin, D. (2009). Master Data Management. Oxford, UK: Elsevier Limited. ISBN: 0123742250.

[2] Berson, A., & Dubov, L. (2010). Master Data Management and Data Governance, 2nd Edition. McGraw-Hill Education. ISBN: 0071744584.

[3] Dreibelbis, A., Hechler, E., Milman, I., Oberhofer, M., Van Run, P. (2008). Enterprise Master Data Management: An SOA Approach to Managing Core Information. IBM Press.

[4] Hillmann, D. I., & Westbrooks, E. L. (2004). Metadata in Practice. American Library Association.

[5] Tannenbaum, A. (2002). Metadata Solutions: Using Metamodels, Repositories, XML, and Enterprise Portals to Generate Information on Demand. Addison-Wesley.

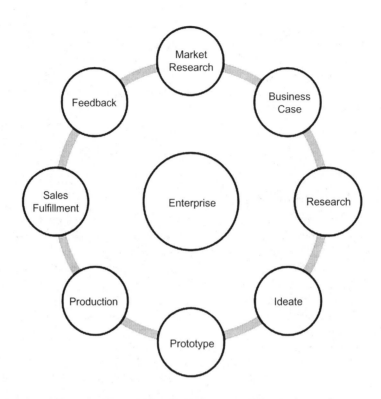

FIGURE 11.2

Enterprise use of data before Big Data.

investigation and analysis. The downside of the process shown in Figure 11.2 is the isolation of each layer of the system, resulting in duplication of data and incorrect attribution of the data across the different systems.

The situation shown in Figure 11.2 continues to happen with the best data governance programs implemented, due to the fact that organizations continue to ignore the importance of corporate metadata and pay the penalty once incorrect information is processed into the systems from source systems all the way to business intelligence platforms.

Figure 11.3 shows the data-driven architecture that can be deployed based on the metadata and master data solutions. This approach streamlines the data assets across the enterprise data warehouse and enables seamless integration with metadata and master data for data management in the data warehouse. While this architecture is more difficult to implement, it is a reusable approach where new data can be easily added into the infrastructure since the system is driven by data-driven architecture. Extending this concept to new systems including Big Data is more feasible as an approach. Let us take a quick look at processing traditional data with metadata and master data before we dive into applying this approach to processing Big Data and enabling the next-generation data warehouse to be more data driven and agile.

Figure 11.4 shows the detailed processing of data across the different stages from source systems to the data warehouse and downstream systems. When implemented with metadata and master

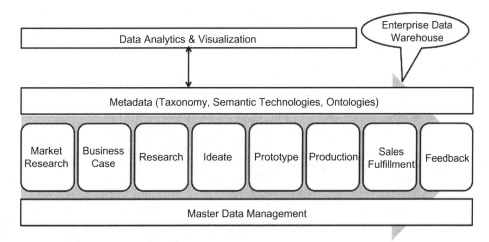

FIGURE 11.3

Enterprise data-driven architecture.

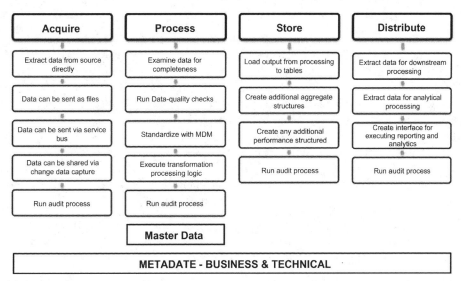

FIGURE 11.4

Data processing cycles with integration of MDM and metadata.

data integration, the stages become self-contained and we can manage the complexities of each stage within that stage's scope of processing. The stages are as follows:

- *Acquire stage.* In this stage we simply collect data from multiple sources and this acquisition process can be implemented as a direct extract from a database to data being sent as flat files or simply available as a web service for extraction and processing.

- Metadata at this stage will include the control file (if provided), and the extract file name, size, and source system identification. All of this data can be collected as a part of the audit process.
- Master data at this stage has no role as it relates more to the content of the data extracts in the processing stage.
- *Process stage.* In this stage the data transformation and standardization including applying data-quality rules is completed and the data is prepared for loading into the data Warehouse, datamart, or analytical database. In this exercise both metadata and master data play very key roles:
  - Metadata is used in the data structures, rules, and data-quality processing.
  - Master data is used for processing and standardizing the key business entities.
  - Metadata is used to process audit data.
  In this processing stage of data movement and management, metadata is very essential to ensure auditability and traceability of data and the process.
- *Storage stage.* In this stage the data is transformed to final storage at rest and is loaded to the data structures. Metadata can be useful in creating agile processes to load and store data in a scalable and flexible architecture. Metadata used in this stage includes loading process, data structures, audit process, and exception processing.
- *Distribution stage.* In this stage data is extracted or processed for use in downstream systems. Metadata is very useful in determining the different extract programs, the interfaces between the data warehouse or datamart, and the downstream applications and auditing data usage and user activity.

In a very efficiently designed system as described in Figure 11.4 we can create an extremely scalable and powerful data processing architecture based on metadata and master data. The challenge in this situation is the processing complexity and how the architecture and design of the data management platform can be compartmentalized to isolate the complexities to each stage within its own layer of integration. Modern data architecture design will create the need for this approach to process and manage the life cycle of data in any organization.

So far we have discussed the use of metadata and master data in creating an extremely agile and scalable solution for processing data in the modern data warehouse. The next section will focus on processing complexities with Big Data and how we can leverage the same concepts of metadata and mater data, and will additionally discuss the use of taxonomies and semantic interfaces in managing data processing within the Big Data ecosystem and the next-generation data warehouse.

Processing complexity of Big Data

The most complicated step in processing Big Data lies not just with the volume or velocity of the data, but also its:

- Variety of formats—data can be presented for processing as Excel spreadsheets, Word documents, PDF files, OCR data, from emails, from content management platforms, from legacy applications, and from web applications. Sometimes it may be variations of the same data over many time periods where the metadata changed significantly.
- Ambiguity of data—can arise from simple issues like naming conventions to similar column names of different data types to same column storing of different data types. A lack of metadata and taxonomies can create a significant delay in processing this data.

- Abstracted layers of hierarchy—the most complex area in Big Data processing are the hidden layers of hierarchy. Data contained in textual, semi-structured, image and video, and converted documents from audio conversations all have context, and without appropriate contextualization the associated hierarchy cannot be processed. Incorrect hierarchy attribution will result in data sets that may not be relevant.
- Lack of metadata—there is no metadata within the documents or files containing Big Data. While this is not unusual, it poses challenges when attributing the metadata to the data during processing. The use of taxonomies and semantic libraries will be useful in flagging the data and subsequently processing it.

Processing limitations

There are a couple of processing limitations for processing Big Data:

- Write-once model—with Big Data there is no update processing logic due to the intrinsic nature of the data that is being processed. Data with changes will be processed as new data.
- Data fracturing—due to the intrinsic storage design, data can be fractured across the Big Data infrastructure. Processing logic needs to understand the appropriate metadata schema used in loading the data. If this match is missed, then errors could creep into processing the data.

Big Data processing can have combinations of these limitations and complexities, which will need to be accommodated in the processing of the data. The next section discusses the steps in processing Big Data.

Processing Big Data

Big Data processing involves steps very similar to processing data in the transactional or data warehouse environments. Figure 11.5 shows the different stages involved in the processing of Big Data; the approach to processing Big Data is:

- Gather the data.
- Analyze the data.
- Process the data.
- Distribute the data.

While the stages are similar to traditional data processing the key differences are:

- Data is first analyzed and then processed.
- Data standardization occurs in the analyze stage, which forms the foundation for the distribute stage where the data warehouse integration happens.
- There is not special emphasis on data quality except the use of metadata, master data, and semantic libraries to enhance and enrich the data.
- Data is prepared in the analyze stage for further processing and integration.

The stages and their activities are described in the following sections in detail, including the use of metadata, master data, and governance processes.

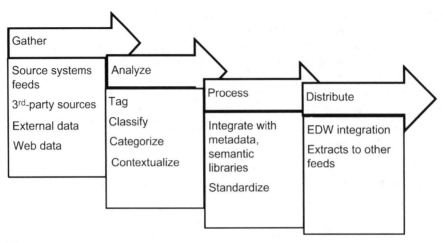

FIGURE 11.5

Processing Big Data.

Gather stage

Data is acquired from multiple sources including real-time systems, near-real-time systems, and batch-oriented applications. The data is collected and loaded to a storage environment like Hadoop or NoSQL. Another option is to process the data through a knowledge discovery platform and store the output rather than the whole data set.

Analysis stage

The analysis stage is the data discovery stage for processing Big Data and preparing it for integration to the structured analytical platforms or the data warehouse. The analysis stage consists of tagging, classification, and categorization of data, which closely resembles the subject area creation data model definition stage in the data warehouse.

- *Tagging*—a common practice that has been prevalent since 2003 on the Internet for data sharing. Tagging is the process of applying a term to an unstructured piece of information that will provide a metadata-like attribution to the data. Tagging creates a rich nonhierarchical data set that can be used to process the data downstream in the process stage.
- *Classify*—unstructured data comes from multiple sources and is stored in the gathering process. Classification helps to group data into subject-oriented data sets for ease of processing. For example, classifying all customer data in one group helps optimize the processing of unstructured customer data.
- *Categorize*—the process of categorization is the external organization of data from a storage perspective where the data is physically grouped by both the classification and then the data type. Categorization will be useful in managing the life cycle of the data since the data is stored as a write-once model in the storage layer.

Process stage

Processing Big Data has several substages, and the data transformation at each substage is significant to produce the correct or incorrect output.

Context processing

Context processing relates to exploring the context of occurrence of data within the unstructured or Big Data environment. The relevancy of the context will help the processing of the appropriate metadata and master data set with the Big Data. The biggest advantage of this kind of processing is the ability to process the same data for multiple contexts, and then looking for patterns within each result set for further data mining and data exploration.

Care should be taken to process the right context for the occurrence. For example, consider the abbreviation "ha" used by all doctors. Without applying the context of where the pattern occurred, it is easily possible to produce noise or garbage as output. If the word occurred in the notes of a heart specialist, it will mean "heart attack" as opposed to a neurosurgeon who will have meant "headache."

You can apply several rules for processing on the same data set based on the contextualization and the patterns you will look for. The next step after contextualization of data is to cleanse and standardize data with metadata, master data, and semantic libraries as the preparation for integrating with the data warehouse and other applications. This is discussed in the next section.

Metadata, master data, and semantic linkage

The most important step in creating the integration of Big Data into a data warehouse is the ability to use metadata, semantic libraries, and master data as the integration links. This step is initiated once the data is tagged and additional processing such as geocoding and contextualization are completed. The next step of processing is to link the data to the enterprise data set. There are many techniques to link the data between structured and unstructured data sets with metadata and master data. This process is the first important step in converting and integrating the unstructured and raw data into a structured format.

Linkage of different units of data from multiple data sets is not a new concept by itself. Figure 11.6 shows a common kind of linkage that is foundational in the world of relational data—referential integrity.

Referential integrity provides the primary key and foreign key relationships in a traditional database and also enforces a strong linking concept that is binary in nature, where the relationship exists or does not exist.

Figure 11.6 shows the example of departments and employees in any company. If John Doe is an employee of the company, then there will be a relationship between the employee and the department to which he belongs. If John Doe is actively employed, then there is a strong relationship between the employee and department. If he has left or retired from the company, there will be historical data for him but no current record between the employee and department data. The model shows the relationship that John Doe has with the company, whether he is either an employee or not, where the probability of a relationship is either 1 or 0, respectively.

When we examine the data from the unstructured world, there are many probabilistic links that can be found within the data and its connection to the data in the structured world. This is the primary difference between the data linkage in Big Data and the RDBMS data.

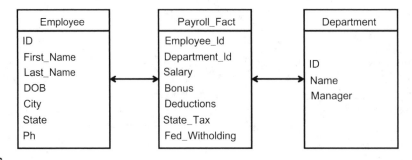

FIGURE 11.6

Database linkage.

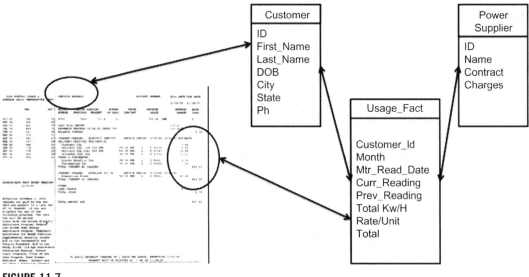

FIGURE 11.7

Connecting Big Data with data warehouse.

Figure 11.7 shows an example of integrating Big Data and the data warehouse to create the next-generation data warehouse. This is an example of linking a customer's electric bill with the data in the ERP system. The linkage here is both binary and probabilistic in nature. This is due to the customer data being present across both the systems.

A probabilistic link is based on the theory of probability where a relationship can potentially exist, however, there is no binary confirmation of whether the probability is 100% or 10% (Figure 11.8). According to the theory of probability, the higher the score of probability, the relationship between the different data sets is likely possible, and the lower the score, the confidence is lower too. Additionally, there is a factor of randomness that we need to consider when applying the theory of probability. In a nutshell, we will either discover extremely strong relationships or no relationships. Adding metadata, master data, and semantic technologies will enable more positive trends in the discovery of strong relationships.

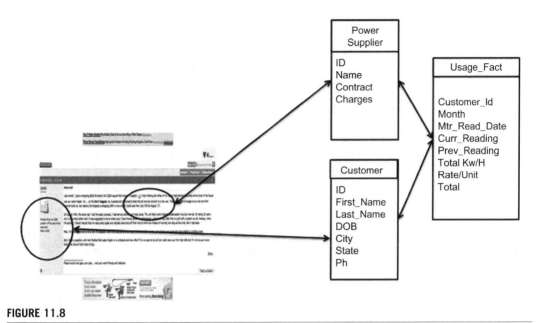

FIGURE 11.8

Probabilistic linkage.

Types of probabilistic links

There are multiple types of probabilistic links and depending on the data type and the relevance of the relationships, we can implement one or a combination of linkage approaches with metadata and master data.

Consider two texts: "long John is a better donut to eat" and "John Smith lives in Arizona." If we run a metadata-based linkage between them, the common word that is found is "John," and the two texts will be related where there is no probability of any linkage or relationship. This represents a poor link, also called a weak link.

On the other hand, consider two other texts: "Blink University has released the latest winners list for Dean's list, at deanslist.blinku.edu" and "Contact the Dean's staff via deanslist.blinku.edu." The email address becomes the linkage and can be used to join these two texts and additionally connect the record to a student or dean's subject areas in the higher-education ERP platform. This represents a strong link. The presence of a strong linkage between Big Data and the data warehouse does not mean that a clearly defined business relationship exists between the environments; rather, it is indicative of a type of join within some context being present.

Consider a text or an email:

From: John.Doe@yahoo.com
Subject: bill payment

Dear sir, we are very sorry to inform you that due to your poor customer service we are moving our business elsewhere.

Regards, John Doe

With the customer email address we can always link and process the data with the structured data in the data warehouse. This link is static in nature, as the customer will always update his or her email address. This link is also called a static link. Static links can become a maintenance nightmare if a customer changes his or her information multiple times in a period of time. This is worse if the change is made from an application that is not connected to the current platform. It is easy to process and create static linkages using master data sets.

Another type of linkage that is more common in processing Big Data is called a dynamic link. A dynamic relationship is created on-the-fly in the Big Data environment by a query. When any query executes, it iterates through for one part of the linkage in the unstructured data and next looks for the other part in the structured data. The linkage is complete when the relationship is not a weak probability. In probabilistic linking we will use metadata and semantic data libraries to discover the links in Big Data and implement the master data set when we process the data in the staging area.

Though linkage processing is the best technique known today for processing textual and semi-structured data, its reliance upon quality metadata and master data along with external semantic libraries proves to be a challenge. This can be overcome over a period of time as the data is processed effectively through the system multiple times, increasing the quality and volume of content available for reference processing.

To effectively create the metadata-based integration, a checklist will help create the roadmap:

1. Definition:
   - Data element definitions
   - Data element business names
   - Data element abbreviations/acronyms
   - Data element types and sizes
   - Data element sources
   - Data-quality observations
2. Outline the objectives of the metadata strategy:
   - Goals of the integration
   - Interchange formats
   - Data-quality goals
   - Data scalability of processing
3. Define the scope of the metadata strategy:
   - Enterprise or departmental
4. Define ownership:
   - Who is the steward of the metadata?
   - Who is the program sponsor?
   - Who will sign off on the documents and tests?
5. Define stewardship:
   - Who own the metadata processes and standards?
   - What are the constraints today to process metadata?
6. Master repository:
   - A best-practice strategy is to adopt the concept of a master repository of metadata.
   - This approach should be documented, as well as the location and tool used to store the metadata. If the repository is to be replicated, then the extent of this should also be noted.

7. Metadata maintenance process:
- Explain how the maintenance of metadata is achieved.
- The extent to which the maintenance of metadata is integrated in the warehouse development life cycle and versioning of metadata.
- Who maintains the metadata (e.g., Can users maintain it? Can users record comments or data-quality observations?).

8. User access to metadata:
- How will users interact and use the metadata?

Once the data is processed though the metadata stage, a second pass is normally required with the master data set and semantic library to cleanse the data that was just processed along with its applicable contexts and rules.

Standardize

Preparing and processing Big Data for integration with the data warehouse requires standardizing of data, which will improve the quality of the data. Standardization of data requires the processing of the data with master data components. In the processing of master data, if there are any keys found in the data set, they are replaced with the master data definitions. For example, if you take the data from a social media platform, the chances of finding keys or data attributes that can link to the master data is rare, and will most likely work with geography and calendar data. But if you are processing data that is owned by the enterprise such as contracts, customer data, or product data, the chances of finding matches with the master data are extremely high and the data output from the standardization process can be easily integrated into the data warehouse.

This process can be repeated multiple times for a given data set, as the business rule for each component is different.

Distribute stage

Big Data is distributed to downstream systems by processing it within analytical applications and reporting systems. Using the data processing outputs from the processing stage where the metadata, master data, and metatags are available, the data is loaded into these systems for further processing. Another distribution technique involves exporting the data as flat files for use in other applications like web reporting and content management platforms.

The focus of this section was to provide readers with insights into how by using a data-driven approach and incorporating master data and metadata, you can create a strong, scalable, and flexible data processing architecture needed for processing and integration of Big Data and the data warehouse. There are additional layers of hidden complexity that are addressed as each system is implemented since the complexities differ widely between different systems and applications. In the next section we will discuss the use of machine learning techniques to process Big Data.

Machine learning

From the prior discussions we see that processing Big Data in a data-driven architecture with semantic libraries and metadata provides knowledge discovery and pattern-based processing techniques where the user has the ability to reprocess the data multiple times using different patterns or, in other

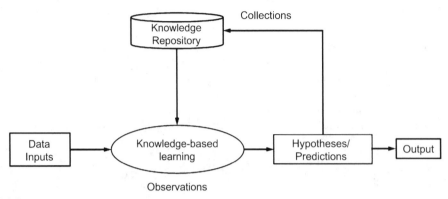

FIGURE 11.9

Machine learning process.

words, process the same data set for multiple contexts. The limitation of this technique is that beyond textual data its applicability is not possible. At this stage is where we bring in machine learning techniques to process data, such as images, videos, graphical information, sensor data, and any other type of data where patterns are easily discernable.

Machine learning can be defined as a knowledge discovery and enrichment process where the machine represented by algorithms mimic human or animal learning techniques and behaviors from a thinking and response perspective. The biggest advantage of incorporating machine learning techniques is the automation aspect of enriching the knowledge base with self-learning techniques with minimal human intervention in the process.

Machine learning is based on a set of algorithms that can process a wide variety of data that normally is difficult to process by hand. These algorithms include:

- Decision tree learning
- Neural networks
- Naive Bayes
- Clustering algorithms
- Genetic algorithms
- Learning algorithms
  - Explanation-based learning
  - Instance-based learning
  - Reinforcement-based learning
  - Support vector machines
- Associative rules
- Recommender algorithms

The implementation of the algorithms is shown in Figure 11.9. The overall steps in implementing any machine learning process are as follows:

1. Gather the data from the inputs.
2. Process the data through the knowledge-based learning algorithms, which observe the data patterns and flags them for processing. The knowledge learning uses data from prior processing

stored in a knowledge repository (an NoSQL- or DBMS-like database) along with the algorithms for machine learning.
3. The data is then processed through the hypothesis workflows.
4. The outputs from a hypothesis and predictive mining exercise are sent to the knowledge repository as a collection with metatags for search criteria and associated user geographic and demographic data.
5. Process the outputs of the hypothesis to outputs for further analysis or presentation to users.

Examples of real-life implementations of machine learning include:

- IBM Watson
- Amazon recommendation engine
- Yelp ratings
- Analysis of astronomical data
- Human speech recognition
- Stream analytics:
  - Credit card fraud
  - Electronic trading fraud
- Google robot-driven vehicles
- Predict stock rates
- Genome classification

Using semantic libraries, metadata, and master data, along with the data collected from each iterative processing, enriches the capabilities of the algorithms to detect better patterns and predict better outcomes.

Let us see how a recommendation engine uses all the data types to create powerful and personalized recommendations. We will use the Amazon website to discuss this process:

1. John Doe searches for movies on Amazon.
2. John Doe receives all the movies relevant to the title he searched for.
3. John Doe also receives recommendations and personalized offers along with the result sets.

How does the system know what else John Doe will be interested in purchasing, and how sure is the confidence score for such a recommendation? This is exactly where we can apply the framework for machine learning shown in Figure 11.9; the process is shown in Figure 11.11.

The first step of the process is a user login or just anonymously executing a search on a website. The search process executes and also simultaneously builds a profile for the user. The search engine produces results that are shared to the user if needed as first-pass output, and adds them to the user profile. As a second step, the search engine executes the personalized recommendation that provides an optimized search result along with recommendations.

In this entire process after the first step, the rest of the search and recommendation workflow follows the machine learning technique and is implemented with the collaborative filtering and clustering algorithms. The user search criteria and the basic user coordinates, including the website, clickstream activity, and geographical data, are all gathered as user profile data, and are integrated with data from the knowledge repository of similar prior user searches. All of this data is processed with machine learning algorithms, and multiple hypothesis results are iterated with confidence scores and the highest score is returned as the closest match to the search. A second pass

FIGURE 11.10

(a) User searches for movie, (b) user gets result sets, and (c) recommendations and personalization.

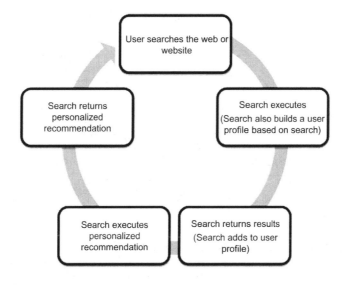

FIGURE 11.11

Search and recommendation process.

of the result set and data from the knowledge repository is processed to optimize the search and this data is returned as personalized offers to the user. Often sponsors of specific products and services provide such offers with incentives that are presented to the user by the recommender algorithm output.

How does machine learning use metadata and master data? In the preceding search example, the metadata is derived for the search elements and tagged with additional data as available. This data is compared and processed with the data from the knowledge repository, which includes semantic libraries, and master data catalogs when the machine learning algorithm is executed. The combination of metadata and master data along with the use of semantic libraries provides a better quality of data to the machine learning algorithm, which in turn produces better quality of output for use by hypothesis and prediction workflows.

Processing data that is very numeric like sensor data, financial data, or credit card data will be based on patterns of numbers that execute as data inputs. These patterns are processed through several mathematical models and their outputs are stored in the knowledge repository, which then shares the stored results back into the processing loop in the machine learning implementation.

Processing data such as images and videos uses conversion techniques to create mathematical data sets for all the nontextual elements. These mathematical data sets are processed through several combinations of data mining and machine learning algorithms, including statistical analysis, linear regression, and polynomial curve-fitting techniques, to create outputs. These outputs are processed further to create a noise-free set of outputs, which can be used for recreating the digital models of images or video data (image only and not audio). Audio is processed as separate feeds and associated with video processing data sets as needed.

Machine learning techniques reduce the complexity of processing Big Data. The most common and popular algorithms for machine learning with web-sale data processing are available in the open-source foundation known as the Apache Mahout project. Mahout is designed to be deployed on Hadoop with minimal configuration efforts and can scale very effectively. While not all machine learning algorithms mandate the need for an enterprise data scientist, this is definitely the most complex area in the processing of large data sets, and having a team of data scientists will definitely be useful for any enterprise.

SUMMARY

As we see from the discussions in this chapter, processing Big Data is indeed a complex and challenging process. Since the room for error in this type of processing is very minimal if allowed, the quality of the data used for processing needs to be very pristine. This can be accomplished by implementing a data-driven architecture that uses all the enterprise data assets available to create a powerful foundation for analysis and integration of data across the Big Data and the DBMS. This foundational architecture is what defines the next generation of data warehousing where all data types are stored and processed to empower an enterprise toward making and executing profitable decisions.

The data in the next-generation data warehouse cannot be growing forever, as the initial size of the new data warehouse starts in the hundreds of terabytes range and normally touches a petabyte very easily. The next chapter will focus on the relevance of information life-cycle management in the age of Big Data, where we need to ensure that the right data sets are always available for processing and consumption by the user at the right time, along with the right metadata. Additionally, the discussion will also focus on when we archive data from Hadoop or NoSQL and how to store that data set if needed for reprocessing.

Information Management and Life Cycle for Big Data

The only things that evolve by themselves in an organization are disorder, friction, and malperformance.
—Peter Drucker

INTRODUCTION

Managing information complexity as data volumes have exploded is one of the biggest challenges since the dawn of information management. In traditional systems the problem has always been the limitations of the RDBMS and the SAN, which over time have continued to be a bottleneck even with the commoditization of hardware and storage. Part of the problem has been about effective information management in terms of metadata and master data management, and part of the problem has been the multiple different technologies that have been deployed in the industry to facilitate data processing, each of which has its own formats. Fast forward and add Big Data to this existing scenario and the problem compounds significantly. How do we deal with this issue, especially considering the fact that Hadoop is being considered as a low-cost storage that can become the enterprise data repository? This chapter deals with how to implement information life-cycle management principles to Big Data and create a sustainable process that will ensure that business continuity is not interrupted and data is available on demand.

Information life-cycle management

Information life-cycle management is the practice of managing the life cycle of data across an enterprise from its creation or acquisition to archival. The concept of information life-cycle management has always existed as "records management" since the early days of computing, but the management of records meant archival and deletion with extremely limited capability to reuse the same data when needed later on. Today, with the advancement in technology and commoditization of infrastructure, managing data is no longer confined to periods of time and is focused as a data management exercise.

Why manage data? The answer to this question lies in the fact that data is a corporate asset and needs to be treated as such. To manage this asset, you need to understand the needs of the enterprise with regards to data life cycle, data security, compliance requirements, regulatory requirements, auditability and traceability, storage and management, metadata and master data requirements, and data stewardship and ownership, which will help you design and implement a robust data governance and management strategy.

Information life-cycle management forms one of the foundational pillars in the management of data within an enterprise. It is the platform on which the three pillars of data management are designed. The first pillar represents process, the second represents the people, and the third represents the technology.

Goals

- Data management as an enterprise function.
- Improve operational efficiencies of systems and processes.
- Reduce total cost of ownership by streamlining the use of hardware and resources.
- Productivity gains by reducing errors and improving overall productivity by automating data management and life cycle.
- Implement an auditable system.
- Reduce system failure risk.
- Provide business continuity.
- Maintain flexibility to add new requirements.

Information life-cycle management consists of the subcomponents shown in Figure 12.1.

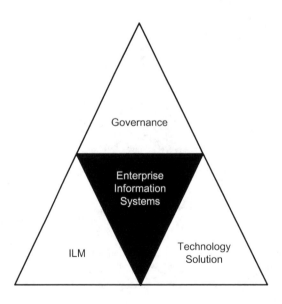

FIGURE 12.1

Information life-cycle management components as applied to the enterprise.

Information management policies

The policies that define the business rules for the data life cycle from acquisition, cleansing, transformation, retention, and security are called information management policies:

- Data acquisition policies are defined:
  - Applications where data entry functions are performed
  - Web and OLTP applications
  - Data warehouse or datamart ETL or CDC processes
  - Analytical databases ETL processes
- Data transformation policies are business rules to transform data from source to destination, and include transformation of granularity levels, keys, hierarchies, metrics, and aggregations.
- Data quality policies are defined as part of data transformation processes.
- Data retention:
  - Traditionally, data retention policies have been targeted at managing database volumes across the systems within the enterprise in an efficient way by developing business rules and processes to relocate data from online storage in the database to an offline storage in the file. The offline data can be stored at remote secure sites. The retention policy needs to consider the requirements for data that mandates support for legal case management, compliance auditing management, and electronic discovery.
  - With Big Data and distributed storage on commodity hardware, the notion of offline storage is now more a label. All data is considered active and accessible all the time. The goals of data retention shift to managing the compression and storage of data across the disk architecture. The challenge in the new generation will be on the most efficient techniques of data management.
- Data security policies are oriented toward securing data from an encryption and obfuscation perspective and also data security from a user access perspective.

Governance

Information and program governance are two important aspects of managing information within an enterprise. Information governance deals with setting up governance models for data within the enterprise and program governance deals with implementing the policies and processes set forth in information governance. Both of these tasks are fairly people-specific as they involve both the business user and the technology teams.

A governance process is a multistructured organization of people who play different roles in managing information. The hierarchy of the different bodies of the governance program is shown in Figure 12.2, and the roles and responsibilities are outlined in the following subsections.

Executive governance board
- Consists of stakeholders from the executive teams or their direct reports.
- Responsible for overall direction and funding.

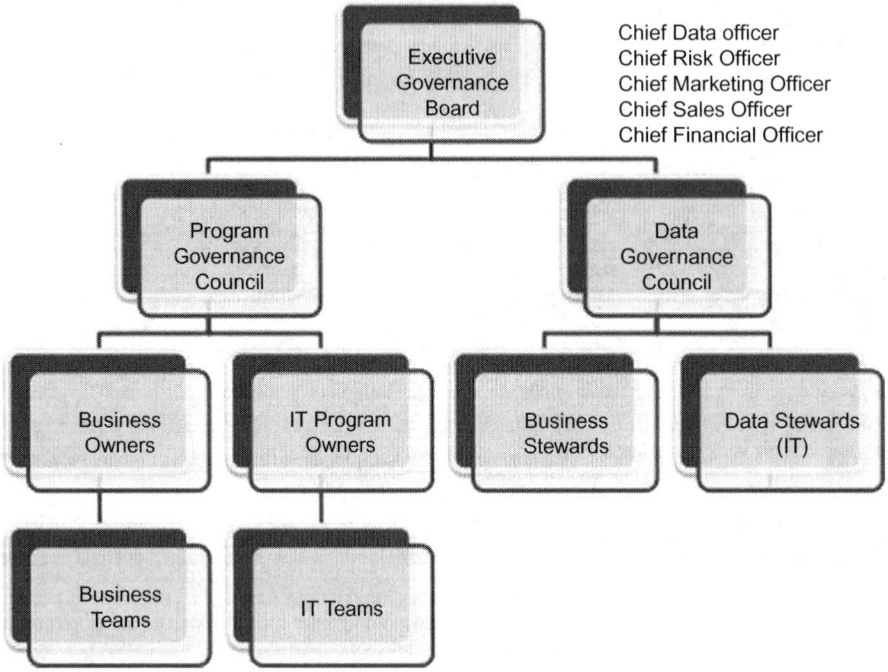

FIGURE 12.2

Data governance teams.

Program governance council
- Consists of program owners who are director-level members of the executive organization. There can be multiple representatives in one team for a small organization, while a large organization can have multiple smaller teams that will fold into a large charter team.
- Responsible for overall direction of the program, management of business and IT team owners, coordination of activities, management of budget, and prioritization of tasks and programs.

Business owners
- Represent the business teams in the council. These are program heads within the business unit (marketing, finance, sales, etc.).
- Responsible for leading the business unit's program initiative and its implementation as a stakeholder.

Business teams
- Consists of members of a particular business unit, for example, marketing or market research or sales.
- Responsible for implementing the program and data governance policies in their projects, report to the council on issues and setbacks, and work with the council on resolution strategies.

IT owners
- Consists of IT project managers assigned to lead the implementation and support for a specific business unit.
- Responsible for leading the IT teams to work on the initiative, the project delivery, issue resolution, and conflict management, and work with the council to solve any issue that can impact a wider audience.

IT teams
- Consists of members of IT teams assigned to work with a particular business team for implementing the technology layers and supporting the program.
- Responsible for implementing the program and data governance technologies and frameworks in the assigned projects, report to the council on issues and setbacks, and work with the council on resolution strategies.

Data governance council
- Consists of business and IT stakeholders from each unit in the enterprise. The members are SMEs who own the data for that business unit and are responsible for making the appropriate decisions for the integration of the data into the enterprise architecture while maintaining their specific requirements within the same framework.
- Responsible for:
  - Data definition
  - Data-quality rules
  - Metadata
  - Data access policy
  - Encryption requirements
  - Obfuscation requirements
  - Master data management policies
  - Issue and conflict resolution
  - Data retention policies

Governance has been a major focus area for large and midsize enterprises for implementing a successful business transformation initiative, which includes data and information management as a subcomponent. Properly executed governance for both data and program aspects have benefitted enterprises by providing confidence to the teams executing business decisions based on the information available in the enterprise. These initiatives have increased ROI and decreased risk when implemented with the right rigor.

Technology
Implementing the program from a concept to reality within data governance falls in the technology layers. There are several different technologies that are used to implement the different aspects of governance. These include tools and technologies used in Data acquisition, Data cleansing, Data transformation and Database code such as stored procedures, programming modules coded as application programming interface (API), Semantic technologies and Metadata libraries.

Data quality
- Is implemented as a part of the data movement and transformation processes.
- Is developed as a combination of business rules developed in ETL/ELT programs and third-party data enrichment processes.

- Is measured in percentage of corrections required per execution per table. The lower the percentage of corrections, the higher the quality of data.

Data enrichment

- This is not a new subject area in the world of data. We have always enriched data to improve its accuracy and information quality.
- In the world of Big Data, data enrichment is accomplished by integrating taxonomies, ontologies, and third-party libraries as a part of the data processing architecture.
- Enriched data will provide the user capabilities:
  - To define and manage hierarchies.
  - To create new business rules on-the-fly for tagging and classifying the data.
  - To process text and semi-structured data more efficiently.
  - Explore and process multilingual and multistructured data analysis.

Data transformation

- Is implemented as part of ETL/ELT processes.
- Is defined as business requirements by the user teams.
- Uses master data and metadata program outputs for referential data processing and data standardization.
- Is developed by IT teams.
- Includes auditing and traceability framework components for recording data manipulation language (DML) outputs and rejects from data quality and integrity checks.

Data archival and retention

- Is implemented as part of the archival and purging process.
- Is developed as a part of the database systems by many vendors.
- Is often misquoted as a database feature.
- Often fails when legacy data is imported back due to lack of correct metadata and underlying structural changes. This can be avoided easily by exporting the metadata and the master data along with the data set.

Master data management

- Is implemented as a standalone program.
- Is implemented in multiple cycles for customers and products.
- Is implemented for location, organization, and other smaller data sets as an add-on by the implementing organization.
- Measured as a percentage of changes processed every execution from source systems.
- Operationalized as business rules for key management across operational, transactional, warehouse, and analytical data

Metadata

- Is implemented as a data definition process by business users,
- Has business-oriented definitions for data for each business unit. One central definition is regarded as the enterprise metadata view of the data.

- Has IT definitions for metadata related to data structures, data management programs, and semantic layers within the database.
- Has definitions for semantic layers implemented for business intelligence and analytical applications.

All the technologies used in the processes described above have a database, a user interface for managing data, rules and definitions, and reports available on the processing of each component and its associated metrics.

There are many books and conferences on the subject of data governance and program governance. We recommend readers peruse the available material for continued reading on implementing governance for a traditional data warehouse.[1-4]

Benefits of information life-cycle management

- Increases process efficiencies.
- Helps enterprises optimize data quality.
- Accelerates ROI.
- Helps reduce the total cost of ownership for data and infrastructure investments.
- Data management strategies help in managing data and holistically improve all the processes, including:
  - Predictable system availability
  - Optimized system performance
  - Improved reusability of resources
  - Improved management of metadata and master data
  - Improved systems life-cycle management
  - Streamlined operations management of data life cycle
  - Legal and compliance requirements
  - Metadata life-cycle management
  - Master data management
  - Optimize spending and costs
  - Reduce data-related risks

With the advance of technology and commoditization of infrastructure it has become easier to implement information life-cycle management processes today than ever before.

Information life-cycle management for Big Data

The advent of Big Data is a boon and a curse to many enterprises. The reason for this sentiment is the unique set of challenges being brought by Big Data in terms of volume, velocity, and variety of data. Many enterprises today are planning to implement a Big Data project and designing an information life-cycle management program to help manage and streamline the Big Data.

[1] Ladley, J. (2012). How to Design, Deploy and Sustain an Effective Data Governance Program. Morgan Kaufmann.
[2] Soares, S. (2012). Big Data Governance: An Emerging Imperative. MC PressLLC.
[3] Orr, J. C. (2011). Data Governance For The Executive. Senna Publishing.
[4] Hill, D. G. (2009). Data Protection: Governance, Risk Management, and Compliance. Taylor & Francis Group.

Big Data acquisition and processing has been discussed in prior chapters in this book. While the technology is inexpensive to acquire the data, there are several complexities with managing and processing the data within the new technology environments and further integrating it with the RDBMS or DBMS. A governance process and methodology is required to manage all of these processes.

Data in the Big Data world is largely created and stored as files. All the processes associated with managing data and processing data are file-based, whether in Hadoop or NoSQL environments. While the new technologies are special file systems, simply deleting files will not be the right solution, and we need to create a robust and well-defined data retention and archiving strategy.

Processing data in the Big Data world uses enterprise metadata and master data. With the volume and data type to be processed, we need to implement policies to manage this environment extremely closely to prevent any unwanted alterations.

Example: information life-cycle management and social media data

Social media data is one of the most popular data assets that every organization likes to tap into for getting a clearer view of their customers and the likes and dislikes that are being expressed by their customers about their products, services, competition, and the impact of the sharing of these sentiments. The data for this exercise is extracted from social media channels and websites, Internet forums and user communities, and consumer websites and reviews.

There is a lot of hidden value within the data from social media and there are several insights that provide critical clues to the success or failure of a particular brand related to a campaign, product, service, and more. The bigger questions are: What is the value of the data once the initial discoveries have been completed? Is there any requirement to keep the data to actually monitor the trend? Or is a statistical summary enough to accomplish the same result?

In the case of social media data, the lifetime value of the data is very short—from the time of acquisition to insights the entire process may take hours to a week probably. The information life-cycle management policy for this data will be storage for two to four weeks for the raw data, six to eight weeks for processed data sets after the processing of the raw data, and then one to three years for summary data aggregated from processed data sets to be used in analytics. The reason for this type of a policy suggestion is the raw data does not have value once it has been processed with the different types of business rules and the processed data sets do not carry value beyond the additional eight weeks. Data is typically discarded from the storage layer and is not required to be stored offline or offsite for any further reuse or reloading.

Without creating a governance policy on information life-cycle management for data, we will end up collecting a lot of data that is having no business impact or value, and end up wasting processing and computing cycles. A strong information life-cycle management policy is necessary for ensuring the success of Big Data.

From this example we can see that managing the information life cycle for Big Data is similar to any other data, but there are some areas that need special attention and can impact your Big Data program negatively if not implemented. Let us look at each aspect in the following section.

Governance

From a Big Data perspective you need both data and program governance to be implemented.

Data governance
- Data retention:
    - What data should be retained?

- What are the associated metadata and master data that need to be processed with the data to be retained?
  - What data will be archived?
- Data security: What are the user security and data security requirements?
- Metadata: What taxonomies will be needed to manage data?
- Business rules: What are the tools and associated business rules for processing?
- Data stewardship: Who owns the data type?
  - Documents—legal, HR, finance, and customer service are all business units to consider
  - Videos, audio, and images
  - Email
  - Call center
  - Social media
  - Content management data
- Audit, balance, and control:
  - What data needs to be audited?
  - What data needs reprocessing in failure situations?
- External data integration:
  - External taxonomies can be integrated to process additional hierarchies and master data enrichment in processing Big Data. You need to understand the granularity and hierarchy of the external data.
  - Third-party data from agencies can be integrated to create reference data and lookup data.
- EDW integration:
  - Data extracts to the data warehouse need to be defined.
  - Metadata integration with the enterprise data needs to be managed and monitored.
  - The integration refresh cycles need to be defined.
  - Data structures to store the Big Data need to be defined and implemented.

Program governance

A strong framework for managing the projects and the people pillars forms the crux of program governance. While there are no significant differences in program governance approaches, the following can be extended:

- What projects are currently being driven to enable information life-cycle management?
- Who are the teams that are assigned to the different programs?
- What is the cost of the implementation for each cycle for each project?
- What are the risks and identified mitigation strategies?
- What are the critical areas that need executive alerts?
- What are the critical priorities and the impact of changes to the priority to the program schedule?
- What are the budgetary constraints that impact the program?

Processing

- The data acquisition process in the world of Big Data has no predefined process. The audit process framework needs to be extended to include Big Data processing. The audit data will consist of the file name, date of process, size, and source (if available).
- Data processing in the world of Big Data contains no predefined schema to model and load the data. In this situation, extra attention needs to be given to metadata management. There

will be multiple cycles of processing of the same data for different subject areas. This is where the complexity of metadata management will need to be addressed in the Big Data processing.
- There is no data-quality processing for Big Data. To enrich and improve the quality of data, you need to include metadata, master data, taxonomies, and other reference data in the processing of Big Data.
- Data storage and management of Big Data requires planning of infrastructure integration and data center planning. This is a part of the planning process for Big Data integration.

Technology
- The technologies for implementing Big Data are Hadoop, NoSQL, and text processing technologies. All these technologies treat the data as files, and create and process multiple files from the various sources as files, producing the output as files.
- In Hadoop, the availability of too many files will cause the NameNode to slow down and impact performance. To mitigate the risk associated with this situation, Hadoop introduced a process called Hadoop Archive (HAR). HAR comes with its own file system implementation and consolidates small- and medium-size files into one large file. The subfiles are available and stored in HAR.
- Since Hadoop is a file system, large data files can be exported and dropped from the primary system. This will create more space for processing. A file can always be restored from the source environment and moved for reconciliation.

Measuring the impact of information life-cycle management

To measure and monitor the impact of governance and processes for information life-cycle management, you can implement scorecards and dashboards and even extend the currently used models for the data warehouse. This is a very nascent and emerging topic, but an important topic to consider implementing when starting a Big Data program. There will be a lot of evolutions and improvements in this area in the next few years, especially in the world of Big Data and the next generation of the data warehouse.

SUMMARY

As we conclude this chapter, you need to understand that governance and information life-cycle management are topics that are extremely important in the world of data management and will be even more important in the world of Big Data and the next generation of data warehousing. The next chapter discusses the evolution of analytics and visualization of Big Data and the emerging role of the data scientist.

Big Data Analytics, Visualization, and Data Scientists

Most people use statistics the way a drunkard uses a lamp post,
more for support than illumination.
—Mark Twain

INTRODUCTION

The biggest impact of Big Data is the ability to analyze events that have happened within and outside an organization and correlate them to provide near-accurate insights into what drove the outcomes. In the case of corporate data or noncustomer-oriented data, there are details that can be explored using powerful algorithms, business rules, and statistical models, and this data includes text, image, audio, video, and machine data. To create the foundational structure for analytics and visualization of the data, you need to have subject-matter experts who can understand the different layers of data being integrated and what granularity levels of integration can be completed to create the holistic picture.

There is a new role in the world of data management that has evolved with Big Data called a data scientist. There are several definitions for this role that are evolving, including data analysts with advanced mathematical degrees, statisticians with multiple specialist degrees, and much more. In simple terms, a data scientist is a role where the person has intimate knowledge of the data being discovered and can effectively explore the data and infer relationships that create the foundation for analytics and visualization.

This chapter focuses on what analytics and visualization are in the world of Big Data, some of the commonly available tools that can be used for data discovery, the role of the data scientist, and the next evolution of Big Data platforms.

Big Data analytics

Analytics programs provide a platform and the opportunity to measure everything across an enterprise. The associated effect of this approach is the creation of transparency across the different layers of data, its associated processes, and methods, and exposing insights into potential opportunities, threats, risks, and issues. Executives, when provided outcomes from analytical exercises, gain better understanding of the decisions and can provide more effective guidance to their enterprise as a whole.

Big Data analytics can be defined as the combination of traditional analytics and data mining techniques along with large volumes of data to create a foundational platform to analyze, model, and predict the behavior of customers, markets, products, services, and the competition, thereby enabling an outcomes-based strategy precisely tailored to meet the needs of the enterprise for that market and customer segment. Big Data analytics provides a real opportunity for enterprises to transform themselves into an innovative organization that can plan, predict, and grow markets and services, driving toward higher revenue.

How does this work in reality? For example, when you engage in a web search for a product, you can see that along with results for the product you searched, you are provided details on sales, promotions, and coupons for the product in your geographical area and the nearest ten miles, as well as promotions being offered by web retailers. Analyzing the data needed to create the search results tailored to meet your individual search results, we can see that the companies who have targeted you for a promotional offer or a discount coupon have used the outcomes of behavioral analytics from clickstream data of thousands of other people who have searched for a similar product or service, and combined them with promotional data targeted for your geographical area to compete for your wallet share. Sometimes all of these activities are done by a third-party company as a service and these third-party vendors use Big Data processing and analytics techniques to provide this kind of service.

Analyzing this data further we can see that clickstream data by itself provides insights into the clicks of a user on a web page, the page from which the user landed into the current page, the page the user visited next from the current page, the amount of time the user spent between clicks, and how many times the user engaged in a search for a category of product or service. By creating a data model to link the web page and all these measurements, we can convert simple clicks into measurable results along with time as an associated dimension. This data can then be integrated with promotional data or campaign data to produce the offers, which are tailored to suit your needs at that point in time. Further to this basic processing, predictive analytical models can be created to predict how many users will convert from a searcher to a buyer, the average amount of time spent by these users, the number of times this conversion happened, the geographies where these conversions happened, and how many times in a given campaign such conversions can happen. While we have had similar processes created and deployed in traditional solutions, we can see by combining Big Data and traditional processes together, the effectiveness of the predictive analytics and their accuracy is greatly improved.

Another example of Big Data analytics is what you experience when you shop online today. The most popular websites offer a personalized recommendation along with products or services that you shop for. These recommendations have positively impacted the bottom line for all the e-retailers that have invested in this approach. What drives a recommendation engine and how does it tailor the results to what each individual shopper searches for? If you take a step back and think through the data needed for this interaction to happen, the recommendation engine principle works on the data collected from search and purchase information that is available as clickstream and market-basket data, which is harvested as lists and integrated using metadata along with geospatial and time information. For example, if you search for a book on Big Data, the recommendation engine will return to you a search result and also a recommendation of popular titles that were searched when other people searched for a similar book, and additionally provides to you another recommendation on a set of books that you can buy similar to other's purchases. This data and number-crunching exercise is a result set of analytics from Big Data.

A consumer-friendly example of everyday analytics is the usage of smart meters to help monitor and regulate power usage. Data from the smart meters can be read on an hourly basis and, depending on the latitude and longitude coordinates, the time of day, and the weather conditions for the hour and next few hours, power companies can generate models to personalize the power consumption details for a customer. This proactive interaction benefits both the parties positively and improves the financial expenditure for the consumer. This type of analytics and personalized services is being implemented on a global basis by many countries.

Big Data analytics can be used to create an effective strategy for healthcare providers. Today, whole-body scanners and X-ray machines store data electronically and this data is hosted by data centers of large equipment manufacturers, and accessed by private cloud services. Harnessing the infrastructure capabilities, different providers can study the patient data from multiple geographies and their reviews can be stored electronically along with recommended treatment options. This data over a period of time can be used as an electronic library of treatments, disease state management, and demographic data. We can create heatmaps on the most effective treatments and predict with confidence what therapies are effective for regions of the world, and even extend this to include gene therapies and genetic traits based on regions of the world and ethnicity. Doctors can derive propensity analytics to predict outcomes, and insurance companies can even harvest this data to manage the cost of insurance.

As we see from these examples, Big Data analytics create an explosion of possibilities when the data is analyzed, modeled, and integrated with corporate data in an integrated environment with traditional analytics and metrics. There are several techniques to create algorithms for Big Data, which we have discussed in earlier chapters. There are several algorithms that are available for implementation in the open-source project Mahout.[1]

To summarize this section, Big Data analytics is the process of discovering patterns and insights from Big Data and modeling them for use with corporate data. The results of Big Data processing for analytics can be modeled as a list of key attributes, and its associated values that can leverage the existing metadata and semantic layers for integration with traditional data.

The next section discusses the data discovery process for Big Data and how to prepare the data for visualization.

Data discovery

The process of data discovery for analytics can be defined in these distinct steps:

- *Data acquisition* is the process of collecting the data for discovery. This includes gathering the files and preparing the data for import using a tool. This can be accomplished using popular data visualization tools like Datameer, Karmasphere, and R.
- *Data tagging* is the process of creating an identifying link on the data for metadata integration.
- *Data classification* is the process of creating subsets of value pairs for data processing and integration. An example of this is extracting website URL in clickstream data along with page-view information.
- *Data modeling* is the process of creating a model for data visualization or analytics. The output from this step can be combined into an extraction exercise.

---

[1] *http://mahout.apache.org/.*

Once the data is prepared for analysis in the discovery stage, the users can extract the result sets from any stage and use them for integration. These steps require a skill combination of data analytics and statistical modeling, which is the role of a data scientist. The question that confronts users today is how to do the data discovery: Do you develop MapReduce code extensively, or do you use software like Datameer or Karmasphere?

The answer to this question is simple; rather than develop extensive lines of MapReduce code, which may not be reusable, you can adopt to using tools like Datameer or Karmasphere that actually can produce the MapReduce code based on the operations that you execute. Datameer has a library of functions that has been developed that can be used in a drag-and-drop fashion to create a powerful discovery module. Karmasphere works on Hive, which lets you write SQL and HQL constructs to interrogate data for discovery processes.

Depending on whichever method you choose to architect the solution your data discovery framework is the key to developing Big Data analytics within your organization. Once the data is ready for visualization, you can integrate the data with mashups and other powerful visualization tools and provide the dashboards to the users.

Visualization

Big Data visualization is not like traditional business intelligence where the data is interactive and can be processed as drilldowns and rollups in a hierarchy or can be drilled into in a real-time fashion. This data is static in nature and will be minimally interactive in a visualization situation. The underlying reason for this static nature is due to the design of the Big Data platform like Hadoop or NoSQL, where the data is stored in files and not table structured, and processing changes will require massive file operations, which are best performed in a microbatch environment as opposed to a real-time environment. This limitation is being addressed in the next generation of Hadoop and other Big Data platforms.

Today, the data that is available for visualization is largely integrated using mashup tools and software that support such functionality, including Datameer, Karmasphere, Tableau, and Spotfire. The mashup platform provides the capability for the user to integrate data from multiple streams into one picture, by linking common data between the different data sets.

For example, if you are looking at integrating customer sentiment analytics with campaign data, field sales data, and competitive research data, the mashup that will be created to view all of this information will be integrating the customer sentiment with campaign data using product and geography information, the competitive research data and the campaign data using geography information, and the sales data and the campaign data using the product and geography information. This data set can be queried interactively and can be used for what-if type of causal analysis by different users across the organization.

Another form of visualization of Big Data is delivered through the use of statistical software like R, SAS, and KXEN, where the predefined models for different statistical functions can use the data extracted from the discovery environment and integrate it with corporate and other data sets to drive the statistical visualizations. Very popular software that uses R for accomplishing this type of functionality is RStudio.

The evolving role of data scientists

The key role that enables the difference between success and failure of a Big Data program is a data scientist. The term was originally coined by two of the original data scientists, D. J. Patil and Jeff Hammerbacher, when they were working at LinkedIn and Facebook.

What defines a data scientist? Is this a special skill or education? How different are these roles from an analyst or engineer? There is no standard definition for the role of a data scientist, but here is a close description: A data scientist is an expert business analyst or an engineer who uses data discovery tools to find new insights in data by using techniques that are statistical or scientific in nature. They work on a variety of hypotheses and design multiple models that they experiment with to arrive at new insights. To accomplish this they use a large volume of data, which is collectively called Big Data.

Data scientists work very closely with data and often question everything that is input or output from the data. In fact, in every enterprise there are a handful of senior business analysts or data analysts who are playing the role of data scientist without being formally called as one.

Data scientists use the data discovery tools discussed in this chapter to create the visualization and analytics associated with Big Data. This role is still in evolution phases, and in the future we will see many teams of data scientists in enterprises as opposed to the handful who we see today. If data is the new oil, then the data scientist is the new explorer. As we evolve the data within enterprises from now into the future, we will need more explorers who can journey through the data asking the questions of why and where looking for insights and patterns. This is the role that will largely fall onto the Data Scientist teams.

SUMMARY

In summary, we can use Big Data to enhance analytics and deliver data for visualization and deeper analysis as needed by an enterprise. There are evolving techniques, methods, and technologies to accomplish this on a regular basis within enterprises. The underlying goal that is delivered with Big Data analytics is the capability to drive innovation and transformation across the enterprise in a transparent and informed manner, where you can tie the outcomes to the predictions and vice versa. The possibilities are endless and can be delivered from the same data set as it is transformed in discovery processes. This kind of a flexible approach is what you should adapt to when designing the solutions for Big Data analytics and visualization.

In the next chapter we will examine three real-life implementations of Big Data within large enterprises where the business transformation was delivered at an exceedingly quick pace with measurable results and actionable insights.

Implementing the Big Data – Data Warehouse – Real-Life Situations

Not everything that can be counted counts, and not everything that counts can be counted.
—**Albert Einstein**

INTRODUCTION: BUILDING THE BIG DATA – DATA WAREHOUSE

The next-generation data warehouse is an integrated architecture of Big Data and traditional data in one heterogeneous platform. This is not the trend but will be the norm that is being adopted by large enterprises. The question that confronts everybody is not why, but rather how to implement such a complex architecture and what is the underlying business case to be developed for this initiative, the cost of deployment, and the value realization from the new platform. This chapter discusses the real-life implementation of the next-generation platform by three different companies and the direction they each have chosen from a technology and architecture perspective.

Customer-centric business transformation

A leading multichannel multifaceted business organization recently started an enterprise transformation program to move from being a product or services organization to a customer-oriented or customer-centric organization. The primary drivers for the business transformation include:

- CEO requests on business insights and causal analysis.
- Competitive research teams want more accurate data from customers, outside of the organizational efforts like surveys, call center conversations, and third-party surveys.
- Customer attrition citing lack of satisfaction.
- Lackluster campaign performance.
- Same store sales and staff performance.
- Executive requests on corporate performance.
- Inventory and warehouse spending and cost issues.
- Improve web channel performance.
- Implement recommendation engines online.
- Implement a robust customer sentiment analytics program.
- Product propensity analytics.
- Demographic analytics.

There are significant issues in the data platforms in the current-state architecture within this enterprise that prevent the deployment of solutions on incumbent technologies. The landscape of the current-state architecture includes:

- Multiple source systems and transactional databases totaling about 10 TB per year in data volumes.
- A large POS network across hundreds of locations.
- Online web transactional databases driving about 7 TB of data per year.
- Catalog and mail data totaling about 3 TB per year in unstructured formats.
- Call center data across all lines of business totaling about 2 TB per year.
- Three data warehouses each containing about 50 TB of data for four years of data.
- Statistical and analytical databases each about 10 TB in summary data for four years of data.

The complexity of this environment also includes metadata databases, MDM systems, and reference databases that are used in processing the data throughout the system.

The current-state complaint points in processing these volumes of data include:

- Data processing does not complete everyday across all the systems:
  - Too many sources to data warehouse extracts.
  - Too many processes for data transformation.
  - Too many repetitive business rules.
  - Too many data-quality exceptions.
- Too many redundant copies of data across the data warehouses, datamarts, statistical databases, and ODS.
- Analytical queries do not complete processing.
- Analytical cube refresh does not complete.
- Drilldown and drill-across dimensions cannot be processed on more than two or three quarters of data.

Figure 14.1 shows the conceptual architecture of the current-state platforms in the enterprise.

To satisfy the business drivers along with current-state performance issues, this enterprise formed a SWAT team to set the strategy and direction for developing a flexible, elastic, and scalable future-state architecture.

The future-state architecture for the enterprise data platform was developed with the following goals and requirements:

- Goals:
  - Align best-fit technology and applications.
  - Reduce overhead in data management.
  - Reduce cost and spending on incumbent technologies.
  - Implement governance processes for program and data management.
- Requirements:
  - Ask any question about anything at any time.
  - Query data from social media, unstructured content, and web database on one interface.
  - Process clickstream and web activity data for near-real-time promotions for online shoppers.

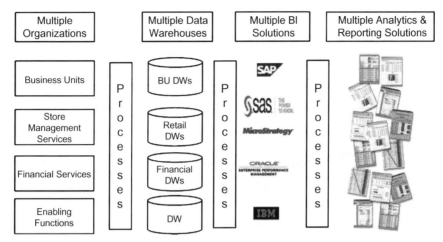

FIGURE 14.1

Current state architecture.

- Provide access to data in a self-service platform from executives to store managers.
- Create a scalable analytics platform for use by data scientists.
- Reduce processing complexity.
- Create an enterprise data repository.
- Increase data quality.

To create a robust future-state architecture that can satisfy all the data requirements, goals, and business requirements, the technology platforms that were considered included incumbent technologies like Teradata and Oracle, Big Data platforms like Hadoop and NoSQL, and applications software like Datameer and Tableau.

The overall architecture was designed on a combination of all of these technologies and the data and applications were classified into different tiers that were defined based on performance, data volumes, cost, and data availability.

The overall benefit of this approach resulted in creating a scalable architecture that utilized technologies from incumbent platforms and new technology platforms that were implemented at a low cost of entry and ownership, and retiring several incumbent technologies and data processing layers, which provided an instant ROI.

The tiered technology approach enabled the enterprise to create the architecture layout as shown in Figure 14.2.

The enterprise architecture team used the tiering approach to present the criteria for the different systems to be allocated to a particular tier in the architecture layers. At the end of the exercise the enterprise data repository was designed and deployed on Hadoop as the storage repository. This included all the current historical data in the multiple data warehouses and other systems. To complete the integration, new data architecture models were developed and data processing rules were assigned to each data layer in the data architecture, along with data quality, auditing, metadata, and master data

	Criteria	Cost	Consumption	Data Volume	Availability	Frequency of Update
Tier 4 Platform – Enterprise Decision Support Platforms Teradata / Oracle / DB2	Tier 4	High	Large amount of users	Large	High	Intra-Day
Tier 3 Platform – Reporting and Analytics Platforms Columnar DB / Appliance	Tier 3	Lower compared to tier 1	Mixed volume of users	High	Lower compared to tier 1	Daily / Batch
Tier 2 Platform – Data Exploration Platforms Hadoop / MySQL / Columnar	Tier 2	Lower compared to tier 1	Mixed volume of users	Extra Large	Lower compared to tier 2	Batch
Tier 1 Platform – Enterprise Data Repository Hadoop	Tier 1	Lower compared to tier 1	Low volume of users	Very Large	Lower compared to tier 2	Near Real Time
Tier 0 Platform – Data Storage Platform Hadoop	Tier 0	Lower compared to tier 1	Low volume of users	Very Large	Lower compared to tier 2	Monthly Batch

FIGURE 14.2

Tiered technology architecture.

solutions. A data map was developed to match each tier of data, which enabled the integration of other tiers of the architecture on new or incumbent technologies as available in the enterprise.

Once the data architecture was deployed and laid out across the new data warehouse, the next step was to address the reporting and analytics platforms. The multiple reporting platforms were retired and three new platforms in total were selected for enterprise analytics and reporting, which resulted in a new program for managing this migration.

The migration and implementation of this new architecture was deployed as a multiple-phased migration plan and it lasted several phases and programs that were executed in parallel.

Outcomes

At the end of about ten months into the migration to the new data architecture platform for the data warehouse, the enterprise began the implementation of the key business drivers that were the underlying reason for the exercise of the data platform. The benefits of a customer-centric business transformation provide the enterprise with immense business benefits that were measurable results in terms of improvement in profitability, reacquisition of customer confidence, ability to understand customer sentiment beyond the call center, ability to execute campaigns with predictable outcomes, manage store performance with deeper insights on customers and competition, and perform profitability analytics by integrating market behaviors to store performance. All of these activities are performed on both Hadoop and RDBMS platforms in different stages and phases of analytics and reporting. The integrated architecture that is deployed in this enterprise is the actual footprint that will begin to exist as the Big Data – data warehouse.

Hadoop and MySQL drives innovation

Another implementation of a Big Data–based data warehouse architecture is driven by integrating and augmenting the incumbent platform with a Hadoop and MySQL architecture. The difference in this architecture approach is the migration from a traditional RDBMS to the new data architecture platform.

The business problem is a leading electronics manufacturer has been having a weak market penetration with its products and services. The biggest threats facing the enterprise include loss of traditional markets, increased customer attrition, poor market performance from a wallet-share perspective, lack of customer confidence, and overall weak performance.

The executive teams within the enterprise were unhappy about the situation and were mandated by the board to regain the brand value in the market. The team started conducting studies to understand the cause of the issues, and found the following:

- The product suite manufactured by the enterprise was not reflecting the market demands of the geographies they were sold to.
- The competition was producing similar products with slightly better features at a lower cost.
- The services provided by the enterprise after the product sale were minimal and lackluster.
- The market pricing strategy did not accurately reflect socioeconomic conditions.
- Customer reviews and feedback about the products and services were largely not considered beyond market research teams.
- Call center teams were not equipped with the right information when customers called for help and advice, resulting in disappointing and embarrassing situations.

Deeper investigation into the current-state issues revealed the following architectural issues:

- The source systems were deployed globally and the data in each of these systems was based on requirements for the local market.
- Each source system had different pieces of information about the product.
- All the product data was buried in textual manuals and was not available digitally.
- Each region of the world had customer feedback both solicited via surveys and unsolicited in web forums and social media.
- Competitive research teams across the world were working on different data sets.
- Vendor management was not a centralized function.
- Financial systems were consolidating data from multiple systems across the world. The integration was not based on auditable data.

The enterprise architecture and data teams were assigned with the task of creating a future-state architecture that enabled the incumbent data warehouse to be extensible and scalable, while meeting the requirements of the enterprise globally. The teams decided to evaluate the following platforms in addition to the incumbent RDBMS platform:

- Hadoop—the Big Data platform can be deployed as the enterprise repository of data. With its lower cost and greater scalability, the platform will bring a lot of performance boost to the overall data architecture.

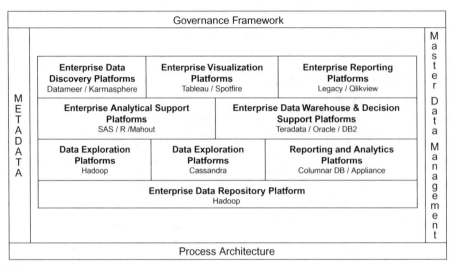

FIGURE 14.3

Big Data modular architecture conceptual model.

- MySQL—this database technology can be deployed to manage the web databases where transactional data needs to be managed. Low-cost and simple replication techniques are the biggest draws for this technology in the data architecture.
- NoSQL—Cassandra or HBase will be useful to manage nontransactional data such as call center data and text analytics data.
- Textual analytics databases—can be useful in managing textual data without having to worry about deploying MapReduce code.
- Datameer, Karmasphere, and R—can be used by the team of analysts and business users to create powerful data mining models.

The technologies were aligned and integrated into a powerful data roadmap, which was visualized as a Lego building block. This approach helped the team of architects to isolate the data by source, type, processing complexity, analytical requirements, security and compliance requirements, performance and service level requirements, data volumes, retention requirements, taxonomy integration, metadata integration, and master data integration. The data isolated with this technique was modeled based on each layer's input and output requirements and the interfaces that needed to be developed.

Once the design approach was finalized as shown in Figure 14.3, the next steps the architecture teams followed were:

- Created additional data governance process for integrating all data types into the new data warehouse.
- Created the data interfaces for each technology layer using metadata-driven interfaces.
- Created a migration plan for moving history and legacy data along with the respective metadata to Hadoop.

- Created a best-practices approach for deploying Cassandra and HBase across the different regions of the world, where the data interfaces were deployed based on corporate standards. The design also included cross–data center replications to ensure availability.
- Integrated a semantic data discovery platform with interfaces to internal and external products and service hierarchies.
- Created and deployed a tagging process for data management and integration, especially with unstructured data.
- Implemented a metadata integration and reference architecture for centralized management of metadata across the enterprise.
- Designed and developed data parsing algorithms for integrating semi-structured and unstructured data components.
- Integrated algorithms for parsing machine logs and clickstream logs to understand the user and device behaviors.
- Integrated algorithms for predictive analytics integration.
- Integrated algorithms for statistical modeling and integration.
- Integrated reporting and visualization platforms into the different data layers.
- Provided business users capabilities to discover, analyze, and visualize data across the enterprise in an integrated platform.

The implementation process was a planned migration to the heterogeneous platform over 24 months on a global basis. The main benefits of the architecture were:

- Design once and deploy in parallel worldwide
- Modular scalability
- Standardization
- Lower cost of maintenance
- Higher scalability and flexibility
- Security standards compliant
- Always available
- Self-service capabilities
- Fault tolerant
- Easy recovery from failure

Benefits

Based on the revised architecture approach to implementing a new data warehouse, the enterprise has started realizing a quick ROI on their analytics and data discovery processes. The business users have been able to measure the performance of the enterprise and its competition with clearer insights and have been able to start recovering some of the brand issues that were not previously salvageable.

Extending the data warehouse and reengineering the architecture was another way of building the next-generation data warehouse. Another technique that was implemented by a leading manufacturing organization was integration of processed outputs from Big Data, which provided them insights into the market, channel performance, and customer sentiment across geographies, and helped them improve efficiencies in procurement and logistics processes.

Integrating Big Data into the data warehouse

The business problem is a large manufacturing company has been observing erratic order patterns from their customers over a period of time. The issue is not related to the quality of the product or any defects associated with the products. Upon research with their distribution network and their customer partners, it was discovered that the products were not being marketed and sold in a uniform pattern across geographies, causing spurts in stock management and ordering processes.

The research team inside the enterprise embarked on a journey to discover what the markets and geographies were actually looking for and how to solve this requirement while not losing focus on the supply chain and orders that have been added to the pipeline. The research process revealed the following:

- The education about the products and their differentiators were not available to all customers across all geographies.
- The sales were triggered by word-of-mouth customer experience with the product.
- There are three other competitors offering similar products but with lesser quality and reliability.
- The products were offered with a lot of discounts to compete on the price, which reduced the value of the product.
- The product was sold at different prices within the same city across two different distributors.

Based on these insights the business team recommended that third-party data on customer sentiment, brand reputation, brand value, competitive analysis, and trends and insights be purchased from different data providers and integrated into the data warehouse for analysis and research purposes.

The architecture teams started working on the data architecture and integration design for incorporating the data purchased from external parties. This architecture design included an audit process to tag the source for each data component to clearly distinguish the granularity and hierarchy of the data sourced. The design included addition of taxonomies and third-party metadata libraries, as all the data was not available to the manufacturing organization. The data architects included interfaces for clients to be able to upload their hierarchies independently.

The implementation of this design included the three different modules that were architected:

- The data architecture interfaces for
  - Internal data
  - External data
  - Third-party data
  - Customer uploads
  - Semantic interfaces for taxonomy integration
- Metadata libraries interfaces
- Hierarchy management

The modules when implemented provided the interfaces to the Big Data results that were purchased from third-party processors. This enabled the team to extend the current platforms of technologies without having to add new infrastructure.

Empowering decision making

Once the major data architecture components were developed, the external data feeds were processed as unstructured data and tagged with the metadata libraries and the semantic data. This process identified the data that needed to be evaluated further and this also led to the implementation of a collaboration suite where the data could be shared across multiple business users for their processing.

The collaboration suite was designed and implemented using Sharepoint and its associated suite of tools. The workflow process in the collaboration suite was implemented to function as follows:

- The system would tag data in an automated discovery process.
- The data content that matched the business rules for processing data would be extracted and stored as a workflow case document.
- The workflow suite would then assign the case document to the relevant teams based on their profiles and business uses for the data.
- The teams can work on the case independent of each other and share back their results.
- The results are all assimilated together and are shared with a governance team that decides the next course of action.

The usefulness of this design in the collaboration environment is the ability for all stakeholders to work on a single version of the truth and also assign priorities to the processing and outcomes for any given data artifact.

Outcomes

The results of implementing the data extensions provided the business teams an opportunity to understand the underlying issues and then work with their distribution partners and customers to educate them on improving their organizational capabilities. This resulted in increased collaboration between the distributors, customers, and end users, which benefitted the manufacturing organization to implement effective supply chain, inventory management, order management, and service management analytics. The overall results from this data integration created a positive impact for the enterprise. The next step of maturity in this journey is the improvement of the research and development processes based on the direct and indirect feedback from the different layers of partners, customers, and the markets.

SUMMARY

In summary, as you can see from these implementation discussions, there are multiple techniques to integrate Big Data, and its associated technologies, platforms, and infrastructure into a data warehouse. Additionally, there are opportunities to create and deploy newer platforms based on the data architecture and integration requirements. While there is no silver bullet to solve any problem, creative thinking and efficient data architecture and integration principles can help you build and manage data warehouses in the age of Big Data. Big Data, as the name goes, is really big until you process it. Once you process this data it becomes highly structured and will be managed and maintained as any structured data component in an enterprise.

This chapter provided you with some real-world examples of how companies integrated Big Data into their data warehouses and provided you with ideas and thoughts on how you can learn and adapt from similar solutions. There are several case studies provided by leading technology vendors in Appendix A of this book and there is a special chapter on a healthcare information factory architecture implementation in Appendix B that will provide you some more insights into this subject. The next chapter focuses on best practices and tips for implementing Big Data technologies, and will be enhanced in the companion website as these technologies continue to evolve over the next few years.

Customer Case Studies

INTRODUCTION

This appendix contains several case studies that have been provided by vendors Cloudera and Teradata for use in this book. The goal of these case studies is to highlight the different use cases on why enterprises adopt technologies like Hadoop, AsterData, and more.

Case study 1: Transforming marketing landscape

Company: Cloudera
Customer: Experian Marketing Services
Program: Transforming the Marketing Landscape with Cloudera
Industry: Digital marketing
Business applications: Matching engine for CCIR engine, facilitating a holistic and current view of consumers
Impact:
- Fifty times performance gains
- Processing 500% more matches per day
- Deployment in<6 months
Outcome:

One of the key enablers that investing in Hadoop with Cloudera will empower is allowing our clients to become obsessed with creating the perfect customer experience. This tool allows us to operate at the speed of business, at the speed where those interactions occur, so our clients can meet their customers with the right message at the right time.
—Jeff Hassemer, vice president of product strategy, Experian Marketing Services

Background

With 15,000+ employees and annual revenues exceeding $4 billion (USD), Experian is a global leader in credit reporting and marketing services. The company is comprised of four main business units: credit information services, decision analytics, business information services, and marketing services.

Experian Marketing Services (EMS) helps marketers connect with customers through relevant communications across a variety of channels, driven by advanced analytics on an extensive database of geographic, demographic, and lifestyle data.

Business challenges

EMS has built its business on the effective collection, analysis, and use of data. As Jeff Hassemer, vice president of product strategy for EMS, explained,

> *Experian has handled large amounts of data for a very long time: who consumers are, how they're connected, how they interact. We've done this over billions and quadrillions of records over time. But with the proliferation of channels and information that are now flowing into client organizations—social media likes, web interactions, email responses—that data has gotten so large that it's maxed the capacity of older systems. We needed to leap forward in our processing ability. We wanted to process data orders of magnitude faster so we could react to tomorrow's consumer.*

In the past, it was normal to send customer database updates to clients once monthly for campaign adjustments, allowing Experian to process large volumes of data through a number of diverse platforms, mostly mainframe based. "We weren't required to provide data in real time. We weren't required to provide the level of volume in terms of the growth rates we've seen from our storage and our data. It's been a total paradigm shift that compelled us to look at other solutions," explained Emad Georgy, CTO for EMS.

Today's consumers leave a digital trail of behaviors and preferences for marketers to leverage so they can enhance the customer experience. Experian's clients have started asking for more frequent updates on consumers' latest purchasing behaviors, online browsing patterns, and social media activity so they can respond in real time. "We serve many of the top retail companies in the world, and they're increasingly looking for a single, integrated view of their customer," noted Georgy. "If a customer is walking into a store in Burlington, MA, is that same customer now liking the company on Facebook? Are they tweeting? We're looking for an integrated view of who that person is so we can determine how to message them in the right way."

But the data exhaust from these digital channels is massive and requires a technological infrastructure that can accommodate rapid processing, large-scale storage, and flexible analysis of multistructured data. Experian's mainframes were hitting the tipping point in terms of performance, flexibility, and scalability. Given the need for immediacy of information and customization of data in real time for clients, EMS set an internal goal to process more than 100 million records of data per hour. That translates to 28,000 records per second.

"Instead of trying to fit a square peg in a round hole, we went out and decided to look for new architectures that can handle the new volumes of data that we manage," said Joe McCullough, IT business analyst at EMS. The team identified about 30 criteria for the new platform, ranging from depth and breadth of offering, to support capabilities, to price, to unique distribution features. They prioritized two criteria above the rest:

- Both batch and real-time data processing capabilities.
- Scalability to accommodate large and growing data volumes.

"We compared Hadoop as well as HBase to a number of other options in the industry," said Georgy. "The North America Experian Marketing Services group has organically led the evaluation of NoSQL technologies within Experian." Hadoop and HBase quickly surfaced as a natural fit for Experian's needs. EMS engineers downloaded raw Apache Hadoop, but quickly saw the gaps that could be filled by a commercial distribution.

EMS critiqued several distributions and "found that, by and far, Cloudera was in the lead. We went with Cloudera for a number of reasons, primarily being the strength of the distribution and the features that CDH gives us," noted Emad Georgy.

EMS' enterprise-level Hadoop needs, such as meeting client SLAs and having 24/7 reliability, led the organization to invest in Cloudera Enterprise, which is comprised of three things: Cloudera's open-source Hadoop stack (CDH), a powerful management toolkit (Cloudera Manager), and expert technical support.

Use case

A few months of exploring Hadoop translated into a production version of Experian's Cross-Channel Identity Resolution (CCIR) engine, a linkage engine that is used to keep a persistent repository of client touchpoints. CCIR runs on HBase, resolving needs for persistency, redundancy, and the ability to automatically redistribute data. HBase offers a shared architecture that is distributed, fault-tolerant, and optimized for storage. And most importantly, HBase enables both batch and real-time data processing.

Experian feeds data into the CDH-powered CCIR engine using custom extract, transform, load (ETL) scripts from in-house mainframes and relational databases, including IBM DB2, Oracle, SQL Server, and Sybase IQ. EMS' HBase system currently spans five billion rows of data, "and we expect that number to grow tenfold in the near future," said Paul Perry, EMS' director of software. Experian also uses Hive and Pig, primarily for Q&A and development purposes. EMS currently has 35 Hadoop nodes across its production and development clusters.

Impact: operational efficiency

Hadoop is delivering operational efficiency to Experian by accelerating processing performance by 50 times. And the cost of their new infrastructure is only a fraction of the legacy environment. Georgy said, "We've been very happy with the implementation of Hadoop. We're less than six months in and are already closing the gap on our 100 million record per hour goal." In comparison, EMS used to process 50 million matches per day. That translates to a 500% improvement.

Further, Cloudera Enterprise allows Experian to get maximum operational efficiency out of their Hadoop clusters. "Cloudera Enterprise gives us an easy way to manage multiple clusters, and because the use cases for clients vary so much, we have to do a lot of tweaking on the platform to get the performance we need. The ability to store different configuration settings and actually version those settings is huge for us," said Perry.

McCullough added, "Not only has Cloudera Manager simplified our process, but it's made it possible at all. Without a Linux background, I would not have been able to deploy Hadoop across a cluster and configure it and have anything up and running in nearly the timeframe that we had."

Cloudera Manager delivers the following operational benefits to Experian:

- Monitors services running on cluster.
- Reports when servers are unhealthy, services have stopped, and/or nodes are bad.
- Automates distribution across the cluster easily.
- Monitors CPU usage across various applications and data storage availability.
- Provides a single portal to see into all cluster details.

Perry summarized the project by saying,

We haven't done anything this cool for a long time. Our developers are excited about it. I'm excited about it. Senior management is excited about it. And the experience we've had with Cloudera—I don't think it could be better. It's been great working with those guys and the architects that they've given us access to are extremely knowledgeable. The only regret I have is that we didn't bring them in sooner.

Impact: driving competitive advantage

Hassemer stated:

> *Our Hadoop infrastructure has become a real transformational change. Deploying Cloudera allows us to process orders of magnitude more information through our systems, and that technological capability in combination with Experian's expertise in bringing together data assets is driving new, real insights into tomorrow's marketing environments. Nobody is doing what we're doing with Hadoop today, especially at this order of magnitude. Ours is the first data management platform of its kind that accepts data, links information together across an entire marketing ecosystem, and puts it into a usable format for a solid customer experience.*

The performance gains offered by Cloudera give Experian new insights and more flexible ways of understanding consumers. EMS no longer relies on a postal address to identify a consumer; they can now match social media IDs, email addresses, web cookies, phone numbers, and more. With the broader match set that Hadoop enables, EMS' clients have a more accurate, current view of who their customers are across multiple channels so they can have better, more informed interactions. Hassemer explained,

> *A consumer might give their email and sign up for a program with one particular brand. The brand doesn't know much about the consumer at that point, thus information sent to the consumer is very bland, not very enticing. The consumer's time is wasted because the emails they receive aren't relevant. By offering a holistic view of the customer in real time, we can increase the relevance of offers that go to the consumer so they say, "This is why I signed up." And they're going to interact with that brand a lot more. One of the key enablers that investing in Hadoop with Cloudera will empower is allowing our clients to become obsessed with creating the perfect customer experience. This tool allows us to operate at the speed of business, at the speed where those interactions occur, so our clients can meet their customers with the right message at the right time.*

Key highlights

Technologies deployed

- Hadoop platform: Cloudera Enterprise
- Hadoop components: HBase, Hive, Hue, MapReduce, and Pig
- Servers: HP DL380
- Data warehouse: IBM DB2
- Datamarts: Oracle, SQL Server, and Sybase IQ

Big Data scale

- 5 billion rows of data, growing tenfold
- Processing 100 million records per hour
- 35 CDH nodes today

Advice to new hadoop users

- Involve expert architects early on.
- Have patience and get trained on Hadoop/HBase before building applications.

Deploying Cloudera allows us to process orders of magnitude more information through our systems, and that technological capability in combination with Experian's expertise in bringing together data assets is driving new, real insights into tomorrow's marketing environments.
—Jeff Hassemer, vice president of product strategy, Experian Marketing Services

Case study 2: Streamlining healthcare connectivity with Big Data

Company: Cloudera
Customer: Healthcare Client
Program: Streamlining healthcare connectivity with Big Data
Industry: Healthcare
Business applications:
- Complex processing and archiving of claims and remittance data.
- Storage and analysis of transactional log data.

Hadoop impact:
- Providers collect payment faster through expedited messaging with payers.
- Industry standard hardware is ten times less expensive than alternative technologies while enabling analytics on stored data.
- Simple deployment, minimal ongoing maintenance.

Company overview

The connectivity and information technology subsidiary of a major pharmaceutical company was created to simplify how the business of healthcare is managed while making the delivery of care safer and more efficient. As more and more of the U.S. healthcare system goes electronic, this organization meets challenges and opportunities through an open network that supports future growth via interoperability among organizations, systems, and solutions.

Business challenges

With regulations such as the Health Insurance Portability and Accountability Act of 1996 (HIPAA), healthcare organizations are required to store healthcare data for extended periods of time. This health IT company instituted a policy of saving seven years' historical claims and remit data, but its in-house database systems had trouble meeting the data retention requirement while processing millions of claims every day.

A software engineer at the company explained, "All of our systems were maxed out. We were constantly having database issues. It was just too much data for what they were meant to handle. They were overworked and overloaded, and it started to cause problems with all of our real-time production processing."

Further, the organization sought a solution that would allow users to do more than just store data. The manager of software development at the company explained, "In today's data-driven world, data really is this huge asset. We wondered, 'What framework, what platform will allow us to optimize the data that we have?'"

The team set out to find a new solution. "We could have gone the SAN route, but it's expensive and cumbersome," said the software engineer. They did some searching online and came across Hadoop, MongoDB, and Cassandra. "We analyzed them and came up with a prototype for each one. In the end, we decided Hadoop was what we wanted."

Initially the organization downloaded Hadoop from Apache and configured it to run on ten Dell workstations that were already in-house. Once the small Hadoop cluster showed its functionality and demonstrated value, the team decided to make a commitment to the platform, but would need support to do so. When evaluating various Hadoop distributions and management vendors, they recognized that Cloudera was different: its Hadoop distribution—CDH—is 100% Apache open source. This allows Cloudera customers to benefit from rapid innovations in the open-source community while also taking advantage of enterprise-grade support and management tools offered with the Cloudera Enterprise subscription.

Use case

When deciding to deploy CDH, the team set out to identify applications that were already seeing performance issues in production. "One of the big advantages of Hadoop has been to be able to segregate Big Data from transactional processing data and allow smoother processing of information. Basically, it allows us to offload a lot of stress from the database," said the company's manager of software development.

They quickly identified two areas that were a strong fit for Hadoop:

- Archiving seven years' claims and remit data, which requires complex processing to get into a normalized format.
- Logging terabytes of data generated from transactional systems daily and storing them in CDH for analytical purposes.

Today the health IT organization uses Flume to move data from its source systems into the CDH cluster on a 24/7 basis. The company loads data from CDH to an Oracle online transaction processing (OLTP) database for billing purposes. This load runs once or twice each day via Sqoop.

Impact: helping providers collect payment faster through operational efficiencies

"If you look at the margin that the average hospital has, it's between 2% and 3%," stated the manager of software development. "So their cash flow is very tight. Anything you can do to reduce the time to get paid is very valuable to a healthcare provider."

Since deploying Cloudera Enterprise, the organization has reduced the time it takes for healthcare providers to get paid by streamlining their transfer of messages to payers. The ability to expedite this process is especially valuable when regulatory changes come into play, such as the recent conversion from HIPAA 4010 to HIPAA 5010.

The company's manager of software development said,

We assist with the conversion and processing of these messages. For example, 4010 messages came in and we'd convert them to 5010 to allow seamless processing. The providers didn't have to upgrade any of their systems when the regulations went into effect. We gave them a bit of a buffer to implement changes. And since we do a lot of electronic processing, we can do basic sanity checks on the messages as they come in and let providers know what adjustments need to be made in order to get paid faster.

Impact: low cost + greater analytic flexibility

Because Hadoop uses industry-standard hardware, the cost per terabyte of storage is, on average, ten times cheaper than a traditional relational data warehouse system. The manager of software development explained,

> One of my pet peeves is: you buy a machine, you buy SAN storage, and then you have to buy licensing for the storage in addition to the storage itself. You have to buy licensing for the blades, and it just becomes an untenable situation. With Hadoop you buy commodity hardware and you're good to go. In addition to the storage, you get a bigger bang for your buck because it gives you the ability to run analytics on the combined compute and storage. The solutions that we had in place previously really didn't allow for that. Even if the costs were equivalent, the benefit you get from storing data on a Hadoop-type solution is far greater than what you'd get from storing it in a database.

Impact: simple deployment and administration

After deciding on the Cloudera solution, "the deployment process into production with Hadoop was actually quite easy," said a software engineer at the company. "Cloudera Manager really helped us a lot. It's as easy as just clicking a few buttons, and you're up and running. It's really simple. And the support staff at Cloudera has been great. They really helped us out with a couple of issues we had along the way." With Cloudera Manager, the team spends very little time managing the cluster.

Further, this health IT organization appreciates the proactive customer support offered by Cloudera Enterprise. Commented their manager of software development,

> We ask questions and we get them answered very quickly. Not only do the Cloudera Support folks answer the question, they come back and say, "Do you have any other questions? Is there anything else we can help you with?" It's very different. The people that are on Cloudera's Support team—you can definitely tell they are Hadoop committers. Not only will they find you the answer but they can tell you, "This may not be the best practice, you may want to change the way you're doing your development to take advantage of other features." The Cloudera Support organization is world class.

Key highlights

Technologies
- Hadoop platform: Cloudera Enterprise
- Hadoop components: Flume, Sqoop, MapReduce, and HDFS
- Data warehouses: Oracle and IBM Netezza

Big Data scale
- 30 TB across 10 CDH nodes in four months
- Archiving seven-plus years' historical data
- 24/7 feeds from source systems processing ~1 TB per day

Advice to new hadoop users
- Step back and evaluate your architecture to take advantage of Hadoop's capabilities.
- Take Hadoop training.

Case study 3: Improving healthcare quality and costs using Big Data

Company: Cloudera
Customer: Explorys Medical
Program: Improving healthcare quality and costs using a Big Data platform
Industry: Healthcare
Business applications:

- Complex data processing and curation of clinical, financial, and operational data.
- Clinical quality measure analytics.
- Proactive care management analytics.

Impact:

- Time to insight reduced from days to minutes.
- Increased business agility.

Reduced total cost of ownership.

We were forced to think about a less expensive, more efficient technology from the beginning, and in hindsight, I'm glad that we were. For us—needing storage, high-capacity index, and analytics—Hadoop really made a lot of sense. And from a partner perspective, Cloudera is one of the most influential that we've had throughout the years.

—Charlie Lougheed, president and CTO, Explorys

Company overview

In 2009, Explorys' cofounders—Stephen McHale, CEO; Charlie Lougheed, president and CTO; and Doug Meil, chief software architect—set forward on a mission to integrate clinical, financial, and operational data to improve delivery of care, resulting in better health outcomes and reduced costs associated with delivering medical services. Explorys has built a cloud-based enterprise performance management (EPM) computing platform for healthcare providers that enables real-time exploration, performance, and predictive analytics of clinical data. Several of the U.S.'s largest integrated delivery networks have deployed Explorys' platform, including Cleveland Clinic, MedStar, University Hospitals, St. Joseph Health System, Catholic Health Partners, and Summa Health System.

Use case

Explorys "bet the company on Hadoop in 2009," stated Meil. Explorys' Big Data platform, known as DataGrid, is based on Cloudera Enterprise and offers three software-as-a-service (SaaS) applications:

- EPM: Explore provides subsecond ad-hoc search across populations, providers, and care venues.
- EPM: Measure is an integrated application and framework for constructing and viewing key performance metrics across providers, groups, care venues, and locations.
- EPM: Engage is an integrated application and framework for coordinating rules-driven registries, prioritized patient and provider outreach, and messaging.

Explorys uses MapReduce to process, organize, and curate large batches of incoming data very quickly into HDFS and HBase. Data sources include HL7, claims data, and third-party feeds from virtual health records (VHRs) such as Epic, Eclipsys, Amalga, McKesson, and Cerner. That data is materialized into structures that can be rapidly accessed and analyzed via off-the-shelf tools or custom-built applications. Those applications then generate data back into HBase for other processing needs. Analytics powered by Hadoop facilitate clinical-quality measure generation, measure calculations for registries, and proactive care management and other critical tasks.

For example, Explorys uses Hadoop-powered analytics for purposes similar to the following scenario. To better serve its community, a county hospital might want to explore why people utilize the emergency room (ER) rather than going to a primary physician for care. This practice is not beneficial for either the patient or hospital, because it is expensive for the hospital and the patient doesn't get the continuity of care that a primary physician would provide.

Additionally, it is important to analyze a bigger problem than just the ER record system. With Hadoop, Explorys can analyze what factors are demographically different about a given population, where patients live, and whether or not care is available in their neighborhoods. Explorys can run these analytics daily to take immediate action, such as sending a letter to a patient the day after she or he has visited the ER that includes information about local healthcare providers and instructions to help prevent readmittance.

Business challenges

McHale explained,

> With a clinical enterprise performance management system built on a relational data warehouse, if healthcare practitioners want to understand something specific about a population or segment of data, they have to go to their IT departments and then wait days or weeks to get that information back. We wanted to provide a platform that would give them an answer as fast as if they were searching on Google.

Rather than managing clinical, financial, and operational data in three data silos, Explorys sought to bring all of that data together. Lougheed explained,

> It's about merging the three elements and telling a story about how an organization is doing, because ultimately what we want to do is improve healthcare and do it at a lower cost. With over 17% of the nation's GDP being spent on healthcare services, we've got to find a better way to deliver healthcare at a cheaper cost point.

McHale added, "We had lots of experience working with traditional database platforms in our careers in banking and telecom, and we just didn't believe they were going to scale economically or from a performance standpoint."

The variety of data would also present a challenge. "Electronic Health Record (EHR) platforms are just now becoming prevalent across the medical landscape," noted Lougheed. "There are more and more devices that generate massive amounts of data. Patients are providing data and feedback on how they're doing. They have devices in the home that provide data. There's a ton of data variety coming in and it's more than the healthcare space can really handle."

Explorys needed to find a cost-efficient technology that would help the company address these Big Data challenges. Hadoop met both of these criteria, and Cloudera stood out to Explorys as the most credible company delivering an enterprise-ready Hadoop solution. McHale, Lougheed, and Meil attended the first Hadoop world conference hosted by Cloudera in 2009, and were sold both on the value of Hadoop and on Cloudera's "ability to deliver." They also appreciated Cloudera's contingent of on-staff Hadoop committers, signifying Cloudera's ability to support production deployments and drive the direction of the technology.

After deploying the DataGrid platform on CDH, Explorys decided to take advantage of the Cloudera Enterprise subscription offering that bundles CDH with Cloudera Support and Cloudera Manager, a software application that delivers visibility into and across Hadoop clusters for stream-lined management, monitoring, and provisioning. Cloudera Enterprise gave Explorys the peace of mind to continue operating its mission-critical Hadoop environment with a lean staff that could focus on the core competencies of the business.

Hadoop impact

Explorys relies on CDH to provide the flexibility, scalability, and speed necessary to answer complex questions on-the-fly. The window for analysis shrank from 30 days using traditional technologies to seconds or minutes with Explorys' CDH-powered system. Meil explained,

> We didn't invent clinical quality measures, but the ability to generate those measures on a rapid basis, support hundreds of them, implement complex attribution logic, and manifest that with a slick user interface on top, that's revolutionary. Cloudera provides the technology that allows us to address traditional challenges in medicine and in operational reporting with a radical new approach.

With traditional systems, it is cumbersome to make changes to the data and then reprocess it. "The ability to have that data ready within a day is game changing," noted McHale. "Without Hadoop, it would be extremely challenging to do and certainly not cost effective."

Because Hadoop uses industry-standard hardware, the cost per terabyte of storage is, on average, ten times cheaper than a traditional relational data warehouse system. Lougheed said,

> We'd be spending literally millions more dollars than we are today on relational database technologies and licensing. Those technologies are important, but they're important in their place. For Big Data analytics, storage, and processing, Hadoop is a perfect solution. It has brought opportunities for us to rechannel those funds, that capital, in directions of being more innovative, bringing more products to bear, and ultimately hiring more people for the company as opposed to buying licenses.

On Cloudera Enterprise, Meil noted, "We have a nontrivial system operations team and any help we can get in terms of operational support and tooling for the management of our cluster is critical. I definitely see the value in Cloudera Enterprise."

Lougheed summarized, "We were forced to think about a less expensive, more efficient technology from the beginning, and in hindsight, I'm glad that we were. For us—needing storage, high-capacity index, and analytics—Hadoop really made a lot of sense. And from a partner perspective, Cloudera is one of the most influential that we've had throughout the years."

Key highlights
Technologies
- Hadoop platform: Cloudera Enterprise
- Hadoop components: HBase, HDFS, and MapReduce
- Metadata mart: MySQL

Big Data scale
- Unlimited data retention, never purge patient data
- Ability to curate 40+ billion clinical and operational data points over 13 million individuals
- 35 TB multistructured data
- Growing to 70 TB by 2013

Advice to new hadoop users
- Leverage lessons learned from early adopters and Apache community.

Case study 4: Improving customer support

Company: Cloudera
Customer: NetApp
Program: NetApp improves customer support by deploying Cloudera Enterprise
Industry: Data storage
Business applications: AutoSupport operations: monitoring, troubleshooting, and health checks of customer storage systems
Impact:
- Database query on 24 billion records reduced from four weeks to less than 10.5 hours.
- Previously impossible database query on 240 billion records runs in less than 18 hours.

Company overview

NetApp creates storage systems and software that helps customers around the world store, manage, protect, and retain one of their most precious assets: data. To better support its customers, NetApp offers AutoSupport, an integrated and efficient monitoring and reporting technology that constantly checks the health of NetApp systems. Customers leverage the My AutoSupport portal on the NetApp Support site for proactive systems management capabilities and insight into storage configuration, capacity, utilization, efficiency, and health-check information.

Business challenge: processing massive volumes of data

AutoSupport collects over 600,000 data transactions weekly, consisting of unstructured logs and system diagnostic information. Approximately 40% of that data is transmitted during an 18-hour period each weekend, creating the potential for I/O bottlenecks that could affect SLA windows.

As the NetApp customer base is expanding, AutoSupport data is growing at approximately 7 TB per month. Related storage requirements are doubling every 16 months. NetApp's AutoSupport team proactively identified the need to upgrade its storage environment to accommodate continued growth.

NetApp's CIO Cynthia Stoddard explained, "I sit on thousands of customers' data and what I do with that data is essential to the company. I need to react and help customers do more with their systems."

AutoSupport needed a Big Data storage and analytic solution that would allow it to store, manage, and analyze increasing volumes of unstructured data; gain insights from these large, complex data sets; and scale for continued growth.

"NetApp AutoSupport data is extremely valuable to us," said Marty Mayer, director of NetApp AutoSupport. "Our customers depend on us to utilize the data to respond in a timely manner when potential problems and issues arise. Additionally, we actively analyze customer storage system data for fitness and health checks that help optimize the investment our customers have made in NetApp."

The solution: netapp open solution for hadoop

The team focused on storage solutions that support the Apache Hadoop open-source software designed for data-intensive distributed applications. Other criteria included scalability, high-performance, and rich analytics capabilities. The AutoSupport group conducted a proof of concept on numerous technologies, evaluating them for key functions, including parsing, ETL capabilities, and data warehousing. The team concluded that the NetApp Open Solution for Hadoop—comprised of NetApp storage coupled with Cloudera Enterprise—surpassed the other solutions in providing the ability to more deeply monitor customer solutions, and executing previously impossible data processing jobs and complex queries. The solution also provided an overall lower total cost of ownership than other Big Data platforms.

NetApp and Cloudera joined forces to offer organizations a solution that is highly scalable with enterprise storage features that improve reliability and performance and reduce costs. NetApp Open Solution for Hadoop customers can leverage the Big Data platform to accelerate adoption of analytic applications that deliver real-time results across intense data and computational workloads. Cloudera is a major enabler for the enterprise adoption and production use of Apache Hadoop. Cloudera Enterprise allows companies to manage the complete operational life cycle of their Apache Hadoop systems with deep visibility into their CDH clusters. It also automates the ongoing system changes needed to maintain and improve the quality of operations.

System architecture

The NetApp AutoSupport team deployed NetApp Open Solution for Hadoop, which includes a 28-node cluster of Cloudera Enterprise on four NetApp E2600 storage systems and a NetApp FAS2040 system. Mayer noted,

> *The NetApp Open Solution for Hadoop system offers us the scalability and flexibility we need to effectively support our growing client base and rapidly expanding data stores. In addition, because the NetApp system addresses our parsing, ETL, and data warehousing needs in a single, comprehensive solution, it reduces our total cost of ownership, freeing up budget for other customer-focused projects.*

The system offers high availability and high performance for even the most demanding AutoSupport workloads. Its balanced performance will sustain the high read and write throughput requirements of the system's data-intensive, high-bandwidth applications, such as the weekend reporting that offers visibility into the health of hundreds of thousands of customer storage systems.

As a customer-facing organization, the NetApp AutoSupport team depends on the reliability of its storage environment 24/7/365. Data ONTAP® 8 on the FAS2040 storage system eliminates the single

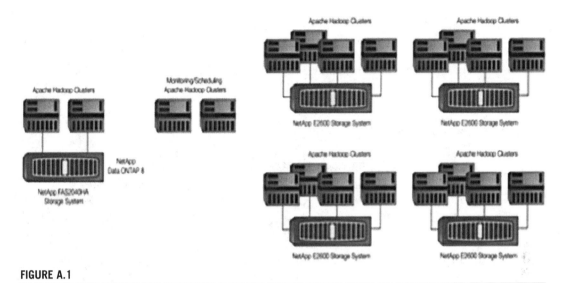

FIGURE A.1

The NetApp AutoSupport team deployed a NetApp Open Solution for Hadoop, which includes Hadoop clusters on NetApp E2600 storage systems and a NetApp FAS2040 system running Data ONTAP 8.

point of failure common in traditional Hadoop-clustered deployments and instead offers full redundancy and automated path failover, along with online administration (Figure A.1).

> *This highly efficient CDH processing will enable our AutoSupport team to quickly mine hundreds of terabytes of data, for real-time analysis of customer system event and performance data and rapid resolution of any issues.*
>
> **—Marty Mayer, director of NatApp AutoSupport**

Impact: high performance for big bandwidth applications

AutoSupport predicts significant performance gains running on the NetApp Open Solution for Hadoop. By supporting even the most bandwidth-intensive applications, the solution will enable the NetApp AutoSupport team to meet stringent SLAs for parsing and loading data. In one case, AutoSupport wanted to correlate disk latency when a disk was hot with the type of manufacturer disk to identify whether there was a relationship between the two. The report requires a query of 24 billion records, which took four weeks to run on the incumbent environment. On the massively parallel NetApp Open Solution for Hadoop, that query returns in 10.5 hours. That's a 64 times query performance improvement. Mayer noted,

> *The productivity and customer service benefits enabled by the NetApp solution are significant. Running the NetApp Open Solution for Hadoop gives us the ability to turn an unwieldy data explosion into a highly manageable environment. It also will allow us to perform deeper analytics than before, which will provide better monitoring and troubleshooting of NetApp customer storage systems.*

In another case, AutoSupport was unable to run a pattern-matching query that would help detect bugs. The report required a query of 240 billion records, which was simply too large to run with the existing infrastructure. Through performance testing on the NetApp Open System for Hadoop, the team was able to run the high-bandwidth query and achieve results in less than 18 hours, using just ten data nodes.

Impact: rich analytics for large data sets

AutoSupport provides skilled resources focused on supporting NetApp customers through analyzing log data for insight into system health. The NetApp Open Solution for Hadoop system enables parallel processing for structured and unstructured data and allows AutoSupport applications to work with thousands of nodes. Weekly AutoSupport logs composed of large, complex data sets offer the team insight into information such as storage capacity trending by customer, country, and other criteria.

The team also runs ad-hoc queries such as investigating an error alert across an entire system set to identify the source, allowing the team to take proactive measures to prevent impact to customer systems. In addition, through automatic AutoSupport system analysis of deep pools of data, the NetApp Technical Support team is immediately notified of critical alerts. The NetApp Open Solution for Hadoop is designed to accelerate these and other AutoSupport queries and processes.

NetApp customers can also benefit directly from the high performance of the NetApp Open Solution for Hadoop system, which offers deeper analytics capabilities than before. With more in-depth visibility into configuration and system health data through the My AutoSupport portal, customers can be more proactive and achieve greater efficiencies with their NetApp storage.

Impact: managing a holistic storage environment

The AutoSupport team will efficiently manage its Big Data environment centrally on the NetApp Open Solution for Hadoop system. The solution will provide high levels of throughput and scalability to meet the growing data demands and intensive performance requirements of AutoSupport applications. Storage managers can efficiently manage huge stores of data in the integrated, unified AutoSupport storage environment, which helps NetApp customers optimize the performance and utilization of their storage solutions.

"The NetApp Open Solution for Hadoop is a holistic rather than point solution," said Kumar Palaniappan, enterprise architect for NetApp. "By design, the NetApp solution offers tight integration between our Hadoop applications and NetApp storage, thereby allowing us to maximize storage utilization and reduce our overall capex and opex. Hadoop analytics will empower us to transform NetApp storage data into business insight for our team and customers."

Key highlights
Technologies
- Hadoop platform: NetApp Open Solution for Hadoop
- Storage systems: NetApp E2600 and FAS2040 HA
- Operating system: Data ONTAP 8.0
- Protocols: NFS and SASL

Big Data scale

- 28-node Cloudera Enterprise cluster
- 600,000+ incoming data transactions processed weekly
- Data volumes growing 7 TB per month
- Storage requirements doubling every 16 months

Case study 5: Driving customer-centric transformations

Company: Cloudera
Customer: Nokia
Program: Using Big Data to bridge the virtual and physical worlds
Industry: Telecommunications
Business applications:
  - Geospatial application development
  - Content/engagement optimization
  - Network sessonization
Outcomes:
  - Enables unprecedented scale and flexibility to build 3D digital maps of the globe.

Hadoop is absolutely mission-critical for Nokia. We can now understand how people interact with the apps on their phones to view usage patterns across applications. We can ask things like, "Which feature did they go to after this one?" and "Where did they seem to get lost?" We wouldn't have gotten our Big Data platform to where it is today without Cloudera's platform, expertise, and support.
—Amy O'Connor, senior director of analytics at Nokia

Company overview

Nokia has been in business for more than 150 years, starting with the production of paper in the nineteenth century and evolving into a leader in mobile and location services that connects more than 1.3 billion people today. Nokia has always transformed resources into useful products—from rubber and paper, to electronics and mobile devices—and today's resource is data.

Nokia's goal is to bring the world to the third phase of mobility: leveraging digital data to make it easier to navigate the physical world. To achieve this goal, Nokia needed to find a technology solution that would support the collection, storage, and analysis of virtually unlimited data types and volumes.

Use case

Effective collection and use of data has become central to Nokia's ability to understand and improve users' experiences with their phones and other location products. "Nokia differentiates itself based on the data we have," stated O'Connor. The company leverages data processing and complex analyses to build maps with predictive traffic and layered elevation models, to source information about points of interest around the world, to understand the quality of phones, and more.

To grow and support its extensive use of Big Data, Nokia relies on a technology ecosystem that includes a Teradata EDW, numerous Oracle and MySQL datamarts, visualization technologies, and, at its core, Hadoop. Nokia has over 100 terabytes (TB) of structured data on Teradata and petabytes (PB) of multistructured data on the HDFS. The centralized Hadoop cluster that lies at the heart of Nokia's infrastructure contains 0.5 PB of data. Nokia's data warehouses and datamarts continuously stream multistructured data into a multitenant Hadoop environment, allowing the company's 60,000+ employees to access the data. Nokia runs hundreds of thousands of Scribe processes each day to efficiently move data from, for example, servers in Singapore to a Hadoop cluster in the U.K. data center. The company uses Sqoop to move data from HDFS to Oracle and/or Teradata. And Nokia serves data out of Hadoop through HBase.

Business challenges

Prior to deploying Hadoop, numerous groups within Nokia were building application silos to accommodate their individual needs. It didn't take long before the company realized it could derive greater value from its collective data sets if these application silos could be integrated, enabling all globally captured data to be cross-referenced for a single, comprehensive version of truth. "We were inventorying all of our applications and data sets," O'Connor noted. "Our goal was to end up with a single data asset."

Nokia wanted to understand at a holistic level how people interact with different applications around the world, which required them to implement an infrastructure that could support daily, terabyte-scale streams of unstructured data from phones in use, services, log files, and other sources.

Leveraging this data also requires complex processing and computation to be consumable and useful for a variety of uses, like gleaning market insights, or understanding collective behaviors of groups; some aggregations of that data also need to be easily migrated to more structured environments to leverage specific analytic tools.

However, capturing petabyte-scale data using a relational database was cost prohibitive and would limit the data types that could be ingested. "We knew we'd break the bank trying to capture all this unstructured data in a structured environment," O'Connor said. Because Hadoop uses industry-standard hardware, the cost per terabyte of storage is, on average, ten times cheaper than a traditional relational data warehouse system. Additionally, unstructured data must be reformatted to fit into a relational schema before it can be loaded into the system. This requires an extra data processing step that slows ingestion, creates latency, and eliminates elements of the data that could become important down the road.

Various groups of engineers at Nokia had already begun experimenting with Apache Hadoop, and a few were using Cloudera's distribution including Apache Hadoop (CDH). The benefits of Hadoop were clear—it offers reliable, cost-effective data storage and high-performance parallel processing of multistructured data at the petabyte scale—however, the rapidly evolving platform and tools designed to support and enable it are complex and can be difficult to deploy in production. CDH simplifies this process, bundling the most popular open-source projects in the Apache Hadoop stack into a single, integrated package with steady and reliable releases.

After experimenting with CDH for several months, the company decided to standardize the use of the Hadoop platform to be the cornerstone of its technology ecosystem. With limited Hadoop expertise in-house, Nokia turned to Cloudera to augment their internal engineering team with strategic technical support and global training services, giving them the confidence with expertise necessary to deploy a very large production Hadoop environment in a short timeframe.

Impact

In 2011, Nokia put its central CDH cluster into production to serve as the company's enterprise-wide information core. Cloudera supported the deployment from start to finish, ensuring the cluster was successfully integrated with other Hadoop clusters and relational technologies for maximum reliability and performance.

Nokia is now using Hadoop to push the analytics envelope, creating 3D digital maps that incorporate traffic models that understand speed categories, recent speeds on roads, historical traffic models, elevation, ongoing events, video streams of the world, and more.

Key highlights
Technologies
- Hadoop platform: Cloudera Enterprise
- Hadoop components: HBase, HDFS, Scribe, and Sqoop
- Data warehouse: Teradata, Oracle, and MySQL

Big Data scale
- 100+ TB structured data
- Multiple PB multistructured data
- Thousands of users in multitenant environment

Case study 6: Quantifying risk and compliance

Company: Cloudera and Datameer
Customer: Financial services
Industry: Financial services
Business applications:
- Asset risk measurement
- Regulatory compliance

Impact:
- 50+ comprehensive data-sanity and -quality checks per record.
- Monthly data-quality reports provided to CRO and CFO to ensure regulatory compliance and accurate forecasts.

Background

To quantify asset risk and comply with regulatory reporting requirements such as the Dodd-Frank Act, this leading retail bank is using Cloudera and Datameer to validate data accuracy and quality.

Integrating loan and branch data as well as wealth management data, a major retail bank's data-quality initiative is responsible for ensuring that every record is accurate. The process includes subjecting the data to over 50 data-sanity and -quality checks. The results of those checks are trended over time to ensure that the tolerances for data corruption and data domains aren't changing

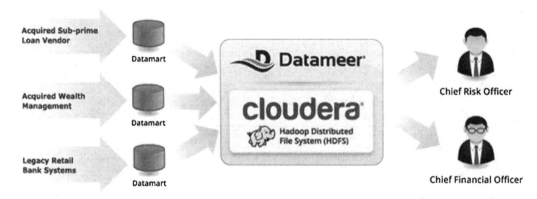

FIGURE A.2

Hadoop with integrated data discovery architecture.

adversely. They also ensure that the risk profiles being reported to investors and regulatory agencies are prudent and in compliance with regulatory requirements.

Prior to deploying Cloudera with Datameer, the bank was using Teradata and IBM Netezza to build out datamarts so they could analyze data quality using their SAS application. The process was time consuming and complex, and the datamart approach didn't provide the data completeness required for determining overall data quality.

Use case

The bank's data quality/data stewardship team of 15 users is utilizing a 20-node CDH cluster. They are analyzing trillions of records, which currently result in approximately one terabyte per month of reports. The results are reported through a data-quality dashboard to the CRO and CFO who are ultimately responsible for ensuring the accuracy of regulatory compliance reporting as well as earnings forecasts to investors (Figure A.2).

Case study 7: Delivering a 360° view of customers

Company: Teradata
Customer: Barnes & Noble
Program: 360° view of customers through faster analytics
Barnes & Noble background:
- 40 million customers
- Internet's largest bookstore
- Sells 300 million books per year
- 30% of electronic book market

Business objectives:
- Outperform competitors via analytics and dominate electronic book market

- Converge data silos for cross-channel insight
- Gain deeper customer personalization for improved targeting
- Improve comarketing initiatives

Business challenges:

- Data silos would not scale
- Poor analytic performance
- Low analyst productivity

Impact

The amounts of data that we're seeing now are unprecedented even from five years ago. So capturing the data is the very first step toward utilizing and analyzing it. Then you have to have systems which will give you the speed of analysis. You have to democratize it around the organization so that you train people and make it a very easy and open access system. So that the people who are business owners can actually use that within their business plans and can get real customer insight very quickly.
      —Marc Parrish, vice president of customer retention and loyalty at Barnes & Noble

Background

As the Internet's largest bookstore, Barnes & Noble sells 300 million books per year to more than 40 million customers. The company that runs 700 retail stores and a popular website commands more than 30% of the electronic book market through its Nook reader, and manages one of the country's largest and best-known loyalty programs.

But with several distinct online and offline distribution channels, Barnes & Noble did not enjoy a deep level of insight into its customers, their preferences, and purchase behaviors across these channels. The company generated massive amounts of data, but could not access it quickly enough at the point of sale, where it could be used most effectively to give customers a superior purchase experience.

To outperform competitors the company needed to use its data far more effectively. By fully leveraging data-driven analytics, Barnes & Noble could develop a deeper, more nuanced understanding of its customers, improve targeting, and create more effective comarketing initiatives to grow its business.

Use case

A deeper understanding of customers: "Part of one family." To differentiate the Barnes & Noble shopping experience and take better advantage of its well-known loyalty program, company executives needed to understand purchase intent and behavior at a much deeper level. Quick access to detailed customer preferences for books, music, and other items would increase brand awareness, enhance customer loyalty, and reduce churn.

By engaging with readers in a more personalized and individual way—at retail, online, and through its Nook reader—the company could treat customers as if they were "part of one family." Unfortunately, Barnes & Noble's systems did not provide a single POS connection that could enable that kind of integrated marketing approach.

Data silos would not scale, so analysis could not be generated in real time. With siloed data there was no practical way to connect online, retail, and Nook purchase and preference information from one location to another. For example, company executives wanted to learn more about its customers—how far they might live from a store, whether they had children, their loyalty and propensity to buy online, etc.—but that data could not be analyzed quickly enough to meet those needs.

So to fully capitalize on one of the company's most significant assets—its data—Barnes & Noble turned to Teradata Aster to take full advantage of more effective strategies for deploying data-driven analytics.

Impact

- Decreasing churn and engaging readers.
- Democratizing access to data.

Many companies capture large sets of customer-oriented data with the goal of adding value to the customer experience and to their brand. But if that data is locked up in hard-to-access silos, it cannot be used throughout the organization to add more value to the brand.

So Barnes & Noble began a project using Teradata Aster's decision tools to accomplish several objectives:

- Learn more about customers by creating one single view into all marketing channels.
- Improve POS systems to enable real-time personalized customer recommendations.
- Analyze trends more quickly to take advantage of tactical opportunities.
- Create more sophisticated models to understand purchase behavior and brand loyalty.
- Gain more visibility into retail and online customers, each of whom had different needs.

Perhaps most importantly, Barnes & Noble wanted to "democratize" access to data—making it available to everyone in the organization who could use it to improve the customer experience. From an analytics perspective, the company needed to shift its overall methodology. Instead of creating individual purchasing behavior theories and testing them over time, the company wanted to run many different theoretical models across the same data set—and do so in a matter of minutes, not days or weeks.

Teradata Aster enabled this process. By using Aster SQL-MapReduce, Barnes & Noble has a single view into all channels, it has much faster response times, and it delivers personalized analytics that enable a more customized purchase experience to all customers.

A 360° view: turning browsers into buyers

The business impact was astounding. Now, with a 360° view of the customer's in-store and online behavior, Barnes & Noble has enhanced its brand and turns more browsers into buyers by more effectively anticipating what customers want.

The company now has a sophisticated real-time POS system that is deployed in the cloud, provides immediate access to information, and can offer special deals to individual customers, for a more personalized sales experience.

Analysis that once took days now takes minutes. For example:

- Payment processing analytics takes just one minute through SQL-MapReduce.
- Web log data processing, which once took seven hours, now takes 20 minutes.
- Interactive dashboards—with all KPIs from the point of order inception—are now generated in just five minutes.

What's more, Barnes & Noble has built revenue attribution models to link every purchase to a site feature and has reduced churn from one day to just 20 minutes. Future plans include using data assets to improve website checkout optimization, enhance store operations, and more—all through deeper consumer insights with Teradata Aster.

Solutions

- Payment processing analytics down from one day to one minute with SQL-MapReduce.
- Web log data processing down from seven hours to 20 minutes.
- Interactive dashboards with all KPIs from the point of order inception down from five hours to five minutes.

Results

- Increased conversions from recommendations with 360° view of customers across all channels.
- Effective revenue attribution models to link every purchase to a site feature.
- Reduced churn from one day to 20 minutes.

Key lessons

- Connecting the POS system to cloud creates effective real-time interaction with customers.
- Data is one of a retailer's most valuable assets.
- Capturing data properly and storing it is the first step to using it to full advantage.

Parrish added, "Now that all our data is in one place, we can understand customer interactions across our entire [retail/online/e-reader] ecosystem. [MapReduce helps researchers] see trends more quickly than possible in systems only using massively parallel processing."

Building the Healthcare Information Factory

Healthcare Information Factory: Implementing Textual Analytics

B

W.H. Inmon, Md Andrew Gettinger, and Krish Krishnan

INTRODUCTION

Healthcare information systems have been a complex subject to deal with for many years until now. With the advent of processing architectures for deep text mining and analytics coupled with Big Data infrastructure, we can create a powerful platform that can integrate data from payors, providers, and patients, creating a holistic view of data across the entire spectrum to optimize revenue, assess and predict risks, and increase quality of care. This chapter is an adaptation from the "Healthcare Information Factory: Implementing Textual Analytics" whitepaper by W. H. Inmon et al. and discusses the usage of text analysis and mining approaches to building the same. This chapter is intended to provide you an overview of potential capabilities with Big Data architectures and algorithms and applying them to integrate and extend the data warehouse.

Note: The whitepaper here has been reproduced with the permission of the authors and the company.

Executive summary

Everyone wants better healthcare and more affordable healthcare. The question is how to achieve these goals.

A really good place to start is with properly managing healthcare information. So what are some of the tractable problems associated with healthcare information? Among other things:

- Healthcare information is approached in an inward-looking manner, where different entities involved in healthcare information management look at their own internal issues and no one steps back and looks at the larger issues of healthcare information management in its totality. Looking at standard codes is a start down this path, but it is only a start. What is needed is a much larger architectural framework that addresses the major issues of global healthcare management,

- There is very little reusability or integrity of research data. Each researcher finds his or her own data and does an analysis. Then the data that has been used sits in a dormant, protected state. As a result each researcher spends huge amounts of time collecting and refining data and relatively little time analyzing the data. With reusability of research data, analysis could be done much more quickly and much less expensively than it is done now. Time to market of new products and medication is greatly speeded up.
- Much of healthcare data is oriented toward text. Any rational approach to managing healthcare information has got to account for the textual orientation of information found in the world of healthcare.

There are undoubtedly other issues with healthcare management of information. But these problems have to be at the top of the list for improvement with healthcare information. Stated differently, any improvements in healthcare information management that do not address these issues will yield only marginal gains in improvement of health and lowering the cost of healthcare.

A change in approaches is necessary. In past times, the problem of information management in the healthcare community has been approached as if the problem were a medical one. Indeed there is an element of medicine in the management of healthcare information. But the issues of healthcare management are also one of information architecture. And it is this element of healthcare information management that has been woefully absent in earlier attempts to address information management in the healthcare environment.

This architectural specification is designed to address these most important issues of information management in the healthcare information.

The healthcare information factory

Over the years there have been several renditions of the architecture of information known as the "information factory." First there was the corporate information factory, which described the vision of the general shape of information systems to come for corporations. Then there was the government information factory, which described the shape of information systems needed by government to deal with the many "siloed" systems found in the government sector. Now there is the healthcare information factory, as described by this paper. The healthcare information factory is a visionary document, describing the way information needs to be looked at holistically when looking at the entirety of health information needs.

One of the essences of the information factory architectures that have been created is the fact that the information factories look across the totality of the needs for information. All too often technicians and users get caught up in looking at just their corner of the world when it comes to understanding the larger structure of information and information requirements. The primary objective of the information factory is to look at *all* the needs for information. This is especially important for healthcare information because healthcare information is needed in places well beyond the doctor's office, the hospital, and the clinic. It is very easy in healthcare to suffer from a severe case of myopia looking at just the immediate or next-to-immediate needs for information. The healthcare information factory looks at the entirety of needs for information that relate to healthcare.

A visionary architecture

The healthcare information factory is a visionary architecture. It does not describe what is, today. Instead it describes what ought to be, tomorrow. In addition, the healthcare information factory is a holistic vision—it looks at the totality of the needs for information across the entire world of healthcare.

The healthcare information factory has been shaped by the combining of the understanding of the needs for information management coupled with the structure of medicine and healthcare. Both standard information practices and the reality of information for healthcare have been factored into the defining of the healthcare information factory.

In many regards the world of healthcare and information systems that service healthcare is similar to the world of information processing found in other environments. And at the same time the world of information systems for healthcare is quite different from information processing found in other environments. This technical paper is about the larger architecture that surrounds the world of information processing for healthcare.

Architectural differences

Information systems for healthcare are quite different from information systems for other endeavors. In the classic commercial rendition of information systems, the information systems are self-contained. All of the information is generated, used, analyzed, and otherwise managed inside the corporation. The corporation is an autonomous capsule of its own information. But in healthcare, the information generated inside the doctor's office, hospital, and clinic has great implication outside of the confines of the provider. From a research standpoint, the clinical information that is generated inside the provider's facility is useful in many other places other than the hospital.

In a word, where corporate information circulates in a closed-loop system, information in the healthcare environment operates in anything but a closed system. The open-system approach to the collection, usage, and management of healthcare information has many far-reaching implications.

Another major difference between information and information processing in the world of healthcare and the other world of commercial systems is that information inside the world of healthcare contains a lot of textual information, while information inside commercial systems is dominated by repetitious, numeric-based transactions. The orientation toward text-based information presents a challenge because the ubiquitous commercial database management systems that are widely used—DB2, Oracle, Teradata, and NT SQL Server—are designed to handle repetitious occurrences of data, primarily numeric data. And the textual data that makes up much of the world of the healthcare information factory is anything but transaction oriented or repetitious.

There are then a whole host of important differences between the worlds of healthcare information processing and commercial information processing.

Architectural similarities

From an architectural standpoint there are many similarities between the two worlds. There are large volumes of data. There is a need for looking at data holistically. There is a need for data transformation. There is a need to support both day-to-day clinical activities and research. In a word, there

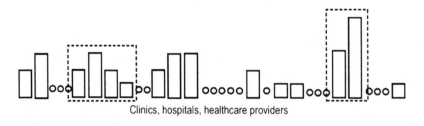

Clinics, hospitals, healthcare providers

FIGURE B.1

Producers and consumers of data.

are many similarities between the world of commercial information processing and that of healthcare information processing.

Separate systems

Doctor's offices, clinics, and hospitals constitute the basic units of collection of information and initial data management in healthcare. Healthcare providers can take many forms. The hospital network may contain many hospitals banded together to process their information in a common fashion. Or a hospital may be as small as an outpatient clinic. In any case, there are many hospitals, clinics, and other providers of care in many configurations. And each of those institutions generates its own information.

Other sources of important healthcare information include ancillary sources such as laboratories, radiology, and pharmacies. Figure B.1 represents the hospitals, clinics, ancillary, and other healthcare providers of the world.

Some of the hospitals in the world operate in a standalone manner. Other hospitals are banded with other hospitals and healthcare providers for jointly collecting and processing data. Some hospitals are part of a large network. Some hospitals are large. Other hospitals are small. There are many different configurations of hospitals, clinics, and healthcare providers.

Like hospitals, there are different structures under which ancillary healthcare providers operate. Some pharmacies operate as a large conglomerate. Other pharmacies are independent. There is a wide variety of operating structures for ancillary healthcare providers.

It is at the provider level that many acts of basic information gathering occur that relate to healthcare. Procedures are done. Checkups are made. Patients are given medication, and so forth. And as each of these activities occur, basic information about healthcare is generated.

A common patient identifier

The first challenge in managing information in this environment is that of creating a common patient identification number for those circumstances where violation of privacy is not an issue. There is a very basic piece of information that must be addressed when violation of patient identity is not an issue. That information is: How does an information analyst identify who is receiving healthcare?

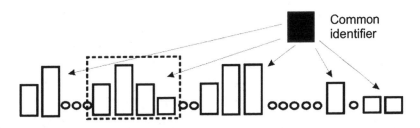

FIGURE B.2

The need for a unique patient identifier.

How does an analyst properly match healthcare information coming from different sources? How does an analyst match together results taken over time for the same patient? It is easy to say that a universal identifier such as social security number needs to be used as a foundation for identifying a patient. But there are some basic problems with a universal identifier such as social security number. What happens if a person doesn't have a social security number? And rarely it occurs that two people have the same social security number. Or what happens if a person has more than one social security number? Or what happens when a father has an operation in one hospital and a week later the father's two-year-old son goes to an emergency room in another hospital and the father uses his own social security number in registering his son?

This most basic problem is pervasive and is the first challenge facing information processing for healthcare. Even in the case of a need to protect identity, there may be occasions where it is to the patient's benefit to have his or her identity recognized beyond the immediate health provider.

Figure B.2 shows the need for technology that creates a unique identification for an individual entering the healthcare system when common identification is legal and beneficial.

There are many good reasons for knowing where healthcare information comes from. From a system-wide standpoint, it is useful to see the many places where a patient has engaged in healthcare. Among other things this kind of information is useful in looking for fraud or abuse of the system. But there is an even more important reason for being able to look at the many places where a patient may have engaged in healthcare. That reason is that by being able to look at a single patient over many episodes of care from different providers, a truly holistic view of the patient emerges. Stated differently, any one provider only has one glimpse of a patient and the patient's healthcare at a moment in time. By being able to track a patient over time and over multiple episodes of care coming from different providers, a much more complete picture of the patient's health is able to be formulated.

Integrating data

As important as unique identification of patients is under the proper circumstances, it is hardly the only problem. The next problem is that of uniform storage and interpretation of data. As an example of this problem, consider the simple information—gender. Gender is found in almost every patient record. The problem is that in hospital ABC, gender is encoded as MALE/FEMALE. In clinic BCD, gender is encoded as M/F. In doctor's office CDE, gender is encoded as X/Y. And in clinic DEF, gender is encoded as 1/0. If there is to be a common treatment of gender in analysis, there needs to be a

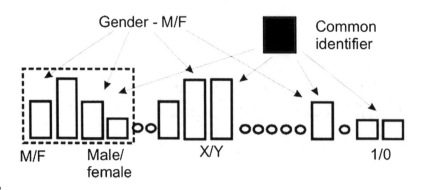

FIGURE B.3

Integrating data.

common specification for the value of gender—say M/F. Then when data is taken from anywhere that gender is not represented that way, a conversion is made from whatever the value is in the provider's system to a common value understood by researchers and analysts. Figure B.3 shows the need to convert data as data is merged into a collective pool.

The larger issue of integration across many data types

But the need for integrated data does not stop at a single data element—gender. There are many other data elements that need to be integrated into a common format as well. As a simple list of common data elements that need to be integrated into a common format and structure, consider:

- Age
- Date of birth
- Place of birth
- Blood pressure
- Weight
- Height
- Ethnic origin

Figure B.4 shows that there is a need to integrate many data elements if a collective database of healthcare information is to be achieved.

ETL and the collective common data warehouse

So how are the important functions of creating a unique identifier and creating a common understanding of data to be achieved? Figure B.5 shows that technology for creating a unique name and ETL technology—that is, extract/transform/load—technology is needed. In today's world the common identifier can be created probabilistically, based on a match of up to 20 different fields. And ETL has been done for a long time now.

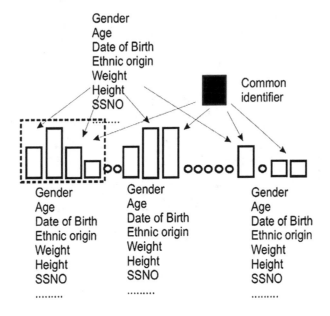

FIGURE B.4

Integrating disparate data.

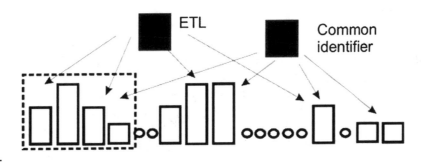

FIGURE B.5

Technologies for data integration.

ETL technology has long been used for integration in the commercial world. ETL applies as readily to healthcare data as it does to commercial data.

The point of collection for this data is shown to be a data warehouse. Two types of data warehouse will be discussed in this paper: a large collective common data warehouse where healthcare information from a wide variety of providers is collected, and a local data warehouse that suits the immediate needs of an individual provider. Local and individual hospitals and clinics contribute their integrated data to the common data warehouse as well as to their own "local" data warehouse. The large collective common data warehouse becomes the place where research is easily done. Large amounts

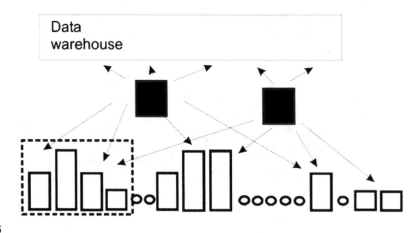

FIGURE B.6

Data integration to the EDW.

of data representing a large population are collected, integrated, and cleaned in the collective common data warehouse. It then becomes the job of the researcher or analyst to do analysis, not to collect data when looking at data in the collective common data warehouse. The local data warehouse that suits the needs of an individual provider is used for information analysis that occurs at the individual provider level. There is great efficiency in this organization of information as witnessed by the many commercial organizations that do architecturally what is being suggested for healthcare information processing. Figure B.6 shows the collection of integrated data into a common data warehouse.

It is noted that the collective common data warehouse—as portrayed here—exists outside the boundaries of a given hospital or hospitals. But it is absolutely normal for there to exist another set of local uncommon data warehouses for an individual hospital or clinic. The distinction between the collective common data warehouse that is being suggested here and the individual data warehouse built for a hospital or clinic will be discussed later in this paper.

One of the issues that arises in the creation of a collective common data warehouse is that of the protection of the privacy of the individual data that generates most of the information that passes into the collective common data warehouse. If there is no need for privacy, then identifying information for each unit of data can be passed from the provider to the collective common data warehouse. If there is a need for privacy, then the instances of data can be passed anonymously to the collective common data warehouse. In this case, data can be used for analysis in the collective common data warehouse but there can never be backward linkage from the collective common data warehouse to the provider. And of course there are instances where healthcare data is sent to the collective common data warehouse where there are no individual identifiers whatsoever.

On occasion there may be a reason for feedback from the collective common data warehouse to the provider. When this is the case the provider may provide an encrypted identifier to the collective common data warehouse when the data is being initially loaded. The provider holds the keys for decrypting the data. Only the immediate provider knows how to make the connection between the individual and the encrypted identifier in this case. If there is feedback from the collected common data warehouse, the encrypted identifier is passed to the provider and the provider subsequently uses

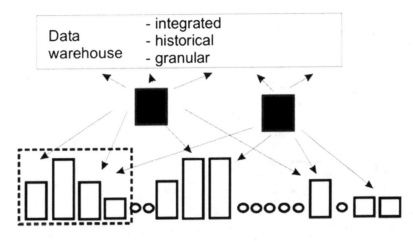

FIGURE B.7

Common traits of data warehouse.

the decryption key to determine the real identification of the patient. In such a manner there may be feedback from the collective common data warehouse to the provider that does not violate the privacy of the individual patient.

Common elements of a data warehouse

There are several recognizable architectural elements to the collective common data warehouse (indeed, these recognizable elements are for *any* data warehouse.) The first of those elements is that data is represented in a single integrated manner in the data warehouse. The second element is that data can be collected over time in the collective common data warehouse. Whereas the hospital OLTP and administrative systems contain reasonably current information, the data warehouse contains historical information, say five to ten years' worth of information. The third element of a data warehouse is that data is at a low level of granularity. These are the three distinguishing characteristics of data in a data warehouse. Depending on the particulars a data warehouse may or may not contain identifying information, depending on the compliance specifications. Figure B.7 shows the general, common characteristics of a data warehouse.

One of the issues that is important as data is sent to the data warehouse is that of the protection of privacy. As a rule, individual identifying data is safe when stored at the transaction level. But as data is placed into a data warehouse, care must be taken not to violate the rules laid down by Health Insurance Portability and Accountability Act (HIPAA). It is noted that the research done on the data found in the data warehouse is normally not dependent on individual identification. When an analyst looks at 10,000 cases of a disease and its symptoms, the analyst is normally not interested in knowing who the individuals are who have contributed information to the study. Instead, the analyst is much more interested in the characteristics, the treatment, the symptoms, and the outcomes of the disease. Therefore, placing data in the data warehouse anonymously is an acceptable practice.

Analytical processing

The data warehouse—either the collective common data warehouse or the local provider data warehouse—is good for many purposes. The reason most people build a data warehouse is for the purpose of doing analytical processing, as opposed to transaction processing. For a variety of reasons it is poor form to build a data warehouse and do transaction processing in the warehouse.

There are many reasons why a data warehouse supports analytical processing. Some of the reasons are:

- Data is found over a spectrum of time in the data warehouse.
- Data is integrated so that many sources of data can be meaningfully combined together.
- Data is at a granular level so that the same data can be looked at in many ways.

This last feature of a data warehouse is one that is of most importance. Because data is at the lowest level of granularity, the same unit of data can be used in many ways. One group of analysts looking at patients can look at the data one way. Another group of analysts looking at procedures can look at the same data another way. Yet another group of analysts can look at the data from the standpoint of physicians.

There are many advantages to having data at a granular level. Looking at the same data in different ways is certainly a huge advantage. But looking at the data from the standpoint of reconcilability is another huge advantage. If one analyst decides to correlate his or her results with another analyst, because the analysis all came from the same granular source, reconcilability is a real possibility.

And yet another tremendous advantage to the organization of data into a data warehouse is that of having a foundation in place when new requirements come along. By having the data infrastructure in place when it is time to do a new analysis, tremendous amounts of time are saved by having existing data organized, integrated, and at the lowest level of granularity at the time the analyst discovers that he or she needs to do a new study.

One way of looking at the value of the data warehouse is that a data warehouse allows data to be reused. It is true that a fair amount of work must be done to create the data in the healthcare data warehouse. But once the data warehouse is created it can be used over and over again. The reusability of data has an amazingly positive effect on research organizations. The reusability of data means that the research analyst can spend his or her time on doing research rather than on collecting and scrubbing data. This means that the cost of research goes down dramatically and that the speed of research is greatly enhanced. Now research takes a fraction of the time than would be required if the research project had to spend a large amount of time finding, accessing, and cleansing research data. There is then enormous value in constructing a data warehouse where data can easily be reused.

But there are other benefits from the building of a data warehouse for the healthcare environment. One of those benefits is the fact that once data has been passed through the integration process, the data becomes very credible. An analyst can have confidence in data that has been passed through the rigor of editing, transformation, and loading. Figure B.8 shows the importance of having the data warehouse built at the lowest level of granularity.

DSS/business intelligence processing

Sitting on top of the data warehouse is a world of DSS or BI (decision support systems or business intelligence). This layer of analytical capability consists of software either designed for an application

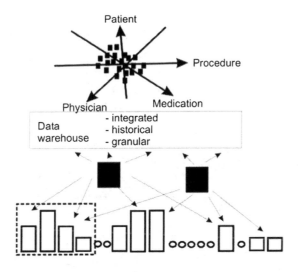

FIGURE B.8

The data warehouse with the lowest "grain of data."

or designed in the form of a tool ready to create a new application. There are many kinds of analytical tools that fit here—SAS, Business Objects, Cognos, Crystal Reports, and many more.

The applications that are built here draw upon the data found in the data warehouse. The tools for analysis that are found here are designed for flexibility, presentation, and diversity of analytical capabilities.

The analytical tools found here are distinctly different from the tools designed to capture and initially organize raw data. OLTP tools and infrastructure are designed for doing the basic transactions that the hospital or clinic needs to capture data initially. But analytical tools are used at the data warehouse level. These two types of tools are as different as chalk and cheese. Some of the defining criteria of these tools include:

- OLTP:
  - Transaction oriented
  - Insertion and update of data
  - Capture of data at a detailed level
  - Response time a real issue
  - Availability a real issue
- DSS/analytical:
  - Ability to access large volumes of data
  - No need to change data values at the record level
  - Ability to summarize and subset data
  - Flexibility of processing
  - Response time not an issue

Figure B.9 shows the different environments and how they relate.

There are many variations on the information structure shown in Figure B.9. Some of the more important of those structures will be discussed later in this paper.

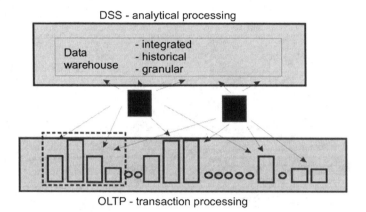

FIGURE B.9

The interrelated components of a data warehouse.

Different types of data that go into the data warehouse

There are essentially two different types of data that flow into a data warehouse: transaction-based data and unstructured data. Transaction-based data is data that is repetitive and predictable. Typical in the healthcare environment of transaction-based data is billing information and a lot of pharmaceutical information. In transaction-based data the same type of data occurs over and over again.

When it comes to unstructured information, it often does not occur repetitively. A doctor makes a report about an operation. The emergency room attendant performs a procedure. The ambulance operator becomes involved in a traffic accident. There is case after case where textual information appears in the rendering of healthcare.

Both of these types of information need to flow into the data warehouse. But there is a fundamental problem. Traditionally trying to mix repetitive data and nonrepetitive data is like trying to plug an American hair curler into an electrical outlet in England. Either nothing happens or you are at the risk of creating a fire. Neither outcome is productive.

Textual data

One way that the world of information systems for healthcare is fundamentally different from the world of information systems for other environments is that in healthcare, the lingua franca is textual data, not transaction-based data. In commercial environments, the dominating mode of information is transactions. Banks cash checks and do ATM activities, airlines make reservations, insurance companies process claims, and so forth. Each of these activities creates a transaction that is in form very similar to thousands of other transactions. And in these commercial environments decisions are made almost exclusively on the basis of the many activities done throughout the day.

But in the healthcare environment there is relatively little transaction processing. Instead there is a wealth of textual data to be processed. Doctors generate text every time they see a patient. Doctors generate text as the result of a procedure. Nurses generate text in a hospital. Insurance companies

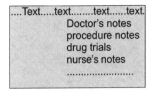

FIGURE B.10

Text found in healthcare.

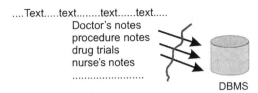

FIGURE B.11

Integrating text to DBMS.

use text in the description of a claim, and so forth. Just as the world of commerce relies on transactions, the world of healthcare relies on text. Figure B.10 shows the generation of text that is found in healthcare.

There is nothing right or wrong about relying on text as the basis for conducting the business of healthcare. But there is one serious drawback, and that is that text does not sit well on standard database management systems. Standard database management systems depend on the same data being repeated over and over, as per transaction processing. But with textual data there is not the same repetition. Text is freeform. The doctor is free to write whatever he or she wants in whatever structure that he or she wants. Trying to read raw text that has been placed on a standard database management system is an act of futility. Certainly raw text can be placed on a disk by using a database management system. But trying to use the raw text after it has been placed there is very, very difficult.

Figure B.11 shows that placing text on a standard database management system can be done but is awkward to process once done.

Processing text in a meaningful fashion—textual integration

The first issue that the analyst faces in building the healthcare information factory is that of converting text to an electronic medium. Certainly when a doctor or nurse writes using a pen or pencil on paper notes, those notes are useless unless they can be converted to an electronic form. Trying to get doctors to write their notes on a computer is a practice that is less than enthusiastically embraced. And trying to get doctors to use a structured screen on a computer is even less enthusiastically accepted.

One approach to the transformation of paper-and-pencil notes to an electronic format is to use the services of a transcriptionist. A transcriptionist reads the paper-and-pencil notes that the doctor has made and electronically transcribes them. There are several advantages to this approach. One approach is that over time the transcriptionist becomes used to the doctor's handwriting. Another advantage is that the transcriptionist starts to become accustomed to the shorthand that doctors inevitably use in making notes. But using a transcriptionist is ultimately tedious and somewhat expensive.

Another approach is to get the doctor to record notes on an audio recording device. Voice recognition software is then used to do the electronic capturing of the notes. There are many advantages to doing the capture of notes by audio. But there are some drawbacks. One drawback is that the voice recognition software is not perfect. In the best of circumstances, some of the words the doctor says will be lost or mangled. The second drawback is that the notes are not immediately available. Some amount of work must be done from the time the doctor says the words until they are ready for review.

FIGURE B.12

Processing text data.

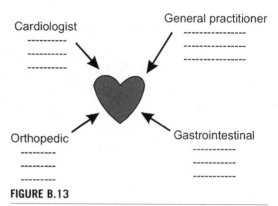

FIGURE B.13

Multiple terms for one subject.

And a third drawback is that this form of electronic capture is not traditional. Many doctors just prefer the way they have been doing it for years.

Figure B.12 shows the need to convert text into an electronic form before the text becomes useful for analytical processing.

As important as the electronic capture of information is, it is only the first step in the process of creating the healthcare information factory. Consider some of the other obstacles facing the analyst wishing to get his or her hands on medical/healthcare data.

The issue of terminology

One of the biggest obstacles is that of terminology. Different doctors speak in different dialects. In medical school cardiologists learn to refer to parts of the human body and conditions of the human body one way. In medical school anesthesiologists refer to the tools and practices of their trade in different language than that used by cardiologists. General practitioners have their set of vocabulary that they use. Nurses have their vocabulary, lab technicians have their vocabulary, and so forth. In a word, people are talking in the same language about the same things, but they are using different terminology. Through schooling, general practice, geographic locality, length of practice, and association with peers, different subcommunities of medical practice are formed, and each of these subcommunities has their own idioms and terms. This state of affairs is natural and normal.

As testimony to the many dialects of healthcare language that are spoken, consider the common term "broken bone." It is said that the term "broken bone" can commonly be stated in as many as 20 different ways.

Figure B.13 shows that different communities have different ways of referring to the same part of the human body.

The problem is that for analysis of text for the healthcare community to occur, there must be some form of a universal language to be created. If an analyst refers to a "broken bone" the analyst does not find the 19 other ways to which a broken bone is referred. This interference of terminology then is one of the important ways in which text becomes its own obstacle to analysis of textual data.

As profound as the obstacle of terminology is, terminology is hardly the only obstacle awaiting the organization that wants to build the healthcare information factory.

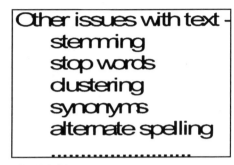

FIGURE B.14

Issues with text processing.

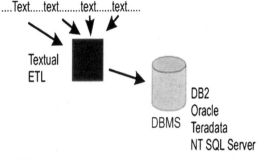

FIGURE B.15

Text processing with textual ETL.

Other obstacles

Text carries with it a whole other set of obstacles. Figure B.14 illustrates some of those obstacles.

Fortunately there is technology that is designed to address the many obstacles of textual analytics. That technology is textual ETL from Forest Rim Technology. The world has long had ETL technology—called classical ETL technology here. The world has had Informatica, Ascential, and Ab Initio. Classical ETL technology is designed to take data from older legacy transaction-oriented systems and integrate the data into a form and structure useful for data warehouse processing. Classical ETL processing is for repetitive transaction processing systems.

Forest Rim Technology, on the other hand, is dedicated to processing textual nonrepetitive information. Forest Rim Technology uses textual information as the input and produces standard databases as the output. As such, you can create your data warehouse using textual data as input with the textual ETL provided by Forest Rim Technology. Forest Rim Technology has developed and heavily patented the process of taking text and preparing text for data warehouse processing. Although ETL for repetitive data and ETL for textual data appears to be conceptually the same, at a detailed level classical repetitive ETL and textual nonrepetitive ETL are very different. (*Note:* If you wish to copy Forest Rim's patented textual ETL technology, please contact Forest Rim (http://www.forestrimtech.com) for licensing rights.)

Textual ETL is designed to take text and do the many things to it that are necessary to prepare the text for entry into a database structure and to integrate the text so that textual analytical processing can be done against it.

The net result of textual ETL is that medical documents can be read, the text integrated, and the results can be placed into a standard database management system. Figure B.15 shows this type of processing.

The process of integration of text is at the heart of being able to do textual analytical processing. (See Forest Rim Technology's patented technology for a detailed explanation of how to do textual integration.) Some of the functions that must be achieved by textual integration include:

- Stop word processing—the removal of extraneous words.
- Stemming—the reduction of words to a common Latin or Greek stem.
- Alternate spelling—the recognition that some words have alternate spellings.

- Multiple language translation—the ability to read text in one language and reference it and create a database in another language.
- Homographic resolution—the ability to take words that are spelled the same way and to expand the words into a properly phrased set of words based on the context of the document.
- Variable pattern recognition—the ability to read a word and recognize its word type merely based on the structure of the word, such as an email address.
- Variable symbol recognition—the ability to recognize and index certain words inside a document.
- Semi-structured data recognition.

Categorizations of data

An important component of textual integration is the ability to recognize external categorizations of data. Once external categorizations of data are recognized, the text can be understood in an abstract manner. In many ways the abstraction of raw text into external categorizations is the equivalent of modeling data. It is through external categorization of data that query tools have the ability to access and analyze textual data.

There are many ways to create external categorizations of data. One of the most important of the ways is to create external categorizations such as taxonomies. Taxonomies can be built internally on a customized basis. Or there are commercially available taxonomies (see Wand, Inc., http://www.wand-inc.com/). A commercially available taxonomy is easy to use and is immediately available. In addition, there are a wide variety of commercially available taxonomies.

As a rule the analyst building the data warehouse from textual data chooses only those taxonomies that are appropriate to the text. For example, if the text was focused on orthopedics, the analyst would not choose to use an external taxonomy for obstetrics for categorization of the text.

One way to look at the value of textual integration is that if text is merely shuffled from one document to a database, no real textual integration has occurred and textual analytics cannot be done.

There are many benefits to doing the processing as described. The major benefit is that the text is integrated. By integrating the text, analytical processing can be done against the text. From a mechanical standpoint, standard analytical tools can be used against the text once the text is placed into a standard database. Analytical tools such as SAS, Business Objects, Cognos, MicroStrategy, Crystal Reports, and others can be run against the textual data found in the textually based database. Figure B.16 shows that once integrated into a database, text can be analyzed by standard tool sets.

Given the granular nature of the textual data and the fact that there is a wide diversity of sources, it is possible to do analytical processing against the integrated text in a variety of ways. Figure B.17 shows that once the integrated textual data has been collected and integrated, that the integrated text can be used in many ways.

One analyst can look at the information that has been gathered and integrated from the perspective of cancer research. Another analyst can use the data that has been gathered and integrated from the standpoint of heart research. Still another analyst can look at and analyze the same data from the standpoint of geriatric research, and so forth. Figure B.17 shows that the textual analytical data that has been collected is very versatile.

An example

As an example of the research that can be done with the textual data, consider a research institution that has treated heart patients for 30 years. Doctors' notes have been collected for 30 years' time as

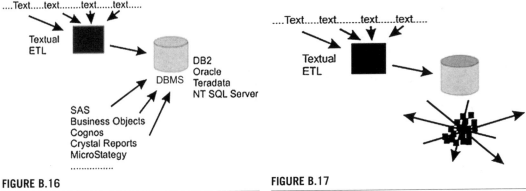

FIGURE B.16

Analytics on textual data.

FIGURE B.17

Textual analytics.

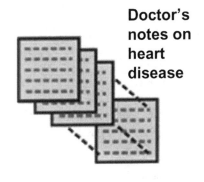

Doctor's notes on heart disease

FIGURE B.18

Doctors' notes.

the result of treating many patients. Some of the doctors' notes are just a few pages long and other doctors' notes are as much as 500 pages in length. There are approximately 10,000 sets of notes that have been collected over the years. Figure B.18 shows these notes.

The doctors' notes that have been collected are passed through the textual ETL process. As part of the processing of textual ETL the terminology found in the doctors' notes is resolved. Given that over time these doctors' notes have been written by many doctors, the resolution of terminology is a non-trivial feat. In addition, stop words are removed, the text is stemmed, alternate spelling is resolved, homographs are processed, and so forth. In a word, the text generated by doctors over 30 years is integrated and is ready for analytical processing. Figure B.19 shows the database that is created as a result of textual ETL.

Visualization

In addition to the creation of a database based on text, the text that has been integrated can be visualized. By visualizing the text, the analyst can easily see important patterns to the information that was contained in the doctors' notes. The analyst can see the correlative factors to heart disease that have

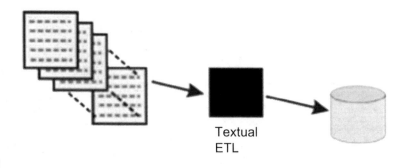

FIGURE B.19

Textual ETL output.

been observed in the doctors' notes over the years. By gathering and integrating the text found in the doctors' notes, the symptoms, side effects, treatment factors, and so forth can all be observed for a large number of patients across a lengthy period of time.

Visualization gives a doctor the opportunity to view textual information over a broad vista. By looking at a broad vista over time, patterns in the data start to emerge that otherwise would not have been easy to see. Visualization makes patterns of treatment and symptoms found in the 30 years of doctors' notes simply "pop out."

Figure B.20 shows that visualization can also be done against the integrated text that has been gathered.

One of the more interesting and incisive activities that can be done with visualizations is that of the creation of comparative visualizations across different demographic sets. For example, in the example being discussed, a visualization for heart disease can be created for a population of 10,000 patients, based on the 30-year history of patients who have been treated. After the correlative collective visualization for 10,000 people has been created, different visualizations for different demographics can be created. The population of 10,000 patients can be divided into separate populations of men and women. Now separate visualizations can be created for men and women. The visualization that can be created for men can be compared to the visualization for the general population, and the effects of heart disease for men can be noted simply by comparing the general population visualization and the visualization created just for men.

Furthermore, the population studies can be divided into subgroups other than men and women. Comparative studies can be made of smokers and nonsmokers, of people over 40 and people under 40, and so forth.

Figure B.21 shows that a general population visualization can be created and that different demographic visualizations can also be created.

Once the different populations have their visualizations created, the difference between the visualizations can be found—called the "delta." The delta shows the most interesting information. For example, in the heart disease study that has been created, the delta between men and women and their journey with heart disease becomes obvious.

Figure B.22 shows the delta between different groups of people insofar as demographic differences are concerned.

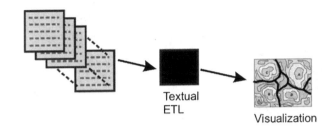

FIGURE B.20

Visualization on textual data.

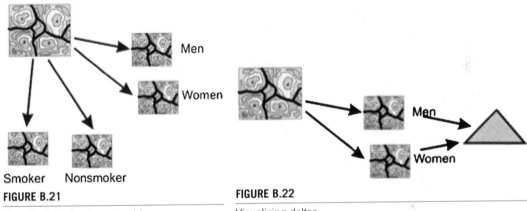

FIGURE B.21

Visualizations by demographics.

FIGURE B.22

Visualizing deltas.

Including text-based databases with classical structured databases

One of the creative uses of the textual data that has been gathered and integrated is the inclusion of the database that contains the textual data into the healthcare information factory. Figure B.23 shows this inclusion.

The system of record

One of the most important features of the healthcare information factory is that of the "system of record." The system of record is the place where an analyst can go to access the data in its "purest" (i.e., original) form. If there ever is any doubt as to the accuracy of data, the system of record is used as the final authority. There are different places in the healthcare information factory where the system of record is found for different types of data. For textual data the system of record is the base document where the original text is contained. For transaction data the system of record resides in the transactions as they were executed. But the system of record moves over time. There is the system of record for very current data, and there is the system of record for historical data. For data that is

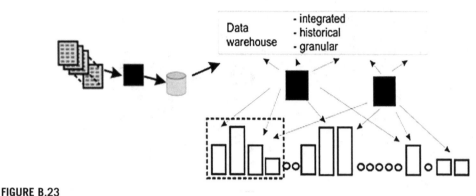

FIGURE B.23

Bridging the two worlds.

historical, the system of record lies in the data warehouse. This means that data goes through a trans-formation as it ages and is placed in a data warehouse. In doing so there may be a difference between the very current values in the system of record data and the historical data warehouse data. In any case the system of record needs to be defined and rigorously enforced.

The value of the system of record is that there is one and only one place where the correct value of data resides. Without the system of record, data tends to be proliferated in many different places and soon there are values of data, which are in contradiction with each other. When there is questionable data that is found in the analytical infrastructure, the integrity of all analytical processing comes into question. Therefore, an integral part of the healthcare information factory is the system of record.

The system of record is the basis for integrity of information in the healthcare information envi-ronment. Figure B.24 shows the system of record in the healthcare information factory environment.

Metadata

Another essential component of the healthcare information factory is metadata. In any information processing environment data can be divided into two camps: actual data and metadata. Metadata is the data needed to describe actual data. The attributes of a file are one form of metadata. The number of records in a file is another form of metadata. The indexes for a file are yet another form of metadata.

Metadata comes in many forms. The simplest form is the technical form where tables, attributes, and physical characteristics are described. The more complex form of metadata is the business-related metadata where definitions, context, and business language are described.

Metadata is essential in the healthcare information factory for many reasons. One reason is the fact that the healthcare information factory is spread across many different platforms of technology. The mechanism needed to coordinate the work done on those platforms is done through communica-tions based on metadata. Another reason why metadata is so important is that the analyst needs to know all about data before the data can be used in an analysis. When an analyst has three sources of data to choose from in doing an analysis, the analyst needs metadata to distinguish the appropriate-ness of any source of data.

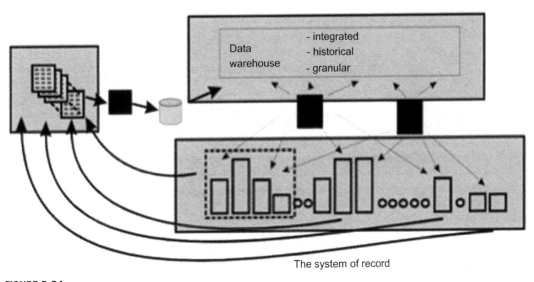

FIGURE B.24

System of record in the healthcare information factory.

Indeed, there are many reasons why metadata is an essential part of the healthcare information factory.

Metadata is found in two levels in the healthcare information factory: at the local level and at the enterprise level. Local metadata is metadata that is focused on a given part of the enterprise. There is metadata for the transaction component. There is metadata for the processing of text. There is metadata for the transformation of data. There is metadata for the description of data residing inside the data warehouse. In a word, local metadata is found in many places in many forms.

But there is also a need for metadata at the global level. Metadata at the global level is metadata that describes how different forms of local metadata are related.

There are two basic forms of metadata: technical metadata and business metadata. Technical metadata is for technicians and describes the different aspects of technology. Business metadata is for the business person and refers to the business understanding of calculations, definitions of data, and structuring of data—all in the language of business, not technology. Figure B.25 shows local metadata and global metadata.

Local individual data warehouses

Another important feature of the healthcare information factory is the need for local data warehouses as well as the collective common data warehouse. As has been discussed elsewhere, medical information has wide value, well outside the boundaries of the hospital or clinic. There is need for a very local rendition of the data warehouse that services the needs of the individual hospital, clinic, or pharmacy. This local data warehouse contains the same type of data as found in the larger collective

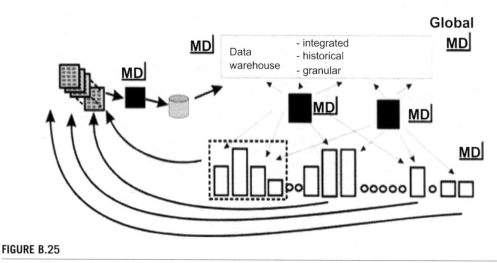

FIGURE B.25

Local and global metadata.

common analytical data warehouse. But the data in the local data warehouse is far less voluminous and far less robust than the data found in the larger collective common analytical warehouse serving the entire medical community. Stated differently, the larger collective common analytical data warehouse is made from the data found in hundreds of hospitals and hundreds of clinics. But the local data warehouse has information specific to the local care provider only. Figure B.26 shows that there are different levels of data warehousing within the healthcare information factory community.

In the ideal case the local hospitals and clinics would create their own data warehouse, then pass data from their data warehouse to the larger analytical data warehouse for all hospitals and clinics. But building a local data warehouse is often beyond the means or ambitions of the local hospital or clinic. Therefore, it often happens that the larger analytical warehouse is fed directly from raw data found in the local hospital or clinic.

Data models and the healthcare information factory

The database design that is done for the different levels of data in the healthcare information factory is initially shaped by the data model. Like all data models, the healthcare information factory data model is an abstraction of the information found in the different data warehouses that constitute the healthcare information factory. Some of the qualities of the data model are:

- Data is organized at a low level of granularity.
- Data is structured according to major subject areas.
- Data is interrelated from one subject area to the next.
- Different groupings of data have identifiers—keys that may be unique or nonunique.

The data model is divided into three distinct levels. Those levels are the high-level, the mid-level, and the low-level data model. Figure B.27 shows these three levels of modeling.

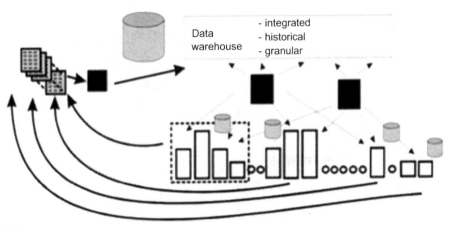

FIGURE B.26

Multistep data warehouse.

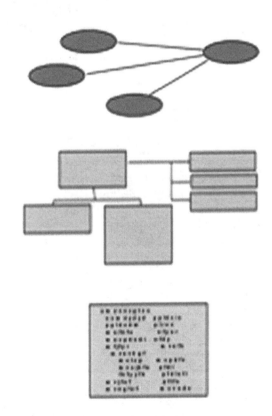

FIGURE B.27

Data models in healthcare information factory.

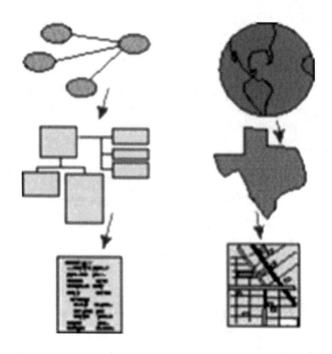

FIGURE B.28

Data model levels—analogy.

The high-level data model is represented by ovals connected by lines. The high-level data model is where the major subjects of the corporation reside. This level of the data model represents the most abstract aspects of the healthcare environment. The lines that connect the high-level subjects depict a relationship between the subject areas. Oftentimes the high-level data model is called an ERD, or an entity relationship diagram.

The mid-level data model is derived from the high-level model. The mid-level data model consists of a much more detailed description of the data, the grouping of the data, and the relationships of the data to each other. Each high-level subject area turns into its own mid-level data model. The mid-level data model is often called the DIS, or data item set. In the diagram the cluster of boxes in the center of the diagram represents the mid-level data model.

The low-level data model is the place where physical characteristics appear. The low-level data model is the first draft of the physical database design. In the diagram, the green box that is full of attribute definitions represents the low-level data model.

The relationship of the different levels of the data model can be described in terms of an analogy. Figure B.28 shows the analogy.

The high-level data model is analogous to a globe (that represents the Earth). The mid-level data model is analogous to a map of the state of Texas. The low-level data model is analogous to the city map of Dallas, TX. Note that there is a relationship between each level of modeling. The state of Texas can be recognized in the globe. And the city of Dallas can be recognized inside the map of Texas.

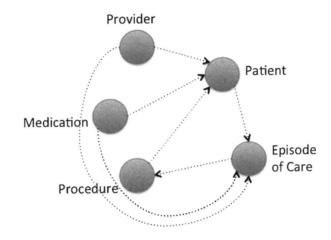

FIGURE B.29

ERD in healthcare information factory.

Also note that as the model goes lower, the completeness of the model diminishes. For example, the state of Texas shows nothing about the state of New York. And the map of the city of Dallas does not show you how to get around El Paso. In addition, as the model goes lower, details increase. You might have a hard time finding the outline of the state of Rhode Island on the globe, and you might have a hard time finding High Street in Dallas in the map of Texas.

As an example of what the high-level data model might look like, consider the ERD shown in Figure B.29.

The ERD in Figure B.29 shows that there are five major subject areas: patient, provider, procedure, medication, and episode of care. The arrows between the subject areas indicate a direct relationship between the major subject areas. The arrowhead on the line indicates the cardinality of the relationship. For example, the arrowhead between patient and episode of care indicates that a patient may have more than one episode of care.

As a rule there are no double-headed arrows. While a single-headed arrow indicates a 1:*n* relationship, a double-headed arrow indicates an *m:n* relationship. As a rule an *m:n* relationship is resolved. The resolution of an *m:n* relationship usually involves the creation of two or more 1:*n* relationships that are at a lower level of granularity than the *m:n* relationship.

Oftentimes the ERD is accompanied by a series of definitions of subject areas and other data, where the different subject areas are carefully defined.

The mid-level data model is created for *each* subject area. As an example, if the patient subject area is expanded into a lower level of detail, it might look like the DIS shown in Figure B.30.

The data in Figure B.30 is for the patient subject area. Data that exists once and only once is found in the root area—the box headed by patient ID. The common patient ID is a probabilistically created value connecting potentially many different records together. The hierarchy of data is extended, showing that a patient can have multiple email addresses, multiple phone numbers, multiple allergies, and multiple relatives. And a relative may have multiple diseases or other conditions.

In addition there may be different types of patients. A patient may be insured or not insured. And a patient may have his or her ethnic background recorded.

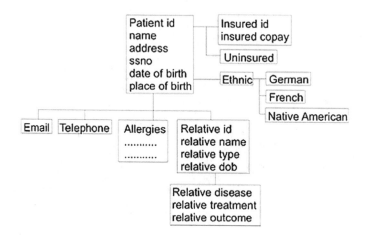

FIGURE B.30

Example subject area.

```
Patient id      varchar(50)      indexed non null
name            varchar(70)      indexed
address         varchar(150)
ssno            '999999999'      indexed
date of birth   date
place of birth  varchar(70)
```

FIGURE B.31

Low-level data model.

In addition to the basic information about a patient recorded, there may be information about how the patient DIS relates to other DIS. In addition keys may be identified and documented. The DIS becomes the next step of data modeling after the ERD is created.

After the mid-level data model is built, it is time to build the low-level data model. In many regards the low-level data model is merely the physical extension of the DIS. Figure B.31 shows the low-level data model.

Each grouping of data in the DIS becomes its own physical low-level model. In the example it is seen that physical characteristics are added as well as other information, such as what attributes are indexed and what attributes cannot be null.

The data model considerations that have been discussed apply generically to any data model. But when it comes time to build the data model for the data warehouse a few other considerations are made. Figure B.32 shows that each grouping of data in a data warehouse has its own unit of time contained in the record.

The unit of time for a record of data is very important because it gives a point of reference for whatever measure or observation is being recorded.

The practice of making sure that each grouping of data is placed in the database for a data warehouse is true for all data warehouses. And it is true for healthcare data warehouses as well. In addition

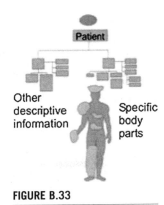

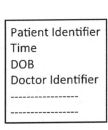

```
Patient Identifier
Time
DOB
Doctor Identifier
-----------------
-----------------
```

FIGURE B.32

Data grouping in a
data warehouse.

Other
descriptive
information

Specific
body
parts

FIGURE B.33

Data model for patient.

to placing data physically in a database, another important database design practice is that of insuring that any data elements that are operational only (such as telephone number) are removed from the data warehouse data model. And summary data is normally removed as well. (Only on rare occasions is it permissible or advisable to store summary data in a data warehouse.)

The data model for the patient in the healthcare data warehouse is almost always divided into three distinctive parts. Figure B.33 shows this division.

Figure B.33 shows that the healthcare data model for the patient is divided into three parts: one part for patient identification, one part descriptive, and one part for body parts and functions. This division makes sense for a variety of reasons. From a functional standpoint there is little or no relationship between a patient's heart rate and the address of the patient. From a database design standpoint, to normalize the data, this division is natural in any case.

So the data model is created with normalization and with a distinct separation of data types. Despite the separation of data, in each grouping of data is always found patient ID. It is necessary to have patient ID as a data element to bring together the many different types of data that are likely to exist for a patient. The data that populates the data model comes from many sources, many of which are generated by the recording of an episode of care.

The data begins as a recording of the activities found in an episode of care. The data is transformed into a form and structure suitable for an individual data warehouse, the kind of data warehouse that a hospital or a clinic might have for its own use. Figure B.34 shows the architecture that is created.

Once the individual or local data warehouse is created, the data flows into the collective common data warehouse. At this point the data is stripped of its identity. The data either becomes anonymous or the data becomes encrypted. The data in the collective common data warehouse is organized by subject area. Then data is taken from the subject areas to form special subject areas. These special subject areas can encompass any type of information useful to research for healthcare.

Note that data can go directly from an episode of care to the collective common data warehouse. In the eventuality that there is no individual provider data warehouse, the data can flow from the episode of care directly into the collective common data warehouse.

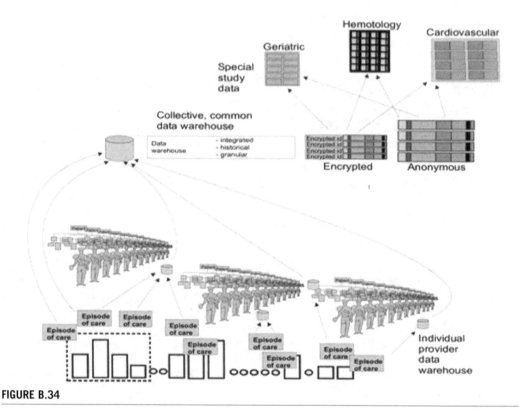

FIGURE B.34

End-state architecture.

Once the collective common data warehouse is created, the data in the collective common data warehouse can easily be interfaced with external data to produce a true scope of analysis. Figure B.35 shows the ability to bring external data into a special subject area.

Creating the medical data warehouse data model

The data model for the medical data warehouse has a unique characteristic not commonly found elsewhere. That characteristic is that the data warehouse model contains many broad classifications of data for a human being. There are of course standard attributes for a human—gender, age, weight, and height. Then there are other common attributes, such as blood pressure and blood type. Then there are many different specific measurements of the human body—liver measurements, kidney measurements, spleen measurements, cholesterol measurements, and so forth. Some of these measurements are commonly tracked and other measurements are rarely tracked. The data model for the human body needs to be able to account for *all* of these measurements.

The problem is that any one checkup or report to the data warehouse will contain only a few of these measurements. In other words there will be many null values in the instance of data embodied

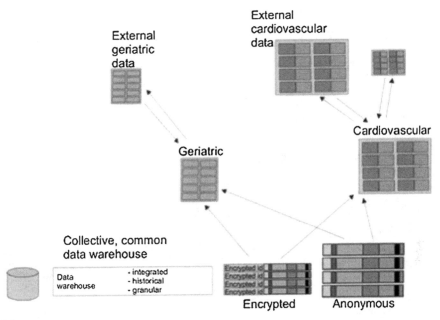

FIGURE B.35

Integrating external data with specific subject area.

by the data model. Modern DBMSs can handle large amounts of null values. But there are other ways to handle this phenomenon of having many elements of data with only a few being measured. One way to handle the data is to encapsulate the different attributes and their measurement so that a variable number of attributes are captured. Notionally, the record of the data in an encapsulated form may look like the following:

Patient: John Doe
Checkup date: Oct. 22, 2008
(Height: 5' 10")
(Weight: 210 lbs)
(Blood pressure: 120/62)
(Blood sugar: 93)

By storing a variable number of attributes, a lot of space is saved. On the other hand, access of the data may be impaired due to the difficulties caused by the lack of uniformity of the medical record.

The collective common data model

One of the most interesting aspects of the healthcare information factory is the data model that is needed for the collective common data warehouse—the data warehouse that is created from all of the

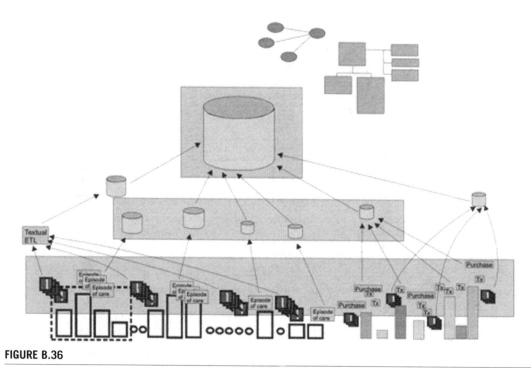

FIGURE B.36

Architecture of medical data warehouse.

healthcare information that comes from all providers and other healthcare entities. There are lots of reasons why this data model is so important. Some of the reasons are:

- The data model is the basis of many different and diverse forms of research. The data model has got to encompass a very wide set of usages.
- The data model cannot have patient information that is identifiable.
- The data model has a very wide scope.
- The data model will have instances of data based on the model where only a few elements of data are present and most elements of data are not present.

Figure B.36 shows the architectural positioning of the data model that needs to be built for the healthcare information factory.

At the heart of the collective common data model is the human body and patient. Any healthcare initiative that does not account for patients is not worth taking seriously. Yet, because of privacy laws, information that is directly known about a patient cannot be in the model. So the data model for the collective common data model contains a lot of indirect information about patients but no information directly known about patients. In this regard the collective common data model is unlike the data models created for other industries. Figure B.37 shows the data model.

The need for privacy makes the collective common data model a bit strange. One the one hand, there is a need for privacy of the individual. On the other hand, there is a need for correlating data

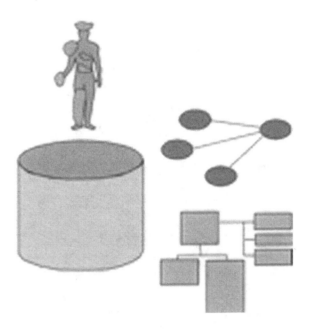

FIGURE B.37

Collective common data model.

FIGURE B.38

Correlation of data.

from many different sources. This dichotomy of needs manifests itself in a way that is not seen often in the domain for the data modeling community. Figure B.38 shows the results of the need for both privacy of the individual and the need for cross-correlation of lots of different kinds of data.

An anonymous identifier is one where the encrypted identity of an individual is known only at the source level. There is the possibility of occasionally entering data into the data warehouse where there is no individual identifier at all.

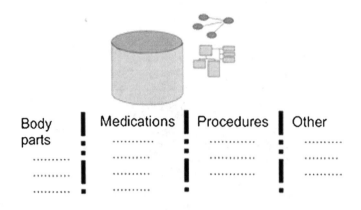

FIGURE B.39

Segments of healthcare information factory.

The collective common data model is broken up into some major and distinct sectors. This is an unusual practice for data modelers because most data models are not broken up into sectors. But most data models do not address anything as large, diverse, and complex as the healthcare environment. Figure B.39 shows the different sectors of the healthcare information factory.

The major sectors of the healthcare information factory data model are:

- Body parts
- Medications
- Procedures
- Other

As an example of what the high-level data model looks like for one of the sectors, consider the simple high-level data model shown in Figure B.40.

The data created for the body parts sector of the collective common data model comes from procedures, checkups, and other direct medical episodes of care. There is always a patient at the heart of each of the pieces of information that has been collected. In addition, there is a date associated with each unit of information. Figure B.41 shows the date component of the information about a body part.

Because of the needs for privatization, the connector of the information is an anonymous identifier. The anonymous identifier is an encrypted key that is generated at the source layer and can only be unlocked at the source. In addition, on occasion information will be placed into the database with a null key. There is limited value to the null data because the data associated with a null identifier cannot be identified or correlated with other data. But there may be some value of having body data that has no anonymous identifier attached to it.

Now consider the data found in another sector of the healthcare data model—medication information. Medication information is structured somewhat differently than data found in the body sector. Figure B.42 shows the basic type of information found in the medication sector of the high-level data model for the collective common data warehouse.

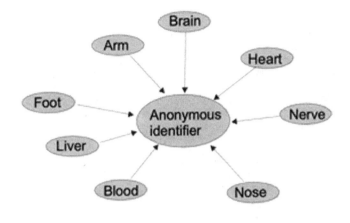

FIGURE B.40

High-level data model.

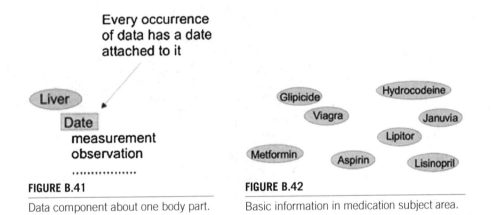

FIGURE B.41

Data component about one body part.

FIGURE B.42

Basic information in medication subject area.

In this sector is found information about the different types of medications. At this place in the data model is found such basic information as manufacturer, recommended dosage, chemical makeup, patent information, and so forth. Important to this data is the ability to relate the data to classes of data. For example, Januvia and Metformin belong to classes of data for the treatment of diabetes. Vicodin and aspirin belong to the class of drug for the treatment of pain, and so forth. Figure B.43 shows the classification of different drugs into different treatment classes.

There is a problem with the classification of drugs by treatment class. The problem is that there often is considerable overlap. One drug may be useful for treating more than one disease or condition. The result is that there may be considerable overlap in the drug fitting into treatment classes. Figure B.44 shows the more realistic case of overlapping treatment classes of drugs.

It is very useful to be able to correlate data in the body class with data in the medication class. This is accomplished by sharing an anonymous ID. When a drug prescription is made, the anonymous ID of the patient is attached to the prescription. This allows the medication data to be connected

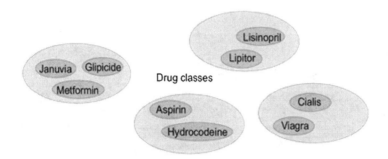

FIGURE B.43

Classification of drugs.

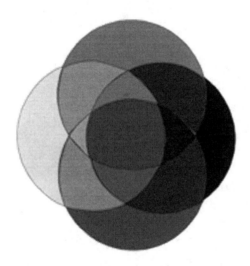

FIGURE B.44

Overlap of different classes.

to the anonymous entity. Figure B.45 shows the usage of anonymous identifiers to act as the bridge between the world of body sector and medication sector information.

The key to being able to make the connections among the different parts of the high-level healthcare data model is the existence of the anonymous identifier in both the medication and body sectors. Figure B.46 highlights this important relationship.

There are many ramifications to the usage of the anonymous identifier as described in the role that has been outlined.

Developing the healthcare information factory

There are different styles of development for systems and environments. The classic form of development is the SDLC, or system development life cycle. The SDLC was first recognized by Ed Yourdon

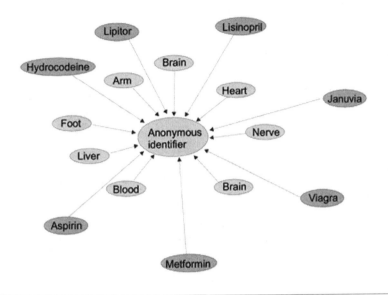

FIGURE B.45

Anonymous identifiers.

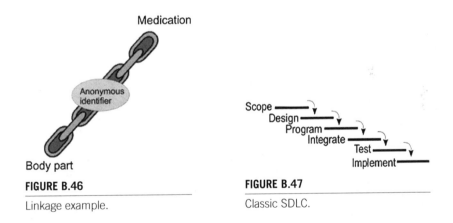

FIGURE B.46

Linkage example.

FIGURE B.47

Classic SDLC.

in the early days of computers. In the SDLC, first one step of development is done, then another step. Figure B.47 shows a classic SDLC.

The SDLC is sometimes called the "waterfall" approach to the development of systems. It is called the waterfall approach because the next step of development does not occur until the current step of development is complete. The SDLC is suited for environments where the requirements for processing are well known and well recognized.

The other style of development is called the spiral development approach. In the spiral development approach a small set of requirements is developed to completion in a short and fast manner. Then another small set of requirements is developed, and so forth. The spiral development approach is shown in Figure B.48.

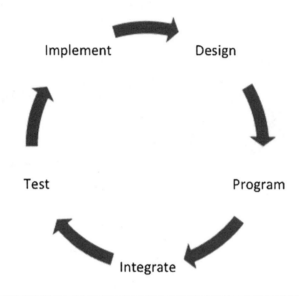

FIGURE B.48

Spiral approach.

In the spiral development approach, the requirements of the system are fluid. When the spiral development commences, there is usually not a static, complete set of requirements for the development of the system.

The third development approach is the "city" approach. In the city development approach development is pretty much an ongoing thing. Like a city that is never complete, some development efforts are ongoing things and are never complete. Figure B.49 shows the city approach to development.

Tto understand the city approach to development, contrast the building of a city versus the building of a house. A house is reasonably finite. The house can either be lived in or cannot be lived in. Relatively speaking, a house takes a short amount of time to build. Once built it is not normal for major new renditions of the same house to be built. Most houses look pretty much the same 20 years after they were completed.

A city on the other hand is undergoing continuous development. Consider Rome, Italy. Rome was first occupied thousands of years ago, yet people are still building Rome today. While parts of Rome are recognizable over the years, other parts of Rome are hardly the same. Major changes are made to Rome. When Rome was first built there were no parking spaces or airports, but there are now.

There is then a very different approach to the building of a city versus the building of a house. The healthcare information factory is much more like a city than a house, when it comes to the general approach to construction.

The different styles of development are found in different places in the healthcare information factory. Figure B.50 shows the different types of development and where they fit in the healthcare information factory architecture.

Figure B.50 shows the individual providers use the SDLC when building their systems at the local provider level. The spiral development approach is used to build the data warehouse at the local

FIGURE B.49

Modular city development.

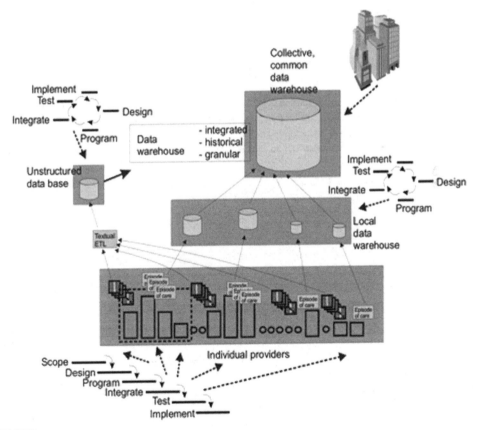

FIGURE B.50

End-state architecture.

FIGURE B.51

Healthcare information factory users.

level. The spiral development approach is also used to build the textual database. And finally, the city approach is used to build the collective common data warehouse.

Healthcare information factory users

At first glance the healthcare information factory appears to be mysterious and alien, because most people have not seen or even considered such a structure. A good way to envision the healthcare information factory and to make it come alive is to understand the healthcare information factory through the many users of the healthcare information factory. There are some predictable types of users found in the healthcare information factory, as shown in Figure B.51.

There are at least five types of users found in the healthcare information factory. Looking from left to right in Figure B.51, these users are:

- The operational user (typically a doctor or a nurse).
- The farmer (typically an accountant).
- The explorer (typically a researcher).
- The miner (typically a researcher steeped in the discipline of statistics).
- The tourist (typically a secretary or a system programmer).

Each of the different type of user has its own characteristics.

The most basic user of the healthcare information factory is the operational, or functional, user (Figure B.52).

The operational user is the user the closest to the episode of care. The operational user knows what has transpired in the episode of care. The operational user may be a doctor, a nurse, a lab technician, an office assistant, and so forth. The operational user most likely knows the patient and the particulars about the episode of care. The details of healthcare activity are recorded here. The operational user has the challenge of translating results to medical codes and conforming to other regulations and governing criteria.

The next user of the healthcare information factory is the farmer (Figure B.53). The farmer is a business analyst (an accountant) where there is a great deal of repetition to his or her job. The farmer is a person who looks for the same type of data repeatedly. The farmer produces typical

FIGURE B.52

Operational user.

FIGURE B.53

A farmer.

end-of-the-month reports. The farmer might look at key performance indicators (KPIs) on a regular basis. The activities the farmer conducts consist of a query that looks for limited amounts of data. In a word, the analytical activities of the farmer are very predictable.

Another type of user found in the healthcare information factory environment is the explorer (Figure B.54). The explorer is very unpredictable. The explorer is someone who looks "outside the box." The explorer submits queries that are very large. Sometimes the explorer goes months without submitting queries, then submits six queries in the same week. The pattern of querying of the explorer is very erratic and unpredictable. Often the explorer finds nothing as a result of query activities. But occasionally the explorer finds huge nuggets of gold.

The data miner is another type of analyst found in the healthcare information factory environment (Figure B.55). The miner is someone who takes a subject and drills down deeply into the subject. The miner looks at many, many cases of data to prove or disprove a hypothesis. The queries that the miner submits are usually quite voluminous, looking at large amounts of data in a single analysis. The miner typically looks at data over a lengthy period of time. The miner uses statistical techniques and may have a lengthy academic background. The miner is steeped in or at least is comfortable with mathematics. The miner begins his or her processing with a hypothesis.

The last type of user found in the healthcare information factory environment is the tourist (Figure B.56). The tourist is not particularly an expert in any given field, but the tourist is familiar with a wide variety of fields. The tourist is someone who knows how to find things. The tourist uses the Internet, directories, and metadata as the tools of the trade.

The healthcare information factory finds these different types of users in different places. Figure B.57 shows the different places in the healthcare information factory where the different types of users are found.

Figure B.57 shows that the operational user is found at the provider level. There are farmers and explorers who are found at the local data warehouse level. There are farmers and explorers found using the unstructured database. And there are explorers, tourist, and miners who are found in the collective common data warehouse.

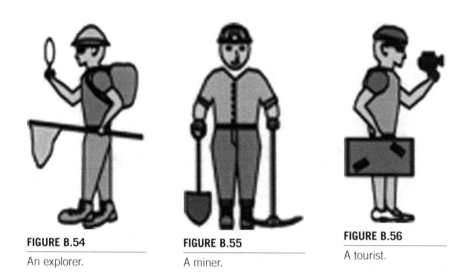

FIGURE B.54

An explorer.

FIGURE B.55

A miner.

FIGURE B.56

A tourist.

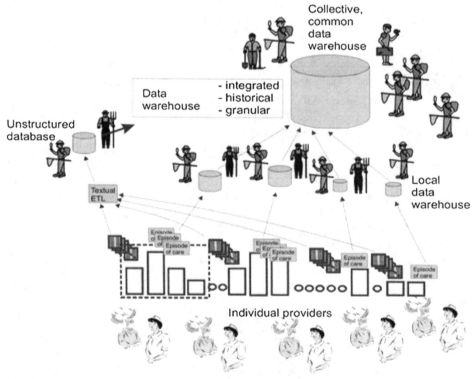

FIGURE B.57

Overall architecture.

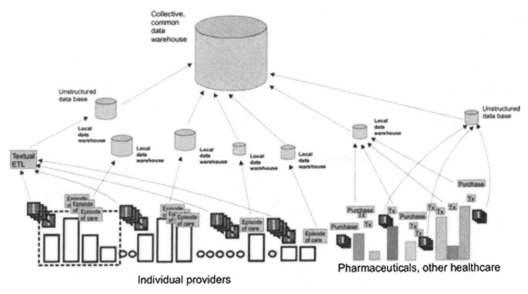

FIGURE B.58

Healthcare entities aligned.

Of course there are occasional exceptions to the rules found here. Occasionally a different type of user will be found in a location not indicated here.

Other healthcare entities

As important as hospitals, clinics, and doctor's hospitals are, they are not the only source of healthcare information. Stated differently, when looking at the larger picture of healthcare, there are other important sources of information other than the classic providers. One such source of information is the pharmaceutical companies. It is entirely compatible for pharmaceuticals to participate in the healthcare information factory. Figure B.58 shows the architectural positioning of the other healthcare entities in the healthcare information factory.

The type of data found in the healthcare information factory when there are other sources of information appears in Figure B.58. In Figure B.58 it is shown that detailed data is generated by the other healthcare sources in the day-to-day operations of the sources. Typically a unit of information that is captured is a sale or other transaction. The detailed data is integrated into a local data warehouse. From the local data warehouse the data is then reintegrated into a collective common data warehouse.

Financing the infrastructure

The differences between the local data warehouse and the larger collective common analytical data warehouse bring to the surface an important question: Who pays for the different data warehouses

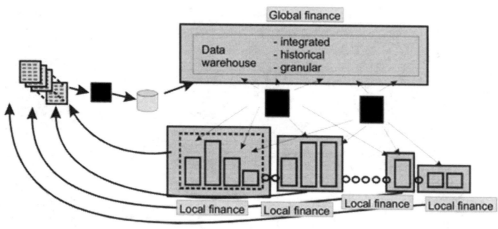

FIGURE B.59

Healthcare information factory.

found in the healthcare information factory? The answer is the local hospital or clinic pays for its own local data warehouse. But the larger analytical data warehouse is paid for by grants and government agencies that benefit from having a global analytical data warehouse. Given the wealth and importance of the data found in the larger analytical database, there are many organizations that will benefit from the massive amount of diverse data found in the global analytical data warehouse.

Figure B.59 shows that different organizations pay for different aspects of the healthcare information factory.

The age of data in the healthcare information factory

The healthcare information factory is a permanent structure. And the healthcare information factory is a dynamic structure. It is always growing and is in a constant state of transformation. Data has its own life cycle within the healthcare information factory. Data enters the healthcare information factory through the providers and other healthcare organizations. Data is used for immediate healthcare needs at the provider level. Then data is transformed into an integrated form fit to enter the local data warehouse. Data stays in the local data warehouse for as long as it is needed. Typically data stays in the local data warehouse about five to ten years. Upon entering the local data warehouse, data is passed to the collective common data warehouse. Upon entering the collective common data warehouse, data stays there indefinitely. Figure B.60 shows the typical age of data throughout the healthcare information factory.

Implementing the healthcare information factory

The healthcare information factory can be implemented with all the data life cycles and management based on the DW 2.0 architecture, as shown in Figure B.61. Additional information about this

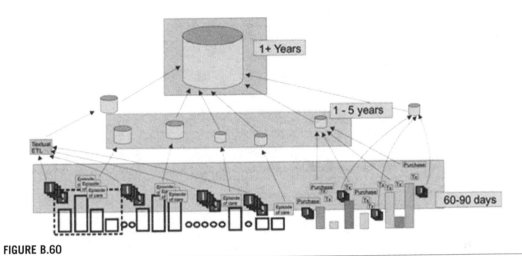

FIGURE B.60

Age of data in the data warehouse.

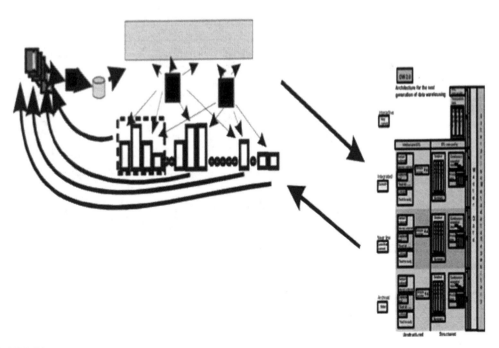

FIGURE B.61

DW 2.0 architecture for healthcare information factory.

architecture is described in detail in the book *DW 2.0: Architecture for the Next Generation of Data Warehousing*, published by Morgan Kaufman.[1]

SUMMARY

This paper is an introduction to the possibilities of how we can implement a new generation of architecture that is data-driven to implement an efficient and useful system for healthcare information management. While there are many techniques to implement this concept, using text analytics and Big Data processing techniques will provide you with a great deal of flexibility, scalability, and ease of integration.

Further reading

Inmon, W. H. (2005). *Building the data warehouse* (4th ed.). New York: John Wiley and Sons.

Inmon, W. H., Fryman, L., & O'Neil, B. (2007). *Business metadata*. Boston: Elsevier.

Inmon, W. H., & Nesavich, T. (2007). *Tapping into unstructured data*. Englewood Cliffs, NJ: Prentice-Hall.

Inmon, W. H. The bill Inmon newsletter. Available at: <*www.b-eye-network.com*>.

Inmon, W. H. (2002). *The corporate information factory*. New York: John Wiley and Sons.

Inmon, W. H. (2001). *The government information factory*. Inmon Consulting.

---

[1] Inmon, W. H. (2008). *DW 2.0: Architecture for the next generation of data warehousing.* San Francisco: Morgan Kaufman.

Summary

In conclusion, the concept of a data warehouse and its primary goal of serving an enterprise's version of the truth, and being the single platform for all sources of information, will continue to remain intact and valid for many years to come.

As we have discussed across many chapters and in many case studies, the limitations that existed with the infrastructures to create, manage, and deploy data warehouses have been largely eliminated with the availability of Big Data technologies and infrastructure platforms, making the goal of the single version of truth a feasible reality.

Integrating and extending Big Data into the data warehouse and creating a larger decision support platform will benefit businesses for years to come. This book has touched upon governance and information life-cycle management aspects of Big Data in the larger program, however, you can reuse all the current program management techniques that you follow for the data warehouse for this program and even implement agile approaches to integrating and managing data in the data warehouse.

Technologies will continue to evolve in this spectrum and there will be more additions of solutions, which can be integrated if you follow the modular integration approaches to building and managing a data warehouse.

The following Appendixes contain many more case studies and a special section on healthcare information factory based on Big Data approaches. These are more guiding posts to help you align your thoughts and goals to building and integrating Big Data in your data warehouse.

Index

Note: Page numbers followed by "*f*" and "*t*" refers to figures and tables, respectively.

Related Titles from Morgan Kaufmann

Principles of Big Data
Preparing, Sharing, and Analyzing Complex
Information
Jules J. Berman
9780124045767

Implementing Analytics
A Blueprint for Design, Development, and Adoption
Nauman Sheikh
9780124016965

Managing Data in Motion
Data Integration Best Practice Techniques
and Technologies
April Reeve
9780123971678

**Web Services, Service-Oriented
Architectures, and Cloud Computing,
2nd Edition**
The Savvy Manager's Guide
Douglas K. Barry
9780123983572

Business Intelligence, 2nd Edition
The Savvy Manager's Guide
David Loshin
9780123858894

**Agile Data Warehousing Project
Management**
Business Intelligence Systems Using Scrum
Ralph Hughes
9780123964632

mkp.com